Early Development of Body Representations

Edited by Virginia Slaughter and Celia A. Brownell

Because we engage with the world and each other through our bodies and bodily movements, being able to represent one's own and others' bodies is fundamental to human perception, cognition and behaviour. This edited book brings together, for the first time, developmental perspectives on the growth of body knowledge in infancy and early childhood and how it intersects with other aspects of perception and cognition. The book is organised into three sections, addressing the bodily self, the bodies of others and integrating self and other. Topics include perception and representation of the human form, infant imitation, understanding biological motion, self-representation, intention understanding, action production and perception and children's human figure drawings. Each section includes chapters from leading international scholars drawn together by an expert commentary that highlights open questions and directions for future research.

VIRGINIA SLAUGHTER is Professor of Developmental Psychology and a principal researcher in the Early Cognitive Development Centre at the University of Queensland, Australia.

CELIA A. BROWNELL is Professor of Psychology and Director of the Early Social Development Lab in the Department of Psychology, University of Pittsburgh.

Cambridge Studies in Cognitive and Perceptual Development

Series editors
Giyoo Hatano[†], University of the Air, Chiba, Japan
Kurt W. Fischer, Harvard University, USA

Advisory board
Gavin Bremner, *Lancaster University, UK*
Patricia M. Greenfield, *University of California, Los Angeles, USA*
Paul Harris, *Harvard University, USA*
Daniel Stern, *University of Geneva, Switzerland*
Esther Thelen, *Indiana University, USA*[†]

The aim of this series is to provide a scholarly forum for current theoretical and empirical issues in cognitive and perceptual development. As the twenty-first century begins, the field is no longer dominated by monolithic theories. Contemporary explanations build on the combined influences of biological, cultural, contextual and ecological factors in well-defined research domains. In the field of cognitive development, cultural and situational factors are widely recognised as influencing the emergence and forms of reasoning in children. In perceptual development, the field has moved beyond the opposition of 'innate' and 'acquired' to suggest a continuous role for perception in the acquisition of knowledge. These approaches and issues will all be reflected in the series, which will also address such important research themes as the indissociable link between perception and action in the developing motor system, the relationship between perceptual and cognitive development and modern ideas on the development of the brain, the significance of developmental processes themselves, dynamic systems theory and contemporary work in the psychodynamic tradition, especially as it relates to the foundations of self-knowledge.

Titles published in the series
1. Jacqueline Nadel and George Butterworth, *Imitation in Infancy*
2. Margaret Harris and Giyoo Hatano, *Learning to Read and Write: A Cross-Linguistic Perspective*
3. Michael Siegal and Candida Peterson, *Children's Understanding of Biology and Health*
4. Paul Light and Karen Littleton, *Social Processes in Children's Learning*
5. Antonio M. Battro, *Half a Brain is Enough: The Story of Nico*
6. Andrew N. Meltzoff and Wolfgang Prinz, *The Imitative Mind: Development, Evolution and Brain Bases*
7. Nira Granott and Jim Parziale, *Microdevelopment: Transition Processes in Development and Learning*
8. Heidi Keller, Ype H. Poortinga and Axel Schölmerich, *Between Culture and Biology: Perspectives on Ontogenetic Development*
9. Nobuo Masataka, *The Onset of Language*

Early Development of Body Representations

Edited by

Virginia Slaughter and
Celia A. Brownell

CAMBRIDGE
UNIVERSITY PRESS

CAMBRIDGE UNIVERSITY PRESS
Cambridge, New York, Melbourne, Madrid, Cape Town,
Singapore, São Paulo, Delhi, Tokyo, Mexico City

Cambridge University Press
The Edinburgh Building, Cambridge CB2 8RU, UK

Published in the United States of America by Cambridge University Press, New York

www.cambridge.org
Information on this title: www.cambridge.org/9780521763820

© Cambridge University Press 2012

First published 2012

Printed in the United Kingdom at the University Press, Cambridge

A catalogue record for this publication is available from the British Library

Library of Congress Cataloguing in Publication data
Early development of body representations / edited by Virginia Slaughter and Celia
A. Brownell.
    p.   cm. – (Cambridge studies in cognitive and perceptual development ; 13)
Includes bibliographical references and index.
ISBN 978-0-521-76382-0
1. Human body – Social aspects.   2. Body image.   I. Slaughter,
Virginia.   II. Brownell, Celia A.   III. Title.   IV. Series.
HM636.E27   2011
305.231–dc23
                                                                        2011023915

ISBN 978-0-521-76382-0 Hardback

Contents

Figures

Tables

Contributors

EMILY J. BLUMENTHAL is a doctoral candidate studying developmental cognitive neuroscience at the Psychology Department and the Institute for Learning and Brain Sciences at the University of Washington.

CELIA A. BROWNELL is Professor of Psychology and Director of the Early Social Development Lab in the Department of Psychology, University of Pittsburgh.

TAMARA CHRISTIE is a developmental psychologist working within the Department of Education and Training, Queensland, Australia.

MAUREEN COX is Emeritus Reader in the Department of Psychology, University of York, UK.

MORITZ M. DAUM is Head of the Infant Cognition and Action research group at the Max Planck Institute for Human Cognitive and Brain Sciences, Leipzig, Germany.

JUDY S. DELOACHE is William Kenan Professor of Psychology at the University of Virginia.

TEODORA GLIGA is a research fellow at the Centre for Brain and Cognitive Development, Birkbeck College, UK.

PETRA HAUF is Canada Research Chair in Cognitive Development and Principal Researcher in the Infant Action and Cognition Lab in the Department of Psychology at St. Francis Xavier University, Canada.

MICHELLE HERON-DELANEY is a postdoctoral research fellow at the Centre of National Research on Disability and Rehabilitation Medicine in Brisbane, Australia.

KAZUO HIRAKI is a professor in the Department of General Systems Studies and Center for Evolutionary Cognitive Sciences in the Graduate School of Arts and Sciences at the University of Tokyo, Japan.

SUSAN C. JOHNSON is a cognitive scientist who studies infant social cognition at The Ohio State University.

SUSAN JONES is Professor of Psychological and Brain Sciences and the Program in Cognitive Science at Indiana University.

CHRIS MOORE is Professor of Psychology and director of the Early Social Development Laboratory in the Department of Psychology, Dalhousie University, Canada.

DEREK G. MOORE is Professor of Developmental Psychology and Director of the Institute for Research in Child Development at the University of East London, UK.

SARA R. NICHOLS is a doctoral candidate studying developmental and clinical psychology at the University of Pittsburgh.

KIRSTEN O'HEARN is a developmental psychologist studying visual processing in autism at the University of Pittsburgh.

DANIEL POVINELLI is Professor of Biology at the University of Louisiana and Director of the National Chimpanzee Observatories Initiative.

MICHELLE POWER is Manager of Ann Bigelow's Infant Development Lab and a researcher in Petra Hauf's Infant Action and Cognition Lab in the Department of Psychology at St. Francis Xavier University, Canada.

WOLFGANG PRINZ is Director Emeritus at the Department of Psychology of the Max Planck Institute for Human Cognitive and Brain Sciences, Leipzig, Germany.

VINCENT REID is a lecturer in the Department of Psychology at Durham University, UK.

PHILIPPE ROCHAT is Professor of Psychology and Head of the Emory Infant and Child Laboratory at Emory University, Atlanta, Georgia.

KARA D. SAGE is a graduate student in developmental psychology and Manager of Dr. Dare Baldwin's Acquiring Minds Lab at the University of Oregon.

VIRGINIA SLAUGHTER is Professor of Developmental Psychology and a principal researcher in the Early Cognitive Development Centre at the University of Queensland, Australia.

JESSICA A. SOMMERVILLE is an associate professor in the Psychology Department and at the Institute for Learning and Brain Sciences at the University of Washington. She also directs the Early Childhood Cognition Lab.

VICTORIA SOUTHGATE is a Research Fellow at the Centre for Brain and Cognitive Development, Birkbeck College, UK.

MARGARITA SVETLOVA is a doctoral candidate studying developmental psychology at the University of Pittsburgh and is a guest researcher in the Department of Developmental and Comparative Psychology at the Max Planck Institute for Human Cognitive and Brain Sciences, Leipzig, Germany.

MANOS TSAKIRIS is Reader in Neuropsychology at the Department of Psychology, Royal Holloway University of London, UK.

DAVID H. UTTAL is Professor of Psychology and Education at Northwestern University, where he studies spatial and symbolic development.

KAITLIN VENEMA is a research coordinator at the University of Washington Autism Center in Seattle, Washington. She formerly worked in the Early Childhood Cognition Lab under Jessica Sommerville.

HANAKO YOSHIDA is an assistant professor in the Department of Psychology at the University of Houston and directs the Cognitive Development Laboratory.

STEPHANIE ZWICKER is a doctoral candidate in the Department of Psychology, Dalhousie University, Canada. She is conducting her PhD research on the temporal parameters of visual-proprioceptive intermodal integration.

Part I

The bodily self

1   Primordial sense of embodied self-unity

Philippe Rochat

Primordial sense of embodied self-unity

Infancy research of the past forty years defies long-held ideas regarding the starting state of mental life. These ideas were justified by the fact that we do not have any explicit recollection of our own infancy. Infantile amnesia was symptomatic of an initial absence of experiential unity and self-awareness. Prior to language, children were regarded as some kind of larvae, eventually emerging from their blind chrysalides to find embodied selfhood, meta-cognition, and explicit self-identity in the light of symbolic functioning and conceptual representations. There is an abundance of evidence now showing that un-memorable infancy does not equate to mindless infants.

The long-held assumptions of mindless and self-less infants, devoid at birth of experiential unity (i.e. a unified embodied experience), can be explained by a lack of consideration of the variety of ways one can be aware, including levels of self-awareness that are more or less explicit and conceptual (Rochat, 2009). Infant studies call for a distinction between experiential and conceptual aware-ness: the awareness that accompanies being and acting in the world toward preferred goals, versus the awareness of a conceptualized and re-cognized world (a phenomenal consciousness that has, in addition, cognitive accessibil-ity), following the recent discussion and distinction proposed by Ned Block (2007).

If in development experiential awareness precedes conceptual awareness, in the same way for example that independent sitting precedes bi-pedal locomo-tion, or that babbling precedes speaking, it does not mean that one is lacking coherence and unity, the other eventually endowed with it. It does not mean, either, that one kind of awareness calls for selfhood and the other does not.

The basic argument made here is that both conceptual (i.e. early body representation, the topic of this volume) and experiential awareness call for

Part of this work was written while supported by a 2006–2007 J. S. Guggenheim Fellowship to the author, who expresses his appreciation to the Foundation. Some of the ideas for this chapter were originally presented at the Conference on Unity and the Self, 30 November 2007, Center of Subjectivity Research, Danish National Research Foundation, University of Copenhagen.

experiential unity and an ascription of selfhood, although at fundamentally different levels of mental functioning. Both conceptual and experiential awareness co-exist in development, particularly from the onset of language. From then on, our awareness tends to fluctuate from the experiential to the conceptual, in the same way that we sometimes sit and sometimes walk; sometimes babble and other times speak. In constantly transitioning through experiential and conceptual awareness, we do not each time lose or re-discover the sense of who we are, nor of what unifies our consciousness of the world.

Embodied sense of self and unity at birth

Empirical observations suggest that infants at birth start off showing all signs of experiential awareness. They feel and are selective in what they feel. They show unity in learning, in representing, and in orienting toward vital resources of their environment: faces, food, caretakers they depend on to survive (Rochat and Senders, 1991; Rochat, 2001 for a review of such evidence). They manifest from the outset some sense of their own body as a substantial and bounded entity among other substantial and bounded entities. They show an experiential awareness of the body that is organized, multimodal, situated, differentiated, and purposeful in the environment, what would correspond to an implicit body schema that is the foundation of later developing explicit body representations (Gallagher and Meltzoff, 1996).

The argument proposed here is that all these features justify the theoretical ascription of embodied unity and selfhood to children from the outset of human development. The questions are, what kind and what changes in development?

Following Kant's classic proposal, for an experience to become conscious *about* something requires embodied unity in the sense that it requires that sensations from the world, including the body itself, be synthesized into intuitions and percepts, these percepts eventually coordinated to grasp patterns and ultimately form concepts (Brook, 1994). Based on these criteria, evidence suggests that infants from birth would manifest unity in the Kantian sense, to the extent that they respond to more than discrete and isolated sensations, and more importantly, to the extent that they differentiate sensations originating *from within or outside the body*. Infants from birth need to be considered as perceivers and actors, not just instinctive reflex machines. They behave as differentiated and organized embodied entities among other entities, and are not born in a primordial state of un-differentiation with the environment.

Recent empirical evidence allows non-trivial conclusions regarding the origins of self-consciousness and what it might be like to be a newborn, calling for radical revisions of strong-held beliefs and premises from which highly influential theories were built. These beliefs include for example the notion that the starting state of development is an exercise of discrete, not yet coordinated hereditary "automatic" reflexes (Piaget, 1936), or Freud's seminal idea that beyond survival instincts, behavior at birth is reduced to some sort of blind, circular, non-objectified and autistic quest toward bodily excitation and suppression (Freud, 1905).

These notions do not allow ascribing to newborns the power of being conscious *about* something that is differentiated from their own bodily experience, hence of their own body as a differentiated entity among other entities in the environment. But, as I will try to suggest, research shows that there is apparently much more than reflexes, a-dualism, blind auto-eroticism, and primary narcissism at the origins of conscious life.

Presumed mental weakness of the pre-verbal child

The fact that we do not have any explicit recollection of our own infancy makes the grasping of our origins in development difficult. Infantile amnesia prevents us from any direct reconstruction by way of introspection of what mental life might be at the origins and what our primeval experience is of being alive in the world. First coined by Freud, the phenomenon of infantile amnesia invites us to speculate that there might be a radically different mental organization at birth, or even *none* whatsoever. It leaves open the possibility of a different and incomparable experience to what we as adults experience of the world. Infantile experience would be yet un-repressed by conscious thoughts and without the awareness of others as "superego."

The memory black hole of the first months in the world outside of the womb has naturally enticed philosophers to think of a primary mental incompetence, the incompetence of infants to create memories, even memories stored for later retrieval. This absence of conscious recollection of our life prior to the third birthday is universal. It is pervasive despite the claims of highly speculative therapies and other rather unscrupulous psychoanalysts reconstructing from patient hearsay what young infants might feel and what might be meaningful events for them.

If we consider infantile amnesia as the symptom of an original incompetence, infants' inability to store and represent sensory information, it is also presumably the symptom of an original incapacity to synthesize sensory impressions into the concepts that give the mind its conscious unity. Children prior to 2–3 years would be incapable of giving sensory experience its unified "mindfulness." Translated in Kantian terms, infantile amnesia would be symptomatic of mental blindness. Babies' intuitions of the world and of their own body arising from sensory experience would be blind, not yet transcended into concepts and representations, not yet synthesized into bodies of knowledge that can be consciously retrieved.

This is what the founders of modern psychology assumed. Wilhelm Wundt, who established the first experimental psychology laboratory in Leipzig in the late nineteenth century, considered that infants could not help in the scientific understanding and conceptualizing of the adult mind. He writes in his *Outline of Psychology* (1897): "The results of experiments which have been tried on very young children must be regarded as purely chance results, wholly untrustworthy on account of the great number of sources of error. For this reason, it is an error to hold, as is sometimes held, that the mental life of adults can never be fully understood except through the analysis of the child's mind" (Eng. Trans. 1907, cited by Kessen 1965). Obviously, Piaget and his followers did not adhere to Wundt's intuition. Nor did the great number of infancy researchers in recent years decrying William James' (1890) idea that we are born into an initial state of "blooming, buzzing, confusion," interpreted as standing for an initial state of disorder and experiential chaos in dire need of organization (see Rochat, 2001 for a review).

Progress in neuroscience might also have reinforced this intuition as we now have ample evidence that the brain of the young child develops continuously in marked ways during the first 2–3 years of life, particularly pre-frontal regions of the neo-cortex that are involved in the higher order synthesis of neural information as in advanced executive function, inhibition in problem-solving and intentional actions (e.g. Zelazo, 2004). Furthermore, and this is what delimits infancy from childhood, by the second year children become symbolic, increasingly proficient with language and begin to manifest an unambiguous conceptual sense of who they are (Bates, 1990). Their vocabulary becomes full of personal pronouns and adjectives like "I," "me" and "mine." All of these mental changes that occur by the second to third year of life correlate with what is typically reported as our earliest, reliable memories.

From this point on, the veil of amnesia appears to be lifted. Memories are stored to become potentially retrievable and communicable in narrative forms (Dennett, 1992; Nelson and Fivush, 2004). From then on only, it would therefore be legitimate to postulate that the child possesses a mind that is explicitly conceptual, showing unity in the Kantian sense. This unity also implies a conceptual sense of who the child is as an entity among other entities, a person among other persons in the world. From the time they speak, children identify (re-cognize) themselves in mirrors and show embarrassment. They start to show off, begin to lie if necessary and to engage in pretense. Arguably, the child's experience rises to mindfulness proper. It is unified over time and space. Representations of representations are synthesized and organized into abstract concepts that can be mentally manipulated at will to generate new truths and true pre-visions about future states of the world.

In short, historically, there has been a natural inclination, albeit with good reason, for many thinkers of the mind to believe that there might be a lack of unity at birth. The lack of unity would persist until children develop the ability to synthesize representations of the world that are memorable and organized along the continuum of time and space. If a concept of self is an a-priori condition of unity in consciousness – as was suggested by Kant – it would be erroneous to speak of any notion of "self" prior to language, prior to the explicit ability to remember, conceptualize, and re-cognize the world symbolically, in particular within symbolic conventions. This, of course, would extend to any other non-symbolic animals that do not possess language, namely creatures that are not capable of representing representations, not capable of organizing thoughts around a-priori truths and within a continuous timeline that gives hindsight to the direct sensory experience of the world.

There are marked qualitative shifts in how and what the mind processes between birth and the onset of language, particularly when the child starts to remember an increasing number of past events in the explicit narrative formats of autobiographical memories (Nelson and Fivush, 2004). However, much research shows now that the phenomenon of infantile amnesia is not due to a lack of unity or sense of self, as alluded to by the founders of modern psychology. In fact, infantile amnesia is becoming increasingly a "misnomer" given the flow of empirical evidence that demonstrates long-term procedural memory in infants of only a few months, infants who presumably should be deep into our memory "black hole" period (e.g. Bauer, 1996; Meltzoff, 1995; Rovee-Collier and Hayne, 2000). In addition, numerous studies show that the timing of first explicit memories (typically between 2 and 4 years) can vary greatly among individuals depending on memory content, gender, family structure and culture (Nelson and Fivush, 2004).

It thus appears that children develop autobiographical memory progressively, incrementally and in parallel to language development. It does not emerge abruptly as if children were overcoming the obstacle of a generalized amnesia, hence a disorganized mind incapable of having organized representations of representation, not functioning rationally on the basis of a-priori concepts, only finding unity and selfhood by their third birthday.

Distinguishing the experiential from the conceptual

Newborns' experience of the world is rich from the start. It is rich within the polarity of pleasure and pain, restfulness and agitation, approach and avoidance. Newborns cry and fuss when hungry or tired. They show irrepressible smiles with eyes rolling to the back of their head after a good feed. They "feel" something, expressing unmistakable pleasure and pains. These expressions have adaptive functions, forming crucial signals for caregivers on whom newborns rely to survive. But how much unity and embodied self-awareness can be ascribed to such emotional, obviously not yet objectified experience of being alive in the world?

To address this question, it is necessary to distinguish two basic forms of being in the world: the *experiential* and the *conceptual*. This is not a new approach, supported and proposed by recent research and theories in cognitive neuroscience, in the footsteps of William James proposing a distinction between the "I" or experiential self and the "me" or conceptual (objectified) self. Damasio (1999) emphasizes the fundamental difference between "core" consciousness and "extended" consciousness about the self and events that are construed over time and emerging with language. Similarly, Edelman and Tononi (2000) call for a distinction between primary and symbolic (language and narrative) driven consciousness. A large body of research in neuroscience supports the experiential diversity of being aware in the world, including blind-sight, hypnotic dissociation of pain and other highly relativist (as opposed to "real" or "core") perceptual phenomena (see Gazzaniga *et al.*, 1998). There are different kinds of awareness, not all necessarily requiring re-cognition, lan-guage, or the capacity to represent representations as in meta-cognition. It is justified to talk about infra- or pre-linguistic awareness. There are indeed markedly different ways of being aware and conscious, as opposed to non-conscious or un-conscious (Rochat, 2009).

Newborns are not yet conceptually aware of being themselves alive in the world, obviously. However, they are *experientially* aware. Newborns, when not sleeping, are not merely in a wakeful state of confusion between what they feel and what causes them to feel. If they see a face or are struck by an object, they do not become this face or this object. Although not yet conceptualizing them as objects of reflection, they do not confound them with their own subjective feeling or sensory experience. This can be assumed to the extent that newborns' feelings and behaviors cannot be simply reduced to automatic reflex responses, like the mechanical adjustments of a thermostat or any kind of automata.

Behavior at birth is more than a collection of automatic reflexes (Rochat, 2007). Rather than reflexes, it is more appropriate to talk about purposeful acts that are expression of innate action systems evolved to sustain infants' survival in the state of prolonged immaturity (Bruner, 1972), what Montagu (1961) calls the human "exterogestation." These systems include orienting, feeding, and exploring, all organizing children's actions around features and resources in the environment that are relevant for their survival (Reed, 1982; Rochat and Senders, 1991).

Behavior at birth is thus more than the expression of highly predictable stimulus–response loops controlled by endogenous, self-contained and auto-matically triggered mechanisms. It is more than breathing or blinking. In addition to reflexes, newborns also manifest bodily movements that are *oriented* toward particular functional goals. These action systems are by definition adapted to tap into available resources that exist *outside* the individual organism, in the surrounding environment: food, surfaces, objects, or people. Furthermore, contrary to reflexes, these movements are organized into systems that are *flexible*, capable of changing based on previous experiences and adjusting to novel circumstances (see Rochat, 2007 for further discussion of the non-rigid and triggered aspect of behavior at birth). Orientation and flexibility are two aspects that argue against the reduction of behavior at birth to simple reflex mechanisms.

Infants are born predisposed to act with purpose, oriented toward indispensable resources in the environment, be it food, comfort, or protection. These innate functional action systems are what unify the experiential awareness of newborns. It is also what justifies the ascription of selfhood from the outset of development. For the rest of this chapter, I will attempt to provide empirical support for these claims (see also Butterworth, 1992 target article and follow up comments for a similar argument based on different perceptual and cognitive evidence).

Criteria and evidence for basic experiential embodied unity at birth

As noted previously, following Kant's view of the mind, sensory inputs from the world need to be unified to become conscious experiences "about something." In other words, for the sense datum to become knowledge about the world, it needs to be synthesized within a temporal and spatial structure at three levels: (1) the transformation of sensory apprehension into intuitions or percepts; (2) the coordination of intuitions or percepts in reproductive imagination (what would correspond to mental simulation in today's neuroscientific jargon); and (3) the recognition of concepts in coordinated intuitions (conceptualization of a-priori categories). Kant proposes that the unity of our conscious experience rests on these three kinds of synthesis, an idea that still prevails in current cognitive sciences.

Within this framework, one can argue that newborns do engage in the synthesizing of sense data, certainly at the first level proposed by Kant, and probably also at the second level. The third level seems to be evident only a few months down the road, possibly before the first birthday. For example, Jean Mandler (1988, 1992) provides some empirical evidence that by 9–12 months, infants might already manifest object categorization that is based on ontological concepts such as animate versus inanimate, self-propelled or not. Although such rich interpretation is disputed by other researchers (see Rakison and Poulin-Dubois, 2001), Mandler proposes that already in the first year infants engage in perceptual analysis that includes the three kinds of synthesis that for Kant are the foundation of unity in consciousness. But, what about newborns, what about infants at birth? Do they show signs of unity in their experience? The most probable answer is yes.

If newborns were lacking unity, just bombarded by meaningless sensory stimulations, we would expect newborns' behavior to be fundamentally disoriented, just a collection of responses that would jerk them around in a disorganized manner. But ample evidence shows that this is not the case (Rochat, 2001). They learn and actively explore their environment, even showing evidence that prenatal experience and learning is transferred into postnatal life. For example, newborns a few hours old orient more toward the scent of their mother's amniotic fluid compared to the scent of the amniotic fluid of a female stranger. They also show active preference in hearing their mother's voice compared to another female voice (Marlier *et al.*, 1998a, 1998b; DeCasper and Fifer, 1980).

There is now substantial evidence demonstrating preference, active selection, learning (e.g. Marlier *et al.*, 1998), and even imitation in neonates (e.g. Meltzoff and Moore, 1977), all pointing to the fact that infants are born to a world they synthesize into meaningful features or affordances (Gibson, 1979). They are born endowed with the ability to detect these affordances and to synthesize them as invariant features of the environment (Rochat and Senders, 1991; Gibson, 1995). These invariants pertain equally to non-self objects and to the body. For example, a drop of sucrose on their tongue leads them to calm down and systematically bring hand to the mouth in the most direct trajectory for biting and sucking (Rochat *et al.*, 1988). The drop of sucrose engages the feeding or appetitive system of the infant that in turn mobilizes the whole body in orienting and rooting activities. These functionally purposeful activities come to rest only when something solid such as a finger or a nipple comes into contact with the face and eventually finds its way into the mouth for sucking (Blass *et al.*, 1989). Evidence of neonatal imitation of tongue protrusion, mouth opening, and finger movements (Meltzoff and Moore, 1977) is the expression of a body schema whereby the sight of active bodily regions in another person (the model) is mapped onto homologous regions of the own body. Another example of expressed body schema at birth is the systematic arm movements observed in neonates with their head turned to the side while lying supine in their crib and plunged in the dark with just a thin beam of light cutting across their visual field. In this condition, newborns are documented systematically bringing their ipsilateral hand and arm into the beam of light for active visual exploration (Van der Meer and Lee, 1995).

The behavioral orientation of newborns and their early propensity to detect invariant features in the environment (including the invariant features of their own body) all point to an experiential awareness at birth that is organized within a stable spatial and temporal structure. Newborns show quick learning, transfer, and use of prenatal experience into postnatal life. They memorize and recall procedural knowledge over time, orienting head and mouth significantly more when, for example, the stimulation is food or any events associated with food and comfort (faces, posture, or certain tastes as well as smells; e.g. Marlier *et al.*, 1998a). Their behavior shows plasticity and is not limited to the here and now of random stimulation (e.g., Van der Meer and Lee, 1995). It is organized as a function of past experience, within an a-priori spatial and temporal structure (e.g. DeCasper and Fifer, 1980).

In short, newborns' behavior expresses an experience of the world that is unified by the detection of meaningful resources and by propensities to act in ways that serve their survival despite the neonate's initial altricial state of great social dependence.

Primordial sense of an embodied self

The basic emotions expressed at birth are reliably identifiable by caretakers as pain, joy, disgust, interest, or anger. They are symptomatic of a rich affective life. Newborns express these emotions with their whole body, becoming spastic and tense in particular ways, emitting particular sounds, when for example crying out of pain as opposed to hunger (Formby, 1967). A rich palette of distinct affective motives underlies newborns' bodily movements and oral expressions.

In relation to the body as a whole, hand–mouth coordination systematically associated with the engagement of the feeding system, as in the case of the drop of sucrose on the tongue (Rochat *et al.*, 1988), is in itself suggestive that newborns possess rudiments of a body schema (Gallagher and Meltzoff, 1996; see Butterworth, 1992 for a similar argument). Such coordination implies some mapping of the body whereby regions and parts of the own body are actively and systematically (as opposed to just randomly) put in contact with each other, in this case hands and mouth with a straight and orchestrated spatio-temporal trajectory. Other expressions of a body schema include neonatal imitation and neonates' systematic exploration of their own arms and hands in the dark, as discussed earlier. In all, body schema and the active propensity of neonates to bring sense modalities and regions of their own body in relation with each other are now well documented.

This supports the idea that infants sense their own body from birth as an *invariant spatial structure*, even as rudimentary and in need of further refinement this spatial structure might be. This structure is obviously not Euclidean in the sense of being synthesized (represented) in the mind of the young infant as a precise map of accurate spatial coordinates and configurations. It does not yet entail that infants already have a re-cognizable image of their own body (a body image). This structure is essentially topological in the sense that it is made of focal attractor regions on the body surface that have many degrees of freedom and a high concentration of sensory receptors such as in the mouth and fingers.

This topology is embodied in action systems that are functional from birth and drive early behavior.

Evidence of a body schema at birth provides some theoretical ground for the ascription of basic selfhood from the outset. Research now demonstrates that neonates behave in relation to their own body in ways that are different, when compared to how they behave in relation to other physical bodies that exist independently of their own. They feel and unquestionably demonstrate from birth a distinct sensitivity to their own bodily movements via *proprioception* and internal (*vestibular*) receptors in the inner ears. Both proprioceptive and vestibular sensitivities are well developed and operational at birth. They are sense modalities of the self par excellence (Lee and Aronson, 1974; Butterworth and Hicks, 1977; Jouen and Gapenne, 1995).

Research shows, for example, that neonates root significantly more with head and mouth toward a tactile stimulation from someone else's finger than from their own hand touching their cheek (Rochat and Hespos, 1997). Other studies report that newborns pick up visual information that specifies ego-motion or movements of their own body while they, in fact, remain stationary. These studies indicate that neonates experience the illusion of moving, adjusting their bodily posture according to changes in direction of an optical flow that is presented in the periphery of their visual field (Jouen and Gapenne, 1995). This kind of observation points to the fact that from birth, infants are endowed with the perceptual, qua inter-modal capacity to pick up and process meaningfully *self-specifying* information.

Questions remain as to what might be actually synthesized or represented as an outcome of the self-specifying perceptual capacity manifested at birth. In other words, what might be the experience of embodied selfhood in neonates? What is the subjective experience of the own body considering that selfhood is first embodied, only later becoming re-cognized as "me."

Embodied self-experience at birth

Neonates experience the body as an invariant locus of pleasure and pain, with a particular topography of hedonic attractors, the mouth region being the most powerful of all, as noted by Freud years ago. Within hours after birth, in relation to this topography, infants learn and memorize sensory events that are associated with pleasure and novelty: they selectively orient to odors associated with the pleasure of feeding and they show basic discrimination of what can be expected from familiar events that unfold over time and that are situated in a space that is embodied, structured within a body schema. But if it is legitimate to posit an a-priori "embodied" spatial and temporal organization of self-experience at birth, what might be the content of this experience aside from pleasure, pain, and the excitement of novelty?

Neonates appear to have an a-priori proprioceptive sense of their own body in the way they act and orient to meaningful affordances of the environment as well as in the way they detect visual information that specifies ego motion, adjusting their posture appropriately in direction and amplitude to compensate for surreptitious changes in gravitational forces (Jouen and Gapenne, 1995). The proprioceptive sense of the body is a necessary correlate of most sensory experiences of the world, from birth on. As proposed by James Gibson (1979), to perceive the world is to *co-perceive* oneself in this world. In this process, proprioception, or the muscular and skeletal sense of the body in reference to *itself*, is indeed the sense modality of the self.

From birth, proprioception alone or in conjunction with other sense modalities, specifies the own body as a differentiated, situated, and eventually an agentive entity among other entities in the world. This corresponds to what Ulric Neisser (1988, 1991) first coined as the "ecological self," a self that can be ascribed to infants from birth. As pointed out by Neisser (1995), criteria for the ascription of an ecological self rest on the behavioral expression by the individual of both an awareness of the environment in terms of a layout with particular affordances for action, and of its body as a motivated agent to explore, detect, and use these affordances.

Newborns fulfill the criteria proposed by Neisser for such awareness. In addition, however, it is legitimate to speculate that they also seem to possess an a-priori awareness that their own body is a distinct entity that is bounded and substantial, as opposed to disorganized and "airy." Newborns perform self-oriented acts by systematically bringing hand to mouth, as already mentioned. In these acts, the mouth tends to open in anticipation of manual contact and the insertion of fingers into the oral cavity for chewing and sucking (Blass *et al.*, 1989; Watson, 1995). What is instantiated in such systematic acts is, once again, an *organized body schema*. These acts are not just random and cannot be reduced to reflex arcs. They need to be construed as functionally self-oriented acts proper. Because they bring body parts in direct relation to one another, as in the case of hand–mouth coordination, they provide neonates with invariant sensory information specifying the own body's quality as bounded substance, with an inside and an outside, specified by particular texture, solidity, temperature, elasticity, taste, and smell.

The a-priori awareness of the own body as a bounded substantial entity is also evident in neonates' postural reaction and gestures when experiencing the impending collision with a looming visual object, an event that carries potentially life-threatening information. Years ago, Ball and Tronick (1971) showed that neonates aged 2–11 weeks manifest head withdrawal and avoidant behavior when exposed to the explosive expansion of an optic array that specifies the impending collision of an object. Infants do not manifest any signs of upset or avoidant behavior when viewing expanding shadows specifying an object either receding or on a miss path in relation to them. Consonant with Ball and Tronick's findings, Carroll and Gibson (1981) reported that by 3 months, when facing a looming object with a large aperture in the middle, such as an open window in a façade, they do not flinch or show signs of withdrawal as they would with a full textured solid object. Instead, they tend to lean forward to look through the aperture. In all, the detection of such affordance in the looming object indicates that there is an a-priori awareness that the own body is substantial. There is a very early, possibly innate awareness that the own body occupies space and can be a physical obstacle to other objects in motion.

Conclusions: from implicit to explicit embodied self-awareness in development

It is necessary to separate the experiential mind of the neonate from the conceptual, explicit, and symbolic mind that emerges with the first words and first reminiscing in narrative, more abstract forms of thinking. From birth on, research shows that infants act and perceive in a meaningful environment made of resources for comfort and satisfying needs as well as affordances for action. Behavior is best described as functionally purposeful from the outset, research showing that we are not born merely "automata" (Gibson, 1995).

I have tried to show that newborns' behavior demonstrates rudiments of an experiential awareness that has unity, this unity justifying an ascription of embodied selfhood. In relation to development, the question is *not* how we eventually become mindful from a starting state of confusion, *not* how we eventually become endowed with a strong mind pulling out of a primitive state of computational weakness, non-differentiation, and selflessness. Rather, based on what we now know about neonates, the question is how does the implicit awareness of the embodied self expressed already at birth come to be explicit and conceptual by the second year when children become self-conscious. How does the experiential *I* come to be also represented as the conceptual *me*? How does the breast that feeds me also become re-described as my mother, when embodied space and time becomes also objectified and measured? What might drive such development? That is the perennial question of developmental psychology.

In the footsteps of Piaget's seminal work, a host of new developmental theories and research try to document the unfolding of conceptual awareness early in life, sometimes trying to characterize corresponding levels of phenomenal awareness in the developing child that can be applied to the awareness of the embodied self (Zelazo, 2004).Trying to accommodate new findings on infant cognition, and as an alternative to Piaget's domain-general constructionist views on cognitive development, Karmiloff-Smith (1992) proposes that the implicit and procedural format of knowledge evident at birth in specific domains of consciousness (e.g. face perception, imitation, number sense) would be *automatically* re-described at a representational level. According to this model, "representational re-description" is the inescapable consequence of practice and the behavioral mastery achieved by infants in their insatiable propensity to learn, master, and discover. Note that such a model applies equally to self-awareness in development (see Zelazo *et al.*, 2007).

Following the model, with practice and improvement perception and action that are first implicit and non-reflexive would be progressively re-described at increasingly abstract levels, each level opening up new intra- and inter-domain relations (see Karmiloff-Smith, 1992 for more details). The spontaneous re-description of implicit knowledge accompanying learning and procedural mastery would eventually lead the child toward explicit and verbalized consciousness. Here, the driving force behind developing consciousness from the outset would be spontaneous and recurrent re-description of representations across domains of knowledge into higher-level format of abstraction and communicability. These domains would obviously include self-knowledge and the own body representation.

What is interesting and relevant in relation to the argument of unity and selfhood at birth is the fact that a mechanism of representational re-description presupposes a representation to begin with (what Zelazo, 2004 labels "minimal consciousness" in his model of consciousness development). It is this minimal "embodied" consciousness in the newborn that I tried to account for in this chapter. However, aside from the empirically informed depiction of a starting state awareness and the distinction between various levels of experiential awareness and representation expressed by children in their development, the question of what might be the *causes* of processes such as the spontaneous representational re-description mechanism described by Karmiloff-Smith remains wide open. This is particularly true in light of the fact that such processes appear to exist prior to language which is often considered as the major determinant of reflexive consciousness and meta-cognitive capacities, what Lev Vygotsky (1978) viewed as internalized thinking derived from language acquisition.

Aside from behavioral evidence, developmental research in the neurosciences reveals neural markers of emerging and putative changes in experiential awareness at birth, and even prior during fetal development. For example, first evidence of consciousness might be attributed to the development of functional neural pathways that link thalamus and sensory cortex already by the third trimester of gestation, or even earlier with the emergence of functional pathways necessarily involved in conscious pain perception (Lee *et al.*, 2005). If there is a renewed effort in mapping pre- and postnatal brain growth, using neural markers that would correlate with levels of consciousness achieved by children in development, we are still far from explaining the actual mechanisms that would drive such development. If there is a positive correlation between brain growth and levels of consciousness, including levels of embodied self-consciousness achieved by the child (see Zelazo *et al.*, 2007), we are still far from a causal explanation.

Language and its progressive mastery do certainly play a causal role in the development of new explicit levels of consciousness. We don't have to assume that language shapes the mind, to recognize that language use by the child in interaction with scaffolding others and its progressive mastery does unquestionably contribute to new levels of abstraction and representational re-description. But to a large extent we are still very much agnostic as to what might trigger such re-description prior to language and what might lead infants in particular to re-describe their innate unity and sense of selfhood to eventually become explicit and conceptual about it. We can assume, however, that from the outset, social interactions with more advanced and linguistically competent others play a central role in infants' advances toward more abstract levels of embodied self-awareness (Vygotsky, 1978; Tomasello, 2008).

These developmental issues form a challenge that is worth embracing because the way children develop and what develops in their experience of the world, including their own body experience, can reveal the building blocks and layers of what we construe as adult forms of consciousness and embodied self-consciousness.

References

Ball, W. and Tronick, E. (1971). Infant responses to impending collision: Optical and real. *Science*, **171**, 818–820.

Bates, E. (1990). Language about me and you: Pronominal reference and the emerging concept of self. In D. Cicchetti and M. Beeghly (eds). *The Self in Transition: Infancy to Childhood* (165–182). Chicago, IL: University of Chicago Press.

Bauer, P. (1996). Recalling past events: From infancy to early childhood. *Annals of Child Development*, **11**, 25–71.

Blass, E. M., Fillion, T. J., Rochat, P., Hoffmeyer, L. B., and Metzger, M. A. (1989). Sensorimotor and motivational determinants of hand–mouth coordination in 1–3-day-old human infants. *Developmental Psychology*, **25**(6), 963–975.

Block, N. (2007). Consciousness, accessibility, and the mesh between psychology and neuroscience. *Brain and Behavioral Sciences*, **30**, 481–548.

Brook, A. 1994. *Kant and the Mind*. Cambridge and New York: Cambridge University Press.

Bruner, J. (1972). Nature and uses of immaturity. *American Psychologist*, **27**(8), 687–708.

Butterworth, G. E. (1992). Origins of self-perception in infancy. *Psychological Inquiry*, **3**, 103–111.

Butterworth, G. E. and Hicks, L. (1977). Visual proprioception and postural stability in infancy: A developmental study. *Perception*, **6**, 255–262.

Carroll, J. J. and Gibson, E. J. (1981). Differentiation of an aperture from an obstacle under conditions of motion by 3-month-old infants. *Paper presented at the Meetings of the Society for Research in Child Development*, Boston, MA.

Damasio, A. (1999). *The feeling of what happens: Body and emotion in the making of consciousness*. New York: Harcourt.

DeCasper, A. J. and Fifer, W. P. (1980). Of human bonding: Newborns prefer their mother's voices. *Science*, **208**, 1, 174–1, 176.

Dennett, D. C. (1992). The self as the center of narrative gravity. In Frank S. Kessel, Pamela M. Cole, and Dale L. Johnson (eds). *Self and Consciousness: Multiple Perspectives* (103–115). Mahwah, NJ: Lawrence Erlbaum Associates.

Edelman, G. M. and Tononi, G. (2000). *A Universe of Consciousness: How Matter becomes Imagination*. New York: Basic Books.

Formby, D. (1967). Maternal recognition of infant's cry. *Developmental Medicine and Child Neurology*, **9**, 293–298.

Freud, S. (1905/2000). *Three Essays on the Theory of Sexuality*. New York: Basic Books Classics series.

Gallagher, S. and Meltzoff, A. (1996). The earliest sense of self and others: Merleau-Ponty and recent developmental studies. *Philosophical Psychology*, **9**, 213–236.

Gazzaniga, M., Ivry, R., and Mangun, G. (1998). *Cognitive Neuroscience: The Biology of Mind*. New York: Norton.

Gibson, E. J. (1995). Are we automata? In P. Rochat (ed.). *The Self in Infancy: Theory and Research* (1–23). Amsterdam: North-Holland/Elsevier Science.

Gibson, J. J. (1979). *The Ecological Approach to Visual Perception*. Boston, MA: Houghton Mifflin.

James, W. (1890). *The Principles of Psychology*. New York: Dover.

Jouen, F. and Gapenne, O. (1995). Interactions between the vestibular and visual systems in the neonate. In P. Rochat (ed.). *The Self in Infancy: Theory and Research* (277–302). Amsterdam: North-Holland/Elsevier Science.

Karmiloff-Smith, A. (1992). *Beyond Modularity: A Developmental Perspective on Cognitive Science*. Cambridge, MA: MIT Press.

Kessen, W. (1965). *The Child*. New York: Wiley.

Lee, D. and Aronson, E. (1974). Visual proprioceptive control of standing in human infants. *Perception and Psychophysics*, **15**, 529–532.

Lee, S. J., Ralston, H. J. P., Drey, E. A., Partridge, J. C., and Rosen, M. A. (2005). Fetal pain: A systematic multidisciplinary review of the evidence. *Journal of the American Medical Association*, **294**, 947–954.

Mandler, J. M. (1988). How to build a baby: On the development of an accessible representational system. *Cognitive Development*, **3**, 113–136.

(1992). How to build a baby II: Conceptual primitives. *Psychological Review*, **99**, 587–604.

Marlier, L., Schaal, B., and Soussignan, R. (1998a). Neonatal responsiveness to the odor of amniotic and lacteal fluids: A test of perinatal chemosensory continuity. *Child Development*, **69**(3), 611–623.

(1998b). Bottle-fed neonates prefer an odor experienced in utero to an odor experienced postnatally in the feeding context. *Developmental Psychobiology*, **33**, 133–145.

Meltzoff, A. N. (1995). What infant memory tells us about infantile amnesia: Long-term and deferred imitation. *Journal of Experimental Child Psychology*, **59**, 497–515.

Meltzoff, A. N. and Moore, M. K. (1977). Imitation of facial and manual gestures by human neonates. *Science*, **198**, 75–78.

Montagu, A. (1961). Neonatal and infant immaturity in man. *Journal of the American Medical Association*, **178**(23), 56–57.

Neisser, U. (1988). Five kinds of self-knowledge. *Philosophical Psychology*, **1**, 35–59.

(1991). Two perceptually given aspects of the self and their development. *Developmental Review*, **11**(3), 197–209.

(1995). Criteria for an ecological self. In P. Rochat (ed.). *The Self in Infancy: Theory and Research. Advances in Psychology*, Vol. 112 (17–34). Amsterdam, Netherlands: North-Holland/Elsevier Science Publishers.

Nelson, K. and Fivush, R. (2004). The emergence of autobiographical memory: A social cultural developmental theory. *Psychological Review*, **111**(2), 486–511.

Piaget, J. (1936). *La Naissance de l'Intelligence* (origins of intelligence in the child). Neuchâtel: Delachaux and Niestlé.

Rakison, D. H. and Poulin-Dubois, D. (2001). The developmental origin of the animate-inanimate distinction. *Psychological Bulletin*, **2**, 209–228.

Reed, E. S. (1982). An outline of a theory of action systems. *Journal of Motor Behavior*, **14**, 98–134.

Rochat, P. (2001). *The Infant's World*. Cambridge, MA: Harvard University Press.

(2007). Intentional action arises from early reciprocal exchanges. *Acta Psychologica*, **124**(1), 8–25.

(2009) *Others in Mind: Social Origins of Self-consciousness*. New York: Cambridge University Press.

Rochat, P. and Hespos, S. J. (1997). Differential rooting response by neonates: Evidence for an early sense of self. *Early Development and Parenting*, **6**, 105–112.

Rochat, P. and Senders, S. J. (1991). Active touch in infancy: Action systems in development. In M. J. Weiss and P. R. Zelazo (eds). *Newborn Attention: Biological Constraints and the Influence of Experience* (412–442). Norwood, NJ: Ablex Publishers.

Rochat, P., Blass, E. M., and Hoffmeyer, L. B. (1988). Oropharyngeal control of hand–mouth coordination in newborn infants. *Developmental Psychology*, **24**, 459–463.

Rovee-Collier, C. K. and Hayne, H. (2000). Memory in infancy and early childhood. In E. Tulving and F. Craik (eds). *Handbook of Memory* (267–374). New York: Oxford University Press.

Tomasello, M. (2008). *Origins of Human Communication*. Cambridge, MA: MIT Press.

Van der Meer, A. and Lee, D. (1995). The functional significance of arm movements in neonates. *Science*, **267**, 693–695.

Vygotsky, L. S. (1978). *Mind in Society*. Cambridge, MA: Harvard University Press.

Watson, J. S. (1995). Self-orientation in early infancy: The general role of contingency and the specific case of reaching to the mouth. In P. Rochat (ed.). *The Self in Infancy: Theory and Research. Advances in Psychology*, Vol. 112 (375–394). Amsterdam, Netherlands: North-Holland/Elsevier Science Publishers.

Zelazo, P. D. (2004). The development of conscious control in childhood. *Trends in Cognitive Sciences*, **8**, 12–17.

Zelazo, P. D., Hong Gao, H., and Todd, R. (2007). *The Development of Consciousness. Cambridge Handbook of Consciousness*. New York: Cambridge University Press.

2   The development of body representations: the integration of visual-proprioceptive information

Stephanie Zwicker, Chris Moore and Daniel Povinelli

Body representations may be considered in terms of both their first- and third-person characteristics. By first-person, we mean those aspects of body awareness and knowledge that are typically exclusively available to the "owner" of the body – the self. By third-person, we mean those aspects of body awareness and knowledge that are at least potentially available to any observer. Although there is overlap between first- and third-person characteristics – I can observe my own hand movements as I type just as anyone who happens to be watching me type can also observe these movements – there are also some qualitatively distinct characteristics. Most importantly, the owner of the body gets various kinds of information in a qualitatively different form and in some sense "privately." For example, the proprioceptive sense yields a type of first-person information that allows for awareness of one's movement and the relative position of various parts of one's body. Thus, even without visual information, it is possible to determine fairly accurately both dynamic and spatial aspects of one's body parts through proprioception. And so, in the dark, I know a lot more about my body than you do.

At least in humans, however, bodies are represented simultaneously in terms of both first- and third-person characteristics. Bodies have both externally observable properties and internal conditions. As adults, our experience and representation of our own bodies, for the most part, consist of integrated multisensory input. That is, when we perform an arm movement, we do not perceive the visual and proprioceptive information as separate yet correlated, but instead as unified and integrated. Similarly, the observed movement of our faces when we look in a mirror is perceived in integration with felt movement of our face. This integration depends upon the perfect temporal coincidence of the relevant information. In illustration, we know that adults will misperceive a fake rubber hand as their own under conditions where they are presented with a tight temporal correlation between first person information (either tactile or proprioceptive) from their own real hand and "third person" visual information from the rubber hand (e.g. Botvinick and Cohen, 1998; Dummer *et al.*, 2009).

It is worth noting here that such integrated multimodal body representations are applied equivalently to both self and other (Barresi and Moore, 1996;

Moore, 2006) – there is a common code. The notion of a common code for the perception of others' and one's own body further demonstrates that body representations must, to some degree, involve an integration of both first- and third-person characteristics of the body (Barresi and Moore, 1996; Moore, 2006). However, it may also be the case that the ability to detect the presence or lack of a correlation between visual and proprioceptive information during observed movement aids in the development of self-awareness, particularly in the ability to discriminate between self-produced effects and other-produced effects (Lewis and Brooks-Gunn, 1979; Bahrick and Watson, 1985). We return to this issue later in the chapter.

Our primary goal in this chapter is to consider the developmental origins of the multimodal first- and third-person integration that supports human body representations. In particular, we focus on studies of visual-proprioceptive intermodal integration. In the first half of the chapter, we review those studies that have examined this topic in infants, ending with some recent work that has examined integration through the manipulation of the synchrony of visual-proprioceptive intermodal perception. This review will reveal that our current understanding of the development of visual-proprioceptive integration remains at a very early stage. Thus, in the second half of the chapter, we consider a variety of issues that may guide future work on this topic.

Visual-proprioceptive intermodal perception in infants

Infants are able to detect the relations between their own action and contingent events in the environment from very early in life. Indeed, such ability would seem to be essential to any form of instrumental learning. For example, Watson and Ramey (1972) placed 8-week-old infants in a crib and gave them experience with a visual event – a moving mobile – contingent upon the production of a particular movement – in this case, a head movement. Infants easily learned the correspondence or contingency between their own head movements and activating the mobile and increased their rate of move-ment. A large literature now exists on the parameters of infants' instrumental learning and attests to the capacity of young infants to detect the relation between the first-person experience of action and the experience of external events (e.g. Rovee-Collier, 1987).

However, visual-proprioceptive body perception and representation is differ-ent. As noted earlier, when we perceive our own body movements we do not have an experience of correlated information. Rather, the multimodal sources of information are perceived as integrated. Integration in this context means a unified percept of the movement that has both visual and proprioceptive characteristics. Following the intersensory redundancy hypothesis of Bahrick and Lickliter (2000), we assume that this integrated perception is generated through selective attention to amodal properties, such as temporal character-istics, present in the intermodal stimulation, although we will not elaborate on this process further.

The method for exploring infants' visual-proprioceptive integration draws on the visual preference method for intermodal perception. For example, in classic work by Spelke and colleagues (e.g. Spelke, 1976, 1979; Spelke and Owsley, 1979), infants watched two movies while listening to a soundtrack played from a centrally located loudspeaker. The soundtrack matched one of the movies as, for example, when regular beats of a drum coincided with an object bouncing on a surface. Under these conditions, visual preference for one or other of the movies indicates that the correspondence between the matched movie and soundtrack has been detected. In general, in Spelke's studies, whereas there was no preference for either movie when played silently, the addition of the matching soundtrack led to a visual preference for the matched movie in infants under 6 months. When applied to visual-proprioceptive intermodal perception, the approach retains the presentation of two streams of visual information presented side-by-side on video monitors. Now, however, one of the monitors presents infants with live video of their own movements, whereas the other presents control video of similar move-ments that are not live. The proprioceptive information provided by the infants' experience of their own movements serves as the information stream that is matched to one of the movies (the live one). Thus, visual preference for one of the videos indicates detection of the correspondence between the visual and proprioceptive information.

A number of studies have employed this general approach to examine infants' visual-proprioceptive intermodal perception. Papousek and Papousek (1974), for example, placed 5-month-old infants in a highchair facing two television screens, one of which displayed a live video of the infant's face and one of which displayed a pre-recorded and therefore non-contingent video of the infant's face. Infants attended to the pre-recorded video for a significantly longer time, thereby demonstrating their ability to discriminate between the videos. Without direct visual information about their own face, infants had to rely solely on the detection of the relationship between the proprioceptive feedback provided by their facial movements and the visual feedback provided on the TV screens.

Employing a similar experimental paradigm, Bahrick and Watson (1985) sought to further elucidate infants' abilities at discriminating between self-produced and other-produced movement. In their first experiment, 5-month-old infants simultaneously viewed both a contingent (live) and a non-contingent video (pre-recorded video of a peer) of their body from the waist down for up to 4 minutes. Infants wore brightly colored, striped stockings to encourage them to attend to the screens and hide any distinctive cues infants may use to discrim-inate between the videos. Bahrick and Watson (1985) used legs as the visual stimuli instead of faces as in Papousek and Papousek (1974) in order to avoid cues such as differential eye contact between the videos that might be used by infants to discriminate between videos. Differential eye contact could occur as a result of using pre-recorded videos of the infant's face. Unless special precautions are taken, live video prevents the infant being able to make direct eye contact with his or her own image, that is, when the infant looks at the live screen the image in the live screen 'looks' back. This is compared to the pre-recorded video in which there will not be eye contact, adding another possible cue the infant could use to discriminate between the two videos. Also, as infants were viewing pre-recorded videos of other infants in Bahrick and Watson's (1985) study, feature recognition, that is identifying a distinctive cue that indicates it is one's own body (e.g. a mole) may have been used as an additional cue by which they discriminated between videos. Therefore having infants all wear the same stockings eliminated this possibility.

Infants looked significantly longer at the non-contingent video suggesting that 5-month-olds are capable of detecting contingencies between their own movement and the movement they view on the video. However, in this study a barrier such as a highchair tray did not impede infants' visual access to their legs. It was therefore impossible to determine whether or not infants identified the visual-proprioceptive contingency or alternatively matched visual-visual information in order to discriminate between self- and other-produced movement.

To better understand the extent to which infants rely solely on visual-proprioceptive contingencies, Bahrick and Watson (1985) repeated the experiment; however, this time they occluded the infants' view of their own legs, which meant that they had to rely solely on proprioceptive feedback from their legs and the visual information presented on the screens. Infants again preferred to look to the non-contingent view of their legs, adding further support to the hypothesis that 5-month old infants are capable of detecting intermodal (visual and proprioceptive) contingencies. A third study was conducted to rule out other possible explanations for discrimination, such as feature detection. Although the infants were all fitted with the same leggings, it is possible that they detected features such as leg length or width that may have aided in discrimination. Bahrick and Watson (1985) eliminated these cues by using a pre-recorded video of the participant for the non-contingent video as opposed to a pre-recorded video of a peer. Again, without the use of feature detection infants still showed a preference for the non-contingent video, further supporting the hypothesis.

Together these results raise other interesting questions. Why do the infants prefer the non-contingent video and is there a time in development when one might observe a preference for viewing the contingent video? In order to investigate this, Bahrick and Watson (1985) repeated the paradigm described above using 3-month-old infants; however, no overall preference for either video was seen. It did appear, though, that 3 months of age is a period of transition as the participants were bimodally distributed, with one group preferring the contingent view and another group preferring the non-contingent view. Bahrick and Watson (1985) suggested that this pattern of results indicates that 3 months of age may serve as a transition period through which infants move from being interested in the contingent pattern of information specifying the self to being interested in the non-contingent pattern of information specifying the other.

Bahrick and Watson's (1985) findings demonstrated that infants as young as 5 months of age are capable of discriminating between a contingent and non-contingent image of their own movement; however, the study did not isolate what kind of information infants used to make this discrimination as it did not control for the temporal or spatial aspect of the videos. Using 3- to 5-month-olds, Rochat and Morgan (1995) manipulated both viewing perspective and directionality in order to investigate the impact of spatial information in the detection of self-produced stimuli. Infants were reclined at a 60-degree angle, which impeded them from viewing their own legs, and presented with two different live views of their own legs on a TV screen. One view was referred to as the "ego" view (i.e. congruent), which presented the infants' legs from the infant's viewpoint. The second view was referred to as the "observer's" view in which the infants' legs were presented as if from an observer's perspective (i.e. non-congruent). The two views differed spatially but were temporally identical. That is, leg movement was temporally synchronous between the two videos but due to the different views being showcased (i.e. ego versus observer) the legs moved either toward (observer) or away from (ego) the infants. Further, directionality was left-right reversed. Both of these manipulations vary spatial information. Results supported Rochat and Morgan's (1995) prediction that infants would prefer the spatially non-congruent video, as nine out of ten infants in both age groups spent more time looking at observer's view of their legs.

In a second experiment, Rochat and Morgan (1995) examined infants' sensitivity to discrepancies in directionality alone. To do this infants viewed two videos as in the first experiment. Both images presented an ego view (thereby controlling for viewing perspective). However, one image displayed a left-right reversal (i.e. non-congruent), thereby manipulating the directionality of movement. Results replicated the findings of the first experiment in that infants showed a preference for the non-congruent view, suggesting that a change in directionality of movement is sufficient for an infant to identify a discrepancy in visual and proprioceptive feedback.

Having shown that infants are sensitive to the directionality of movement, Rochat and Morgan (1995) next isolated the viewing perspective (i.e. ego and observer) in order to determine whether or not it was a sufficient enough cue to discriminate between congruent and non-congruent information. In a third experiment, only viewing perspective was manipulated by again presenting infants with both an ego and observer's view of their legs, while maintaining directionality and temporal information. Contrary to expectations, infants did not show a preference for either the spatially congruent (i.e. ego view) or non-congruent (i.e. observer's view) video. This suggests that the preference observed in the first two experiments was driven by differences in directionality and not differences in perspective.

The studies described so far have either compared a live video with a recorded one (e.g. Bahrick and Watson, 1985) or two live videos in which spatial information alone was manipulated (e.g. Rochat and Morgan, 1995). The latter approach has demonstrated that 3- to 5-month-olds are capable of discriminating between two live videos of their own body on the basis of directionality. However, discrepancy in viewing perspective does not appear to be sufficient for discrimination if the temporal information remains contingent. This may be due to their inability to form a representation of their body from an observer's perspective. The former approach compares attention to synchronous and contingent intermodal information with attention to asynchronous and non-contingent information. As such, it is well designed to examine the discrimination of contingent intermodal information from non-contingent intermodal information. The results using this approach appear to be similar regardless of whether faces (Papousek and Papousek, 1974), legs and feet (Bahrick and Watson, 1985; Rochat and Morgan, 1995), or arms and hands (Schmuckler, 1996) are used as stimuli. The latter approach compares attention to two cases of intermodally synchronous but spatially divergent information. This approach is useful for examining the extent to which common spatial information is detectable from visual-proprioceptive intermodal sources.

However, we suggested at the outset of the chapter that human body representations involve an integration of first-person and third-person information, an integration that depends on the synchrony (or simultaneity) of those forms of information. Thus, a third approach is to compare attention to two cases where contingency is maintained but synchrony is disrupted. The idea here is to present infants with a visual preference situation in which one of the video monitors displays live visual feedback of the infants' movements while the other displays visual feedback of the infants' movements that has been delayed by a short amount of time. The goal is to determine the degree of temporal lag that can be detected. From our point of view, this approach is of particular importance for the examination of the *integration* of first- and third-person information because contingency is controlled – both videos display visual information that is contingent on the proprioceptively perceived information – but temporal coincidence is varied. Therefore, this approach isolates the temporal properties of visual-proprioceptive – or first- and third-person information – integration. Studies of the temporal properties of visual-proprioceptive integration may be seen as an examination of the window of simultaneity within which infants have a unified percept of the body.

Rochat and Striano (2000) were the first to report such a study. Using the preferential-looking paradigm, they presented 1- to 5-month-old infants with two views of their legs; one view was live while the other was delayed by 0.5, 1, 2, or 3 seconds. Infants viewed each delay for 1 minute in counterbalanced order. Infants did not show preferential looking in any of the delay conditions and this led Rochat and Striano (2000) to conclude that for young infants visual and proprioceptive information could be integrated over all delays between 0 and 3 seconds. However, given that this study produced only null results, it is in fact impossible to draw any firm conclusions. It is possible, especially given the relatively short exposure (i.e., 1 minute) at each level of delay, that the lack of preference observed reflected essentially random performance. Further, a failure to discriminate between the two videos based on a failure to demonstrate a preference should not exclusively be interpreted as an inability to detect a discrepancy as it is equally plausible that infants were capable of discriminating between the delayed and live images but simply did not have a preference.

To further investigate this phenomenon, Hiraki (2006) had 5- and 7-month-old infants view two displays of their own legs. One screen was live while the other was delayed by 2 seconds. The short delay ensures that the spatial information presented on each screen was as similar as possible. Seven-month-olds looked significantly longer at the delayed screen; however, there was no difference in looking time at the two screens for the 5-month-olds. Hiraki (2006) also reported that in a pilot study infants did not show a preference when the delay was 1 second, although it did not appear to be the case that delay was systematically manipulated. This study was the first to report a discrimination of a short delay in visual feedback of self-produced movements in infants and suggests that the temporal threshold for discrimination is between 1 and 2 seconds. The failure to find discrimination at 5 months might suggest that infants' ability to detect an asynchrony between the visual and proprioceptive stimulation changes over this period of development, although such a conclusion must remain tentative, given the difficulty of making firm inferences from a failure to show visual preference in the younger infants.

We (Collins and Moore, 2008) have also conducted preliminary research following on from Hiraki's approach. Like others, we used a visual preference approach. We presented forty-six infants (5–12-months-old) with two video images of themselves simultaneously – one live and one delayed by varying degrees (we used 1 second, 2 seconds, and 10 seconds as conditions in a between subjects design) for about 4 minutes. The delayed video was achieved through the use of a video delay unit (Prime Image Pipeline D1), which can insert delays in playback between 0 and 30 seconds in frame increments. Infants viewed video of their own faces in our study, as our pilot attempts using infants' legs were not able to sustain infants' attention for long enough. We then examined looking times to the delayed and live image and calculated the proportion of time spent looking at the delayed screen. Our initial results showed that older infants in this age range demonstrated a preference for the delayed image when the delay was 2 seconds, but no infants demonstrated a preference when the delay was either 1 or 10 seconds. This initial study is encouraging in that it is consistent with the results of Hiraki (2006) as well as extending his findings to faces. The non-linear pattern of results is intriguing because it suggests that there may be two separate explanations for the lack of preference at 1 and 10 seconds respectively, although it needs to be replicated in a larger sample. The results from these three studies seem to suggest a developmental pattern in which infants younger than 5 months of age are integrating visual and proprioceptive input (e.g., not discriminating a temporal delay) whereas infants 7 months and older, as seen in both our own work and Hiraki's (2006) study, become capable of identifying short temporal discrepancies between their visual and proprioceptive inputs.

We can see that very little research examining the temporal parameters of visual-proprioceptive integration has been conducted with infants. When one examines the research findings to date, it is clear that the current understanding of infants' visual-proprioceptive temporal discrimination threshold is far from complete. As we have seen, all of the relevant studies have used the visual preference paradigm, which is a method with intrinsic limitations, and, apart from evidence of a discrimination of a 2-second delay in infants in the second half of the first year, they have generated mostly null results. The downside to the use of this visual preference paradigm is that if infants do not demonstrate a looking-time preference, the inference from the results is ambiguous. Indeed, there are three competing explanations for the null results. First, of course, is that the infants are unable to make the discrimination under study. A second is that the discrimination is possible for the infants but that they do not have a preference for either stimulus. Finally, a third is that there is a preference but that the method is not sensitive enough to detect it. We believe that there is good reason to believe that the null results so far achieved may reasonably be attributed to a lack of preference as well as a lack of sensitivity, rather than a lack of discrimination. In the next section, we consider a variety of issues that may inform our inferences from the available data and suggest further empirical approaches to determine more accurately the nature of the development of visual-proprioceptive integration.

What is the temporal threshold of visual-proprioceptive integration?

We draw on two sources of evidence to inform our understanding of this question. First, a small number of experiments with adults have provided relevant data on visual-proprioceptive integration. Over a series of trials,

Leube *et al.* (2003) asked adults to slowly open and close one hand while watching the produced movement on a video monitor. The video feedback was randomly delayed between 0 and 400 milliseconds (ms) with each trial lasting 3 seconds. Participants were asked to identify whether or not the resulting video they were viewing was delayed or live. Adults responded at about chance levels when presented with a delay of 80 ms. That is, when adults were presented with an 80 ms delay, approximately 50 percent of the time they identified the video as delayed, and approximately 50 percent of the time they identified the video as live. Delays shorter than 80 ms were predominantly reported as being live and, conversely, delays longer than 80 ms were predominantly correctly identified as delayed. We have recently replicated this approach, with adults requested to make arm movements that they could only view using video feedback. Our results also indicated a threshold of about 80 ms (between 2 and 3 video frames, or between 66 and 99 ms). These findings suggest that, at least in adults, the lower limit of discrimination is much shorter than what studies with infants have so far revealed, but leaves open whether the difference between current estimates of discrimination in infants and adults corresponds to genuine developmental differences or only methodological differences.

Second, other studies of infants have examined the temporal parameters of bimodal integration across visual and auditory streams of information (see e.g. Lewkowicz, 1996, 2000). The use of these two streams of information has the advantage that both are under experimental control, and thereby allows a precise assessment of the temporal window over which bimodal information may be integrated. Using a habituation/test method, Lewkowicz (1996) first presented infants from 2–8 months with simple events involving synchronous visual and auditory information. After habituation, test events with delays varying from 100 to 550 ms were presented. Lewkowicz reported that when the auditory information led the visual information by as little as 350 ms, infants showed discrimination of live from delayed stimuli. When the visual information led the auditory information, discrimination of live from delayed occurred at as little as 450 ms. This level of temporal discrimination is substantially shorter than that observed in the research on infant visual-proprioceptive integration (Hiraki, 2006).

It is possible, of course, that the temporal parameters of intersensory integration for visual and auditory information are different than for visual and proprioceptive information. Interestingly, however, the threshold estimates for visual-proprioceptive integration and visual-auditory integration in adults are remarkably similar. For example, Lewkowicz (2000) habituated adults to a bouncing object in which the auditory and visual information was synchronous. Following habituation, participants were presented with a variety of asynchronous trials in which the auditory stimuli (i.e. percussive bounce) preceded the visual stimuli (i.e. the object hitting a surface). Adults in this study were able to detect temporal asynchrony when presented with a 65 ms delay between the sound and the bounce. The close correspondence between the temporal parameters for visual-proprioceptive and visual-auditory integration suggests no significant difference in the temporal information processing properties between the two types of bimodal integration. If the same is true for infants, then one might predict that temporal discrepancies discriminable for visual-proprioceptive events would be similar to those for visual-auditory events, i.e. about 350 ms.

From this brief review of other relevant research a reasonable conclusion is that the research on visual-proprioceptive integration in infants has not yet used appropriately sensitive methods. It appears that the current methods being used to explore this phenomenon need to be revised and improved upon in order to more clearly delineate infants' capabilities with regards to asynchrony detection. We would recommend a number of modifications. First, it is important to note that the discrimination threshold for infants' integration of visual and auditory information was established using a habituation/test methodology (Lewkowicz, 1996). Therefore, use of the habituation method for visual-proprioceptive integration is warranted. Ideally, infants should first be habituated or familiarized with live visual feedback of their movements and subsequently presented with visual feedback delayed by varying amounts of time.

Second, the study of visual-proprioceptive integration is compromised in comparison to visual-auditory integration in that it is not possible to exert control over one of the streams of information – proprioception – in the same way as one can with visual or auditory information. Furthermore, it is not possible with infants, as it is with adults, even to instruct them to move. In these paradigms, infants are free to move, or not move, as they wish. There tends to be considerable variability in the amount of movement that infants produce in these studies, with some producing little or no movement. But, for an infant to have even a chance of discriminating between the test videos they must move; if they do not, both videos will be appear identical. Therefore, those infants that produce little or limited movement are unlikely to be able to discriminate the test videos. Clearly it would be an advantage to be able to encourage infants to produce sustained movement during the trial, as adults tend to do. One solution to this issue might be to increase the salience of the visual stimuli by a dressing up the body part infants are to view. For example, when the focus is on leg movements, one might consider attaching tassels or lights to the infants' socks that react to movement, thereby increasing the infants motivation to move their legs and producing enough movement to allow them to discriminate between videos.

In short, it is very unlikely that we currently have an accurate picture of the temporal threshold for visual-proprioceptive integration in infants. We propose that a more valid approach to determining the threshold would be to use a habituation/test procedure along with strategies to maximize the movement that infants produce during the session as they attend to the visual feedback.

How might the temporal discrimination threshold vary?

We have suggested that the temporal threshold for visual-proprioceptive integration may vary with development. Adults can discriminate visual-proprioceptive asynchronies of around 80 ms, whereas the limited data to date show that infants can discriminate no less than a 2-second asynchrony, and even an optimistic estimate based on ideal experimental conditions would suggest that about 350 ms may be the lower limit for infants. However, our knowledge of the possible developmental pattern is extremely primitive. All we know at present is that infants during the second half of the first year have a threshold for asynchrony detection that is considerably longer than that of adults. We know nothing about how that developmental difference changes with age. Thus, future research will need to be directed at a cross section of ages in an attempt to map the change in threshold with age. This work will be of most interest when carried out in relation to other measures of self and body awareness. For example, it will be interesting to examine whether there are significant changes in visual-proprioceptive integration associated with developments in objective self-awareness, such as self-recognition during the second year. We return to this issue in the final section of the chapter.

A second issue researchers are confronted with when studying variability in the temporal discrimination threshold is the lack of control not only over the amount of movement, as discussed in the previous section, but also over the type of movements produced by the infants. Although it is likely that there is a real developmental difference in discrimination threshold, it is important to consider that the apparent difference in threshold between adults and infants may be, in part, dependent upon a difference in the extent to which the participants take an active role in trying to determine whether an asynchrony exists. One major difference between adult and infant delay detection studies is that adults are explicitly told the purpose of the study – to detect an asynchrony – whereas infants are simply left to observe their own movements. As a result, adults' movements will tend to be oriented toward the conscious goal to determine whether or not the visual input is delayed from the proprioceptive experience. If discrimination threshold also varies according to type of move-ment, then it is possible that adult participants quickly learn during the experi-ment to produce the kinds of movements that are most helpful. In contrast, infants are more likely to produce random movements, which will not neces-sarily be advantageous for detecting small temporal delays between visual and proprioceptive feedback.

Recent work with adults in our lab suggests that the type of movement produced is an important factor in asynchrony detection. We hypothesized that movements that involved a sudden onset and offset would facilitate the participants' ability to detect delays, whereas movements that were of a continuous nature with no sudden start or stop would diminish their ability to detect delay between visual and proprioceptive information. To test this idea, we manipulated the type of movement participants produced while viewing video of their hand either live or delayed by small lags. Participants were seated at a table facing a video monitor and asked to place their arm behind a vertical divider attached to the table thereby blocking visual access to their arm. The monitor provided the participants with a view of their arm that was either live or delayed by 1, 2, 3, 4, or 5 video frames. For each trial, participants were asked to move their hidden hand and arm from side to side in either a continuous motion (i.e. back and forth without stopping) or discretely (i.e. back and forth with a quick start and stop). Trials were 5 seconds in length. In order to control the amount of movement produced, participants were asked to move from one side of the table (i.e. right to left) every second thereby producing five side-to-side movements during every trial. Participants completed five trials for every delay; one for their right and one for their left hand, in a counterbalanced order in either the discrete or continuous condition. After each trial, participants were asked to verbally report whether the trial was delayed or live.

Analyses examined whether the type of hand and arm movement produced differentially affected participants' ability to detect temporal delays between visual and proprioceptive perceptual input. There was a significant difference in performance across condition, in that the threshold for participants producing discrete movements was approximately 81 ms, as compared to participants producing continuous movements whose threshold was about 113 ms. This study, therefore, demonstrates that the type of movement produced, that is discrete or continuous, significantly affects adults' ability to detect delays between visual and proprioceptive input.

The significance of this finding for studies with infants is that we can be reasonably certain that infants are not spontaneously producing the kinds of movements that would allow optimal asynchrony detection and therefore that the current measures of that threshold overestimate it. Further, apart from the type of movement, it is conceivable that infants may simply not be producing enough movement in order to provide them with a sufficient amount of information, therefore undermining their ability to discriminate. This may be particularly true for studies that use the infant's face as the stimulus in that legs and feet perform gross motor movements as opposed to one's face, which primarily performs fine motor movements. Given the difference in the type of movement, it is possible that discriminating small temporal delays between one's own movement and the visual feedback of that movement is easier with gross motor movements as seen with feet and leg movement. Further, the movements produced by legs and feet are more discrete than the movement produced by the face. Perhaps the more continuous movement produced by the face will make temporal asynchrony detection much more difficult in that there was not a sudden onset and offset of movement as seen with legs and feet.

Visual-proprioceptive integration and the development of the objective self

The kind of integration of visual and proprioceptive information based on synchrony reviewed in this chapter so far provides an important basis for body representations. However, it is well known that infants do not acquire a more objective or explicit sense of the self's body until the middle to end of the second year (Brownell et al., 2007; Moore, 2007; Moore et al., 2007). The paradigmatic manifestation of this development is mirror self-recognition, whereby infants show self-directed behavior when confronted with an unusual mirror image of themselves (Amsterdam, 1972), although there are other manifestations of the objective self (see Brownell et al., 2007; Moore et al., 2007). For some years, it has been claimed that the self-awareness underlying mirror self-recognition depends upon the integration of the visual and proprioceptive information available when attending to a mirror image of the self (e.g. Lewis and Brooks-Gunn, 1979; Mitchell, 1993; Povinelli, 1995).

We know that for toddlers, self-recognition depends upon the *synchrony* of the dynamics of the visually perceived mirror image and the dynamics of the proprioceptively perceived movements in front of the mirror. When synchrony is disrupted in the self-recognition task in toddlers, they fail to treat the visual image in the same way. A number of experiments have explicitly tested children's awareness of the self using modified versions of the self-recognition task that use delayed video feedback as opposed to a mirror or live video feed. For example, Povinelli et al. (1996) videotaped an experimenter secretly placing a sticker on children's heads while they played a game with the experimenter. Children were 2, 3, or 4 years or age – substantially older than those that can pass mirror self-recognition tasks under normal conditions. About three minutes after the placement of the sticker, the child viewed the video. They found that almost no 2-year-olds, 25 percent of 3-year-olds, and 75 percent of 4-year-olds reached toward the sticker. These results have been taken to demonstrate that children younger than 4 years of age did not understand how the delayed video image related to their current self (Povinelli et al., 1996). However, by 4 years, children are able to connect their current self with previous states of self into a temporally continuous sense of self. Therefore, based on these results, Povinelli et al. (1996) distinguished between an "online" sense of self developed at the end of infancy and a "proper" or temporally extended self developed later in the pre-school period (see also Povinelli and Simon, 1998).

More recently, Miyazaki and Hiraki (2006) presented children with a similar video self-recognition task in which a short delay of 1 or 2 seconds was imposed. They argued that such short delays would be within the limits for online processing of visual-proprioceptive information and thus that 3-year-olds would be capable of "passing" the delayed self-recognition task with such short delays in the visual feedback. Following the surreptitious placement of the sticker on the children's heads, the researchers then asked the children to attend to a TV. The image presented on the TV was either a live image of the child or an image delayed by 2 seconds. They found that over 80 percent of 4-year-olds reached up and touched the sticker on their heads in both the live and delayed conditions. In contrast, almost 90 percent of 3-year-olds touched the sticker in the live condition but only 38 percent in the delayed condition. Miyazaki and Hiraki (2006) repeated the experiment using a shorter delay of 1 second and found that 71 percent of 3-year-olds were capable of passing the task, suggesting that the temporal limit for an online visual-proprioceptive information processing system is between 1 and 2 seconds. This finding suggests that even a delay as short as 2 seconds might be too much for children's ability to detect the correlation between the visually presented image and their body representation.

It is worth noting here that the degree of delay – between 1 and 2 seconds – that has been shown to disrupt self-recognition in toddlers (Miyazaki and Hiraki, 2006) corresponds to the degree of delay shown to be discriminable by infants in the visual-proprioceptive integration tasks (Hiraki, 2006). Does this coincidence suggest that both self-recognition and visual-proprioceptive intermodal integration manifest the same temporal parameters? And, if so, does this mean that mirror self-recognition depends on the same information processing mechanisms as visual-proprioceptive intermodal integration? We suggest that this coincidence actually masks a significant difference between these types of task. As we have seen earlier in the chapter, the degree of asynchrony that can be detected in visual-propioceptive integration tasks shows a *decline* over development such that by adulthood, people can detect an asynchrony of 80 ms. In contrast, the degree of asynchrony that children are able to ignore in self-recognition tasks shows an *increase* over development, so that by 4 years children show self-recognition over delays of minutes, not just seconds. The fact that the temporal thresholds for these two types of task change developmentally in opposite directions suggests that the tasks depend on different processes with different developmental histories. Nevertheless, we argue that these processes are not independent; indeed they may well interact in the development of body representations of the self.

Visual-proprioceptive intermodal integration is fundamentally a basic perceptual-attentional-motor process. Coincident and correlated visual and proprioceptive information during movement are processed from early in life with the net results being the generation of integrated visual-proprioceptive representations of the body – what, in the context of its evolution, Barth *et al.* (2004) refer to as the "self evolved for locomotor flexibility" (SELF) system. It is important to emphasize that this self representation operates "on-line," i.e. during movement, but that it also incorporates (in the original meaning of that term) both first-person (e.g. proprioceptive) and third-person (e.g. visual) information. Established through the infancy period, the self-representation forms a necessary basis for the more explicit body representations that emerge at the end of infancy. In self-recognition tasks, the child is faced with a situation in which they have to relate the acquired self representation to the available image in the visual medium (mirror or video) in such a way that that visual image is taken to be "of" the self representation. This comparison is at first facilitated by the common information available in both – the dynamics of the mirror or video image match those of the online self representation – and thus the image in the mirror is linked back to the self.

This process that we have described for self-recognition is a representational one rather than a perceptual one, even if it is at first tied to online processing. Later, as children become able to hold in mind the self representation for longer, they become able to bridge longer temporal discrepancies between the presented visual image and the self representation.

Are there implications for the temporal parameters of visual-proprioceptive integration? The empirical work remains to be done, but one suggestion is that the development of the more explicit self-representation feeds back into visual-proprioceptive integration. Earlier we pointed out that there are likely real developmental differences between infants and adults in the degree of asynchrony that can be detected between proprioceptive information and visual feedback. Infants can detect asynchronies of 2 seconds (Hiraki, 2006), whereas adults can detect asynchronies of as little as 80 ms. It is possible that this developmental difference reduces with age in a continuous way as information processing systems mature. However, perhaps a more intriguing possibility is that the difference is overcome in a more discontinuous way as children acquire a more explicit self-representation. If so, then one might predict that assessments of visual-proprioceptive asynchrony detection would show rapid changes at just those points in development that are associated with changes in self representation. For example, we are currently investigating whether the onset of mirror self-recognition is associated with a significant decrement in the asynchrony detection threshold. Toddlers between between 15 and 21 months of age will be tested on mirror self-recognition and on their performance in a visual-proprioceptive integration task, in which the visual feedback delay will be manipulated. A direct comparison of visual-proprioceptive asynchrony detection for children who do and who do not show self-recognition will be carried out to allow us to determine if the asynchrony detection threshold is indeed associated with self-recognition. If such an association is found, this will provide evidence that a discontinuous developmental pattern of asynchrony detection is linked to the onset of an objective sense of self.

Conclusion

Human body representations involve both first- and third-person characteristics. Thus the integration of synchronous visual and proprioceptive information about the body and its movements is fundamental to body representation in infants and adults. Over the past twenty years extensive progress has been made concerning our understanding of the development of visual-proprioceptive integration, but there is still much work to be done. We believe that infants' temporal discrimination threshold for visual-proprioceptive integration has been greatly overestimated. Comparison of infant research and that with adults suggests that this work has been hampered by a lack of sensitivity of the methods as well as by the challenge of exerting control over the experimental preparations. Nevertheless, there does appear to be real development in the temporal parameters of visual-proprioceptive integration. Further work is required to elucidate the nature of the developmental pattern and, in particular, the relation between visual-proprioceptive integration and the development of more explicit concepts of self. A more complete understanding of infant visual-proprioceptive integration will allow us to not only understand how infants learn about themselves but also how they learn to discriminate between themselves, others, and the world around them.

References

Amsterdam, B. (1972). Mirror self-image reactions before age two. *Developmental Psychobiology*, **5**, 297–305.

Bahrick, L. E. and Lickliter, R. (2000). Intersensory redundancy guides attentional selectivity and perceptual learning in infancy. *Developmental Psychology*, **36**, 190–201.

Bahrick, L. E. and Watson, J. S. (1985). Detection of intermodal proprioceptive-visual contingency as a potential basis of self-perception in infancy. *Developmental Psychology*, **21**, 963–973.

Barresi, J. and Moore, C. (1996). Intentional relations and social understanding. *Behavioral and Brain Sciences*, **19**, 107–154.

Barth, J., Povinelli, D., and Cant, J. (2004). Bodily origins of SELF. In D. Beike, J. Lampinen, and D. Behrend (eds). *The Self and Memory*. New York: Psychology Press.

Botvinick, M. and Cohen, J. (1998). Rubber hands "feel" touch that eyes see. *Nature*, **391**, 756.

Brownell, C., Zerwas, S., and Ramani, G. (2007). "So big": The development of body self-awareness in toddlers. *Child Development*, **78**, 1,426–1,440.

Collins, S. and Moore, C. (2008). *The Temporal Parameters of Visual-proprioceptive Perception in Infancy*. Poster presented at the International Conference on Infant Studies, Vancouver, Canada (March).

Dummer, T., Picot-Annand, A., Neal, T., and Moore, C. (2009). Movement and the rubber hand illusion. *Perception*, **38**, 271–280.

Hiraki, K. (2006). Detecting contingency: A key to understanding development of self and social cognition. *Japanese Psychological Research*, **48**, 204–212.

Leube, D. T., Knoblich, G., Erb, M., Grodd, W., Bartels, M., and Kricher, T. T. (2003). The neural correlates of perceiving one's own movements. *NeuroImage*, **20**, 2,084–2,090.

Lewis, M. and Brooks-Gunn, J. (1979). *Social Cognition and the Acquisition of Self*. New York; London: Plenum Press.

Lewkowicz, D. J. (1996). Perception of auditory-visual temporal synchrony in human infants. *Journal of Experimental Psychology: Human Perception and Performance*, **22**, 1,094–1,106.

(2000). The development of intersensory temporal perception: An epigenetic systems/limitations view. *Psychological Bulletin*, **126**, 281–308.

Mitchell, R. W. (1993). Mental models of mirror-self-recognition: Two theories. *New Ideas in Psychology*, **11**, 295–325.

Miyazaki, M. and Hiraki, K. (2006). Delayed intermodal contingency affects young children's recognition of their current self. *Child Development*, **77**, 736–750.

Moore, C. (2006). *The Development of Commonsense Psychology*. Mahwah, NJ: Lawrence Erlbaum Associates.

(2007). Understanding self and other in the second year. In C. A. Brownell and C. B. Kopp (eds). *Transitions in Early Socioemotional Development: The Toddler Years* (43–65). New York: Guilford Press.

Moore, C., Mealiea, J., Garon, N., and Povinelli, D. (2007). The development of body self-awareness. *Infancy*, **11**, 157–174.

Papousek, H. and Papousek, M. (1974). Mirror image and self-recognition in young human infants: I. A method of experimental analysis. *Developmental Psychobiology*, **7**, 149–157.

Povinelli, D. (1995). The unduplicated self. In Rochat, P. (ed.). *The Self in Infancy: Theory and Research* (481). Amsterdam, Netherlands: North-Holland/Elsevier Science Publishers.

Povinelli, D. J. and Simon, B. B. (1998). Young children's reactions to briefly versus extremely delayed images of the self: Emergence of the autobiographical stance. *Developmental Psychology*, **43**, 188–194.

Povinelli, D., Landau, K., and Perilloux, H. (1996). Self-recognition in young children using delayed versus live feedback: Evidence of a developmental asynchrony. *Child Development*, **67**, 1,540–1,554.

Rochat, P. and Morgan, R. (1995). Spatial determinants in the perception of self-produced leg movements by 3- to 5-month-old infants. *Developmental Psychology*, **31**, 626–636.

Rochat, P. and Striano, T. (2000). Perceived self in infancy. *Infant Behavior and Development*, **23**, 513–530.

Rovee-Collier, C. (1987). Learning and memory in infancy. In J. D. Osofsky (ed.). *Handbook of Infant Development* (2nd edn; 98–148). Oxford, UK: John Wiley & Sons.

Schmuckler, M. A. (1996). Visual-proprioceptive intermodal perception in infancy. *Infant Behavior and Development*, **19**, 221–232.

Spelke, E. (1976). Infants' intermodal perception of events. *Cognitive Psychology*, **8**, 553–560.

(1979). Perceiving bimodally specified events in infancy. *Developmental Psychology*, **15**, 626–636.

Spelke, E. and Owsley, C. (1979). Intermodal exploration and knowledge in infancy. *Infant Behavior and Development*, **2**, 13–27.

Watson, J. and Ramey, C. (1972). Reactions to response-contingent stimulation in early infancy. *Merrill–Palmer Quarterly*, **18**, 219–227.

3 Emergence and early development of the body image

Celia A. Brownell, Margarita Svetlova and Sara R. Nichols

The body is the means by which we interact and communicate with one another, and as such it both connects us to one another and conveys fundamental social information about us, including personal identity as well as general character-istics like age, gender, and social roles, and psychological characteristics such as intentions, feelings, and attitudes. Although our own bodies are in the back-ground during much of our ordinary activity, serving simply as vehicles for our movements and interactions, there are many circumstances when they do become the intentional focus of conscious attention and we represent them explicitly and reflect on them. For example, we attend to our body size when we decide whether a chosen shirt or pair of pants is likely to be too small or too large; we carefully arrange our bodies and body parts in specific, sometimes atypical ways as we learn a new golf stroke or T'ai Chi form; we adjust our body's movements and posture deliberately to relay meaningful information non-verbally, including shared understandings; we change our body's appear-ance by intentionally concealing, adorning, or marking parts of it to enhance self-presentation; we use our bodies strategically as assistive devices or tools when we lean into something to move it or perch our children on our shoulders so they can see better; and we often evaluate the integrity, function, or appear-ance of our bodies, whether in action or at rest. Thus, we purposely configure and alter our bodies and body parts for particular purposes as we consciously engage the social and physical world. We voluntarily attend to and represent our bodies objectively, forming explicit concepts, beliefs, attitudes, and feelings about their physical characteristics and functional capabilities. And we project our bodily views of ourselves into the past and the future.

When and how do such conscious, voluntary, self-aware representations of one's own body arise in development? The purpose of the current chapter is to review and illustrate the developmental roots of children's objective own-body

The research reported in this chapter was supported in part by grants from the National Institute of Child Health and Human Development, HD043971 and HD055283, to the first author. We thank the parents and children whose participation made this research possible.

awareness. In research with adults a distinction is made between the automatic, unconscious, continuously updated sensorimotor representation of the body that specifies one's posture and the location of one's body in space, and which accompanies and directs intentional action, and the conscious, self-aware, visuo-spatial form of body representation that requires the ability to reflect on one's body as an object with characteristics such as shape, size, and spatial organization (Gallagher, 2005; Knoblich *et al.*, 2006). Developmental psychologists have similarly distinguished between the non-reflective, pre-conscious, embodied self-perception of infancy and the later-developing ability to make such self-perceptions available to consciousness, to label them, compare them, and remember them (Butterworth, 1995; Neisser, 1993; Rochat, 1995). The former is sometimes labelled the *body schema* and the latter the *body image* (e.g. Gallagher, 1995, 2005; Maravita, 2006), a convention we will follow in the current chapter. Whereas the body schema exists at birth and possibly even before, in the pre-natal period (Bertenthal and Longo, 2007), the body image develops over the course of childhood (Davison *et al.*, 2003; Mangweth *et al.*, 2005; Smolak, 2004).

In this chapter we examine the early developmental foundations of the body image in young children, specifically, the emergence and very early growth of what has been termed *body self-awareness* (Brownell *et al.*, 2007; Moore *et al.*, 2007). This is the ability to reflect on and reason about the body objectively, from without rather than from within, as it were. When and how do children integrate a first-person, felt and visually experienced body with a third-person visual perception of others' bodies to be able to imagine their own body, its structure, size, shape, and other physical qualities (Barresi and Moore, 1996; Meltzoff, 2007)? What is the nature and developmental course of children's earliest visuo-spatial, structural representations of their own bodies (see Slaughter, Heron-Delaney, and Christie, Chapter 5 in this volume, for early representations of others' bodies)?

To address these questions we present recent research exploring initial developments in children's explicit, self-reflective stance on their own bodies' shape, size, and configuration. We show that own-body representations develop slowly over the first three or more years of life, with the transition from implicit, pre-conscious body perception to explicit and conscious body self-awareness beginning in the second year of life, and that different aspects of children's early own-body representations develop along slightly different trajectories. We propose that an explicit visuo-spatial representation of one's body progresses from early awareness of individual body parts to representation of the body as a whole in which the body parts together constitute a typical configuration that corresponds to others' bodies. In particular, our data suggest that children first become aware of their individual body parts in isolation from one another, then begin to represent their body as an obstacle in relation to other things in the world, then become able to consider their own body size explicitly, which is followed by representing how their body parts are arranged in relation to one another. We hypothesize that these various components consolidate and become integrated over the pre-school years to yield a stable, coherent body image which is part of one's emerging self-identity and autobiographical self-representation (e.g. Howe *et al.*, 2009; Welch-Ross, 2001), and which can ultimately be estimated, evaluated, and altered to suit one's individual purposes.

Neural representation of the body and body parts

Because of a dearth of theory concerning the early development of body image, these proposals have been driven, in part, from empirical evidence in neuroscience research with adults. Specifically, there is growing evidence that the body is uniquely represented in multiple, only partially overlapping areas in the adult brain. Bodies are processed separately from faces in the brain (see Minnebusch and Daum, 2009; Peelen and Downing, 2007, for reviews), and processing the body's actions occurs in different areas from processing the body's form (Moro *et al.*, 2008; Urgesi, Candidi, *et al.*, 2007). Peelen and Downing (2007) argue that visual representations of bodies in the brain are not only functionally dissociable from movement-related representations of the body, but also from the cortical network involved in the putative human mirror system, the system involved in both perception and production of object-directed actions. Thus, the structure of the human body is represented in the brain independently of both its movements and its actions directed toward the physical world.

With respect to structure, visual perception of body parts and features activates different areas than perception of the whole body. The former is located in the extrastriate body area (EBA) in the lateral posterior fusiform gyrus, whereas the latter activates a fusiform body area (FBA) in the inferior temporal sulcus (Peelen and Downing, 2007; Taylor *et al.*, 2007; Urgesi, Calvo-Merino, *et al.*, 2007). There is also evidence that distinct areas detect one's own body over others' bodies (the FBA and inferior parietal lobe), and that these are different from areas associated with an abstract self-concept in the fronto-parietal network (Devue *et al.*, 2007; Hodzic, Kaas, *et al.*, 2009; Hodzic, Muckli, *et al.*, 2009). That is, the areas involved in visual perception of the body (EBA and FBA) do not respond to identity or ownership of body parts, and seem to be most activated by allocentric rather than egocentric views of body parts (Saxe *et al.*, 2006). This suggests distinct neural representations for one's own versus others' bodies.

Based on these findings, and on the assumption that the brain becomes more specialized for particular processes and representations over the course of development through accumulating experiences with relevant aspects of the world (Carter and Pelphrey, 2006; Johnson and Munakata, 2005) including integration with self-specifying sensory information (Botvinick, 2004; Lewis and Carmody, 2008), there may be reason to believe that these multiple networks for representing and processing information about the body develop somewhat independently and become progressively integrated over childhood. In particular, it is possible that children's earliest objective, visuo-spatial representations of their own bodies are not isomorphic with their representations of others' bodies, and that these complementary aspects of body representation do not develop entirely in parallel. It also seems reasonable to expect that early developments in children's own-body representations might differ for different components of these representations, such as body shape, body size or extent, and the spatial relationships among body parts and part–whole organization of body.

Thus, we begin by considering the sensorimotor body schema of infancy briefly, arguing that the body schema and the body image are distinct developmental phenomena. We then consider the evidence, including our own, for the emergence and early development of a primitive body image in the second year of life as the body schema is brought into conscious awareness. In particular, after Moore (2007; Moore *et al.*, 2007) we posit that young children first become consciously aware of and able to reflect voluntarily on their own bodies in concert with the emergence of objective self-awareness. Further, we propose that early own-body representations progress from body parts to the body as a whole, and that different components of own-body representation such as body size representation and the topographic organization of the body develop along slightly different trajectories. We conclude by considering some promising directions for additional research.

Precursors in infancy: the body schema

A rich corpus of research with adults has shown that perception of one's own body involves the integration of multiple sensory inputs and that altering the information from any one of those inputs can change the basic perception of one's body (see Holmes and Spence, 2006; Maravita, 2006, for reviews of this literature). For example, presenting visual information about the location of a body part, such as the hand, which conflicts with tactile or proprioceptive information about its location, produces a sense that the body part is in a different location than it actually is. One typically perceives that the hand is located where it appears to be visually rather than where it is felt to be. Own-body perceptions can be similarly altered to include physical extensions such as clothing, as well as tools when they are used intentionally. Somewhat amazingly, integration of visual and tactile information specifying the body can even include fake body parts: adults can be induced to feel that a rubber hand is their own hand when they watch the rubber hand being stroked at the same time as they feel their own out-of-sight hand being stroked (Botvinick and Cohen, 1998; Tsakiris and Haggard, 2005). When visual information about one's actions conflicts with kinaesthetic and proprioceptive feedback about the location of the body part or the direction of the action, the visually specified body part is perceived as one's own. For example, when adults draw a straight line under visual guidance but see their hand unexpectedly deviate from the line (via a mirror-based illusion in which they actually see an experimenter's hand), they maintain the sense that the observed hand is their own and attribute the unexpected movements to an external force like a magnet momentarily controlling their actions (Gullaud and Vinter, 1996; Nielsen, 1963). Interestingly, therefore, experimental alterations of the body schema do not lead to the conscious sense that one's body is not one's own, and the perception of one's own visually specified body is at least partially distinct from sensing the body's own movements, even though these are typically integrated in the adult brain with a sense of body ownership.

Like adults, young infants also sense that their bodies are their own and can detect a change in the information that specifies their own bodies. For example, by 3–5 months of age, infants can visually discriminate their own moving body parts from those of others, even though they cannot yet independently recognize themselves. While viewing themselves moving in real time on video, they distinguish images of their own limbs from paired images of another infant's moving limbs (Bahrick, 1995; Rochat, 1998; Schmuckler, 1996). Young infants can also discriminate images of reversed or upside-down contingently moving images of their own limbs from right-side up, canonical views of their limbs (Morgan and Rochat, 1997; Rochat and Morgan, 1995). At a minimum, these findings suggest that infants detect their own movements and the intermodal match or mismatch between their own felt movements and the movements they see on the video. Still earlier, by 2–3 months of age, infants perceive the temporal links between specific actions they direct toward objects or people and the sights, sounds, tastes, and tactile experiences associated with their own actions, and they can maintain or recreate the movements that generate these events (Rochat and Striano, 1999). Finally, research on infants' motor decisions has demonstrated that reaching, sitting, and crawling infants adjust their motor activity to take account of variations in the physical characteristics of the space through which they move (see Adolph and Berger, 2006, for a review). Thus, within the first half year of life, infants integrate multiple sources of information specifying their own bodies to differentiate their own bodies from the world, pointing to the early development of an initial body schema. Richer interpretations grant the young infant a representation of its own body (Meltzoff et al., 1995), but few argue from these findings that the infant is consciously, reflectively self-aware of its body. There is nevertheless general agreement that these abilities do form the perceptual, sensorimotor foundations for later-developing conceptual knowledge of the human body and objective self-awareness and the body image (Butterworth, 1992; Rochat, 2001; Slaughter and Heron, 2004).

Because the body schema is integrated with the body image in unimpaired adults, experimental procedures to examine the body schema in adults often rely on their ability to attend to, reflect on, and report their body's features, character-istics, or sensations, i.e. their explicit, conscious representation of their own bodies (Gillihan and Farah, 2005). However, this strategy cannot be used with infants and toddlers who are not yet consciously aware of and voluntarily able to reflect and report on their own bodies. But in adults with brain damage the body schema and the body image are sometimes dissociated. Thus, neuropsychology research has the potential to provide both models and procedures for studying early development of body representations, especially insofar as the body schema and body image are also dissociated in infancy. We will return to this point below as we present evidence for the emergence of a nascent body image in the second year of life. As a complement, understanding the development and integration of the body schema and body image in very early childhood can potentially provide insights into underlying neural mechanisms, including both how the body and brain are "put together" and how they can "come apart" following traumatic brain injury or in relation to disorders like autism or schizophrenia.

Emergence of the body image: early developments in body self-awareness

Evidence from neuropsychology demonstrates that the multiple systems under-lying adults' body knowledge can be independently disrupted or preserved (e.g. Felician *et al.*, 2003; Goldenberg, 1995; Guariglia *et al.*, 2002; Schwoebel and Coslett, 2005; Sirigu *et al.*, 1991). For example, in stroke patients it has been observed that the body schema is selectively impaired following lesions in the dorsolateral frontal and parietal regions, whereas configural and semantic knowledge about the human body are impaired after lesions of the left temporal lobe (Schwoebel and Coslett, 2005). On the basis of such evidence, these researchers concluded that a triple dissociation exists among sensorimotor (body schema), structural (body image), and lexical/semantic representations of the body. Likewise, as noted above, imaging evidence with unimpaired adults has shown that different brain regions are associated with visuo-spatial repre-sentations than with sensorimotor representations of one's own body. Also as noted previously, neuroscience research has shown that there are distinct neural representations for body parts and the whole body, as well as for one's own versus others' bodies and body parts. This work establishes grounds for hypothesizing unique developmental patterns for own-body representations, in addition to different patterns for the body image versus the body schema, and for body part representation versus whole body representation. In the ensuing sections we describe our findings on the earliest developments in children's self-aware representations of their own bodies and body parts.

Body structure

The development of children's objective awareness of their own bodies is grounded in the matching of self-produced movement with proprioceptive-kinaesthetic and visual feedback about the self which begins in infancy, and which becomes explicit and accessible to conscious awareness in the second year. Thus our work has focused on developments that occur between 18 and 30 months of age. We began our studies in this area in part because of a puzzling behavior we frequently observed informally with one- and young two-year-olds in our lab. In one particular study, for example, children would sometimes pull a small child-sized chair up to a large, solid box. They almost always pushed the chair right up to the solid front of the box so that the seat of the chair was tight against the box. Oddly, however, they would then try to sit in the chair, becoming puzzled and frustrated when they did not fit into the fraction of an inch between the edge of the chair and the front of the box. To explore the generality of this curious behavior, we tried to induce it by introducing a small table and chairs into the lab room, separating the chairs from the table, and encouraging the children to bring a chair over to the table to sit on. Once more, some children pushed the chair up to the table so that the seat was entirely under the table and then struggled to fit their own bodies, impossibly, onto the chair, often requiring an adult to intervene to pull the chair out so that the child had room to sit. The overwhelming impression in all of these instances was that the children were not consciously considering their own bodies and the space taken up by their bodies as they moved their chairs into position, and that once a chair was in position they were again failing to consider that their bodies would not fit into the space available. We never saw an "aha" or "silly me" or "what was I thinking" moment when a child discovered or figured out that what she or he had been planning or trying to do was physically impossible.

It was about then that DeLoache and colleagues (2004) published their landmark study of "scale errors," a similar phenomenon in which they showed that one-year-olds would attempt to fit themselves into doll-sized replica cars, try to sit on doll-size chairs, and try to slide down a doll-size slide unbidden. Also, at approximately the same time, Moore and colleagues showed that children in this age range failed to remove themselves from a mat they were standing on so that they could push a shopping cart to which the mat was attached (Moore et al., 2007), and they attempted to squeeze themselves impossibly through a too-small opening in a wall to retrieve something on the other side (Garon and Moore, 2002). These investigators thus provided some of the first experimental evidence for young children's failure to take their own body's physical dimensions explicitly into account while engaging the world – in one case failing to consider their body's size, and in the other case failing to consider that their own body could serve as an obstacle that obstructed their goal-directed actions. Even Piaget, many years before, had noted that his own 18-month-old daughter did things like trying to pick herself up by her own feet to remove herself from a hole (Piaget, 1954, obs. 122), or trying to pick up a rug while standing on it (Piaget, 1952, obs. 168). Thus, we were inspired to explore these phenomena more fully and systematically, motivated by the general question of how children come to represent and reflect explicitly on their own bodies as objects.

In the first study (Brownell *et al.*, 2007) we extended the work of DeLoache *et al.* (2004) and Moore (2007) to examine developmental patterns in: (1) young children's objective representations of their body's size, and (2) the possibility that their own body could obstruct or encumber the use of other objects. Children between 17 and 30 months of age (in three age groups: 18, 22, and 26 months) were administered a set of five tasks, three of which indexed body-size awareness and two of which indexed awareness of the body as obstacle. To assess *body-size awareness*, they were given doll's clothes (hat, jacket, shoes) to wear, a set of doll toys to play with (car, chair, slide) all of which were much too small for the child to use realistically (adapted from DeLoache *et al.*, 2004), and a choice of two doors to pass through to reach a parent, one of which was too small (adapted from Garon and Moore, 2002). To assess the ability to reflect on their *body as an obstacle*, they were placed, standing, on a blanket attached to the rear axle of a stroller and encouraged to push the stroller (adapted from Garon and Moore, 2002), and they were seated on a small mat and then encouraged to hand the mat over to the experimenter (adapted from Bullock and Lutkenhaus, 1990). For each task, failure to consider the objective characteristics of their own body would result in an error such as trying to put the doll's clothes on, trying to squeeze through the too-small door, and so on. Thus, attempts to use the doll toys and clothes as if they were full-sized were recorded as errors, as were attempts to squeeze through the too-small door. Likewise, attempts to push the stroller without stepping off the blanket and attempts to hand over the mat without first moving off it were counted as errors.

Nearly all of the children made at least one error on the three body-size tasks (90–100 percent at each age), with the mean number of errors declining between 22 and 26 months of age (M = 2.61, 2.79, 1.56 at 18, 22, and 26 months respectively), $F(2, 54) = 3.52$, $p = .04$. Some children were errorless on individual tasks, but only 3 percent were error free across all three of the body-size tasks. The average age of children who were errorless on at least one task was 24 months, while the average age of those few children who were errorless on all three was 27 months. However, even at 30 months of age, children continued to make errors with respect to their own body size

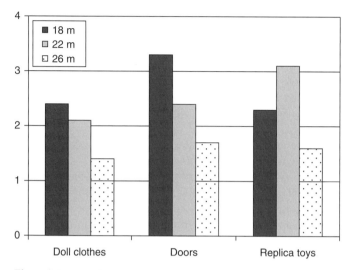

Figure 3.1 Age-related decline in body-size errors for each of three tasks

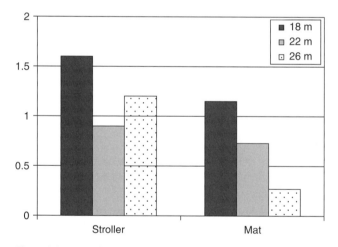

Figure 3.2 Age-related decline in body-as-obstacle errors for each of two tasks

(see Figure 3.1). Thus, *body-size awareness* appears to emerge at the end of the second year of life, with the earliest age of mastery occurring in the third year.

For the body-as-obstacle tasks fewer children made errors, especially at the older ages, although a majority at each age did so (77–100 percent). Again, the number of errors declined significantly with age, especially between 18 and 22 months (see Figure 3.2), somewhat earlier than for the body size tasks

(M = 1.41, .69, .73 at 18, 22, and 26 months respectively), $F(2, 34)$ = 4.14, p = .03. Between 21 percent and 56 percent of children were errorless on at least one task, a higher percentage than for the body size tasks. However, the average age of errorless performance was once more 24 months. Eighteen percent were error free on both tasks, with an average age of 25 months, slightly younger than for the body-size tasks. These data suggest that children may become aware of their *bodies as obstacles* somewhat earlier than they are able to consider the size of their bodies.

Performance across the three body size tasks was significantly related, as was performance across the two body-as-obstacle tasks (r's = .19–.56). However, there were no significant relations between scores on the body-size tasks and the body-as-obstacle tasks (r's = −.06–.02). Thus, these two aspects of early objective body awareness appear to be developing at least partly independently. Because even the oldest children in the sample continued to make errors on many of the tasks, it is clear that children's representations of their own bodies' size and structure continues to develop well into the third year of life.

Importantly, there were no relations between performance on the five body self-awareness tasks and performance on a parallel set of comparison tasks that did not require the children to reflect on their own bodies. Reasoning about one's own body therefore appears to be developmentally distinct from reasoning about physical objects. In sum, these findings show that representing and reasoning about one's own body explicitly, in relation to other things in the world, emerges late in the second year of life, and at slightly different ages for awareness of one's own body size and awareness of one's body as something with mass and solidity that can serve as an encumbrance or obstruction in relation to other objects.

Body topography

As adults, we know the spatial organization of our bodies, for example, where the knee is relative to the thigh, the ear relative to the eyebrow, and so forth. This is sometimes referred to as "body topography" knowledge (Reed, 2002). In a second study we explored this aspect of young children's developing knowledge of their body, that is, how their individual body parts are spatially organized (Brownell *et al.*, 2010). Slaughter and Heron (2004) have shown that in the second year of life children recognize that others' bodies have a particular configuration, shape, and structure, and they are sensitive to the canonical spatial relationships among body parts; during the third year, this knowledge of human body configuration becomes more explicit (Heron and Slaughter, 2008). Because we had previously shown that this is the period when awareness of one's own body as an object emerges, we reasoned that configurational or topographical knowledge of one's own body might also be emergent.

We focused on two components of this aspect of body knowledge: the locations of one's own body parts (body part localization), and the spatial relationships among one's own body parts (body configuration knowledge), because clinical neuropsychological research with adults has shown these to be distinct components of mature body representations. For example, patients with injury to the left parietal area sometimes exhibit autotopagnosia, in which they find it challenging to locate or describe the locations of their own body parts such as their elbow or knee when an examiner names them, even though they can generate the correct name for each body part upon hearing it defined, and can point to similar body parts on animals as well as individual parts of inanimate objects such as bicycles (Felician *et al.*, 2003; Guariglia *et al.*, 2002; Semenza, 1988). Investigators attribute the problem to a disruption in patients' topographic representation of their own body, independent of the semantic representations of body parts. Patients with ideomotor apraxia as a consequence of left parietal damage often find it difficult to imitate meaningless gestures which the examiner positions at particular body locations. For example, a patient might watch an examiner model a salute-like hand gesture next to the ear, but when asked to imitate it would reproduce the gesture next to the nose (Buxbaum and Coslett, 2001; Goldenberg, 1996). Because meaningless gestures directed to locations on one's own body must take account of the relations among individual body parts and their spatial organization, errors like these suggest disruptions in patients' structural knowledge of their own body (Chaminade *et al.*, 2005; Goldenberg and Hagmann, 1997; Goldenberg and Karnath, 2006). Recent imaging research is consistent with these findings and has identified the left caudal IPS in the posterior parietal cortex as specific to the processing of visuo-spatial relations among body parts (Dell'Acqua *et al.*, 2008).

In this study we adapted these neuropsychological procedures for identifying deficiencies in adults' topographic knowledge of their own bodies to address early developments in children's knowledge of their body topography. To assess children's ability to *locate their own body parts*, 20- and 30-month-old children were asked to place a sticker on twelve different unnamed body locations on themselves, one at a time, after watching an experimenter place a sticker at each location on another adult. The locations were chosen to include body parts for which the children were likely to have names (nose, hand) as well as those for which they were unlikely to have names yet (forehead, wrist); they also included visible and non-visible locations (from the child's egocentric perspective). To assess children's ability to *represent the spatial relationships among their body parts*, they were asked to imitate a meaningless gesture (a clenched fist) positioned at six different body locations, some visible (e.g. forearm) and some not (e.g. chin). For each one the experimenter placed her closed fist on a specific body location and then encouraged the child to imitate her. To control for differences in general motor and imitative ability, children were also asked to imitate novel actions with objects, all directed to the table top (e.g. pat a plastic dishwashing scrubby on the table). Children's sticker placements and imitations were scored for accuracy within 1 inch of the demonstrated body location (without penalty for left/right reversals).

Results showed that older children placed twice as many stickers on or adjacent to the correct body location as younger children (proportion correct, 20 months $M = .23$; 30 months $M = .47$), $F (1, 59) = 4.87$, $p < .05$). On the imitation task children at both ages performed well and equivalently when they imitated actions directed toward the table (proportion correct, $Ms = .76, .78$ at 20 and 30 months, respectively). But when they imitated a gesture directed to their own body, younger children performed much less accurately ($M = .08$) than older children ($M = .26$), as shown by the interaction between age and gesture location, $F (1, 55) = 3.69$, p < .06. Accuracy on the sticker and imitation tasks was significantly correlated ($r = .53$). So it appears that children's body part localization and their body configuration knowledge constitute related components of a general topographic representation of their own bodies which emerges between 20 and 30 months of age. These same children were also administered the body-size awareness tasks used in the prior study. A composite measure of body-size awareness from the three body-size tasks was unrelated to a composite measure of body topography from the sticker and imitation tasks. This suggests that there are two distinct aspects of early body self-awareness developing in this period, one related to children's knowledge of their own body size and one related to the topographic representation of their body and its parts.

Body parts

Our recent data suggest a still earlier developmental achievement in children's explicit own-body knowledge – awareness and representation of one's individual body parts. This, we believe, precedes the development of a conscious, coherent, hierarchically organized whole body representation which subsumes the individual parts and defines the spatial relationships among them. As previously noted, neuroscience research has demonstrated that the neural substrate underlying body-part processing in the adult brain is somewhat different than the substrate for whole body processing (Minnebusch and Daum, 2009; Reed *et al.*, 2006). For example, using ERPs, individual body-part processing has been found to occur at a temporally earlier, bottom-up processing stage, followed by a subsequent, top-down processing stage in which body parts are integrated to constitute a whole agent (Neri, 2009). Consistent with this distinction, imaging studies have shown that the cortical regions involved in visual processing of body parts and features are different from those that integrate body parts into a spatially organized whole (Hodzic, Kaas, *et al.*, 2009; Hodzic,

Muckli, *et al.*, 2009; Peelen and Downing, 2007; Taylor *et al.*, 2007; Urgesi, Calvo-Merino, *et al.*, 2007).

Young children begin learning the names of individual body parts by the end of the first year of life (MacWhinney *et al.*, 1987; Witt *et al.*, 1990). This typically means that they can point to a body part on themselves, or sometimes on a doll, when someone names it, e.g. "Where's your nose?" However, as reviewed above, our research has shown that even at 30 months of age, children find it difficult to locate their own body parts by pointing to them or placing a sticker on them after watching someone else point to the same body part on a different person without naming or labeling it. DeLoache and Marzolf (1995) have similarly shown that two-year-olds are quite poor at visually matching their own body parts to those of a doll when the body parts are not labeled. Thus, one-year-olds can point to their own body parts in response to a verbal label, but they find it challenging to match someone else's body parts to their own using visuo-spatial information alone.

This all suggests that individual body parts and their labels may be learned before children possess a configural, whole-body representation that includes the organized, spatial relationships among their individual body parts. To examine this possibility, we asked the parents of the children who participated in the study of early body topography described above to report which individual body parts their children knew. Parents were presented with a checklist of twenty-eight distinct, nameable body parts ranging from the common (nose, eye, hand, foot) to the uncommon (temple, collarbone, wrist, underarm). They were asked to indicate those which their children knew by name, using whatever response was relevant and meaningful in that family. For example, one boy closed and opened his eyes when asked where his eyes were, sniffed when asked about his nose, and opened his mouth when asked where it was. So it was not necessary that a child be able to produce body part names or labels, or even point to a body part, for a parent to credit the child with knowing that body part.

As one would expect, the number of body parts that children knew when named by an adult increased with age (Ms = 15.4 and 20.0 at 20 and 30 months, respectively), F (1, 59) = 23.59, p < .001. Furthermore, across ages, children knew many more named body parts (M = 17.5) than they could locate on themselves by placing a sticker on their own body part to match the location on an adult model (M = 3.2), F (1, 59) = 44.09, p < .001. Restricting the parent report items to just those twelve from the body part localization (sticker) task, children still knew significantly more labeled body parts according to parent report (M = 6.0), than they could demonstrate by matching from another's body to their own (M = 3.2), F (1, 59) = 35.10, p < .001.

The data further show that there was no relation between the number of body part names that children knew according to parent report and their performance on the body topography tasks, even when restricted to the twelve locations tested on the body part localization (sticker) task (r's = .002 – .07). If children who knew more body part names had also been better at the body topography tasks (independent of age), then we might have inferred that parts and whole are acquired together as a single, coherent representation of the body and its parts. In the absence of such an association, it seems reasonable to conclude that body part awareness and topographic own-body representations derive from underlying representations that are initially acquired separately even if they are ultimately integrated.

We observed anecdotal evidence for this conclusion in the body topography tasks as we frequently observed that two-year-olds would try to search visually or manually for a particular body location on themselves while they carefully studied the sticker or fist locations on the model. One boy, for example, repeatedly felt about his face as he referenced the sticker on the model's forehead, trying to determine where, exactly, his own forehead was. He finally placed the sticker on his cheek. Another child tried to turn around to look at her own back so that she could see where to place the sticker; she finally placed it on her side. These children knew many individual body part names and could point to specific, named body parts on request. But they didn't yet have a good general sense for where other, unrehearsed body locations were on themselves, or how to map unknown body locations on themselves from another's body. It's as if their own body maps were a collection of landmarks, without a larger cognitive map that defined the locations of the landmarks in relation to one another.

Thus one-year-old, pre-verbal children learn to identify the locations of selected body parts when these are associated with distinct labels. However, they do not seem to use this knowledge to map body part locations between themselves and others more generally. That is, being able to point to a given body part when requested does not translate into being able to locate that body part on oneself by visually mapping from someone else's body to one's own. This seems somewhat surprising – that a non-verbal means for indexing children's ability to locate specific body parts on themselves should produce poorer performance than a task that requires children to match the name for a body part with its location. What might explain this disparity?

One hypothesis is that children's early body-part knowledge as indexed by responses to adults' labels reflects a set of rote-learned, highly practiced routines tutored by adults, and is not grounded in complex, configural, hierarchically organized body representations. Children often attend to their own hands and feet, and even discover previously unknown parts of themselves such as their "belly-button," much to their own surprise and delight. Likewise, parents draw attention to children's body parts as they tend to them – labelling noses, mouths, and hands as they wipe them clean, for example – and as children themselves attend to or handle their own body parts. It is no doubt practical for children to learn "arms up" when a parent is attempting to place a shirt over the child's head, or to present a face for cleaning when requested. Parents also often take pleasure in teaching particular body parts and playing games like "where's your nose?" with their children. Thus, there are plenty of opportunities for rote learning of specific body parts to occur.

However, attending to one's own individual body parts, whether with or without the help and direction of an adult, permits only a partial perspective on one's own body. For example, when children play with their hands, it provides them with an egocentric visual perspective on their hands; but it cannot provide the information for a third person (imagined) perspective on how their hands are positioned and spatially related to other parts of their own body like their shoulders, neck, or knees. Such hierarchical, spatially organized own-body knowledge requires integrating a third person perspective on *others'* bodies with one's perspectives on one's own body. Thus, it is possible that infants could learn to indicate individual body parts on themselves as parents draw their attention to specific body parts, label them, and tutor children to respond to those labels. Children would thereby come to associate body part names with particular body part locations, movements, or gestures. But this would not require any higher order, organized, third-person visual representation of one's whole body and the spatial relationships among the various body parts and regions.

Efforts by parents to teach body parts and their names to infants and young children may nevertheless constitute an important source of input and a first step in the developing ability to attend to and reflect on self voluntarily and to objectify one's own body. Susan Jones and Hanako Yoshida (Chapter 11 of this volume) offer the interesting speculation that adults' repeated imitation of infants' actions may constitute another means for transforming and integrating early knowledge of particular body parts with subsequent representations of relations among body parts and locations. We know of no research that addresses parental efforts to draw children's attention to and label their bodies and body parts, nor how such efforts relate to the child's age, language abilities, or growing self-awareness, nor how effective they are. Thus, for the moment, these suggestions must remain speculative. Nevertheless, it appears that children may represent body parts as individual, independent, nameable entities before they can integrate them into an explicit, organized, visuo-spatial representation that characterizes the whole person.

Summary: early own-body knowledge

We have shown that children first begin to exhibit reflective awareness of their own bodies late in the second year of life. By this we mean that they can consciously represent their body as an object with characteristics such as size, shape, and mass, and that they also understand how their body parts are arranged in relation to one another, permitting them to map even novel locations from someone else's body to their own, and vice versa. We have also shown that different dimensions of explicit own-body knowledge are developmentally distinct. Children first begin to objectify their own bodies as they take interest in their body parts and as adults begin to refer to individual body parts by name. In the first half of the second year children begin pointing to their individual body parts on request, when adults name them. Subsequently, between 18 and 22 months in our studies, children begin to represent their whole bodies, understanding them as objects that take up space and that can serve as obstacles or encumbrances, getting in the way of something else, weighing things down, and so on, much like other objects in the world. Somewhat later, between 22 and 26 months in our research, children begin to understand their bodies as objects that can be bigger or smaller than other objects. By 30 months of age, they are beginning to understand their bodies in terms of a more detailed topographic representation; they know where particular body parts are located and how their body parts are arranged in relation to one another. Thus, during their second and third years of life, children's objective own-body representations progress from a collection of independent body parts, to a representation of the whole body with size, shape, and a hierarchically organized spatial structure.

It is important to note that the data pointing to this progression are exclusively cross-sectional; longitudinal data are required to be fully confident of this developmental picture. Moreover, a limited number of tasks have been used to index the various aspects of body self-awareness and to identify age-related changes. Nevertheless, these findings provide a first look at the emergence and early growth of children's explicit knowledge of the shape, size, and structure of their own bodies. Interestingly, these different components of explicit own-body awareness, while all emerging over the second and third years of life, also appear to be distinct and unrelated. That is, a child who is more advanced or competent in one component is not necessarily so in others. This suggests that even though these multiple aspects of body self-awareness are integrated in adults as part of a coherent, stable body image, there appears to be some dissociation among them developmentally, with integration likely occurring later in childhood.

Future directions

As noted previously, research with non-human primates, adult neurological patients, and normal, healthy adults has identified distinct cortical regions dedicated to specific aspects of body representation. This research generates useful questions and hypotheses for the developmental study of body representation and associated neural networks, as illustrated in the current chapter.

Likewise, learning more about how body representations develop and their underlying neural networks will provide an additional source of evidence to corroborate or to disconfirm hypothesized links between brain structure and body perception in adults.

As one example, using multiple methodologies in healthy adults and an adult with epilepsy, Blanke and his colleagues have shown that the temporoparietal junction (TPJ) is involved in mental representation and visuo-spatial perspective-taking with respect to one's own body, and importantly, that this function is dissociable from the mental spatial transformation of objects (Blanke *et al.*, 2005). They additionally found that interference with neural activity at the right TPJ can produce an "out of body experience," an aberrant model of one's own body in which the normal integration of self with the body's physical location is disrupted. This work suggests that the TPJ is probably involved in integrating a visuo-spatial perspective on one's own body (the body image) with the felt experience of an agentic self at a particular location (the body schema). This area is also involved in other aspects of body-related processing, including own-body vestibular information and visual perception of human bodies and body parts (see Blanke *et al.*, 2005, for details). Given what we know about the early development of the body image in children, it seems reasonable to hypothesize that the TPJ may be relatively immature until the second and third years of life. Correspondingly, if as Blanke and colleagues (2005) hypothesized, the TPJ is "a neural locus for self processing within a widely distributed network of cortical areas," and "the TPJ mediates ... visuo-spatial perspective, self location, and experienced spatial unity," then it is possible that the various components of body self-awareness become integrated into a coherent structural own-body representation as relevant cortical areas mature and as the functionality of the TPJ develops.

Interestingly, a recent magnetic resonance imaging (MRI) study of infants between 15 and 30 months of age showed this pattern. Lewis and Carmody (2008) examined the maturation of specific brain regions thought to be associated with early developments in self-representation, namely the TPJ and medial prefrontal cortex (MPFC). Controlling for age, they found that maturation of the left TPJ was related to children's ability to reflect explicitly on self as indicated by mirror self-recognition, personal pronoun usage, and representing their own and others' behavior in pretense. The data from adults, however, point to the right TPJ as the locus of own-body processing (see also Tsakiris *et al.*, 2008). Lewis and Carmody (2008) suggest that the right hemisphere may be more involved in processing information relating self to other, whereas the left is more involved in representing self and one's own actions. In any case, such findings are intriguing and suggest that it may be fruitful to pursue the neural mechanisms underlying developments in own-body representation beginning in early childhood, particularly in relation to other aspects of self and other representation.

Finally, the role of experience in forming and maintaining body representations during development is a key issue (see also Jones and Yoshida, Chapter 11 of this volume). In adults the role of experience in body perception is sometimes studied using short-term experimental manipulations (e.g. prismatic eyeglasses, Holmes and Spence, 2006) or patterns of recovery from trauma to or lesions in particular parts of the brain. However, neither of these approaches adequately mirrors the continual, dynamic interplay of experience and the growth of body representations during infancy and early childhood. Thus, studying how both universal and specific experiences early in development influence the developing body image may yield unique insights into the more general role of experience in shaping the human brain and human behavior and cognition.

References

Adolph, K. and Berger, S. (2006). Motor development. In D. Kuhn and R. Siegler (eds). *Handbook of Child Psychology, Vol. II: Cognition, Perception and Language* (6th edn). New York: Wiley.

Bahrick, L. (1995). Intermodal origins of self-perception. In P. Rochat (ed.). *The Self in Infancy: Theory and Research* (349–374). Amsterdam, Netherlands: North-Holland/Elsevier Science Publishers.

Barresi, J. and Moore, C. (1996). Intentional relations and social understanding. *Behavioral and Brain Sciences*, **19**, 107–154.

Bertenthal, B. I. and Longo, M. R. (2007). Is there evidence of a mirror system from birth? *Developmental Science*, **10**(5), 526–529.

Blanke, O., Mohr, C., Michel, C., Pascual-Leone, A., Brugger, P. *et al.* (2005). Linking out-of-body experience and self processing to mental own-body imagery at the temporoparietal junction. *The Journal of Neuroscience*, **25**, 550–557.

Botvinick, M. (2004). Probing the neural basis of body ownership. *Science*, **305**, 782–783.

Botvinick, M. and Cohen, J. (1998). Rubber hands "feel" touch that eyes see. *Nature*, **391**, 756.

Brownell, C. A., Nichols, S., Svetlova, M., Zerwas, S., and Ramani, G. (2010). The head bone's connected to the neck bone: When do toddlers represent their own body topography? *Child Development*, **81**, 797–810.

Brownell, C. A., Zerwas, S., and Ramani, G. (2007). "So Big": The development of body self-awareness in toddlers. *Child Development*, **78**, 1,426–1,440.

Bullock, M. and Lutkenhaus, P. (1990). Who am I? Self-understanding in toddlers. *Merrill Palmer Quarterly*, **36**(2), 217–238.

Butterworth, G. (1992). Origins of self-perception in infancy. *Psychological Inquiry*, **3**(2), 103–111.

    (1995). The self as an object of consciousness in infancy. In P. Rochat (ed.). *The Self in Infancy: Theory and Research* (35–51). Amsterdam, Netherlands: North-Holland/Elsevier Science Publishers.

Buxbaum, L. J. and Coslett, H. (2001). Specialized structural descriptions for human body parts: Evidence from autotopagnosia. *Cognitive Neuropsychology*, **18**, 289–306.

Carter, E. J. and Pelphrey, K. A. (2006). School-aged children exhibit domain-specific responses to biological motion. *Social Neuroscience*, **1**(3–4), 396–411.

Chaminade, T., Meltzoff, A. N., and Decety, J. (2005). An fMRI study of imitation: Action representation and body schema. *Neuropsychologia*, **43**(1), 115–127.

Davison, K. K., Markey, C. N., and Birch, L. L. (2003). A longitudinal examination of patterns in girls' weight concerns and body dissatisfaction from ages 5 to 9 years. *International Journal of Eating Disorders*, **33**(3), 320–332.

Dell'Acqua, C., Hesse, M., Rumiati, R., and Fink, G. (2008). Where is a nose with respect to a foot? The left posterior parietal cortex processes spatial relationships among body parts. *Cerebral Cortex*, **18**, 2,879–2,890.

DeLoache, J. and Marzolf, D. (1995). The use of dolls to interview young children: Issues of symbolic representation. *Journal of Experimental Child Psychology*, **60**, 155–173.

DeLoache, J., Uttal, D., and Rosengren, K. (2004). Scale errors offer evidence for a perception–action dissociation early in life. *Science*, **304**, 1,027–1,029.

Devue, C., Collette, F., Balteau, E., Degueldre, C., Luxen, A. *et al.* (2007). Here I am: The cortical correlates of visual self-recognition. *Brain Research*, **1**,143, 169–182.

Felician, O., Ceccaldi, M., Didic, M., Thinus-Blanc, C., and Poncet, M. (2003). Pointing to body parts: A double dissociation study. *Neuropsychologia*, **41**(10), 1,307–1,316.

Gallagher, S. (1995). Body schema and intentionality. In J. L. Bermudez, A. Marcel, and N. Eilan (eds). *The Body and the Self* (225–244). Cambridge, MA: MIT Press.

(2005). *How the Body Shapes the Mind*. New York: Oxford University Press.

Garon, S. and Moore, C. (2002). *Development of the Objective Self.* Paper presented at the International Conference on Infant Studies, Toronto, Canada, April.

Gillihan, S. J. and Farah, M. J. (2005). Is self special? A critical review of evidence from experimental psychology and cognitive neuroscience. *Psychological Bulletin*, **131**(1), 76–97.

Goldenberg, G. (1995). Imitating gestures and manipulating a mannikin: The representations of the human body in ideomotor apraxia. *Neuropsychologia*, **33**(1), 63–72.

(1996). Defective imitation of gestures in patients with damage in the left or right hemispheres. *Journal of Neurology, Neurosurgery and Psychiatry*, **61**(2), 176–180.

Goldenberg, G. and Hagmann, S. (1997). The meaning of meaningless gestures: A study of visuo-imitative apraxia. *Neuropsychologia*, **35**(3), 333–341.

Goldenberg, G. and Karnath, H.-O. (2006). The neural basis of imitation is body part specific. *Journal of Neuroscience*, **26**(23), 6,282–6,287.

Guariglia, C., Piccardi, M., Puglisi, A., and Traballesi, M. (2002). Is autotopagnosia real? EC says yes. A case study. *Neuropsychologia*, **40**, 1,744–1,749.

Gullaud, L. and Vinter, A. (1996). The role of visual and proprioceptive information in mirror-drawing behavior. In M. L. Simner, C. G. Leedham, and A. J. W. M. Thomassen (eds). *Handwriting and Drawing Research: Basic and Applied Issues* (99–113). Amsterdam, Netherlands: IOS Press.

Heron, M. and Slaughter, V. (2008). Toddlers' categorization of typical and scrambled dolls and cars. *Infant Behavior and Development*, **31**, 374–385.

Hodzic, A., Kaas, A., Muckli, L., Stirn, A., and Singer, W. (2009). Distinct cortical networks for the detection and identification of human body. *NeuroImage*, **45**, 1,264–1,271.

Hodzic, A., Muckli, L., Singer, W., and Stirn, A. (2009). Cortical responses to self and others. *Human Brain Mapping*, **30**, 951–962.

Holmes, N. P. and Spence, C. (2006). Beyond the body schema: Visual, prosthetic, and technological contributions to bodily perception and awareness. In G. Knoblich, I. M. Thornton, M. Grosjean, and M. Shiffrar (eds). *Human Body Perception from the Inside Out: Advances in Visual Cognition* (15–64). New York: Oxford University Press.

Howe, M. L., Courage, M. L., and Rooksby, M. (2009). The genesis and development of autobiographical memory. In M. L. C. N. Courage (ed.). *The Development of Memory in Infancy and Childhood* (2nd edn, 177–196). New York: Psychology Press.

Johnson, M. H. and Munakata, Y. (2005). Processes of change in brain and cognitive development. *Trends in Cognitive Sciences*, **9**(3), 152–158.

Knoblich, G., Thornton, I. M., Grosjean, M., and Shiffrar, M. (eds) (2006). *Human Body Perception from the Inside Out*. New York: Oxford University Press.

Lewis, M. and Carmody, D. P. (2008). Self-representation and brain development. *Developmental Psychology*, **44**(5), 1,329–1,334.

MacWhinney, K., Cermak, S., and Fisher, A. (1987). Body part identification in 1- to 4-year-old children. *American Journal of Occupational Therapy*, **41**, 454–459.

Mangweth, B., Hausmann, A., Danzl, C., Walch, T., Rupp, C. I. *et al.* (2005). Childhood body-focused behaviors and social behaviors as risk factors of eating disorders. *Psychotherapy and Psychosomatics*, **74**(4), 247–253.

Maravita, A. (2006). From "body in the brain" to "body in space": Sensory and intentional components of body representation. In G. Knoblich, I. M. Thornton, M. Grosjean, and M. Shiffrar (eds). *Human Body Perception from the Inside Out: Advances in Visual Cognition* (65–88). New York: Oxford University Press.

Meltzoff, A. N. (2007). The "like me" framework for recognizing and becoming an intentional agent. *Acta Psychologica*, **124**(1), 26–43.

Minnebusch, D. A. and Daum, I. (2009). Neuropsychological mechanisms of visual face and body perception. *Neuroscience and Biobehavioral Reviews*, **33**, 1,133–1,144.

Moore, C. (2007). Understanding self and others in the second year. In C. A. Brownell and C. B. Kopp (eds). *Socioemotional Development in the Toddler Years: Transitions and Transformations* (43–65). New York: Guilford Press.

Moore, C., Mealiea, J., Garon, N., and Povinelli, D. (2007). The development of body self-awareness. *Infancy*, **11**, 157–174.

Morgan, R. and Rochat, P. (1997). Intermodal calibration of the body in early infancy. *Ecological Psychology*, **9**(1), 1–23.

Moro, V., Urgesi, C., Pernigo, S., Lanteri, P., Pazzaglia, M., and Aglioti, S. M. (2008). The neural basis of body form and body action agnosia. *Neuron*, **60**, 235–246.

Neisser, U. (1993). The self perceived. In U. Neisser (Ed.), *The perceived self: Ecological and interpersonal sources of self-knowledge* (pp. 3–21). New York, NY: Cambridge University Press.

Neri, P. (2009). Wholes and subparts in visual processing of human agency. *Proceedings of the Royal Society Biological Sciences*, **276**, 861–869.

Nielsen, T. (1963). Volition: A new experimental approach. *Scandinavian Journal of Psychology*, **4**, 225–230.

Peelen, M. V. and Downing, P. E. (2007). The neural basis of visual body perception. *Nature Reviews Neuroscience*, **8**(8), 636–648.

Piaget, J. (1952). *The Origins of Intelligence in Children*. New York: International Universities Press.

(1954). *The Construction of Reality in the Child*. New York: Ballantine Books.

Reed, C. L. (2002). What is the body schema? In A. Meltzoff and W. Prinz (eds). *The Imitative Mind* (233–246). Cambridge: Cambridge University Press.

Reed, C. L., Stone, V. E., Grubb, J. D., and McGoldrick, J. E. (2006). Turning configural processing upside down: Part and whole body postures. *Journal of Experimental Psychology: Human Perception and Performance*, **32**(1), 73–87.

Rochat, P. (1995). Early objectification of the self. In P. Rochat (ed.). *The Self in Infancy: Theory and Research* (53–71). Amsterdam: Elsevier.

(1998). Self-perception and action in infancy. *Experimental Brain Research*, **123**(1–2), 102–109.

(2001). Origins of self-concept. In G. Bremner and A. Fogel (eds). *Blackwell Handbook of Infant Development* (191–212). Malden, MA: Blackwell Publishers.

Rochat, P. and Morgan, R. (1995). Spatial determinants in the perception of self-produced leg movements in 3- to 5-month-old infants. *Developmental Psychology*, **31**(4), 626–636.

Rochat, P. and Striano, T. (1999). Emerging self-exploration by 2-month-old infants. *Developmental Science*, **2**(2), 206–218.

Saxe, R., Jamal, N., and Powell, L. (2006). My body or yours? The effect of visual perspective on cortical body representations. *Cerebral Cortex*, **16**, 178–182.

Schmuckler, M. A. (1996). Visual-proprioceptive intermodal perception in infancy. *Infant Behavior and Development*, **19**(2), 221–232.

Schwoebel, J. and Coslett, H. (2005). Evidence for multiple, distinct representations of the human body. *Journal of Cognitive Neuroscience*, **17**(4), 543–553.

Semenza, C. (1988). Impairment in localization of body parts following brain damage. *Cortex*, **24**(3), 443–449.

Sirigu, A., Grafman, J., Bressler, K., and Sunderland, T. (1991). Multiple representations contribute to body knowledge processing: Evidence from a case of autotopagnosia. *Brain*, **114**, 629–664.

Slaughter, V., and Heron, M. (2004). Origins and early development of human body knowledge. *Monographs of the Society for Research in Child Development*, **69**(2), 1–102.

Smolak, L. (2004). Body image in children and adolescents: Where do we go from here? *Body Image*, **1**(1), 15–28.

Taylor, J. C., Wiggett, A. J., and Downing, P. E. (2007). Functional MRI analysis of body and body part representations in the extrastriate and fusiform body areas. *Journal of Neurophysiology*, **98**, 1,626–1,633.

Tsakiris, M., Constantini, M., and Haggard, P. (2008). The role of the right temporoparietal junction in maintaining a coherent sense of one's body. *Neuropsychologia*, **46**, 3,014–3,018.

Tsakiris, M. and Haggard, P. (2005). The rubber hand illusion revisited. *Journal of Experimental Psychology: Human Perception and Performance*, **31**, 80–91.

Urgesi, C., Calvo-Merino, B., Haggard, P., and Aglioti, S. M. (2007). Transcranial magnetic stimulation reveals two cortical pathways for visual body processing. *The Journal of Neuroscience*, **27**(30), 8,023–8,030.

Urgesi, C., Candidi, M., Ionta, S., and Aglioti, S. M. (2007). Representation of body identity and body actions in extrastriate body area and ventral premotor cortex. *Nature Neuroscience*, **10**(1), 30–31.

Welch-Ross, M. (2001). Evaluative self-awareness and the development of autobiographical memory. In C. Moore and K. Lemmon (eds). *The Self in Time: Developmental Perspectives* (401–422). Mahwah, NJ: Lawrence Erlbaum Associates.

Witt, A., Cermak, S., and Coster, W. (1990). Body part identification in 1- to 2-year-old children. *American Journal of Occupational Therapy*, **44**, 147–153.

4 Gulliver, Goliath and Goldilocks: young children and scale errors

Judy S. DeLoache and David H. Uttal

Consider the familiar story of *Goldilocks and the Three Bears*. When this famous folklore heroine entered the home of the three-member ursine family after having been lost and wandering through the woods for some time, she was desperately tired. Spying a set of three chairs, she decided to sit down to rest. She first tried to sit in the biggest one, but found that it was far too high for her to get onto. She discovered that the second chair was much too wide to be comfortable for her small body. Finally, trying the third, the smallest, chair, she was relieved that it was "just right" for her and promptly sat down.

In Goldilocks' efforts to seek comfort in the home of the bears, her actions were regulated by her visual recognition that certain of the objects present belonged to the familiar category, "chair." Having correctly categorized those objects, and feeling fatigued, she went about using them in the standard way. Her initial two attempts to sit down were foiled by the inappropriate size of two of the chairs for a little girl. Only the third was appropriately scaled to the size of her body and therefore (in the terms of Gibson, 1977) offered an *affordance* for sitting.

Goldilocks' first two sitting attempts were highly unusual, because object-directed actions are typically quite precisely scaled to the size of the object relative to the person carrying out the action. Such actions are regulated both by what one perceives when looking at the object and what one already knows about what *kind* of object it is. Thus, the sight of a chair – even an atypical one – activates our knowledge representation of the category "chairs," as well as our mental representation of the motor act of sitting in chairs. Whether or not we actually sit down depends upon, among other things, whether we are currently motivated to do so. Goldilocks was very tired from wandering through the woods and hence highly motivated to sit down and rest – motivated enough to make a prolonged effort to find a suitable chair. The acceptability of a sitting surface can depend on how tired we are, what the social situation is, how comfortable the available surface appears to be, and so on.

Of particular importance in this decision process is our judgment of the *feasibility* of the contemplated action – whether the particular chair in question would afford sitting for the particular individual contemplating plopping down on it. Is it too small or too large, too soft or too hard, too fragile or adequately sturdy *for that person to sit on comfortably*? Baby Bear's chair afforded sitting for him, but not for the much larger, heavier Goldilocks. (The same is true in many homes, in which a given chair is the province of one family member, whereas another favors a different chair with very different characteristics. For a sloucher, a soft couch affords comfortable sitting, but a dining-room chair is more amenable for someone who prefers sitting bolt upright.)

Adults typically make such feasibility judgments automatically and accurately. There is no need to carry on an inner dialogue to decide whether a particular chair is "sittable." In J. J. Gibson's (1977) terms, the *affordance* for sitting is directly perceived. This ability develops as a function of experience, as has been so elegantly demonstrated in research by Karen Adolph (2005; Adolph and Berger, 2006). Only through experience exercising a given motor skill do children become capable of making accurate judgments about whether they can successfully execute a particular action in a particular situation. Thus, infants who have just started crawling have remarkably poor judgment regarding when they will or will not be able to crawl successfully. New crawlers will, for example, heedlessly launch themselves down sloping surfaces far too steep for them to get down without falling. However, after a few weeks of crawling experience, infants judiciously pause at the top of a slope to consider whether or not to proceed.

The perception of affordances occurs similarly with respect to young children's object-focused actions. Even 2-year-olds understand the function of a chair and possess a well-practiced motor program for sitting. Regardless of age, sitting in an appropriately sized chair involves approaching the chair, turning around with one's back to it, bending one's knees, and lowering oneself onto its horizontal surface. In the vast majority of young children's interactions with chairs, their actions are accurately scaled to the size of the object. Occasionally, however, that's not the case; something goes awry. In spite of knowing what kind of thing a chair is and having sat on many different chairs, very young children sometimes fail to bring that knowledge and practice to bear in a given instance of sitting on a given chair. A 2-year-old might, for example, sit down on a dollhouse-sized chair or attempt to squeeze her foot into her doll's shoe – a shoe so small that she may not be able to get more than her big toe in. Another toddler might try in all seriousness to get into his toy truck.

This type of fruitless behavior is known as a *scale error*. Specifically, scale errors involve children making extremely dramatic errors when interacting with miniature objects, such as a dollhouse-sized chair or a small toy car (DeLoache, 2010; DeLoache *et al.*, 2004). Specifically, they attempt to carry out an action that is *impossible* due to the large difference in the size of the child's body and that of the target object. In such errors, the child misperceives the affordances of the objects and momentarily fails to take representation of his or her own body into account.[1]

The work summarized here originated with a series of informal observations. In many years of doing research with toddlers interacting with scale models of rooms, I had occasionally observed toddlers trying, in all seriousness, to sit on the miniature chair in the scale model. They would walk over to the tiny chair, turn around, bend at the knees, and lower themselves directly onto it. (Only by alertly snatching it away did we prevent the chair's premature demise.)

Everyday observations constituted the other original source of evidence for the existence of scale errors. David Uttal's young daughter tried to lie down for a nap in her doll's bed. Karl Rosengren had once observed his child persistently attempting to get into a small toy car. Being surprised and fascinated that any children would perform such remarkably misdirected actions, we initiated a formal investigation into this never-before reported phenomenon.

Figure 4.1 shows a prototypical example of a common scale error. As described above, this little boy is seriously attempting to get into the small toy car. The remarkable nature of scale errors can be appreciated best by viewing them being committed, so illustrative film clips are available at: www.faculty. virginia.edu/childstudycenter/clips.html.

Documentation of the existence of scale errors

The initial investigation of scale errors was conducted with children between 18 and 30 months of age (DeLoache *et al.* 2004). The crucial materials for this research were three pairs of very appealing commercial toys, each pair comprising a child-sized plaything and a miniature version of it. The larger items included a car that a child could get inside and move around the room, a small armchair that a child could comfortably sit in, and an indoor slide that a child could climb up and slide down.

The two-part session started with the child interacting with each of the three large target objects at least twice. Specific prompts were given for particular actions with the target objects: "Wanna go down the slide?" and "Come sit in your chair, and I'll read you a story."

Then the child was escorted from the room for a short break. In the child's absence, the three large toys were replaced by the miniature replicas, each of which looked just like its larger counterpart, except for size. When the child

---

[1] Clearly children can attempt to interact with large objects that are not scaled to their body size, and they can often be successful. For example, with enough determination and effort, a toddler might be able to get up on a chair with a high seat. In these cases, an action is difficult and in some ways inappropriate, but it is *possible*. In contrast, scale errors are defined as attempted actions that are *impossible* due to the relative sizes of the child's body and the target object.

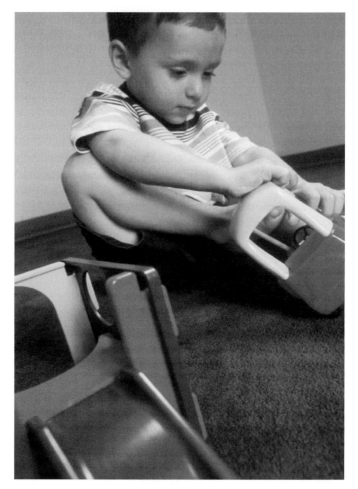

Figure 4.1 This child is committing a scale error: he is in all seriousness trying to force his foot into the miniature toy car

returned, nothing was said about the changes that had been made. The experimenter responded non-committally to any comments or questions that the child offered. The experimenter encouraged the child to interact with the miniature objects, using the same prompts that were given with respect to the large ones.

The children's responses to discovering the tiny toys in place of the large ones varied greatly. A few seemed delighted by it, one absolutely whooping at the sight of the substitute items. A few were distressed, including one child who asked plaintively, "Where my big car?" Another picked up the miniature slide and hurled it across the room in disgust, and one boy literally kicked the small slide all the way around the room. Most surprisingly, some children offered no clear evidence that they had even noticed the change!

Most of the time, the children ignored the experimenter's encouragement to interact with the toys. Instead, they simply played with the small toys in standard ways, pushing the toy car around on the floor while producing motor sound effects or sending a doll down the miniature slide.

Some of the children behaved in unusual and intriguing (and often amusing) ways. Approximately half of them attempted to interact with the miniature objects as if they were the original, larger objects. Some children sat down on the tiny chair, sometimes remaining perched on top of it for a surprisingly long time before noticing its actual size. They sat on the miniature slide and attempted to go down it, sometimes falling off in the process. Most remarkably, they tried to squeeze into the toy car, usually by opening the tiny door and then trying to force their foot through the much-too-small opening. In trying to interact with the tiny car, one child tried to solve the problem by taking her shoe off, apparently thinking that she might be able to get into the car if she were barefoot!

A crucial criterion for judging a given behavior to constitute a scale error is that it is *serious;* a scale error by definition involves a serious attempt to interact with a much-too-small object. Thus, it is crucial to distinguish scale errors from pretense. When children are executing a scale error, there is no "knowing smile" of pretense.

As described earlier, the original impetus for studying scale errors was the fact that we had informally observed them in a variety of different settings. Formal documentation of the occurrence of everyday scale errors outside laboratory settings was recently done by Liza Ware and colleagues via a web-based survey (Ware *et al.*, 2010). Parents were asked whether they had ever observed their children committing scale errors and, if so, to describe them in detail. To make it clear what we were interested in, the instructions on the website included detailed descriptions of scale errors, as well as a film clip of a child committing a prototypical scale error. The respondents provided a wide variety of accounts of scale errors, establishing empirically that scale errors are an everyday phenomenon. Table 4.1 presents a few examples of representative scale errors.

Independent evidence for the existence of scale errors comes from the laboratory of Celia Brownell (Brownell *et al.*, 2007; Brownell, Chapter 3 of this volume). She and her colleagues replicated the occurrence of the specific scale errors reported by DeLoache *et al.* (2004), that is, young children trying to get into the same miniature car, to go down the miniature slide, and to sit on the tiny chair. In addition, they designed several other tasks to examine young children's proclivity to take their own body size into account in a wide variety of situations. For example, one task involved getting through vertical slits cut in a

Table 4.1^a *Examples of parents' descriptions of scale errors*

Object type	Size description	Child's actions	Child's reaction
Doll's shoe	About half the size of a newborn's shoe.	Tried to put it on.	Cried out in frustration.
Toy truck	Size of a little car that you can hold inside your hand, like a Hot Wheels® car.	Tried to put leg inside the door as if he was going to drive it.	He was very mad. He asked me to help him get in the truck.
Doll's bed	Fisher Price® dollhouse bed.	Tried to get into bed with foot, pulling the blanket over her toe, then lay down on top of the whole bed.	Anger and frustration, then hurt because of the uncomfortable bed under her back.
Toy horse	About the right scale for a dollhouse doll to ride.	Tried to get on the horse's back and ride it.	She tried a few times, seeming determined to ride it.

Note: Some descriptions have been edited for length or grammar.
^{a} This table also appears in Mandler and DeLoache (in press)

wall. Some of the slits were wide enough and tall enough for a child to squeeze through, but others were far too narrow or too short. Performing behaviors reminiscent of classic scale errors with replica objects, many of these young children persistently attempted to force their way through or under the impossibly small openings. Brownell *et al.* (2007) also described a different version of scale error – young children struggling in an effort to get into their doll's clothes.

The documentation of the occurrence of scale errors in four independently conducted sets of studies (Brownell *et al.*, 2007; DeLoache *et al.*, 2004; Rosengren *et al.*, 2010; Ware *et al.*, 2010) provides compelling evidence for the existence of scale errors. This evidence also suggests that scale errors are a relatively common occurrence in the lives of very young children.

Now the question is why: what leads a child to commit a scale error? Or to put it another way, what underlies these common but nevertheless remarkable behaviors early in life? Any account of scale errors must interpret them as a type of perfectly normal, everyday behavior, given the fact that they are committed so commonly by so many typically developing children.

Scale errors and the use of visual information for planning versus executing actions on objects

In the original report of scale errors, DeLoache *et al.* (2004) proposed that they originate from a momentary failure to integrate visual information for planning a series of actions and for executing those actions. This account is based on the dual processing theory of vision of Milner and Goodale (1995). According to these theorists, visual information for planning versus executing actions is processed in different parts of the visual system. Visual stimulation is transmitted from the eye to the visual area in the occipital cortex, and from there it travels forward in two streams. One, the ventral stream, uses visual information for the identification of objects. The dorsal stream uses visual information to guide the execution of actions on objects.

The initial evidence for this theory came from brain-damaged patients who showed dissociations in the use of visual information; that is, these individuals were able to use visual information in the service of some behaviors, but not others. Those who had suffered damage to the brain areas involved in the ventral stream might not be able to identify a common object based on looking at it. Thus, if a cup were placed in front of them, they would be unable to state its name or tell anything about it. However, if the object were placed in their hands, they could use it appropriately. They could grasp the cup by its handle and bring it to their lips. In contrast, individuals with damage to the dorsal stream might be able to identify a given object, but then be incapable of carrying out appropriate actions with it. These individuals could say, "That's a cup," but could not use it to drink. These dramatic dissociations provide strong evidence that successful action requires the integration of the two streams of visual information.

Adapting this framework in the interpretation of scale errors, DeLoache *et al.* (2004) proposed that a scale error originates when a young child sees a miniature replica of a familiar type of object such as a chair. The child identifies the replica as a member of a given category – chairs – and decides to interact with it. In the formation of an action plan, however, the child fails to incorporate information about the actual size of the object; instead, the plan is based on a particular familiar large object or the general class of objects that the miniature one represents. Thus, the child identifies a replica object as a "chair," but of particular relevance to scale errors, the child's mental representation of the object as "a chair" does not include "tiny, non-functional." A moment later, however, as the faulty action plan is initiated, visual information about the actual size of the object is brought to bear to accurately scale the child's actions on it. The error is in the failure to use visual information to identify an object as a miniature object, not in the child's actual interaction with that object.

In committing a scale error with the miniature car, for example, the child first approaches it, just as he or she would do with the larger car, and opens its tiny door, just as would be required to get into the large car. Finally, the child tries to get inside, attempting to insinuate a foot through the open door. Similarly, with the chair, the child approaches it, turns around right in front of it, bends at the knees, and lowers his or her body precisely onto it. The crucial point is that the *execution* of each of these actions is governed by visual information about the *actual* size of the miniature object and is appropriately scaled to it.

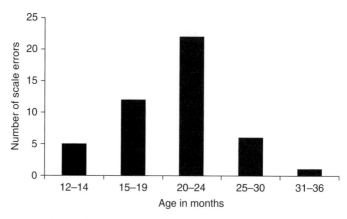

Figure 4.2 Incidence of scale errors by age

This account of young children's scale errors is based on Milner and Goodale's (1995) theory positing dissociation in the use of visual information for the planning versus the control of actions. Interpreting scale errors in their framework, we have proposed that in young children's interactions with replica objects, their ventral stream/planning system occasionally fails to integrate size information in the process of identifying an object and forming a plan to act on it. Once the faulty action plan is initiated, however, the dorsal stream/control system employs visual information about the actual size of the object in the doomed effort to carry it out.

According to this account of scale errors by very young children, the inverted U-shape function of their incidence reflects *immaturity* in the functioning of the ventral stream early in life. The incidence of scale errors by age (see Figure 4.2) suggests a complex developmental course. Initially, infants' conceptual representations of object categories are relatively impoverished. As a consequence, scale errors are initially rare; the level of activation of the relevant category that results from interacting with a given replica object is not strong enough to override infants' visual perception of its actual size.

With the burgeoning conceptual development that occurs in the second year of life, children's representations of object categories become increasingly rich and elaborated, and the associated motor routines become increasingly well integrated. As a result, the sight of a familiar kind of object can now override perception of its actual size, resulting in the initiation of a scale error. Eventually, with the advent of other developmental changes that occur at this age, especially substantial increases in the capacity for inhibitory control (e.g. Carlson *et al.*, 2005), the formation of inherently faulty action plans becomes progressively less common.

Conclusion

Writing this chapter induced various musings, including speculation on the rather remarkable prominence of issues concerning scale in the classic literature for children. Consider – in addition to *Goldilocks and the Three Bears* discussed in the opening of the chapter – *Alice in Wonderland*, *Tom Thumb*, and *Gulliver's Travels* (which was not originally a book for children, but was transformed into one through many re-tellings). The prominence of scale in these and many other children's books suggests that the topic is of inherent interest to young children.

This preoccupation with scale should probably not be surprising. After all, children live in a world that is, for the most part, not amenable to them in this regard. Most household furniture is designed with respect to the bodies of adults; simply getting onto the living room couch can be a challenging task for a toddler.

These musings led me to recall one of the favorite events of my childhood – visiting Tiny Town in the mountains north of Denver. Tiny Town is (I was delighted to discover via the web that it still exists) a "village" composed of miniature replicas of various buildings, including a jail, stores, and houses. A small train transports visitors around the town. Surely the enduring popularity of this attraction has much to do with children's delight in the rare experience of exploring a town in which everything is perfectly scaled for them.

References

Adolph, K. E. (2005). Learning to learn in the development of action. In J. Lockman, J. Rieser, and C. A. Nelson (eds). *Action as an Organizer of Perception and Cognition during Learning and Development: Minnesota Symposium on child Development* (Vol. 33, 91–133). Hillsdale, NJ: Erlbaum.

Adolph, K. E. and Berger, S. A. (2006). Motor development. In W. Damon and R. Lerner (series eds), and D. Kuhn and R. S. Siegler (vol. eds). *Handbook of Child Psychology: Vol. II: Cognition, Perception, and Language* (6th edn). New York: Wiley, 161–213.

Brownell, C. A., Zerwas, S., and Ramani, G. B. (2007). "So big": The development of body self-awareness in toddlers. *Child Development*, **78**, 1,426–1,440.

Carlson, S. M., Davis, A., and Leach, J. G. (2005). Less is more: Executive function and symbolic representation in preschool children. *Psychological Science*, **16**, 609–616.

DeLoache, J. S. (2010). Everyday scale errors. *Developmental Science*, **13**, 28–36.

DeLoache, J. S., Uttal, D. H., and Rosengren, K. S. (2004). Scale errors offer evidence for a perception–action dissociation early in life. *Science*, **304**, 1,027–1,029.

Gibson, J. J. (1977). The theory of affordances. In R. Shaw and J. Bransford (eds). *Perceiving, Acting, and Knowing*. Hillsdale, NJ: Erlbaum.

Mandler, J. and DeLoache, J. S. (in press). Early development of the understanding and use of symbolic artifacts. In S. Pauen (ed.). *Early Development of the Understanding and Use of Symbolic Artifacts*.

Milner, A. D. and Goodale, M. A. (1995). *The Visual Brain in Action*. New York: Oxford University Press.

Rosengren, K. S., Schein, S. S., and Gutierrez, I. T. (2010). Individual differences in children's production of scale errors. *Infant Behavior and Development*, **33**, 309–313.

Ware, E. A., Uttal, D. H., and DeLoache, J. S. (2010). Everyday scale errors. *Developmental Science*, **13**, 28–36.

Commentary on Part I

The embodied mini-*me*: tracing the development of body representations and their role for self-awareness

Manos Tsakiris

We are certainly born with a body, but are we also born with a body in our brain? The four chapters that deal with the development of body representations in the present volume touch upon a timely issue in developmental psychology, cognitive and experimental psychology, and cognitive neurosciences. Back in the old days of the cognitive revolution, multisensory processing and sensorimotor integration were placed on the margins of psychological research on the human mind, mainly because the psychological community thought that whatever interesting goes on in our minds has little or nothing to do with the organs that we use to perceive the world and move around it. However, recent interdisciplinary advances suggest that higher cognitive functions are indeed grounded in basic sensorimotor processes (Barsalou, 2008; Rossetti *et al.*, 2007). Embodied cognition accounts emphasize the crucial role of body representations for every act of perception, but even for other cognitive functions such as reasoning and mentalizing. Even psychological models of the self tend to ground the most basic sense of self to its body, rather than to autobiographical memories and cognitive schemata that was the trend for much of the research on self done during the "cognitive revolution." The four chapters presented here deal with a series of topics ranging from basic processes of sensorimotor integration during visual perception (see DeLoache and Uttal, Chapter 4 of this volume) to the organization of body-schematic and multisensory processes (see Chapter 1 by Rochat and Chapter 2 by Zwicker, Moore, and Povinelli), and from the awareness of one's body image (see Chapter 3 by Brownell, Svetlova, and Nichols) to self-identity (see Chapter 2 by Zwicker, Moore, and Povinelli).

Economic and Social Research Council (ESRC, UK) First Grant RES-061–25–0233.

The body in the wonderland

DeLoache and Uttal focus on the striking scale errors performed by some infants when confronted with miniature replicas of larger-sized toys. For example, some infants would try to get into a miniature car, if they had previously played with a larger car. DeLoache and Uttal make an interesting claim about the development of the synergies between the ventral and dorsal streams that are required for efficient object recognition and manipulation. This hypothesis seems plausible given our knowledge on the behavior of neuropsychological patients. However, while reading this chapter, the reader inevitably wonders what would happen if we were to reverse the order of presentation of the two critical conditions. Typically, infants are first invited to play with small chairs and cars whose size affords real-life type of interactions (e.g. sitting on the baby chair, or getting into the small car). They are then asked to leave the room, and when they return, their toys have been replaced by miniatures that are almost identical in appearance. A certain percentage of infants would then perform the typical scale errors by trying to sit on a chair or get into a car that is now as small as their foot. Would infants make the same scale errors if they were not exposed to the larger toys in the first place? Apparently, only anecdotal evidence exists that infants do make scale errors spontaneously (e.g. trying to sit on the doll's chair), but one could not rule out the role of priming effects in the standard experimental paradigm or the existence of a highly malleable representation of their body size that has not yet matured to the level needed for constraining motivational states (e.g. "I want to play with this toy") and informing efficient interaction with all the environmental challenges. A strong motivation to explore whatever there is out there that attracts their attention and interest, in combination with the absence of stable representations of body size or awareness of their body competence, may result in spontaneous unsuccessful interactions with the external world. After all, it is by trial and error that we get to learn, not only about the world, but also about ourselves. Scale errors are just another instance of this process arising when interacting in the wonderland.

Interestingly, the chapter by Brownell, Svetlova, and Nichols provides an overview of the development of body image that might also be relevant for the understanding of scale errors, among other behavioral patterns reviewed in their chapter. The concept of body image has a long and troubled history in psychology. Usually, the terms "body image" and "body schema" are used indiscriminately, with ever-changing meanings between authors. The body schema has been interpreted as the knowledge or conscious awareness of the body (Gerstmann, 1927; Klein, 1930, cited in Poeck and Orgass, 1971); as an image (Lhermitte, 1939); as cerebral representation of the body (Hauptmann, 1928; Lange 1936, cited in Poeck and Orgass, 1971); and as a pre-conscious physiological function (Head and Holmes, 1911; for a review see Poeck and

Orgass, 1971). In recent years, the body schema has been linked to innate, sub-personal body representations hardwired in the brain, whereas body image usually refers to one's perceptual relationship to one's own body. According to Gallagher (2005), the concept of body image refers to the appearance of the body in the perceptual field. In contrast, the concept of body schema denotes the way the body shapes the perceptual field. Another way by which the body schema can be distinguished from the body image has been proposed by Paillard (1999). In a way that resembles the two visual systems (the "where" and the "what" systems, see Ungerleider and Mishkin, 1982), Paillard (1999) suggested that the body schema is in fact the "where" system of kinaesthetic information, whereas the body image is the "what" system of perceptual identification of body features. It was then assumed that proprioceptive infor-mation is necessary for updating the body schema, whereas exteroceptive multimodal information, mainly visual, underpins the central representation and percept of the body image. This analogy between body image and the "what" system, and body schema and the "where" system, might be relevant for understanding the scale errors, given that from 18 to 30 months children fail to take their physical dimensions explicitly into account, as Brownell and col-leagues show.

The consensus in the recent literature is that body image involves mainly a conscious mental representation of the visual appearance of one's body. Brownell, Svetlova, and Nichols adopt a similar approach, by adding that body image is the explicit visuo-spatial representation of one's body. The findings they review suggest that children become aware of their individual body parts in isolation from one another, while later (at the end of their second year), they become able to represent their body size explicitly and finally to represent their body parts as connected in relation to one another. These stages emerge gradually during the first two to three years of life. Children will first manage to objectify their own body because, according to Brownell and colleagues, they "take interest in their body parts." Around 18 months of age, they will start pointing to individual body parts upon request. This conquest will be followed by a more global representation of the whole body between months 18 and 22, as evidenced by their understanding that bodies take up space. They will then display an understanding that bodies are bigger or smaller than other objects, and eventually by the thirtieth month they will display a topographical understanding not only of the location of body parts, but crucially of the arrangements of one body part in relation to another. This developmental path-way aptly demonstrates how what was once a bunch of body parts comes to be represented as an integrated whole body that is constituted by body parts that are related to each other in specific and dependent ways imposed by their anatomy and functionality. This coherent body has size, shape and a clear spatial structure that is now mentally represented.

The multisensory body

Even though the mastering of a coherent and global body image (i.e. the visuo-spatial representation of one's body) does not occur until approximately the end of the third year, Rochat (Chapter 1) argues in favor of a primordial sense of self-unity present at birth. This primordial sense of self should be understood in two ways. First as the experiential awareness, distinct from conceptual aware-ness, of being embodied in the world, and second as a motor potentiality (See also Gallese and Sinigaglia, 2010), which is *ready-at-hand* from birth, and is guided by innate body schematic processes. Rochat argues that from birth, infants are capable of processing self-specifying information in a highly effi-cient way. For example, Rochat and Hespos (1997) have shown how neonates can distinguish between self- and externally generated touch on their face. Of more relevance to the chapter by Brownell and colleagues, the work reviewed, and to a large extent performed by Rochat and his colleagues, suggests that contrary to the slow and incremental development of body image, at least some body representations are innate. For example, Morgan and Rochat (1997) showed that 3-month-old infants, with relatively little experience of seeing their legs, are sensitive to left-right reversal of their own legs shown on a screen and to differences in the relative movements and/or the featural characteristics of the legs (i.e. the relative bending of the legs at the knees and ankles), supporting the idea of innate representations of the anatomical and structural features of a normative body. In a way, Rochat's research deals with what can be considered as a prerequisite for the emergence of body image. An interesting line of future research would be to actually use performance on the body-schema paradigms reviewed by Rochat to predict the onset of the different stages of an explicit body awareness as studied by Brownell and colleagues. It is often the case that body schema and body image are treated as dissociable representations, and in fact few, if any, studies have looked at the interaction between body-schematic and body-image processes. However, to the extent that the experience of one's body is at the same time sensorimotor, affective, and perceptual, and if we want to understand the neurocognitive processes that underpin the versatile nature of embodied experience, it will be essential to look for interactions between the body in action and the body perceived as an object. The interactions between the experience of the body in action and the experience of the body perceived as an object might also be crucial for under-standing the building blocks of the ability to shift perspectives; that is, to understand how the change from a first person perspective to a third person perspective takes place. This perspective change might turn out to be essential for grounding the ability to mentalize, but also the ability to form a representa-tion of one's identity as an "objective self," as suggested in Chapter 2 by Zwicker, Moore, and Povinelli.

While Rochat uses the abundance of data that favor a primordial experiential self-awareness in infants, Zwicker and colleagues extend the research on multisensory processing to ask how such processes might lead to a full-blown awareness of one's self. Here, the difference between self-awareness and awareness of one's self might be understood as the difference between experiential and conceptual awareness (see Chapter 1 by Rochat), that is, the difference between the body as the active perceiver of the world and the body perceived as an object. Zwicker and colleagues provide an engaging review of the studies that looked at multisensory, and in particular visuo-proprioceptive, integration in infants, and in particular they show how multisensory processing may underpin the awareness of one's body, but also the awareness of one's identity.

As Zwicker and colleagues explain, infants are capable of detecting visuo-proprioceptive incongruencies from early on. The study by Bahrick and Watson (1985) shows that at around 3 months of age infants start spending more time viewing an incongruent pattern of body movement where the relationship between visual and proprioceptive feedback is experimentally manipulated, rather than a congruent one. Similar findings were reported in replications and modifications of this paradigm, but the critical issue here is the actual temporal threshold for detecting mismatches. The results are not conclusive as detection thresholds depend on the sensory modalities used (e.g. auditory-visual, visuo-proprioceptive), but the consensus seems to be that for visual-proprioceptive asynchronies presented to adults the threshold is around 80 ms, whereas the limited data to date suggest that infants between 5 and 12 months can discriminate no less than a 2-second asynchrony. Overall, intermodal matching seems to be a prerequisite for a sense of body ownership and self-identification (Rochat and Striano, 2000; Tsakiris, 2010; and see also Zwicker, Moore, and Povinelli, Chapter 2 in this volume). The extent to which multisensory input is the sole driver of body ownership or not is a controversial issue at the heart of the neurocognitive understanding of body ownership in particular, and of body representations more generally (Berlucchi and Aglioti, 1997; Carruthers, 2008; Dijkerman and de Haan, 2007; Graziano and Botvinik, 2001; Holmes and Spence, 2006; Sirigu et al., 1991; Tsakiris and Fotopoulou, 2008).

Several of the tasks used to test infants' ability to detect visuo-proprioceptive incongruencies are similar to the experimental paradigms developed in Marc Jeannerod's lab at the Institut des Sciences Cognitives, Lyon, France. In self-recognition experiments on adults, afferent signals such as vision and proprioception need to be integrated with efferent signals in order to generate a coherent self-representation (for a review see Jeannerod, 2003). Participants see a body part, which may or may not be related to their own body, and judge whether it is their own body part or not. The information available to support this judgment is systematically varied across conditions, for example by manipulating the identity of the hand, by moving the hand, by introducing delays between the movement and the visual feedback, or by rotating the hand image. Self-recognition requires the monitoring and integration of various sources of information such as intention, efferent signals, and afferent signals in a short time-window. The tasks require an explicit self-recognition judgment: the participant's body part is objectified, that is, a body part is presented like an external object projected on a screen, and the experimental manipulations focus on the conditions under which this body part will be judged as "mine." The participant's response is accompanied by an explicit form of awareness of one's self (e.g. "this is me"). Interestingly, if we remove efferent information by asking participants to judge the identity of passively moving hands, then self-recognition performance deteriorates dramatically (Tsakiris *et al.*, 2005). This significant difference suggests that efference improves the comparison and integration of private (e.g. proprioception) and public (e.g. vision) sensory signals. Efferent information might provide an advantage in monitoring the timing of sensory events. In the case of a self-generated action, forward models of the motor system use the efferent information so as to generate a prediction about the anticipated sensory feedback (Frith *et al.*, 2000). Afferent-driven body awareness alone may not be sufficient for reliable explicit self-recognition. Even when there is a perfect match between proprioception and vision, efference provides a significant advantage for self-recognition performance (Tsakiris *et al.*, 2005). Therefore, self-recognition, in the sense of correctly recognizing a visual object or event as "me" or "mine" seems to depend largely on efference and agency. This is a crucial point that is only briefly mentioned by Zwicker and colleagues as their focus is on the detection of intersensory match/mismatch. However, we should not underestimate the role that the efferent signals might play in these situations. Research on adults suggests that the detection threshold is significantly altered once efferent information becomes available, and therefore the change in the detection threshold of infants as they develop might reflect the development of the internal predictive models of the motor system (Frith *et al.*, 2000), rather than simply an improvement in the temporal and/or spatial resolution of multisensory processing. Of course, it would be difficult to contrast passive to active movements and the detection of the resulting visuo-proprioceptive effects in infants, but efferent information seems crucial for infallible self-recognition in adults, and it might also contribute greatly to the detection of visuo-proprioceptive incongruencies in infants.

Looking for myself

For the last part of their chapter, Zwicker and colleagues turn their attention to the question of mirror self-recognition and the emergence of an awareness of oneself as a diachronic individual entity that is the same over time and distinct from other people. They put forward an intriguing question: "It is worth noting here that the degree of delay – between 1 and 2 seconds – that has been shown to disrupt self-recognition (Miyazaki and Hiraki, 2006) in toddlers corresponds to the degree of delay shown to be discriminable by infants in the visual-proprioceptive integration tasks with infants (Hiraki, 2006). Does this coincidence suggest that both self-recognition and visual-proprioceptive intermodal integration manifest the same temporal parameters?" Their answer is negative because the temporal thresholds for these two tasks (e.g. detection of visuo-proprioceptive incongruencies and recognition of one's self in the mirror or videos) change developmentally in opposite directions. Detection thresholds for visuo-proprioceptive discrepancies tend to decrease, while the temporal delays at which infants continue to recognize images of themselves increase as they grow up.

No one would deny that the consolidation of a mnemonic representation of one's physical appearance (e.g. how one's face looks) plays a key role for mirror self-recognition or for recognition of video-images of one's self. However, I would like to argue that Zwicker and colleagues raise an interesting issue that has only recently become a topic of psychological research. Recent experimental research on the physical aspects of self (Gillihan and Farah, 2005) has focused on two main aspects: self-face recognition, and body ownership. Even though our physical sense of self is jointly constituted by our physical appearance, of which the face is perhaps its most distinctive feature, and by our sensory-motor body, there has been no direct research link between these two main aspects of selfhood, face, and body. In a sense, psychological research has focused either on "face-less bodies" by using self-face recognition tasks that depend on the retrieval of visual representations of one's face (Keenan et al., 2000), or on "body-less faces" by investigating how current sensory inflow interacts with motor signals and body representations (Tsakiris, 2010). Both traditions have advanced our understanding of self-face and self-body representations respectively, even though, to date, the interaction between the two has not been investigated. Body recognition studies conclude that multisensory integration is the main cue to selfhood (Tsakiris, 2010). Self-face recognition studies conclude that visual recognition of stored visual features and visual configurations inform self-face recognition. However, the evidence used in one tradition may have an unrecognized importance in the other. Thus, multisensory evidence for selfhood is widely recognized for bodies, but it may also be important for self-face recognition.

In fact, recent studies have asked this question by investigating whether current multisensory input may influence the sense of self-identity. Tsakiris (2008) extended the paradigm of multisensory integration to self-face recognition. Participants were stroked on their face while they were looking at a morphed face being touched in synchrony or asynchrony. Before and after the visuo-tactile stimulation participants performed a self-recognition task. The results showed that synchronized multisensory signals had a significant effect on self-face recognition. Following synchronous, but not asynchronous, stimulation, and when asked to judge the identity of morphed pictures of the two faces, participants assimilated features of the other's face in the mental representation of their own face. This effect provides direct evidence that our mental representation of our self, such as self-face representation, is not solely derived from stable mnemonic representations, but instead these representations are susceptible to current multisensory evidence (see also Paladino *et al.*, 2010; Sforza *et al.*, 2010). Therefore, it is possible that self-face representation is not solely dependent on mnemonic or conceptual representations, but, instead, is dependent on current multisensory input. Multisensory integration can update cognitive representations of one's body, such as the sense of body ownership (Tsakiris, 2010), the physical appearance of one's body (Longo *et al.*, 2009), and the representation of one's identity in relation to other people (Tsakiris, 2008).

Mind the body

Central to all four chapters that review the state-of-the-art in current developmental research on body representations is the idea that understanding the way infants use and experience their bodies is essential for our understanding of how the brain (and the body) learns to deal with the external world, but also how the brain (and the body) makes self-awareness possible. Inevitably, the former is essential for understanding the behavior of every biological organism, but the latter is what seems to be one of the major scientific questions: how do we get from basic information processing of sensory and motor signals to self-awareness? Self-awareness in this context should be understood as the awareness of one's embodied existence that is at the same time in constant interaction with the environment and other embodied creatures, but also distinct from others. The four chapters on the development of body representations considered how multisensory integration together with internal models of the body modulate the experience of the body as being one's own, as well as the demarcation or distinction between one's body and other objects. One of the key questions in the neurocognitive study of self is that of specificity (Gillihan and Farah, 2005). The experience and awareness of one's body may represent a critical component of self-specificity as evidenced by the different ways in which multisensory integration in interaction with internal models of the body can actually manipulate important physical and psychological aspects of the self.

References

Bahrick, L. E. and Watson, J. S. (1985). Detection of intermodal proprioceptive visual contingency as a potential basis of self-perception in infancy. *Developmental Psychology*, **21**, 963–973.

Barsalou, L. W. (2008). Grounded cognition. *Annual Review of Psychology*, **59**, 617–645.

Berlucchi, G. and Aglioti, S. (1997). The body in the brain: Neural bases of corporeal awareness. *Trends in Neurosciences*, **20**, 560–564.

Carruthers, G. (2008). Types of body representation and the sense of embodiment. *Consciousness and Cognition*, **17**, 1,302–1,316.

Dijkerman, H. C. and de Haan, E. H. (2007). Somatosensory processes subserving perception and action. *Behavioral and Brain Sciences*, **30**, 189–201.

Frith, C. D., Blakemore, S. J., and Wolpert, D. M. (2000). Abnormalities in the awareness and control of action. *Philosophical Transactions of the Royal Society B: Biological Sciences*, **355**, 1,771–1,788.

Gallagher, S. (2005). *How the Body Shapes the Mind*. Oxford: Oxford University Press.

Gallese, V. and Sinigaglia, C. (2010). The bodily self as power for action. *Neuropsychologia*, **48**(3), 746–55.

Gillihan, S. J. and Farah, M. J. (2005). Is self special? A critical review of evidence from experimental psychology and cognitive neuroscience. *Psychological Bulletin*, **131**, 76–97.

Graziano, M. S. A. and Botvinik, M. M. (2001). How the brain represents the body: Insights from neurophysiology and psychology. In W. Prinz and B. Hommel (eds). *Common Mechanisms in Perception and Action, Attention and Performance XIX*. Oxford/New York: Oxford University Press.

Holmes, N. P. and Spence, C. (2006). Beyond the body schema: Visual, prosthetic, and technological contributions to bodily perception and awareness. In G. Knoblich, I. Thornton, M. Grosjean, and M. Shiffrar (eds). *Human Body Perception from the Inside Out* (15–64). Oxford: Oxford University Press.

Jeannerod, M. (2003). The mechanism of self-recognition in humans. *Behavioural Brain Research*, **142**, 1–15.

Keenan, J. P., Wheeler, M. A., Gallup, G. G. Jr., and Pascual-Leone, A. (2000). Self-recognition and the right prefrontal cortex. *Trends in Cognitive Sciences*, **4**(9), 338–344.

Lhermitte, J. (1939). *L'Image de Notre Corps*. Paris: Nouvelle Revue Critique.

Longo, M. R., Schüür, F., Kammers, M. P. M., Tsakiris, M., and Haggard, P. (2009). Self awareness and the body image. *Acta Psychologica*, **132**(2), 166–172.

Morgan, R. and Rochat, P. (1997). Intermodal calibration of the body in early infancy. *Ecological Psychology*, **9**, 1–24.

Paillard, J. (1999). Body schema and body image. A double dissociation in deafferented patients. In G. N. Gantchev, S. Mori, and J. Massion (eds). *Motor Control. Today and Tomorrow* (197–214). Bulgaria: Akademicno Izdatelstvo.

Paladino, M. P., Mazzurega, M., Pavani, F., and Schubert, T. W. (2010). Synchronous multisensory stimulation blurs self-other boundaries. *Psychological Science*, **21**(9), 1,202–1,207.

Poeck, K. and Orgass, B. (1971). The concept of the body schema: A critical review and some experimental results. *Cortex*, **7**, 254–277.

Rochat, P. and Hespos, S. J. (1997). Differential rooting response by neonates: Evidence for an early sense of self. *Early Development and Parenting*, **6**, 105–112.

Rochat, P. and Striano, T. (2000). Perceived self in infancy. *Infant Behavior and Development*, **23**, 513–530.

Rossetti, Y., Haggard, P., and Kawato, M. (eds) (2007). *Sensorimotor Foundations of Higher Cognition, Attention and Performance XXII*. Oxford/New York: Oxford University Press.

Sforza, A., Bufalari, I., Haggard, P., and Aglioti, S. M. (2010). My face in yours: Visuo-tactile facial stimulation influences sense of identity. *Social Neuroscience*, **5**(2), 148–162.

Sirigu, A., Grafman, J., Bressler, K., and Sunderland, T. (1991). Multiple representations contribute to body knowledge processing. Evidence from a case of autotopagnosia. *Brain*, **114**, 629–642.

Tsakiris, M. (2008). Looking for myself: Current multisensory input alters self-face recognition. *PLoS One*, **3**(12), e4,040.

   (2010). My body in the brain: A neurocognitive model of body-ownership. *Neuropsychologia*, **48**(3), 703–12.

Tsakiris, M. and Fotopoulou, A. (2008). Is my body the sum of online and offline body-representations? *Consciousness and Cognition*, **17**, 1,317–1,320, discussion at 1,321–1,323.

Tsakiris, M., Haggard, P., Franck, N., Mainy, N., and Sirigu, A. (2005). A specific role for efferent information in self-recognition. *Cognition*, **96**, 215–231.

Ungerleider, L. G. and Mishkin, M. (1982). Two cortical visual systems. In D. G. Ingle, M. A. Goodale, and R. J. Q. Mansfield (eds). *Analysis of Visual Behavior*. Cambridge, MA: MIT Press.

Part II

The bodies of others

5   Developing expertise in human body perception

*Virginia Slaughter, Michelle Heron-Delaney
and Tamara Christie*

Adults see the human body shape in all manner of stimuli, including highly abstract stick figures that barely specify the human body configuration and point-light displays (PLDs) that specify only the characteristic motion patterns of the human form. This capacity to quickly and effortlessly perceive the human form reflects our expertise at visually processing human bodies. In this chapter we will argue that expertise in perceiving bodies occurs by virtue of their ubiquity and social significance, not because of any kind of innate representation or privileged learning mechanism. We are claiming this because visual discrimination of human bodies is slow to develop in infancy, and because it is initially stimulus-dependent, becoming more and more generalisable over time in a typical learning trajectory.

Body perception involves several processing steps. First, viewers detect that a visual object is a human body, as distinct from other object classes such as cars or dogs. At later stages of processing, viewers may identify features of an individual body, such as the posture, the gender or attractiveness, and they may also recognise the body's personal identity. All of this information is ultimately interpreted for its social-communicative relevance and meaning in context. In this chapter, we will be focusing on the initial step of body processing: body detection, here defined as the capacity to visually discriminate bodies from other objects. We will describe a series of experiments in which we have investigated infants' responses to typical human bodies versus scrambled bodies. The typical body stimuli portray the human form in various postures (e.g. arms raised above the head, legs spread wide, etc.). To create the scrambled body stimuli, we move the arms and/or legs to non-canonical locations (e.g. arms coming out of the head, legs and arms switched on the torso, etc.). We compare these two stimuli because scrambling bodies preserves the low level visual elements of typical

Much of the experimental work reported in this chapter was funded by Australian Research Council Discovery Project awards to the first author. Some of the experimental findings were submitted in partial fulfilment of Michelle Heron-Delaney's PhD degree and others formed part of Tamara Christie's PhD degree. Both Heron-Delaney and Christie were supported by Australian Postgraduate Awards. We sincerely thank the many families who participated in these experiments.

bodies including total contour, contrast and visual detail, and distorts only the configural properties, that is, the unique overall shape by which viewers detect that a visual object is a human body as opposed to something else (see Figure 5.1 for examples). This technique has been used widely to investigate perception of

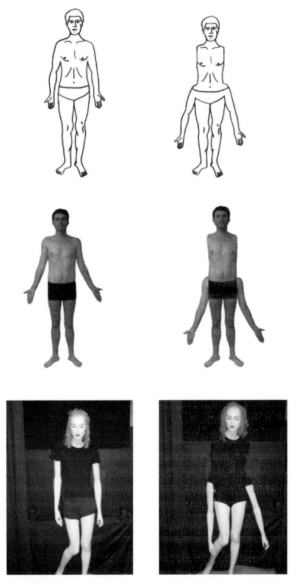

Figure 5.1 Typical and scrambled human body stimuli varying in realism

faces (Johnson *et al.*, 1991) as well as bodies (Peelen and Downing, 2005; Reed *et al.*, 2006).

To compare infants' responses to typical and scrambled bodies, we use two testing paradigms. In the visual habituation experiments, infants view a series of typical bodies until they are bored (defined as a 50 percent reduction in visual attention to the body stimuli), at which point they are shown a series of scrambled bodies on the test. This procedure measures whether or not infants notice the difference between typical and scrambled bodies based either on previous experience or as a function of learning in the context of the experiment. This paradigm does not allow us to conclude that infants identify bodies as bodies, but it does demonstrate their capacity to detect the typical body configuration as compared to a scrambled configuration. In other experiments we use a visual preference technique, in which infants are simultaneously shown a typical and a scrambled body, and their attention to each is measured. Longer looking at one or the other indicates that infants both notice the difference between the typical body and the scrambled body, and spontaneously prefer either the familiar (typical) or the novel (scrambled) body stimulus. Spontaneous preferences vary with infant age, stimulus complexity and exposure (Cohen, 2004), so these are generally interpreted post hoc. However, the presence of a spontaneous preference indicates that infants are familiar with the typical human body configuration since they have no other basis on which to systematically prefer to look at the typical or scrambled bodies.

Expert body perception in adulthood

It has long been known that humans are particularly sensitive to human faces, and that adults are expert in perceiving faces. Recent work on body perception indicates that the same is true for adults' visual processing of human bodies.

Visual expertise is indexed in various ways. One of the key behavioural markers is configural processing. This refers to visual object perception that relies on a holistic assessment of how the parts of an object relate to each other, as well as the shapes of the individual parts. Configural processing is most consistently demonstrated for visual perception of faces (Robbins and McKone, 2007), but has also been observed for other object classes that are highly structurally similar, and with which perceivers have a good deal of experience (Maurer *et al.*, 2002). Configural processing is evident when object detection and recognition are disrupted by inversion. This indicates configural processing because turning familiar objects upside down disturbs the viewer's ability to rapidly process the spatial relations between the object's different parts (Maurer *et al.*, 2002). Furthermore the steepness of the inversion effect provides an indication of the amount of configural processing; objects that are subject to the most configural processing are the ones whose perception is most disrupted by inversion.

Reed *et al.* (2003) demonstrated that recognition of human bodies is subject to an inversion effect, indicating that bodies are processed configurally. They asked participants to view paired images of human bodies that either matched exactly or varied according to an element of the body's posture, such as the way the arm was bent or the width of the stance. The task was to determine whether or not the body images matched. Human bodies were more difficult to match when they were presented upside down than when they were presented upright, in contrast to houses which were as easy to recognise inverted as upright. Reed *et al.* (2003) also found a reduced inversion effect for bodies with biomechanically impossible postures, indicating that non-canonical body shapes are subject to less configural processing than bodies with more normal shapes.

Ramm *et al.* (2010) also demonstrated configural processing of human bodies in adults, this time with a simple detection task. They showed participants photographs of human bodies that were either intact or scrambled. The task was to detect as quickly as possible whether or not the body was 'normal'. Participants were fast and accurate at the task when the images were upright, but when the bodies were inverted their reaction times declined. Furthermore, reaction times for the normal bodies were more adversely impacted by inversion than were reaction times for the scrambled bodies. Thus when presented upside down, the normal bodies were particularly difficult to detect, confirming that the normal bodies were subject to strong configural processing. This work, like that of Reed *et al.* (2003) suggests that adults most readily detect and identify human bodies by analysing their global configurations.

Downing *et al.* (2004) used a different paradigm to demonstrate expertise in human body perception. In their study, adults judged whether the vertical or horizontal arms of a cross were longer. While doing this, images of human bodies and other non-body objects were briefly flashed in one of the inner corners of the cross. When human bodies were flashed, their presence was more readily noticed than when other objects were flashed, and participants were more accurate at detecting what they were (e.g. human bodies as opposed to something else). A similar finding exists for faces (Mack and Rock, 1998). These results indirectly confirm that faces and bodies are objects of expertise, because they both capture attention and are rapidly and accurately detected.

Brain imaging studies also indicate that human bodies are objects of expertise. Like faces, human bodies are processed by distinct areas in the brain. Although there is some debate about how such data should be interpreted (see e.g. Xu, 2005), the presence of specialised brain regions for body perception supports the claim that bodies are objects of expertise for normal adult perceivers (Peelen and Downing, 2005). Functional magnetic resonance imaging (MRI) studies indicate at least two overlapping cortical areas are active when bodies are being detected or recognised. One is the extrastriate body area (EBA; Downing *et al.*, 2001; Taylor *et al.*, 2007). This area in the lateral occipitotemporal cortex appears to be specialised for representing the whole body as well as peripheral body parts like hands. Another body-specific cortical area is the fusiform body area (FBA), which is located near the fusiform face area (FFA) in the lateral posterior fusiform gyrus, and is primarily implicated in detection and recognition of the whole body configuration (Peelen and Downing, 2005; Schwarzlose *et al.*, 2005).

Evoked response potential (ERP) studies also suggest that adults have specific expertise in body perception. Viewing intact human bodies produces an enhanced negative event-related potential, known as the N190. The N190 is not evident when viewing scrambled bodies (Thierry *et al.*, 2006). Viewing inverted bodies produces a delayed N170 for faces (Bentin *et al.*, 1996) and for bodies (Minnebusch *et al.*, 2009; Stekelenburg and de Gelder, 2004), though no inversion effects have been reported for the body-specific N190. As with the functional magnetic resonance imaging (fMRI) work, the meaning of these neurological data is debated, but many authors conclude that these unique evoked response potential (ERP) signals indicate configural processing and therefore expertise (see Maurer *et al.*, 2002 for a discussion).

How does visual expertise for the human body arise?

As yet, there is little research to indicate at what point these indicators of expertise in human body perception are evident in development. We can therefore make no strong claims about when or how human bodies become objects of visual expertise for adults. There is, however, an ongoing debate in the face perception literature about how facial expertise effects, including configural processing and unique brain responses, come about. A review of these may inform our speculations about early body perception.

One view is that faces are objects of expertise because specialised mechanisms for processing them have evolved in the human brain, and these mechanisms can be mapped onto the face-specific brain regions that have so far been discovered (McKone *et al.*, 2007; Rhodes *et al.*, 2004). This view posits more generally that some visual object classes are privileged by virtue of being processed via dedicated mechanisms. This view does not make explicit claims about the origins of expertise for faces; however, two proposals are considered. If facial expertise is dependent on dedicated processing mechanisms, then these may be innate. This idea is supported by evidence showing that newborn infants discriminate upright face patterns from inverted or scrambled ones, suggesting that specialised attention and/or detection mechanisms for faces are present at birth (Cassia *et al.*, 2004; Johnson and Morton, 1991). There is also evidence for a sensitive or critical period for face perception postpartum, in which visual experience of faces is necessary for expertise to develop in later life (Le Grand *et al.*, 2003, 2004). This is also consistent with the idea that in adults, expert face perception is supported by specialised processing mechanisms. Note that these developmental scenarios do not preclude that further development occurs in the domain of face processing; this is well documented for various aspects of face recognition (see, e.g. Carey, 1992; Goodman *et al.*, 2007). However, these perspectives on face expertise do claim that faces constitute a privileged class of visual object from birth or very early in infancy, and that status contributes to the expertise effects seen in adults.

A competing view holds that perceptual expertise for faces comes about via domain-general learning mechanisms. On this view, there is nothing privileged about faces or any other objects for which we have visual expertise, other than our extensive perceptual experience with them (Bukach *et al.*, 2006; Gauthier and Tarr, 1997). This view is supported by research suggesting that adults demonstrate some perceptual expertise effects for novel objects following intensive visual training (Gauthier *et al.*, 1998). The proposal from this perceptive is that expertise is dependent solely on exposure and practice and it can be acquired at any time during development.

With these views in mind, we may consider the question of how expertise in human body perception is acquired. In line with the different explanations for expertise in face perception, there are three potential developmental trajectories for body perception, leading to expertise in adulthood, that can be considered:

(1) Expert processing of bodies is innate. This proposal holds that human bodies are detected from birth with reference to an inborn template that specifies the human body configuration. This would be an experience-independent representation, determined by genetic processes and expressed in the developing brain at birth, or else derived from *in utero* proprioceptive feedback specifying the structure of our own bodies in a representation that was generalisable to third person body perception (see Sugita, 2009 for an elaboration of this argument). This would mean that bodies are privileged visual objects from the start; no learning would be required in order for infants to detect them, at least.

(2) Expert processing of bodies is acquired via specialised learning mechanisms during a sensitive or critical period in infancy. This would be an experience-expectant representation, rapidly developed via genetically prepared systems for observation of others' bodies and extraction of the configural representation. This proposal states that bodies become privileged through rapid learning via dedicated mechanisms.

(3) Expert processing of bodies is acquired via domain-general learning processes. This proposal implies that the human body configuration that adults detect and recognise with expertise, develops via experience-dependent processes. These include visual analysis of bodies in the environment and

generalisation of a representation of the typical body configuration. This would mean that bodies become objects of expertise over a relatively extended learning period via repeated exposure.

Some research on the early development of face perception supports proposals of both experience-independent and experience-expectant mechanisms in the development of face perception (Johnson *et al.*, 1991; Nelson, 2001; see also Sugita, 2008 for a relevant experiment with Japanese monkeys). It is reasonable to consider that the development of perceptual expertise for bodies may be similar. First, bodies and faces have similar configural properties, including strong spatial orientation (e.g. an unambiguous top and a bottom) and symmetry along the vertical axis. Second, bodies are physically attached to faces; where one is present, so is the other. We acknowledge that visual access to faces and bodies are different in early development, since young infants' poor visual acuity and inability to hold an upright posture may limit their visual exposure to whole human bodies. However, it could still be argued that the processes governing the development of face perception should apply to the perception of bodies – perhaps with some delay to accommodate limited visual access to bodies in early infancy – by virtue of their connectedness. Third, bodies are like faces in being experienced from both first- and third-person perspectives, and only bodies and faces have this feature. Thus both have the potential for there to be an innate template or representation guiding perception of others' faces/ bodies based on the structure of one's own face/body.

Despite the potential strength of these arguments, our data suggest that body expertise is acquired via general learning mechanisms. For those who subscribe to nativist models of face perception, this is in stark contrast to the development of expertise for the faces that are attached to them.

Body detection develops relatively late in infancy

Our work indicates that the ability to discriminate the typical human body shape from scrambled bodies is late-developing in general, particularly in comparison to the early development of face perception. As Table 5.1 indicates, the very earliest that we see reliable discrimination is at age 4–6 months, when the stimuli are real live human bodies moving naturally. The latest we see reliable typical-scrambled body discrimination in infants is 15–18 months when the stimuli are static two-dimensional representations of human bodies. This late acquisition and long generalization period effectively eliminates proposal (1) above, and calls proposal (2) into question. That is, if body perception were based on experience-independent processes, then we would expect discrimination of scrambled human bodies from typical bodies at birth, in line with newborns' capacity to discriminate scrambled from typical facial patterns (Johnson and Morton, 1991). If it were based on

Table 5.1 *Earliest age at which infants detect the human typical body shape, across stimulus realism conditions*

Body stimulus	Visual preference test	Visual habituation test
Line drawings	18 months (preference for scrambled)	15 months
Photographs	18 months (preference for scrambled)	18 months
Dolls		12 months
Mannequins		9 months
Real people (static)		9 months
Photographs with simultaneous human voice		9 months
Animated photographs (incorporating biologically possible movement)	9 months (preference for typical)	9 months
Real people moving arms and head naturally		4–6 months

experience-expectant processes, then we should see a period of rapid development, either soon after birth or at a later stage when all typically developing infants could expect to have access to the appropriate visual input. In human infants this might be when they begin to sit up and thereby gain visual access to whole bodies, in the second half of the first year of life. However, there is no clear point for punctuated development, rather, body discrimination develops gradually. Furthermore, in the first 18 months of life infants' discrimination of human bodies interacts with the extent to which the test stimulus is perceptually similar to real humans. This stimulus-dependency is consistent with learning patterns typical of infants in the first 2 years of life (Hartshorn *et al.*, 1998; Hayne *et al.*, 2000).

Table 5.1 shows that there is a relationship between the abstractness of human body stimuli and the age at which infants discriminate scrambled from typical bodies. These data make reference to whether or not groups of infants respond differently to typical and scrambled bodies, using a pass/fail criterion for the different age groups. Figures 5.2 and Figures 5.3 provide a complementary perspective on the same data, portraying patterns of performance within two different age groups that we have tested extensively. These figures depict the proportions of 9-month-olds (Figure 5.2) and 12-month-olds (Figure 5.3) who noticed the transition from typical to scrambled bodies across a number of distinct visual habituation experiments that differed according to the abstraction of the body stimulus. Note that 9- and 12-month-olds have not participated in all of the same studies, so some of the stimulus types do not appear on both figures. Figure 5.2 and Figure 5.3 both show clear generalisation gradients from the most realistic human body stimuli (on the right of both graphs) to the least realistic (on the left). We will now briefly review these experiments.

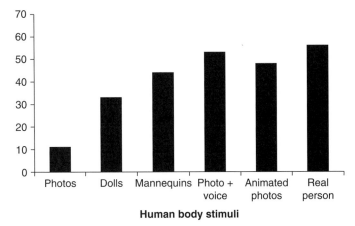

Figure 5.2 Proportions of 9-month-olds who discriminate scrambled from typical human body shapes, by stimulus type

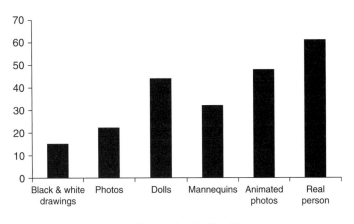

Figure 5.3 Proportions of 12-month-olds who discriminate scrambled from typical human body shapes, by stimulus type

Stimulus generalisation effects in infants' body detection

In trying to establish the earliest age at which infants visually discriminate human bodies, we have completed a number of studies in which the realism of the body stimuli varied. We have manipulated the physical characteristics of body stimuli, including perceptual detail (e.g. line drawings versus colour photographs), size (e.g. small photos or replicas versus life-sized bodies) and dimensionality (images versus statues or real people). We have also introduced movement (static versus moving bodies) and multi-modality (simultaneous presentation of a human voice with the body stimulus). On each of these dimensions, the more realistic portrayal leads to facilitated body perception by infants. There are also cumulative effects of adding realism.

Our initial experiments involved testing infants' responses to black and white line drawings and colour photographs of human bodies (see Figure 5.1). These were presented on a screen that was 130 centimetres (cm) away from the infant. The line drawings were approximately 30 cm tall and the photos were approximately 52 cm tall. We tested twenty-four infants at each of three age groups: 12, 15 and 18 months of age, on the preference test. When the body stimuli were two-dimensional images, only the 18-month-olds showed a preference, and it was for the scrambled body shapes (Slaughter *et al.*, 2002). The younger infants did not have a preference for either typical or scrambled bodies. Subsequent habituation experiments were carried out, testing approximately twenty infants at each of three age groups: 12, 15 and 18 months. These experiments revealed that infants could discriminate scrambled bodies after habituation to typical bodies by 15 months when the stimuli were line drawings, and by 18 months when the stimuli were photographs. This was somewhat surprising given that photographs are more detailed and realistic than line drawings; however, a subsequent study (unpublished) indicated that discrimination of scrambled human body photographs was also evident in 15-month-olds. The important point is that in all of our studies to date using static, two dimensional human body photographs and drawings, 12-month-olds consistently fail to discriminate scrambled bodies (Christie and Slaughter, 2011; Slaughter and Heron, 2004).

Our next series of experiments systematically varied the size and dimensionality of the body stimuli. In these experiments we created three-dimensional typical and scrambled bodies using dolls, mannequins and real people (Heron and Slaughter, 2010).

We chose to investigate infants' responses to doll bodies because these are three dimensional, as are real people, and dolls are potentially more familiar to infants than whole body drawings or photos, in the first year of life. We created typical and scrambled doll bodies from a set of identical plastic girl dolls, approximately 14 cm tall, with peach-coloured skin and blond hair. The dolls were presented on a stage 105 cm away from the infant. The typical doll was presented in four distinct postures until infants habituated, then the scrambled dolls, whose arms were moved to either the head or to the hips, were presented. We only relocated the arms in creating scrambled doll bodies because we wanted to compare infants' responses to dolls and mannequins (see below) and it was impossible to take off and re-position the mannequin's legs. Groups of 9-, 12- and 15-month-olds (N = 18 per age group) were tested using the habituation paradigm. With dolls as the body stimuli, 12-month-olds discriminated scrambled bodies, as did the 15-month-olds. However, 9-month-olds did not respond to the scrambled bodies. This finding indicates that a three-dimensional body stimulus is more effective than a two-dimensional stimulus in eliciting infants' body perception, since the key visual discrimination was made 3–6 months earlier than infants tested with drawings or photos.

Next, we investigated the significance of the size of the body stimulus. The majority of human bodies that infants would have seen are life-sized. Therefore we tested infants with typical and scrambled mannequin bodies (see Figure 5.1). The typical and scrambled mannequin bodies were configurally identical to the previous study with dolls. To run this study, infants sat in a high chair 150 cm away from and facing a curtained stage. An experimenter opened the curtain to reveal the mannequin on each looking trial during habituation and test. In this experiment we tested groups of approximately twenty infants aged 9-, 12-, 15- and 18-months-old. After habituation to the typical bodied mannequin in different postures, all age groups reliably discriminated the scrambled mannequin bodies. Thus, with a life-sized three-dimensional body, infants as young as 9 months old are sensitive to the human body configuration.

In discussing the results of our habituation experiments using two-dimensional body images, we speculated that '2-month-olds would express surprise if presented with a real human whose arms grew out of his head' (Slaughter and Heron, 2004: 78). To investigate whether or not this was true, we went as far as possible along the realism continuum to create typical and scrambled 'real' human bodies. Two female experimenters worked together to accomplish this. One woman stood against a floor-length black curtain. Her arms were hidden by extending them behind her through holes in the curtain. The second woman was hidden behind the curtain but with her arms poking through additional holes cut in either the correct location to create a typical human body composite (e.g. at the visible woman's shoulders), or in an incorrect location (e.g. at the visible woman's hips or head) to create scrambled bodies like those presented in the doll and mannequin experiments described above. The visible model was 172 cm tall, female, white, of slim stature, and had red curly hair. She was presented in the same stage set-up as the previous experiment using mannequin bodies. We tested groups of approximately twenty infants at ages 6-, 9-, 12- and 18-months-old. Under these highly realistic conditions, the 9-, 12- and 18-month-olds reliably discriminated the scrambled bodies, but 6-month-old infants did not. Thus the pattern of results across experiments when we manipulate dimensionality and size of the body stimulus is that infants discriminate scrambled human body shapes as young as 9 months when the bodies are three-dimensional and life-sized. Furthermore, a continuum of realism emerged, suggesting that infants may generalise from their visual experience of real human bodies to less and less realistic body representations in a developmental process that occurs between the ages of 9 and 18 months (Heron and Slaughter, 2010).

In another experiment, we explored whether or not the presence of a voice would facilitate infants' body perception. Sai (2005) showed that newborns rapidly learn the specific features of their mother's face, provided they are also exposed to her voice. Sai (2005) concluded that infants' rapidly learned preference for their mothers' faces is produced by an intermodal learning process, in which the voice directs attention to the relevant visual stimulus (the mother's face). Similarly, albeit over a longer timeframe, learning about the human body may also involve, or be influenced by, intermodal stimulation. To test this, we replicated our standard visual habituation experiment using photographs as the body stimuli (see Figure 5.1) and added a simultaneous vocal track of a young man talking to the infant, as follows: 'Hello baby, look at me, peekaboo, peekaboo, look at me'. The vocal track looped throughout the experiment. We tested sixteen infants at ages 6- and 9-months-old, and found that with the addition of a voice, infants as young as 9 months discriminated scrambled from typical human body photographs. In a control condition with music playing instead of the human voice, 9-month-olds failed to discriminate scrambled human bodies, indicating that it was the specific features of a human voice that facilitated infants' body detection.

Another characteristic of human bodies is that they move. Both adults and infants readily detect the specific movement patterns of human bodies and these may help perceivers extract the body structure (Johansson, 1977; Thornton *et al.*, 1998). Research on infants' perception of PLDs indicates that sensitivity to various perturbations of human bodies portrayed in PLD movement (e.g. scrambled PLDs, inverted PLDs, phase-shifted PLDs) is evident within the first year of life (Marshall and Shipley, 2009; Reid *et al.*, 2008). Furthermore, sensitivity to biological movement in general appears to be experience-independent, as Simion *et al.* (2008) recently demonstrated that human newborns preferentially attend to a PLD of a walking hen compared to a scrambled PLD hen. In adults, human bodies in motion are processed not just by the body-specific EBA and FBA cortical regions, but also by the superior temporal sulcus, which is specialised for processing biological movement (Beauchamp *et al.*, 2002, 2003). Thus we speculated that moving body stimuli may enhance infants' perception since moving bodies are both more similar to the bodies they have seen and more likely to engage multiple brain systems to facilitate discrimination of scrambled from typical bodies.

For the moving body experiments (Christie and Slaughter, 2011) we first animated the human body photos (e.g. those portrayed in Figure 5.1) so that the head, arms and legs oscillated simultaneously from their connection points on the torso. Thus the movement was biologically possible, but not highly realistic.

Even so, the addition of movement facilitated infants' perception of the bodies. We tested groups of eighteen infants at 6-, 9- and 12-months-old using the same physical set-up and procedure as in the static photograph discrimination experiments described above. Infants who were habituated to moving typical bodies noticed the transition to moving scrambled bodies by 9 months of age. However, 6-month-olds did not discriminate the scrambled moving bodies. We also ran a control condition to demonstrate that the facilitation effect of adding movement was specific to bodily movement and not simply an artefact of increased attention to a display that moved: a spiral turning behind static human body shapes did not facilitate body discrimination in 9-month-olds.

Next we tested 6-, 9- and 12-month-olds (N = 16 per group) in a preference test, during which they were simultaneously presented with moving typical and scrambled bodies, rather than being shown scrambled human bodies only after habituation to typical bodies. In this experiment, the 9-month-olds again demonstrated that they could discriminate scrambled and typical bodies, and at this age they preferred the familiar, typical bodies. The 6-month-olds showed no preference, and the 12-month-olds had a significant preference for the scrambled bodies, suggesting that by this age, they were most interested in the novel, scrambled body shapes.

Finally, we replicated the real human body experiment described above, with the addition of movement. In this case, the woman whose arms poked through the curtain was instructed to wave her arms back and forth continuously in both the typical body and scrambled body configurations. The visible model, whose head was visible, tipped her head from side to side at the same time so that arms and head were always moving during presentations of both typical and scrambled bodies. Anticipating that this body stimulus would be the most realistic and therefore easiest to discriminate, we tested 4- and 6-month-olds, with eighteen per age group. We found that 6-month-olds reliably discriminated scrambled bodies after habituation to typical bodies in this experiment, and 4-month-olds were also capable of doing so, though the effect was weak (only 39 percent of 4-month-olds genuinely recovered interest when the scrambled bodies were presented at test, as compared to 50 percent of 6-month-olds). Thus this experiment demonstrated that by 4 months of age, infants begin to show some sensitivity to scrambled bodies when the stimuli are as realistic as possible – real humans who are moving naturally. By 6 months, infants showed robust discrimination of scrambled bodies under these stimulus conditions.

Across all of these experiments, the results collectively demonstrate that the realism of the stimulus influences infants' body perception. Increasing the realism of the body across different dimensions appears to have an additive effect such that earliest discrimination is of real human bodies, realistic in size, dimensionality and movement. However, we do have to acknowledge that in the real moving bodies experiment, it was only the arms and head that moved, and only the arms were relocated to create the scrambled body shapes. This was due to physical limitations on the postures that the two women in front of and behind the curtain could maintain. Because the movement and scrambling in this study were both focused on the body's arms, the discrimination task may have been made easier compared to the other studies since the movement may have drawn attention to the only body elements that were relevant for detecting the transition to scrambled body shapes.

It is important to note that sensitivity to bodies may develop before it is expressed in infants' visual discrimination and/or preference. Gliga and Dehaene-Lambertz (2005) found evidence of typical versus scrambled body discrimination in an ERP study with 3-month-old infants. They showed typical and scrambled body images of headless women to infants while a continuous electroencephalogram (EEG) recorded ERPs. The ERP recordings indicated that the mean amplitudes for the P1 and N290 components were significantly larger for the scrambled images than the intact images, suggesting that infants discriminated between the scrambled and typical body shapes. However, as the authors noted, the headless bodies were highly novel and infants may have responded simply to the low-level configural information in the stimuli (such as overall symmetry), rather than recognizing the images as human bodies (Gliga and Dehaene-Lambertz, 2005). Thus infants may be implicitly sensitive to the human body configuration before they demonstrate that sensitivity in looking tasks; however, more research is required to confirm this possibility.

The stimulus dependency effects we have observed in infants' body detection are consistent with learning trajectories in other domains of early cognitive development. For example, infants' learning of a behaviour–outcome contingency, such as pressing a lever to make an entertaining train run briefly on a track, is dependent upon the features of the train and the context of learning (Hartshorn *et al.*, 1998). In this and similar learning paradigms, younger infants' performance is more stimulus dependent than that of older infants. Hayne *et al.* (2000) propose that young infants' learning is constrained by representational specificity such that they can only retrieve information from memory when there is a close match between encoding and retrieval contexts. With respect to body detection, this suggests that younger infants only discriminate scrambled bodies in the higher realism conditions because these most closely match the real human bodies from which they are extracting the configural regularities. With increasing exposure to different portrayals of human bodies, as well as age-related changes in memory and retrieval, infants can generalise their knowledge to more and more abstract body stimuli.

While consistent with general learning patterns in infancy, the stimulus realism effects we observed in infants' body perception contrast sharply with the early development of face perception. Johnson and Morton (1991) proposed an experience-independent face detection mechanism that directs newborns' attention to faces and responds as robustly to abstract faces portrayed with three dark blobs (two eyes and a mouth) as to realistic face images (see also Cassia *et al.*, 2004). So newborns attend equally to more or less abstract face stimuli. This may be because highly abstract face stimuli match an innate face template, or because the newborn visual system is highly sensitive to their low-level visual features (e.g. more high-contrast elements at the top of a bounded region). In support of the second proposal, Cassia *et al.* (2004) have shown that even non-face patterns with more contrast at the top are preferred, and they argue that infants' inborn preference for human faces is driven by a broad attentional mechanism that orients newborns to patterns with more contrast at the top. These authors concede that in the natural environment, this is tanta-mount to a face template (Simion *et al.*, 2001), since newborns' visual acuity is likely to limit the objects with high contrast at the top of a bounded region that they can resolve. The important point here is that the experience-independent representation or attentional bias that drives infants to discriminate faces from other objects from birth is tuned to highly abstract patterns, in contrast to their much later-developing discrimination of the rest of the body.

Returning to the three proposals for the origins of expertise in body percep-tion, two aspects of our overall pattern of data stand out. First, even under optimal conditions, human body perception is a late development. It is not until the second half of the first year of life that infants consistently discriminate scrambled bodies from typical ones. This suggests that visual experience with bodies is required and, furthermore, that visual experience may not be available until infants' visual acuity approaches adult levels, around age 6 months, and they begin to be able to maintain body postures that allow them to get a good look at other people as they move around the environment.

Second, the hierarchy of stimulus types that engender body recognition between 4 and 18 months of age suggests that infants' perception of the human body configuration is intertwined with other elements of person percep-tion including biological movement, object size and texture, and the presence of a human voice.

With these points in mind, it appears that developmental trajectory (3), which posits that expert processing of bodies is acquired gradually via domain-general learning processes, is most tenable. The other two proposals predict that infants should discriminate scrambled versus typical bodies early in development, either from birth (proposal 1) or soon after exposure to others' bodies (proposal 2). As noted above, one could argue that experience-expectant learning to perceive bodies is delayed until infants are out of arms – maybe the infants' transition to sitting upright turns on the experience-expectant learning process, so that once they can see people's bodies in full, then the structure is learned. However, we found no correlation between infants' ability to discriminate scrambled from typical bodies and their gross or fine motor development

(Christie and Slaughter, 2009). This targeted investigation extended our previous observations that infants' body perception was not linked to their locomotor status, across the vast majority of our studies using various body stimuli. It is risky to build theories on null correlations, but the fact that we found no associations between motor development and human body perception in infants between 6 and 15 months of age, calls into question the idea that body perception develops as a result of a punctuated experience-expectant process that is triggered by visual exposure to the whole human form.

Proposal (3) predicts a gradual acquisition and, furthermore, if infants are extracting body structural invariants from experience, then richly realistic body stimuli would be easier to generalise to, compared to abstract body stimuli. Once expertise in body processing is acquired, then there are no longer stimulus effects, as in the example of adults who easily perceive human bodies in highly abstract stick figures. We do not yet know when stimulus effects no longer influence infants' perception of human bodies, although by 18 months, infants look longer at a novel, scrambled body even if it is portrayed in black and white line drawings, as in Figure 5.1. Infants' responses to even more abstract body stimuli have yet to be investigated. By adulthood, human body stick figures, line drawings, and photos are equally effective in activating the body-specific EBA (Downing *et al.*, 2001), so stimulus effects are no longer evident, at both behavioural and neurocognitive levels of analysis, once expertise is acquired.

Conclusion and future directions

We have argued that the capacity to accurately detect human bodies comes about via an experience-dependent developmental process that occurs gradually over the first 18 months of life. Initially, discrimination of scrambled bodies is only available when infants view realistic body stimuli that approximate the physical, movement or multimodal characteristics of real people. This suggests that infants generalise their knowledge about the body shape from direct experience with real people. Thus it appears that infants are not equipped with a configural representation of the human body, but have to extract one from visual experience. This process may well be assisted by innate mechanisms directing attention to faces and to biological motion (Simion *et al.*, 2008), both of which could increase infant's visual access to human bodies.

To test this model, further work is required. One fruitful approach would be to manipulate infants' visual exposure to the whole human form. For instance, infants younger than 6 months might be enticed to regularly view human body images, videos or dolls. Would this allow them to pass the discrimination and/or preference tests sooner than their peers who did not get the same exposure? Similarly, we might make use of the fact that cultures differ in dress styles which can influence how well the human form can be visually resolved. Studies investigating developmental trajectories for early body knowledge across cultures could be informative.

We have found no evidence that infants discriminate scrambled from typical bodies before 4 months of age at the very earliest; however, to date no one has tested newborns' visual responses to typical and scrambled human forms. Given that U-shaped curves in development are evident in a number of domains, this should be investigated in order to confirm our proposal that body detection develops gradually.

It will also be important to systematically investigate when the hallmarks of visual expertise, such as configural processing, emerge in development. A recent preliminary study found configural human body processing by pre-schoolers when they were tested with a body part naming task (Christie *et al.*, 2009). Children viewed pictures of upright and inverted normal bodies, as well as upright and inverted scrambled bodies. Each body had one limb highlighted with a multicoloured pattern and children were instructed to name the limb as quickly as possible. The children were significantly faster at naming the high-lighted body part on the normal upright body compared to the other body stimuli, indicating that their identification of the individual body parts was enhanced when configural processing was possible. Further exploring the onset of these and related perceptual expertise effects will help flesh out our understanding of the developmental trajectory from early perceptual learning and generalisation to expert visual processing of the human body.

References

Beauchamp, M. S., Lee, K. E., Haxby, J. V., and Martin, A. (2002). Parallel visual motion processing streams for manipulable objects and human movements. *Neuron*, **34**, 149–159.

  (2003). fMRI responses to video and point-light displays of moving humans and manipulable objects. *Journal of Cognitive Neuroscience*, **15**, 991–1,001.

Bentin, S., Allison, T., Puce, A., Perez, E., and McCarthy, G. (1996). Electrophysiological studies of face perception in humans. *Journal of Cognitive Neuroscience*, **8**, 551–565.

Bukach, C., Gauthier, I., and Tarr, M. (2006). Beyond faces and modularity: The power of an expertise framework. *Trends in Cognitive Science*, **10**, 159–166.

Carey, S. (1992). Becoming a face expert. *Philosophical Transactions of the Royal Society of London*, **335**, 95–103.

Cassia, V. M., Turati, C., and Simion, F. (2004). Can a nonspecific bias toward top-heavy patterns explain newborns' face preference? *Psychological Science*, **15**, 379–383.

Christie, T. and Slaughter, V. (2009). Exploring links between sensori-motor and visuo-spatial body representations in infancy. *Developmental Neuropsychology*, **34**, 448–460.

  (2011). Movement facilitates infants' recognition of the whole human form. *Cognition*, **114**, 329–337.

Christie, T., Slaughter, V., and Oka, T. (2009). Configural body processing in pre-schoolers. *Poster presented at the Experimental Psychology Conference*, Wollongong, Australia.

Cohen, L. B. (2004). Uses and misuses of habituation and related preference paradigms. *Infant and Child Development*, **13**, 349–352.

Downing, P. E., Bray, D., Rogers, J., and Childs, C. (2004). Bodies capture attention when nothing is expected. *Cognition*, **93**, B27–B38.

Downing, P. E., Jiang, Y., Shuman, M., and Kanwisher, N. (2001). A cortical area selective for visual processing of the human body. *Science*, **293**, 2,470–2,473.

Gauthier, I. and Tarr, M. J. (1997). Becoming a 'greeble' expert: Exploring mechanisms for face recognition. *Vision Research*, **37**, 1,673–1,682.

Gauthier, I., Williams, P., Tarr, M. J., and Tanaka, J. (1998). Training 'greeble' experts: A framework for studying expert object recognition processes. *Vision Research*, **38**, 2,401–2,428.

Gliga, T. and Dehaene-Lambertz, G. (2005). Structural encoding of body and face in human infants and adults. *Journal of Cognitive Neuroscience*, **17**, 1,328–1,340.

Goodman, G., Sayfan, L., Lee, J., Sandhei, M., Walle-Olsen, A. *et al.* (2007). The development of memory for own- and other-race faces. *Journal of Experimental Child Psychology*, **98**, 233–242.

Hartshorn, K., Rovee-Collier, C., Gerhardstein, P., Bhatt, R., Klein, P. *et al.* (1998). Developmental changes in the specificity of memory over the first year of life. *Developmental Psychobiology*, **33**, 61–78.

Hayne, H., Boniface, J., and Barr, R. (2000). The development of declarative memory in human infants: Age-related changes in deferred imitation. *Behavioral Neuroscience*, **114**, 77–83.

Heron, M. and Slaughter, V. (2010). Infants' responses to real humans and representations of humans. *International Journal of Behavioral Development*, **34**, 34–45.

Johansson, G. (1977). Studies on visual perception of locomotion. *Perception*, **6**, 365–376.

Johnson, M. H., Dziurawiec, S., Ellis, H., and Morton, J. (1991). Newborn preferential tracking of face-like stimuli and its subsequent decline. *Cognition*, **40**, 1–19.

Johnson, M. H. and Morton, J. (1991). *Biology and cognitive development: The case of face recognition*. Oxford, UK: Blackwell.

Le Grand, R., Mondloch, C. J., Maurer, D., and Brent, H. P. (2003). Expert face processing requires visual input to the right hemisphere during infancy. *Nature Neuroscience*, **6**, 1,108–1,112.

(2004). Impairment in holistic face processing following early visual deprivation. *Psychological Science*, **15**, 762–768.

Mack A. and Rock, I. (1998). *Inattentional Blindness*. Cambridge, MA: MIT Press.

Marshall, P. and Shipley, T. (2009). Event-related potentials to point-light displays of human actions in 5-month-old infants. *Developmental Neuropsychology*, **34**, 368–377.

Maurer, D., Le Grand, R., and Mondloch, C. J. (2002). The many faces of configural processing. *Trends in Cognitive Sciences*, **6**, 255–260.

McKone, E., Kanwisher, N., and Duchaine, B. (2007). Can generic expertise explain special processing for faces? *Trends in Cognitive Science*, **11**, 8–15.

Minnebusch, D., Suchan, B., and Daum, I. (2009). Losing your head: Behavioral and electrophysiological effects of body inversion. *Journal of Cognitive Neuroscience*, **21**, 865–874.

Nelson, C. A. (2001). The development and neural bases of face recognition. *Infant and Child Development*, **10**, 3–18.

Peelen, M. V. and Downing, P. E. (2005). Within-subject reproducibility of category-specific visual activation with functional MRI. *Human Brain Mapping*, **25**, 402–408.

Ramm, B., Cummins, T., and Slaughter, V. (2010). Specifying the human body configuration. *Visual Cognition*, **18**, 898–919.

Reed, C. L., Stone, V., Bozova, S., and Tanaka, J. (2003). The body inversion effect. *Psychological Science*, **14**, 302–308.

Reed, C. L., Stone, V., Grubb, J., and McGoldrick, J. (2006). Turning configural processing upside down: Part and whole body postures. *Journal of Experimental Psychology: Human Perception and Performance*, **32**, 67–83.

Reid, V. M., Hoehl, S., Landt, J., and Striano, T. (2008). Human infants dissociate structural and dynamic information in biological motion: Evidence from neural systems. *Social Cognitive and Affective Neuroscience*, **3**, 161–167.

Rhodes, G., Byatt, G., Michie, P. T., and Puce, A. (2004). Is the fusiform face area specialized for faces, individuation, or expert individuation? *Journal of Cognitive Neuroscience*, **16**, 189–203.

Robbins, R. and McKone, E. (2007). No face-like processing for objects-of-expertise in three behavioural tasks. *Cognition*, **103**, 34–79.

Sai, F. (2005). The role of the mother's voice in developing mother's face preference: Evidence for intermodal perception at birth. *Infant and Child Development*, **14**, 29–50.

Schwarzlose, R. F., Baker, C. I., and Kanwisher, N. (2005). Separate face and body selectivity on the fusiform gyrus. *Journal of Neuroscience*, **25**, 11,055–11,059.

Simion, F., Cassia, V., Turati, C., and Valenza, E. (2001). The origins of face perception: Specific versus non-specific mechanisms. *Infant and Child Development*, **10**, 59–65.

Simion, F., Regolin, L., and Bulf, H. (2008). A predisposition for biological motion in the newborn baby. *Proceedings of the National Academy of Sciences (USA)*, **105**, 809–813.

Slaughter, V. and Heron, M. (2004). Origins and early development of human body knowledge. *Monographs of the Society for Research in Child Development*, **69**(2).

Slaughter, V., Heron, M., and Sim, S. (2002). Development of preferences for the human body shape in infancy. *Cognition*, **85**, B71–B81.

Stekelenburg, J. and de Gelder, B. (2004). The neural correlates of perceiving human bodies: An ERP study on the body-inversion effect. *Neuroreport*, **15**(5), 777–780.

Sugita, Y. (2008). Face perception in monkeys reared with no exposure to faces. *Proceedings of the National Academy of Sciences (USA)*, **105**, 394–398.

  (2009). Innate face processing. *Current Opinion in Neurobiology*, **19**, 39–44.

Taylor, J., Wiggett, A., and Downing, P. (2007). fMRI analysis of body and body part representations in the extrastriate and fusiform body areas. *Journal of Neurophysiology*, **98**, 1,626–1,633.

Thierry, G., Pegna, A. J., Dodds, C., Roberts, M., Basan, S., and Downing, P. (2006). An event-related potential component sensitive to images of the human body. *Neuroimage*, **32**, 871–879.

Thornton, I., Pinto, J., and Shiffrar, M. (1998). The visual perception of human locomotion. *Cognitive Neuropsychology*, **15**, 535–552.

Xu, Y. (2005). Revisiting the role of the fusiform face area in visual expertise. *Cerebral Cortex*, **15**, 1,234–1,242.

6   Children's representations of the human figure in their drawings

Maureen Cox

One of the first recognisable things that children draw is the human figure and it remains a popular topic throughout their school years. It is usually composed of a number of parts, drawn in sequence and fitted together in a particular spatial way. Typically, the head is drawn first and consists of a contour, which encloses the facial features. The body is drawn below the head. The legs are often, but not always, added next and then the arms last. Hair, hands and feet, and other embellishments may also be included. Older drawers already know how to draw such a figure, even though it may not be very sophisticated and may turn out to be rather sketchy and more like a cartoon. Very young children, however, have to learn how to make this drawing and it is by no means a simple process. They have to decide which components to include, remember these key body parts, decide which order to draw them in, know where to locate each one on the figure, choose the appropriate kind of line or shape for each part and know how to fit them together. And of course they need adequate visuo-motor skills and cognitive abilities to be able to bring all this about.

In this chapter I will review the research on children's developing ability to represent the human figure in their drawings and the extent to which this reflects their knowledge of the human body. I will discuss the various influences on its development, including the culture that children grow up in as well as their own individual characteristics and experiences. Understanding this development and the influences on it is important for those professionals working in an educational or therapeutic context who use children's human figure drawings, as without such knowledge they may underestimate children's ability and misinterpret their emotional state. A fuller account of some of the data, claims and arguments referred to in this chapter can be found in Cox, 2005.

Children's early mark-making

Around their first birthday most children are beginning to be interested in mark-making. They see their parents or older siblings drawing pictures – usually on paper with a pencil or crayon. Between the ages of 12 and15 months children

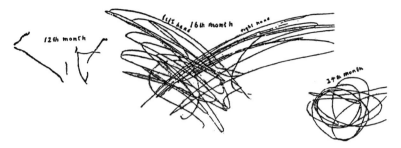

Figure 6.1 Tentative scribbles at age 1 year (left); side-to-side scribbles at 16 months (centre); and spiralling scribbles at 2 years (Major, 1906)

will request their mothers to draw, by looking at them intently and offering them the drawing materials. And by 18 months children will suggest the topic of the drawing they want their mothers to produce (Yamagata, 1997). More or less at the same time, young children want to try this activity for themselves.

Some of the earliest marks that children make are the result of stabbing movements towards the paper. Soon, we see sideways sweeps and also 'push-pull' movements, all leaving distinctive kinds of marks on the page (Matthews, 1984). As children gain more control over the pencil they produce spirals and, eventually, are able to control these to such an extent that a closed shape is formed, albeit an irregular one (Piaget and Inhelder, 1956). The emergence of this closed shape is important, according to Arnheim (1974), because it seems to suggest a solid object against a background. Gradually, then, children develop and expand a repertoire of marks, marks that they will be able to select when constructing a more complex representational drawing later on (see Figure 6.1).

The beginnings of representation

During this early phase of development it is often unclear whether or not the marks on the page are meant to represent anything. The scribbles certainly don't look recognisable! But this can be misleading. It may be the movement or action of, for example, a person running that the child has tried to mimic. The marks left on the page are the visual trace of this action, not an attempt to capture what a person actually looks like. Matthews (1984) calls them 'action representations'.

Before they can draw a recognisable object by themselves, children can often select appropriate lines and shapes to complete an adult's drawing. When I drew a head and a torso for my daughter, aged 1 year 11 months, she added some side-to-side scribbles for the arms and some vertical scribbles for the legs. Then she drew a curved line overlapping the face, which she said was a hat (see Figure 6.2). She had selected roughly appropriate marks for the different parts of the figure and had

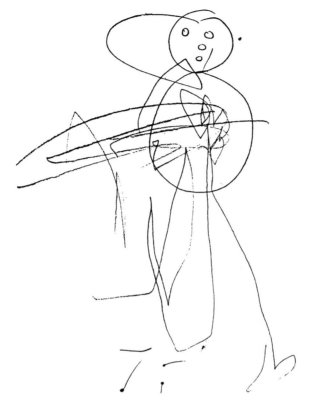

Figure 6.2 Amy, aged 1 year 11 months, added arms, legs and a hat to an adult's pre-drawn head and torso

also placed them in roughly the right locations (Cox, 1992). Golomb (1974, 1981) has also shown that children who normally only produced apparently mean- ingless scribbles had a good understanding of the spatial organisation of the human figure. As the body parts of a figure were dictated to them these young children correctly located the hair, the head, the tummy, and then the legs in a spatially correct order, and they could do this even when the spoken items were jumbled up. Children's performance in these kinds of assisted tasks shows that their understanding of the arrangement of the main parts the human body is quite robust. They are also beginning to choose appropriate kinds of marks that might best represent these body parts. And all this occurs somewhat earlier than they can demonstrate in their own free drawings.

When these young children are asked to draw a figure without any assistance they often draw just a line or a squiggle. If they are able to they may draw an

Figure 6.3 'It's my Mummy', by Simon, aged 3 years (left); 'Mummy and Daddy', by Simon at 3 years 2 months (right)

Figure 6.4 Tadpole figures drawn by pre-school children

irregular but closed shape. These lines or shapes may stand for a whole person, but they belie what the children actually know about the human body (see Figure 6.3). Gradually, with age and experience, children will differentiate the parts of the figure in their drawings and will find ways to make them look recognisable. This search for or invention of 'equivalents' involves the children in finding lines and shapes that stand for and bear some resemblance to the body parts they represent (Arnheim, 1974; Goodnow, 1977; Golomb, 2002). To some extent they have already embarked on this task, as indicated in the example of my daughter's completion of a figure by selecting different kinds of lines for different body parts.

The first, recognisable figures

One of the earliest recognisable figures that children draw is the 'tadpole' form (see Figure 6.4). In my data the youngest child to have drawn a tadpole figure was aged 2 years 9 months, but Eng (1931) reported that her niece drew one when she was 1 year and 10 months old. Tadpole figures are so common that they are probably drawn by almost all young children (Freeman 1980).

The tadpole figure is often simply a rough circle set upon two legs, although it may also have facial features and perhaps some arms and may even have further details such as hands and feet – and, occasionally, eyelashes! If the arms are included they seem to be emerging from the sides of the head. What the tadpole figure appears to lack is a torso. It is not clear, though, whether it really does lack a torso. It may be, as Arnheim (1974) has suggested, that the head and the torso are both included in the figure, albeit undifferentiated: either the enclosed shape stands for both the head and the torso *or* the torso may be located, implicitly, between the legs of the figure. Luquet (2001), however, was more inclined to the view that the torso is actually missing, not because the children have failed to notice it but because they do not regard it as important.

Young children certainly know that a real person has a torso. In a study of 100 tadpole drawers aged from 2 years 10 months to 4 years 10 months all of them readily pointed to their 'bodies' or 'tummies' when asked by the experimenter (Cox and Batra, unpublished data), and in Brittain and Chien's (1983) study pre-school children could give appropriate names for the main body parts, including the torso, when an experimenter pointed to them on a pre-drawn figure.

Perhaps children omit the torso from their figure drawings simply because they have forgotten it. After all, this complex task requires that they remember a number of different body parts, how to draw them and where to put them. In a dictation task, in which the experimenter named each body part as the child drew it, only one tadpole-drawer ignored the torso; twenty-four others made a dot or a squiggle either inside the head contour or below the head (Cox, 1992). So, when prompted to include the torso these children had a good idea where on the figure it should go. However, they had little idea of *how* to draw the torso. It seems to me that they had not devised a suitable schema for it. When we provided one, by including it in a selection of pre-cut pieces of card representing each of the main body parts (head, torso, arms and legs), the children were much more successful at producing a conventional figure (Cox and Mason, 1998).

So, although young children know about the torso and where it is located on the human figure they very often do not include it as a separate region in their human figure drawings. This may be because they do not regard it as important or may simply have forgotten it. Either way, they have not invented or acquired a way of drawing it at this early stage. Apparently, the difficulty is with the drawing task, not with the child's conceptualisation of the human body. We must be aware that there is not necessarily a direct one-to-one mapping between children's knowledge of the human figure and what they draw on the page.

The development of a conventional figure

By the age of 5 years most children (67 percent, according to Gesell, 1925) have given up the tadpole form and have moved on to constructing a conventional figure with a separate and distinct torso placed below the head, and arms and legs attached to this torso (Cox and Parkin, 1986). Up to the age of about 12 or 13 years children add more body parts and details to their human figure drawings (Goodenough, 1926; Harris, 1963; Koppitz, 1968), but this changes by the teenage years when they become more interested in drawing portraits than whole-body figures, and also tend to concentrate on shading in order to produce a more solid, three-dimensional effect.

Each of the body parts in children's first conventional figures tends to have its own contour, and Willats (1985, 1987) has suggested how the shape of each one might be chosen, depending on the salient dimensions of the body parts of a real human being. The choice is not arbitrary but is based on children's knowledge of real body parts. As the head and torso are bulky, three-dimensional objects, children are likely to choose shapes (or 'regions', as Willats calls them) to depict them, rather than single lines. Rather few children draw a single line for the torso, as I have found in my own studies and as Kellogg (1969) also reported in hers. In contrast to the bulky head and torso, limbs are long objects, extending mainly along one dimension, so young children, according to Willats, are likely to represent them with single lines. And, indeed, this is the case, although by the age of 6 years most children have switched to using outlining contours for the arms and the legs of their figures (Cox, 1993).

Up until the age of about 5 or 6 years children's figures have a segmented appearance, with each body part having its own boundary (see Figure 6.5, left). Increasingly, though, parts of the body are combined with a continuous contour, which Goodnow (1977) has called 'threading'. Typically, the arms and the upper torso are combined, and the lower torso and the legs. The effect is that the figures appear to be wearing a jumper or trousers, although it is not clear whether the children intend their figures to be clothed (see Figure 6.5, right). By the age of 7 to 8 years most children are using threading in their drawings and by 9 to 10 years nearly all of them are doing so (Cox, 1993).

A young child's drawings of the human figure often look very similar, as if he or she is tipping out the same formula or stereotype. In Amy's drawing of her family, for example, the three figures are constructed in exactly the same way (see Figure 6.6). It's as if the child has discovered a way of drawing a person and then runs that same 'program' regardless of the individual differences in appearance among the people being depicted. Karmiloff-Smith (1990) has argued that young children are compelled to run the program because they are unable to modify the sequentially ordered set of movements that they have practised. The evidence does not support this explanation, however. A number of studies have shown that children do vary the order of movements over a series of drawings, and that they are also capable of making mid-procedure alterations to their drawings (Van Sommers, 1984; Spensley and Taylor, 1999; Barlow, 2003). I prefer Van Sommers' explanation that the drawing or schema

Figure 6.5 This figure (left), drawn by a 6-year-old, is in a canonical orientation; this figure (right), drawn by an 8-year-old, is in side-view and appears to be walking: the arm occludes the contour of the torso

Figure 6.6 Amy, aged 5 years 2 months, drew her family using the same basic schema for each figure

that children work out when they first start to draw the human figure then acts as a *visual* goal towards which subsequent drawing attempts are directed. Bearing in mind this visual goal, children then try to replicate it but do not necessarily follow the same order of movements each time. Nonetheless, they appear to be very conservative in their drawing, persisting with a particular style for some time before they see the need to revise it.

Most figures drawn by young children have a frontal orientation – they face the viewer with their legs apart and their arms held away from the torso. This stance is often referred to as the 'canonical' orientation (Freeman, 1980; Dziurawiec and Deregowski, 1992), the one that best displays all the salient and defining features of a person. It's rarely the case that the canonical view could also be a real view of a figure since not all the body parts have been drawn from one particular viewpoint. For example, the feet are often turned to the sides, pointing in opposite directions; the nose may be drawn from a side view whereas the eyes and mouth have been drawn from the front. Such a figure is an example of what Luquet (2001) called 'intellectual realism', children's intention to show what they know about the human figure, to display each of the main parts to its best advantage rather than to draw the whole figure as it would look from a particular point of view (see Figure 6.5, left).

A number of studies have shown that children are not completely inflexible, and can vary their figures if requested to do so. When children were asked to draw a plastic toy figure from different viewpoints all 6-year-olds and 75 percent of 4-year-olds successfully drew a back view, and all 6-year-olds and 49 per cent of the 4-year-olds successfully drew a side view (Cox and Moore, 1994). They were able to make the necessary alterations to their drawings so that these views were different from their drawings of the frontal orientation of the figure.

By the age of about 7 or 8 years children begin to attend more to 'visual realism', which indicates an awareness of the need to depict the figure from a particular viewpoint. Children begin spontaneously to experiment with different orientations of the figure (placing it in a side view, for example), often showing it engaged in some action or movement, and occluding parts of the body that are obscured when other parts overlap them (see Figure 6.5, right). Instead of drawing a generic form they try to individualise their figures by adding features (e.g. spectacles, a beard, a long nose) that are related to each particular person. The figures are now differentiated by gender, although at first often in a rather stereotyped way – with long hair and ribbons for girls and short hair for boys (Arazos and Davis, 1989; Sitton and Light, 1992) – and are often clothed, again in gender-stereotyped ways at first. Children also become interested in the emotional expression of their figures, altering the shape of the mouth or the eyebrows to show happiness or anger and adding features such as tears to denote sadness (Golomb, 1992; Cox, 2005). It is likely that the developments we see in children's drawings are attempts to make the figures appear more realistic, at first in terms of intellectual realism (what they know about real figures) and later in terms of visual realism (how the figure looks from a particular point of view), although of course visual realism is informed by knowledge too.

How universal are children's attempts to draw the human figure?

The pattern of development in children's drawings of the human figure that I have outlined above is widespread. Does this mean that children everywhere start off representing the human figure in the same way – with scribbles and simple shapes, followed by tadpole forms – and then develop increasingly realistic conventional forms? It is certainly the case that most children in most cultures scribble and make simple shapes before they move on to creating recognisable figures. And, as I have already indicated, it is often a tadpole form that is the first recognisable figure that children go on to produce. None the less, there are other forms that some children experiment with.

In their study of children's drawings in the Jimi valley of Papua New Guinea, Martlew and Connolly (1996) found the tadpole form and some other kinds of figures too, notably a contour figure and, to a much lesser extent, a stick figure. When I analysed the longitudinal data collected in the UK by Amelia Fysh (Cox 1997) I also found that although many children produced a tadpole form as their first recognisable human figure some produced alternatives (see Figure 6.7). Some drew facial features but did not enclose them with a surrounding head contour; others drew contour figures; a few produced stick figures. Interestingly, though, in this collection most of those children who produced an alternative form did not continue with it nor developed it into a more complex form; rather,

Figure 6.7 A figure with no outline around the facial features (left), drawn by a 4-year-old; a contour figure (centre), drawn by a boy aged 4 years 3 months; a stick figure (right), drawn by a 4-year-old

they switched to tadpole figures quite early. Unfortunately, the Martlew and Connolly study was not longitudinal so we cannot know whether or not their children would have switched to drawing tadpole figures as the UK children did. What these findings indicate, however, is that there are different ways that the human figure can be depicted and that not all young children come up, initially, with the same solution.

One presumes that the more unusual forms are drawn by those children who have not been shown exactly how to draw a human figure, but have tried to achieve a passable figure by mentally extracting shapes from pictures or from real people and then finding appropriate lines or shapes to represent them. In some cases, however, it may be that an adult or another child has actually shown the child how to draw – a stick figure, for example – even though most children, in developed countries at least, do not draw their figures in this way.

That most young children draw tadpole figures or rapidly switch to drawing them suggests that they have a particular goal in mind when they intend to depict a human being. That goal will be the depiction of the human body that is typical in their society. In western societies it is perhaps the head that is the most obvious feature; indeed, it is usually drawn first and is disproportionately large, often leaving little space on the page for the rest of the body (Freeman, 1980; Thomas and Tsalimi, 1988). Although the tadpole form itself is not common among older children's and adults' drawings it may be that it is the best attempt that novice-drawers, such as small children, can make in trying to achieve their goal. Tadpole figures have even been noted among rural adults in Turkey who had had no prior experience of drawing and had been asked to draw a person for the first time (Cox and Bayraktar, 1989).

The representation of the human figure in different cultures

When children progress to drawing a conventional figure, with more details, we can see differences among cultures in the way they are drawn. Features that are particularly distinctive are styles of hair and dress. Pfeffer (1984), for example, found that 40 percent of a sample of Yoruba children in Nigeria drew their figures with African hairstyles, 25 percent of them drew them in traditional dress and 50 percent drew African facial features (see Figure 6.8). These percentages may not seem particularly high and this may reflect the fact that the children were not explicitly asked to draw African figures in traditional dress. When Frisch and Handler (1967) asked black children to draw a *Negro* figure 80 percent of them drew obvious African features.

It is perhaps not surprising that children's figure drawings will reflect these culturally distinctive hairstyles, facial features and dress; after all, these features are characteristic of real people and are very familiar to the children. There are

Figure 6.8 These figures, drawn by a 9-year-old boy (left) and a 10-year-old girl (right) from Nigeria, display African features and rectangular torsos (thanks to Dr Karen Pfeffer for collecting these drawings)

other differences, though, that do not seem to reflect regional differences in the way people look or dress but, rather, are simply different choices of graphic conventions. One example is the way that the torso is drawn. Typically, in young western children's pictures, the torso is circular or oval in shape, although older children adapt it to indicate the clothes worn by boys or girls – for example, a dress or blouse and skirt, or a shirt or jacket and trousers (Cox 1992, 1993). Interestingly, children in some African countries and in the Middle East draw a rectangular torso (see Figure 6.8). This is so common that Wilson and Wilson (1984) call it the 'Islamic' torso. In the early 1930s (Paget, 1932), a bi-triangular torso was found in the drawings of children in South West Africa (now Namibia). Over 60 years later, in 1995–7, Andersson (2003) collected drawings from children in this region and also in the neighbouring part of Zimbabwe and found examples of this same kind of torso (see Figure 6.9).

The torso of a real person does not have a regular geometric shape. It may be rather angular at the shoulders, but also has rounded contours. It is usually longer than it is wide, but not always. It is often narrower at the waist but, again, not always. Because of this range of differences there are a number of possible solutions to the problem of how best to draw it. It is interesting that some cultural groups favour one shape rather than another.

Figure 6.9 These bi-triangular figures were drawn by a 14-year-old Zimbabwean girl (printed with the permission of Dr Ingrid and Dr Sven Andersson)

Although we see these differences in the human figure drawings among different cultural groups we can all recognise that they are meant to represent people. After all, they have defining features such as heads, torsos, arms and legs, and the location of these features in the drawing corresponds roughly to their location on real people (Paget, 1932). Thus, the representations reflect the drawers' knowledge of the human form. And one might presume that the decision to include these main features is universal. In general this seems to be true although the emphasis may vary. For example, although in most cultures the face is prominent Paget recorded several pin-head figures drawn by children in South West Africa in which there was no space for facial features.

There is a dramatically different solution to the way that a person should be depicted in the art of some Australian Aboriginal groups (Munn, 1973; Wales, 1990; Cox and Hill, 1996; Cox, 1998). For example, the U-shaped form used by the Warlpiri in central Australia to represent a whole person seems very strange to westerners who may think that it bears no relation to the shape of a real person and has been chosen completely arbitrarily. It may be, however, that this form represents an aerial view of a person seated on the ground, perhaps engaging in an act of story-telling, or involved in a community meeting (see Figure 6.10). Since this form can be drawn quickly in the sand to accompany their oral story-telling it may originally have been devised by the adults for this particular purpose. Warlpiri children become adept at drawing the human figure in this way too. But they also draw in a western style and, if we examine their western-style figures, we see a similar kind of development as we see among children in western societies – tadpole forms followed by conventional depictions.

Figure 6.10 A group of people chatting around a campfire, drawn by an 8-year-old Warlpiri girl, central Australia; the U-shaped symbol has been used for most of the figures but the baby is a conventional western form (traced from an original drawing collected by Rosemary Hill; thanks to the Warlpiri Media Association and the people of Yuendumu, Central Australia)

The sources of cultural influence on children's drawings

Children's human figure drawings may be influenced by the pictorial images they see in their particular culture. In western societies these sources are often the mass media – books, magazines, comics, cartoon films and so on. However, some regional forms may have been influenced by the styles used by local artists or craftsmen. For example, the bi-triangular figures drawn by children in Namibia and Zimbabwe have been observed on woven baskets and the carved sides of drums as well as on other artefacts in this region (Andersson, 2003). Other forms, such as the Warlpiri U-shaped figures, have been copied from the sand sketches of community story-tellers and, in more recent times, can be seen in the paintings of local adult artists, many of which hang in permanent collections in art galleries to great international interest and acclaim.

The kinds of images prevalent in the education system can have a profound effect on the style that children adopt. In China, where art is a high status school subject and art teaching has been very formal, at least up until the 1990s, characteristic Chinese styles of drawing have been retained (Winner, 1989; Cox *et al.*, 1998). And in Japan where, again, art teaching is very structured, children's human figure drawings have a distinct Japanese flavour about them, often influenced by the manga comics and films, popular among both children and adults (Wilson, 2000; Cox *et al.*, 2001). In the Warlpiri culture, images on the walls of classrooms and in books show western styles of representing the human figure as well as the traditional U-shaped form. So, both styles are valued.

In some cultures, however, in which there has been no prior form of pictorial representation or even when there has, it is often a western style of representation that has been promoted. When Fortes (1940) collected drawings from children in what was then the Gold Coast of West Africa he found that the figures drawn by children attending a boarding school were noticeably western in style compared with those requested from village children who did not attend school. Fortes (1981) returned 35 years later and collected drawings from local school children, many of whom were the descendants of those in the original sample. These drawings were western in style, and more skilfully produced than those drawn by the earlier generation. Martlew and Connolly (1996) also found that, in their sample in the Jimi Valley of Papua New Guinea, the more schooling children had had the more western in style were their drawings.

Children themselves can be the source of a particular style, influencing other children who then adopt this form. Wilson (1985) found that nearly all of a sample of Spanish-speaking children in California in the years from 1917 to 1923 drew the legs of their figures in a particularly complicated and intersecting way not seen elsewhere. It is not known whether this style originated with one particular child, but it seemed to be passed on by one child copying from another. Paget (1932), an early collector of children's human figure drawings, suggested that this may be one of the main ways that particular styles are passed on from one 'generation' of children to the next in a similar way that playground games are passed on.

The cultural differences in the details and the structure of human figure drawings indicate that children are influenced by the kinds of depictions that are common in their particular society. This should not surprise us, as children's development does not take place in isolation but within a culture (Vygotsky, 1978). In most cases, children are not drawing *de novo* but in relation to the ways in which the human body is routinely represented in the pictures they see around them – in books and magazines, on TV, in the art gallery – as well as those drawn by teachers, parents, older siblings and same-age friends. So, although children understand a lot about the human body, the way they represent it in their drawings is also influenced by the context in which they have grown up. However, it is important to emphasise that children are not imbibing cultural influences in a passive way, but are actively engaged in the process of cultural transmission. Development progresses through social interactions with parents and teachers as well as with other children, all within a wider cultural context.

Individual characteristics and experiences

It was very obvious to the early investigators of children's drawings that as children get older their figures become more detailed and the proportions of the body parts become more realistic (Schuyten, 1904; Lobsien, 1905), and it was also clear that this process was slower among the less intellectually able children (Rouma, 1913). A number of studies of children with a non-specific intellectual disability has shown that these children perform less well than typically developing children of the same chronological age (Cox and Howarth, 1989; Cox and Cotgreave, 1996). There has been some attempt to establish tests of intelligence or intellectual maturity based on the normal range of children's human figure drawing. These tests include the Draw-a-Man Test (Goodenough, 1926), the revised Goodenough-Harris Test (Harris, 1963), the Draw-a-Person Test (Koppitz, 1968) and the Draw-a-Person Test (Naglieri, 1988). Children's human figure drawings are scored mainly according to the number of details included, but points are also awarded for the proportions and integration of the parts of the figure. Although the reliability of these tests is high their validity is not, leading many researchers to advise against using them for diagnostic purposes.

There have been a few studies of the drawings by children with an intellectual disability related to a specific cause – such as Down's syndrome, for example (Clements and Barrett, 1994; Eames and Cox, 1994; Cox and Maynard, 1998; Laws and Lawrence, 2001) or autism (Eames and Cox, 1994). Again, however, these children tend to lag behind typically developing children of the same age, and in fact they perform even lower than younger children matched on mental age.

Another special population that has been quite intensively studied in relation to drawing ability is the blind. It may seem surprising that blind children can understand or even produce drawings, as we might assume that drawing is essentially a visual activity. However, it's through the use of the raised-line technique that blind people are able to appreciate and produce pictures. A raised line is produced when drawing on a rubber-coated board with a ball-point pen. Using this technique, Millar (1975) found that young blind children, aged 6 and 8 years, were not very successful at drawing a human figure and often did not produce anything recognizable at all. At age 10, though, they had much more success, drawing the main body parts and placing them in the correct spatial relationship to each other. What's more, they used the same kinds of shapes as did sighted (but blindfolded) children – for example, a circle was used to represent the head – indicating that shapes used for body parts are not arbitrary but preserve something of the shape of the real items. It is interesting that this discovery can be made not solely through vision but also through touch. A study of one particular blind girl (Kennedy, 2003) also indicates that, although there is a developmental lag, drawing development proceeds in a similar way among the blind as among the sighted. Clearly, a lack of vision does not impede our ability to recognise or produce pictures. As Kennedy argues, pictorial representation engages us at a broader perceptual and cognitive level.

The various tests designed to assess children's human figure drawings have sometimes been used to compare the intellectual level of children from different cultures. There are dangers in this. In cultures where drawings of the human figure are less popular children will be less practised at producing them. A less confidently drawn figure or a less detailed one will score lower on tests such as the Draw-a-Man Test (Goodenough, 1926; Harris, 1963). Similarly, in cultures where a very different type of figure is commonly produced children's scores on these tests may be lower and their intellectual ability may be underestimated. It is therefore inappropriate to use these kinds of tests with children from a particular cultural group unless test norms have been established for them.

Many people assume that human figure drawings will reflect children's personality or emotional problems, or their experience of traumatic events such as conflict, war, or physical, sexual, or psychological abuse. There have been several attempts to develop tests based on human figure drawings, which might enable the therapist to assess children's personality, emotional difficulties and distress. Such tests include the Draw-a-Person Test devised by Machover (1949) and another of the same name devised by Koppitz (1968). As with the tests developed for assessing children's intellectual level, these tests have also been found wanting (see reviews by Swensen, 1968; Kahill, 1984; Motta *et al.*, 1993). In fact, both their reliability *and* their validity are so weak that many researchers believe that their use as diagnostic tools cannot be supported.

Despite these criticisms many therapists – particularly art therapists – continue to use children's drawings as a basis for interpreting children's emotional problems, believing that a child's picture will reveal emotional problems. There are difficulties with this view. If we compare the drawings of, for example, traumatised and non-traumatised groups of children there are generally no significant differences in the content of their drawings or in the way that the figures are drawn (Hibbard *et al.*, 1987; Forrest and Thomas, 1991). In fact, to date, no general rules have been established for differentiating between the drawings of normal children and those with emotional problems (Catte and Cox, 1999; Cox and Catte, 2000). What's more, it has been shown that art therapists are unable, reliably, to pick out the drawings made by emotionally disturbed children and normal children. It seems that emotionally distressed children may be functioning at a level more consistent with those of a younger age, and that their drawings may therefore resemble a younger child's drawing. In other words, their drawing ability may be delayed in its development but not aberrant.

Summary

With increasing age, children in developed countries add more details and construct their human figure drawings with better proportions and in more realistic ways. By the teenage years, if they are still drawing, they become more interested in portraits rather than the whole figure and in techniques such as shading in order to create a more three-dimensional image. It is important that we realise there is no direct relationship between children's human figure drawings and what they actually know about the human body. It is highly likely that, at any age, children know a lot more than they include in their drawn figures. Therefore we should proceed with caution when attempting to infer something about their intellectual or emotional state from what they draw.

Children are not immune from the culture around them and it is not surprising that we see some evidence of this influence in their drawings. These differences seem to reflect the adults' artwork in any particular culture and also the emphasis that each society or educational system puts on children's artwork. As well as the influence of culture the pattern of drawing development may be modified according to children's individual characteristics and experiences. Development will be slower for children who are intellectually less able or who have a physical disability, such as blindness. In fact, those who are intellectually less able may perform even lower than younger children who have the same mental age. Although we often assume that the emotional distress that some children suffer as a result of illness, conflict, or abuse will be reflected in their drawings and that, therefore, we can use their drawings to assess their emotional state of mind, there is actually little convincing research to support this.

Professionals – in education or in therapy – need to be aware of the normal development in children's drawings of the human figure so that they do not misinterpret what the children produce. Not only should they know about the typical changes with age but also the differences that might occur in different cultural groups or with children who have an intellectual, physical, or emotional disability. Without such knowledge there is a danger that they may under-estimate a child's ability or mistake as aberrant what is in fact a perfectly normal portrayal of the human form. They also need to recognise the limitations of the tests based on human figure drawings and treat them with caution.

References

Andersson, S. B. (2003). Local conventions in children's drawings in the Namibian region. Unpublished manuscript, University of Linköping.

Arazos, A. and Davis, A. (1989). Young children's representation of gender in drawings. Presented at the British Psychological Society's Developmental Section Annual Conference, University of Surrey.

Arnheim, R. (1974). *Art and Visual Perception: A Psychology of the Creative Eye. The New Version* (2nd edn). Berkeley, CA: University of California Press.

Barlow, C. M. (2003). Rigidity in children's drawings and its relationship with representational change. Unpublished DPhil. thesis, Staffordshire University.

Brittain, W. L. and Chien, Y-C. (1983). Relationship between preschool children's ability to name body parts and their ability to construct a man. *Perceptual and Motor Skills*, **57**, 19–24.

Catte, M. and Cox, M. V. (1999). Emotional indicators in children's human figure drawings. *European Child and Adolescent Psychiatry*, **8**, 86–91.

Clements, W. and Barrett, M. (1994). The drawings of children and young people with Down's syndrome: a case of delay or difference? *British Journal of Educational Psychology*, **64**, 441–452.

Cox, M. V. (1992). *Children's Drawings*. Harmondsworth, UK: Penguin.

(1993). *Children's Drawings of the Human Figure*. Hove, UK: Lawrence Erlbaum.

(1997). *Drawings of People by the Under-5s*. London: Falmer Press.

(1998). Drawings of people by Australian Aboriginal children: The intermixing of cultural styles. *Journal of Art and Design Education*, **17**, 71–79.

(2005). *The Pictorial World of the Child*. Cambridge, UK: Cambridge University Press.

Cox, M. V. and Bayraktar, R. (1989). A cross-cultural study of children's human figure drawings. Presented at the Tenth Biennial Conference of the International Society for the Study of Behavioural Development, University of Jyväskylä, Finland.

Cox, M. V. and Catte, M. (2000). Severely disturbed children's human figure drawings: Are they unusual or just poor drawings? *European Child and Adolescent Psychiatry*, **9**, 301–306.

Cox, M. V. and Cotgreave, S. (1996). The human figure drawings of normal children and those with mild learning difficulties. *Educational Psychology*, **16**, 433–438.

Cox, M. V. and Hill, R. (1996). Different strokes. *Times Higher Educational Supplement*, 9 August, **18**.

Cox, M. V. and Howarth, C. (1989). The human figure drawings of normal children and those with severe learning difficulties. *British Journal of Developmental Psychology*, **7**, 333–339.

Cox, M. V. and Mason, S. (1998). The young child's pictorial representation of the human figure. *International Journal of Early Years Education*, **6**, 31–38.

Cox, M. V. and Maynard, S. (1998). The human figure drawings of children with Down's syndrome. *British Journal of Developmental Psychology*, **16**, 133–137.

Cox, M. V. and Moore, R. (1994). Children's depictions of different views of the human figure. *Educational Psychology*, **14**, 427–436.

Cox, M. V. and Parkin, C. E. (1986). Young children's human figure drawing: Cross-sectional and longitudinal studies. *Educational Psychology*, **6**, 353–368.

Cox, M. V., Koyasu, M., Hiranuma, H., and Perara, J. (2001). Children's human figure drawings in the UK and Japan: The effects of age, sex and culture. *British Journal of Developmental Psychology*, **19**, 275–292.

Cox, M. V., Perara, J., and Xu, F. (1998). Children's drawing ability in the UK and China. *Psychologia*, **41**, 171–182.

Dziurawiec, S. and Deregowski, J. B. (1992). Twisted perspective in young children's drawings. *British Journal of Developmental Psychology*, **10**, 35–49.

Eames, K. and Cox, M. V. (1994). Visual realism in the drawings of autistic, Down's syndrome and normal children. *British Journal of Developmental Psychology*, **12**, 235–239.

Eng, H. (1931). *The Psychology of Children's Drawings*. London: Routledge and Kegan Paul.

Forrest, M. and Thomas, G. V. (1991). An exploratory study of drawings by bereaved children. *British Journal of Clinical Psychology*, **30**, 373–374.

Fortes, M. (1940). Children's drawings among the Tallensi. *Africa*, **13**, 239–295.

(1981). Tallensi children's drawings. In B. Lloyd and J. Gay (eds). *Universals of Human Thought: Some African Evidence* (46–70). Cambridge, UK: Cambridge University Press.

Freeman, N. H. (1980). *Strategies of Representation in Young Children: Analysis of Spatial Skills and Drawing Processes*. London: Academic Press.

Frisch, R. G. and Handler, L. (1967). Differences in negro and white drawings: a cultural interpretation. *Perceptual and Motor Skills*, **24**, 667–670.

Gesell, A. (1925). *The Mental Growth of the Preschool Child*. New York: Macmillan.

Golomb, C. (1974). *Young Children's Sculpture and Drawing*. Cambridge, MA: Harvard University Press.

(1981). Representation and reality: The origins and determinants of young children's drawings. *Review of Research in Visual Art Education*, **14**, 36–48.

(1992). *The Child's Creation of a Pictorial World*. Berkeley, CA: University of California Press.

(2002). *Child Art in Context*. Washington, DC: American Psychological Association.

Goodenough, F. L. (1926). *Measurement of Intelligence by Drawings*. New York: Harcourt, Brace and World.

Goodnow, J. (1977). *Children's Drawing*. London: Fontana/Open Books.

Harris, D. B. (1963). *Children's Drawings as Measures of Intellectual Maturity: A Revision and Extension of the Goodenough Draw-a-Man Test*. New York: Harcourt, Brace and World.

Hibbard, R. A., Roghmann, K., and Hoekelman, R. A. (1987). Genitalia in children's drawings: An association with sexual abuse. *Pediatrics*, **79**, 129–136.

Kahill, S. (1984). Human figure drawing in adults: An update of the empirical evidence, 1967–1982. *Canadian Psychology*, **25**, 269–292.

Karmiloff-Smith, A. (1990). Constraints on representational change: Evidence from children's drawing. *Cognition*, **34**, 1–27.

Kellogg, R. (1969). *Analysing Children's Art*. Palo Alto, CA: Mayfield.

Kennedy, J. M. (2003). Drawings from Gaia, a blind girl. *Perception*, **32**, 391–406.

Koppitz, E. M. (1968). *Psychological Evaluation of Children's Human Figure Drawings*. New York; London: Grune and Stratton.

Laws, G. and Lawrence, L. (2001). Spatial representation in the drawings of children with Down's syndrome and its relationship to language and motor development: A preliminary investigation. *British Journal of Developmental Psychology*, **19**, 453–473.

Lobsien, M. (1905). Kinderzeichnung und Kunstkanon. *Zeitschrift für Pedagogische Psychologie*, **7**, 393–404.

Luquet, G. -H. (2001). *Children's Drawings* (translated with an introduction by A. Costall). London: Free Association Books. (Original work published in 1927.)

Machover, K. (1949). *Personality Projection in the Drawings of the Human Figure.* Springfield, IL: C. C. Thomas.

Major, D. R. (1906). *First Steps in Mental Growth.* New York: Macmillan.

Martlew, M. and Connolly, K. J. (1996). Human figure drawings by schooled and unschooled children in Papua New Guinea. *Child Development*, **67**, 2,743–2,762.

Matthews, J. (1984). Children drawing: Are young children really scribbling? *Child Development and Care*, **18**, 1–39.

Millar, S. 1975. Visual experience or translation of rules? Drawing the human figure by blind and sighted children. *Perception*, **4**, 363–371.

Motta, R. W., Little, S. G., and Tobin, M. I. (1993). The use and abuse of human figure drawings. *School Psychology Quarterly*, **8**, 162–169.

Munn, N. (1973). *Walbiri Iconography: Graphic Representation and Cultural Symbolism in a Central Australian Society.* Ithaca, NY: Cornell University Press.

Naglieri, J. A. 1988. *Draw a Person: a quantitative scoring system.* Psychological Corporation.

Paget, G. W. (1932). Some drawings of men and women made by children of certain non-European races. *Journal of the Royal Anthropological Institute*, **62**, 127–144.

Pfeffer, K. (1984). Interpretation of studies of ethnic identity: Draw-a-person as a measure of ethnic identity. *Perceptual and Motor Skills*, **59**, 835–838.

Piaget, J. and Inhelder, B. (1956). *The Child's Conception of Space.* London: Routledge and Kegan Paul.

Rouma, G. (1913). *Le Langage Graphique de l'Enfant.* Paris: Misch and Thron.

Schuyten, M. (1904). De oorspronkelijke "Ventjes" der Antwerpsch schoolkindern. *Paedologisch Jaarboek*, **5**, 1–87.

Sitton, R. and Light, P. (1992). Drawing to differentiate: Flexibility in young children's human figure drawings. *British Journal of Developmental Psychology*, **10**, 25–33.

Spensley, F. and Taylor, J. (1999). The development of cognitive flexibility: Evidence from children's drawings. *Human Development*, **42**, 300–324.

Swensen, C. H. (1968). Empirical evaluations of human figure drawings: 1957–1966. *Psychological Bulletin*, **70**, 20–44.

Thomas, G. V. and Tsalimi, A. 1988. Effects of order of drawing head and trunk on their relative sizes in children's human figure drawings. *British Journal of Developmental Psychology*, **6**, 191–203.

Van Sommers, P. (1984). *Drawing and Cognition.* Cambridge, UK: Cambridge University Press.

Vygotsky, L. (1978). *Mind in Society: The Development of Higher Psychological Processes.* Cambridge, MA: Harvard University Press.

Wales, R. (1990). Children's pictures. In R. Grieve and M. Hughes (eds). *Understanding Children* (140–155). Oxford, UK: Basil Blackwell.

Willats, J. (1985). Drawing systems revisited: The role of denotation systems in children's figure drawings. In N. H. Freeman and M. V. Cox (eds). *Visual Order: The Nature and Development of Pictorial Representation* (78–100). Cambridge, UK: Cambridge University Press.

(1987). Marr and pictures: An information processing account of children's drawings. *Archives de Psychologie*, **55**, 105–125.

Wilson, B. (1985). The artistic tower of Babel: Inextricable links between culture and graphic development. *Visual Arts Research*, **11**, 90–104.

(2000). Empire of signs revisited: Children's manga and the changing face of Japan. In L. Lindström (ed.). *The Cultural Context: Comparative Studies of Art Education and Children's Drawings* (160–178). Stockholm University Press.

Wilson, B. and Wilson, M. (1984). Children's drawings in Egypt: Cultural style acquisition as graphic development. *Visual Arts Research*, **10**, 13–26.

Winner, E. (1989). How can Chinese children draw so well? *Journal of Aesthetic Education*, **22**, 17–34.

Yamagata, K. (1997). Representational activity during mother–child interaction: The scribbling stage of drawing. *British Journal of Developmental Psychology*, **15**, 355–366.

Understanding of human motion, form and levels
      of meaning: evidence from the perception of
      human point-light displays by infants and
      people with autism

Derek G. Moore

The study of the development of infant responses to the visual representation of the human form in photographs and drawings is clearly important, but equally so is consideration of the role that human motion plays in delivering meanings about the bodies of other people. Much is still to be learned about infants' abilities to represent the whole human form, and to establish which of the material properties of humans are used and encoded by infants. Moreover, we need to consider the role that specific patterns of motion might play in the formation of these representations. Evidence on these issues has emerged from the study of responses to human point-light displays (PLDs). In this chapter I review evidence on the emergence of abilities to perceive different 'levels of meaning' conveyed by human PLDs and then outline how consideration of these levels of meaning can help in understanding potential difficulties that people with autism may have in perceiving and making sense of human bodily motion.

Levels of human bodily motion

Before we proceed we need to clarify the distinction between the terms human motion, biomechanical motion and biological motion. These terms are sometimes used without sufficient consideration. The term biological motion can be considered to cover all forms of motion shown by animals, with the most basic level of motion being that of self-starting irregular, partially contingent motion. Biomechanical motion is a more specific aspect of biological motion that is associated with having articulated moving limbs. This is movement that humans and many, but not all, animals show. While human motion is biological and contains biomechanical movement that overlaps with that of many animals, human motion also has specific properties that are constrained by the human form, with the arms and legs being vertically aligned, and that also convey important conspecific social and psychological meanings. Thus there are levels of subtlety to the patterning of human motion that we may be particularly attuned to. The point is that we should not consider that human motion is simply equivalent to or synonymous with biological or biomechanical motion, and when considering the literature on the development of these abilities we must keep in mind these distinctions.

By distinguishing those aspects of human motion that are similar and different to those of other biological creatures, we also begin to recognise the importance of the development of sensitivity to these different layers of bodily motion, ranging from movement associated with simple motions like walking to more complex patterns of intentional actions and then the overlaid, subtle patterns of motion that reflect a person's internal subjective states.

Peter Hobson and I (Moore *et al.*, 1997) have referred to different components of person perception – distinguishing between the perception of a human as a human on the basis of basic human walking, and the perception of a person's specific intended actions and perception of the person's subjective states – all of which can be conveyed through different 'layers' of human bodily movement, and all detectable even in highly abstracted forms such as PLDs.

The idea that these different levels could be examined independently of form was supported by the work that had been done in Uppsala by Johansson and colleagues (Johansson, 1973, 1976; Maas *et al.*, 1971); and the suggestion that there are different levels of meaning in human motion was certainly not a unique claim, and one that many have revisited since. For example, Troje and Westergoff (2006) refer to a range of motion processing from the biological basic 'life detection', through the recognition of structure from motion, and through action recognition and style recognition (see also Opfer, 2002; Rakison and Poulin-Dubois, 2001). This shows the multiple challenges facing cognitive and perceptual systems in extracting meaning from human motion, and any developmental account of the understanding of the human body needs to take into account the development of sensitivities to multiple layers of meaning; we are only at the beginning of understanding how these abilities emerge in infants and children.

Human motion and PLDs

The idea of using lights attached to humans to construct dynamic displays that would allow the study of human motion was developed at the University of Uppsala in the 1970s (Maas *et al.*, 1971). Human PLDs were originally created by attaching reflective patches to a person's body, specifically to the joints of the arms and legs, and to the shoulders and hips. During the construction of the displays a light is shone towards these patches and the person then moves around the room (usually presenting a side on view to the camera). The light is then reflected back towards the camera by the patches. With alterations to the aperture settings, lighting conditions, and now with the use of digital filters, one can produce an image where all that is visible are the point lights attached to the

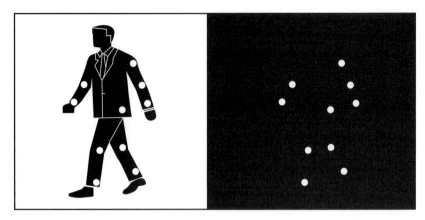

Figure 7.1 How a human point-light display appears as a static image

person, not the person themselves (see Figure 7.1 for a static representation of a display). Subsequently researchers have developed algorithms for re-creating walking displays, or have used now commonly available motion-capture equipment. Importantly, these displays present motion patterns but do not provide the surface information that might normally be used for recognition. Indeed, static versions of PLDs provide little information and are rarely recognised, often being described as a collection of stars or as a Christmas tree by naïve observers.

The number of point lights and positioning has been varied from study to study, and it appears that five is the minimum number that will produce a convincing display, but more commonly between ten and twelve are used. The most striking thing is that to the naïve perceiver human walking PLDs are compellingly and effortlessly seen as a person walking in the dark with lights on their body. They are not simply perceived as a pattern of unrelated lights. Critically this is not a trivial computational problem. For fixed rigid structures like a box there is only one structure that could fit the available array of moving lights. For human displays, however there are many rigid structures that could account for the spatial relationships between the moving lights (Johansson, 1973) yet despite this, human PLDs are recognised very rapidly (in less than a tenth of a second) and more quickly than PLDs of objects (Moore *et al.*, 1995, 1997).

The first studies examining this phenomenon were designed to establish whether human motion alone was sufficient for understanding human actions and to determine how rapidly this was achieved. These early studies used naïve perceivers to explore how quickly it was possible to tell that a PLD was a human (Johannson, 1976). Others then explored whether it was possible using these displays to recognise the identity of others (Cutting and Kozlowski, 1977; Frykholm, 1983), their gender (Kowzlowski and Cutting, 1977) and even their intended and deceptive intentions (Runeson and Frykhom, 1983;1986), and more recently the emotional qualities of interpersonal dialogue and dance (see Atkinson *et al.*, 2004; Clarke *et al.*, 2005; Dittrich *et al.*, 1996).

There has subsequently been considerable work that has established the robustness of the phenomenon and ascertaining the circumstances under which the perception of coherence of displays is affected in adults and older children (see for example Pavlova *et al.*, 2001, 2006; Pavlova and Sokolov, 2000, 2003). This has involved comparing the perception of normal upright walking displays with the perception of displays that have been inverted, been overlaid with a masking pattern of moving dots, or in which the motion patterns of the lights are altered or transposed. This work is reviewed extensively elsewhere, for example the excellent review by Blake and Shiffrar (2007).

In this review, rather than focusing on work on the parameters that determine the perception of the coherence of the motion of human PLDs and debates regarding the neurological underpinnings of the process, I concentrate on the findings from behavioural studies in infancy that have explored the perception of higher order levels of meaning depicted by PLDs, and what these studies allow us to conclude about developing representations of the human form. Secondly I consider recent findings of the perception of PLDs by children with autism, and what these suggest about the critical role of motion perception and body representations in social development. This review is therefore concerned not so much with the basic processes underlying perception of the coherence of PLDs and what this says about perceptual systems, but with what appears to be perceived beyond the surface information in terms of levels of meanings and emerging representations of the human form and actions, how this develops and what evidence there is that some children may have specific difficulties with components of this process.

Development of levels of understanding in infancy

As already outlined, human motion can be considered to be multilayered in terms of the information it conveys about similarities and differences between humans and other animals (see Arterberry and Bornstein, 2001, 2002; Pauen, 2000) and in the information conveyed about more subtle facets of humans such as their gender, age, identity, intentions and subjective states (Runeson and Frykhom, 1983, 1986); and using PLDs provides a useful technique for assessing the relationship between motion and form. A key question is when and how this emerges in infancy.

Early sensitivity to human motion

One of the first studies of infant perception of human PLDs was by Fox and McDaniel (1982). They studied the perception of human PLDs in 2-, 4- and

6-month-old infants. They used a preferential looking paradigm and presented infants concurrently, with a human PLD and a control foil consisting of the same number of dots in the same configuration but which moved about 'randomly'. This display was constructed with the aid of a number of assistants who waved about a collection of poles with reflectors attached to their ends. What Fox and McDaniel found was that the 4- and 6-month-olds, but not the 2-month-olds, preferred the human PLD to the 'random' PLD. There were, however, differences between the foil and target in the motion patterns and for this reason in a second experiment they paired an upright and inverted display. Again, Fox and McDaniel found that both 4- and 6-month-old infants looked more towards the upright display. In a third experiment, Fox and McDaniel explored whether infants would show a preference for a PLD of a whole body versus a PLD of two hands clapping – a similarly complex animate form. Under these conditions 2- and 4-month-olds showed no visual preference for one display over the other, but 6-month-olds looked more at the human bodily display rather than the hands.

The findings suggested that infants perceive human PLDs as of particular interest by around 4 months of age but specifically see the human form as salient by 6 months of age. Also, Fox and McDaniel suggested that the results of the second task implied that infants discriminate between displays on the basis of their meaning rather than just on movement –because both an upright and an inverted display contain the same absolute and relative motions. Having said this, it is possible that infants only attend to part of the displays – i.e. the top or bottom thirds. If this was the case then, to the infants, the two displays would appear to present different movements, and this might have explained infants' preference behaviour.

The finding that 2-month-olds did not show preferences between any of the display patterns may be interpreted in a number of ways. It may be that 2-month-olds had not developed enough perceptual acuity towards movement to discriminate between the displays, but that the neuronal architecture was present. It may be that they register movement but that such movements do not have meanings. It may be that the neuronal 'hardware' does not develop until 3–4 months old, or alternatively it may be that infants require exposure to humans over the first three months of life before they are able to perceive the commonality between the movements of a display and the movements of a real person, and that the perception of PLDs requires a certain degree of learning. Fox and McDaniel suggested that the process of perceiving these displays is 'largely intrinsic', but that a certain amount of post-natal maturation is required before a mechanism for perception becomes functional.

In a more recent study Simion *et al.* (2008) have reported that newborn infants will show a preference towards biological motion in PLDs where the PLDs are representations of a walking chicken. This suggests that, contrary to Fox and McDaniel, infants may at birth have a visual filter tuned to the characteristic biomechanical motion of limbs and animals in locomotion. Simion *et al.* claim that this may be a general detector that would apply in the perception of any articulated vertebrate. However, it has not been ascertained whether the same or different effects are found for human PLDs.

Bertenthal and colleagues investigated further the perception of human PLDs by infants. They too assessed infants' perception of upright and inverted PLDs, but used computer-generated displays to do so (Bertenthal *et al.*, 1984). In contrast to Fox and McDaniel, they employed a discrimination procedure, an infant-control, habituation–dishabituation paradigm, rather than a preference task, to see whether infants could discriminate between displays. They performed two experiments. In the first they presented two displays to infants. Half the participants were presented with a number of trials showing an upright walking figure (trials continued until looking on consecutive trials dropped to 50 percent), followed by a number of trials presenting an inverted display. The human PLDs moved (walked) in the same direction across the screen, and did not remain in one place as in the Fox and McDaniel experiment. The other half of the participants were shown the stimuli in reverse order – i.e. they were first habituated to an inverted display. Also, participants were presented over a number of trials with static versions of the two displays. When the displays were moving, both the 3- and 5-month-old infants showed recovery of attention to the change from one form of display to the other, either upright to inverted or inverted to upright, but when the displays were presented in static form the infants showed no such sensitivity.

Although the results of Fox and McDaniel (1982) suggested that infants are sensitive to structure and possibly meaning as revealed through dynamic human motion, the findings were also consistent with a number of other possible interpretations (Bertenthal *et al.*, 1984). For example, one possibility is that the reason infants discriminate the upright from the upside-down image is because they attend to only one portion of the display, maybe the bottom third; if this were the case then the two displays would present different 'amounts' of motion, thus enabling discrimination. Another possibility is that infants are sensitive to the different absolute movements of the displays, the upside-down display having a different tilt and phase.

In a second task, Bertenthal *et al.* attempted to test these alternative explanations by presenting a normal canonical, 'treadmill' display, that is a display where the person appears to be walking on a conveyor belt and remains in the centre of the monitor, and a display in which the point lights showed exactly the same absolute motions (left and right, up and down), but where the positioning of the point lights were scrambled i.e. the point light of the ankle was now in the position of the shoulder; this was made possible because the displays were computer-generated. In this 'scrambled' display all relative motion was removed while all absolute movement remained constant. Such a display is said by adult observers to be reminiscent of a swarm of bees. For this part of the experiment, only 5-month-old infants were tested. There were six groups of infants. Two groups were tested for discrimination between the 'upright-normal' and 'upright-anomalous' display (two orders of presentation), and the second two groups for discrimination between the 'anomalous' display, and the same display inverted. The third two groups were tested for discrimination between static versions of the displays.

The findings were that infants were sensitive to differences between the normal 'treadmill' and anomalous display, but were not sensitive to differences in absolute motions created by presenting the anomalous display in upright and inverted form. Infants also showed no discrimination between static displays. This suggests that infants perceive some form of 'figural coherence' in the human PLD which was not perceived in the less coherent anomalous display, and that this coherence is specified by the relative, rather than absolute motions of the point lights.

In other studies, Bertenthal and colleagues have explored further the importance of relative motion for infants' capacities to discriminate between displays (see Bertenthal, 1993; Bertenthal *et al.*, 1985, 1987; Bertenthal and Pinto, 1994; Booth *et al.*, 2000). They have found that infants are sensitive to changes in phase, that is when point lights remain at fixed distances but differ as to when they change direction from a normal display, for example where the 'wrist' moves backwards while the 'elbow' is still moving forwards. Also, they have found that, whereas 5-month-old infants are sensitive to changes in local rigidity (where point lights change direction simultaneously as in a normal display but do not remain at fixed distances from each other) in upright displays but not in upside-down displays, 3-month-old infants are sensitive to these changes in both upright and upside-down displays (Bertenthal *et al.*, 1987). There have also been many studies exploring the brain systems involved in the perception of displays in adults (see, for example, Allison *et al.*, 2000; Bonda *et al.*, 1996; Downing *et al.*, 2001; Grossman *et al.*, 2005; Grezes *et al.*, 2001; Vaina *et al.*, 1990) and more recently there have been a series of studies of neurological processes in infants (i.e. Hirai and Hiraki, 2005; Hirai *et al.*, 2009; Marshall and Shipley, 2009; Reid *et al.*, 2006, 2008). These issues are discussed in detail by Reid (Chapter 8).

'Knowledge constraints'

The critical point in terms of the development of representations of the human body, is that Bertenthal proposed that there may be knowledge-based constraints that begin to act on the perception of PLDs at around 3 months old, such that the discrimination of human biological motion becomes orientation specific. Further evidence for the role of experience and knowledge in the perception of displays comes from a study by Pinto and Davis (1991, cited in

Bertenthal, 1993). In this study infants were presented with a series of human PLDs (non-computer generated), moving and walking in directions that showed views other than the side-on canonical view typically used in these studies. Following these (habituation) trials, a computer canonical generated PLD was presented alternately in inverted and upright orientation for a number of trials. The hypothesis was that if an infant extracts a common property over the familiarisation trials, then they will show less recovery of attention on presentation of the upright display than the inverted display. The findings were that, whereas 5-month-olds showed such a generalisation, 3-month-olds did not show such a strong recovery.

Although these and other data suggest that 3-month-olds are not as sensitive as 5-month-olds to orientation, and therefore may not be perceiving the displays as possessing the same level of meanings, these data were not conclusive. It is possible that in fact infant sensitivity to changes in the motion of right-way-up human displays may occur simply because, by 5 months of age, an infant's perceptual system will have had far more exposure to human arms and legs operating under gravity constraints in an upright orientation. Thus, one might parsimoniously explain infants' selective responses to upright PLDs purely in terms of familiarity with upright human motion. Furthermore, even if some knowledge constraints are applied to human PLDs and a developing human representation is mapped onto the motion patterns of the PLD, it is not necessarily the case that infants would incorporate the same physical properties into this representation as they would for a physical object (Kuhlmeier *et al.*, 2004). Specifically, even though they may bind a form to the human PLD they may not perceive a PLD as having solid and inviolable properties like a material physical object.

Evidence for perception of the physical properties of the hidden human form

Colleagues and I (Moore *et al.*, 2007) explored these issues further: we wished to determine whether, in the second half of the first year, infants bind some prototypic representation to upright human motion depicted in human PLDs, and to ascertain whether this representation would incorporate some of the same physical properties that are applied to other material objects, as might be predicted, for example, by Saxe *et al.* (2006), who reported that infants are sensitive to the violation of the solidity of visible arms. Specifically, we wished to see if infants represented the hidden body represented by a human PLD as a solid form, and if infants would see it as a violation of this principle if the hidden solid form underlying the display occupied the same physical space as a visible solid object. As we were unclear whether or not 6-month-old infants would apply solidity to these displays, we tested groups of 6-month-old and 9-month-old infants.

We created three experimental tasks; in each a PLD was repeatedly presented, but the relationship between the display and the physical world changed across three phases. During the first phase of the first task, infants were shown an upright human PLD walking across a computer screen. In the second phase, the point-light walker repeatedly passed *behind* a three-dimensional perspective representation of a table. In the critical final phase, the walker appeared to pass *through* the space occupied by the table top (see Figure 7.2). It is known that, from 4 months of age, infants can use perspective and gradient cues in two-dimensional computer arrays to represent three dimensions (Durand and Lecuyer, 2002), thus it was expected that infants would interpret the table as a solid object. The question addressed by the first task, was whether infants would also consider the walking human PLD to be solid, and consequently would show increased attention when the hidden human form passed through the space occupied by the table top.

In the second experiment we assessed infants' sensitivity to violations of a scrambled PLD, which contained the same overall movement as a human display and was arranged along the same vertical dimension, but in which the motion patterns of the point lights were 'phase-shifted' and transposed. Finally in the third experiment we tested the orientation-specificity of the effect, by

Figure 7.2 Still image showing violation of the solidity of a human point-light display

seeing whether or not infants would show an equivalent response to the violation of an inverted version of the walking human display, which is equally as coherent as an upright display.

The results suggested that both age groups of infants interpreted the in-depth representation of the table and the upright human PLD as representing solid objects (Durand and Lecuyer, 2002). Critically, even 6-month-old infants showed greater recovery of attention when the solidity of the human point-light display was apparently violated as it passed through the space occupied by the table, compared to when it passed behind the table. No comparable effect was observed when infants were shown either a scrambled or an inverted PLD passing through the table top. Specifically, the amount of recovery shown by infants to the apparent violation of the solidity of the human display was around twice the amount shown by infants who witnessed the control stimuli pass through the table. The response to the apparent violation of the human PLD cannot be explained simply in terms of sensitivity to changes in occlusion patterns, or in terms of the change in spatial relations between the table and a rigid pendular system, as changes in occlusion, and in spatial relations between the display and the table, occurred for the upright, scrambled and inverted displays alike. Furthermore, the human and control displays all equally allow for an arbitrary mapping of rigid connections between lights.

Attribution of psychological properties in infancy

These findings indicate that from the middle of the first year infants are now in a position to form a representation of a single unified form that is linked to human motion, opening the way to the development of understanding of those aspects of motion and form that specify human psychological properties such as intentions, emotions and so forth. An example of where form and motion combine and interact is when an infant views a person moving towards or away from an animal (or object or person). If the person they see is backing away while facing towards the animal, then this conveys a different meaning, one of wariness or fear, from that conveyed when a person turns their back and walks away from the animal. Indeed, there is evidence for specialist neurons that independently process the direction the human trunk is facing versus the overall direction of a person's movement (Perrett et al., 1990).

These abilities to integrate motion and form are likely to be dependent on the development of the dorsal and ventral streams of the brain (Johnson et al., 2001; Ungerleider and Haxby, 1994) and our findings are consistent with suggestions that these neural streams mature some time around the middle of the first year (Atkinson, 2000; Johnson et al., 2002). It may be that only once this integration occurs are infants able to begin to utilise information about both motion and human form and begin to interpret other aspects of human behaviours.

This proposal is consistent with the recent findings of Kuhlmeier *et al.* (2010) who have found that 6-month-old infants are sensitive to the direction human treadmill walkers are facing. This may form a part of the critical development of infants' understanding of directed attention that emerges in the middle of the first year and has been demonstrated by Yoon and Johnson (2009). Further work might look at when infants first differentiate the direction of a person's trunk independently of the direction of motion, and assess the importance that trunk direction plays in understanding others' intentions relative to the importance of the direction of a person's eyes, face and head. Indeed, it may be the case that infants' abilities to represent the human form and the qualities of the human body, such as the direction of the trunk and the location of arms and legs, plays an important role in the development of an understanding of intentional human action (Moore *et al.*, 2007). Thus we need to consider how infants' development of a whole-body prototype fits with accounts of the development of bodily imitation and the development of the understanding of the intentions and agency of self and others (Gallagher, 2005; Gergley *et al.*, 2002).

Summary

To summarise, infants face a number of challenges to understand the meaning inherent in human motion and these abilities are demonstrated by a number of behavioural and neuro-physiological responses to human PLDs (neurological processes are outlined in detail in Chapter 8 by Reid). In behavioural terms infants seem to show preferences for biomechanical motion at birth (Simion *et al.*, 2008). By 2 to 3 months they show abilities to discriminate between and prefer coherent versus scrambled motions, and by 5 months this capacity is restricted to displays in the correct orientation. By 6 months infants may be binding a solid form to human displays but not to scrambled or inverted displays, and are sensitive to the direction of facing of displays (Moore *et al.*, 2007; Kuhlmeier *et al.*, 2010). Thus, as infants move into the middle of the first year they appear to have developed capacities for integrating motion with the human form that underpins that motion and applies this to the perception of human PLDs. This is not trivial, and the question is to what extent the representation of the human form that infants are developing is related to, and bound up with, information from motion patterns.

The importance of motion for accessing canonical representations of humans has been shown recently by Christie and Slaughter (2010, and this volume): when scrambled configurations of the human arms and legs in static pictorial representations are shown to infants they do not appear to be sensitive to these until 12 to 18 months (Slaughter *et al.*, 2002). However when the pictorial displays are made to show viable human motion patterns infants do show discriminations between the displays. Thus, there is some converging evidence that both motion and form are part of infants' early developing representations of human bodies (and possibly animals too, see Pinto and Shiffrar, 2009). It has yet to be determined precisely how motion and form information are combined by infants, but motion seems not only to be salient and important, but also to provide access to meanings that static forms alone may not.

From the middle of the first year infants then begin to show an understanding of the relationship between human motion, form and intentions. This is clearly evident in infants' developing responses to the intended actions of others and in their own production of actions intended to influence others. The relationship between human action and form in this period is further demonstrated in infants' responses at 12 months to human PLDs that indicate the direction of attention of a person. Infants already seem able to apply these properties to human PLDs. This suggests that bodily representations available to infants at 12 months are already incorporating information about direction and psychological properties that are used to directly influence infants' attention (Yoon and Johnson, 2009).

Table 7.1 presents a summary of these findings on infants' developing sensitivity to biological, biomechanical and human motion in the first year. The table indicates the meanings that emerge in the first year in infants, that

Table 7.1 *Sensitivity to levels of motion and form in human PLDs in infancy and age capacity may emerge*

Sensitivity shown by infant to PLDs	Implications for emerging representation	Age of emergence	Citation
Orientation specificity for biomechanical movements	General biomechanical life preference	Newborn	Simion *et al.* (2008)
Preference for human versus random motion	Specific human biomechanical preference	2–4 months	Fox and McDaniel (1982)
Sensitivity to phase shifts	Motion must be biologically plausible	3 months	Bertenthal *et al.* (1985)
Sensitivity to speed of actions (running v walking)	Speed of motion is relevant to action perception	3 months	Booth *et al.* (2002)
Orientation specificity for humans	Motion is constrained by gravity	3–5 months	Bertenthal *et al* (1984)
Sensitivity to local rigidity	Consistency of rigid form	5 months	Bertenthal *et al.* (1987)
Sensitivity to violation of solidity of body	Vertically aligned and solid	6 months	Moore *et al.* (2007)
Sensitivity to different directions of facing of body	Directionally specified with front and back	6 months	Kuhlmeier *et al.* (2010)
Sensitivity to direction of attention	Movement directionality is linked to psychological processes	12 months	Yoon and Johnson (2009)

suggest that by the middle of the first year, infants have overcome many of the complex computational problems that appear necessary to interpret the motion patterns of humans, are beginning to use bottom-up and top-down pathways (see Giese and Poggio, 2003) and can draw on form and motion to enrich their understanding of human interactions. This then opens up the way for the development of more psychologically complex understanding of the 'higher' order meanings conveyed through motion.

Differences in the perception of levels of meaning: evidence from autism

Trying to understand the role that motion plays in conveying subjective and emotional states was what originally stimulated my interest in human PLDs. They clearly afford a novel way of exploring difficulties that children might have in social understanding by providing stimuli that are novel, engaging and ecologically valid, and that remove face information. This is of particular importance when considering people with Autistic Spectrum Disorders (ASDs). People with ASDs have specific difficulties with social communication and social engagement and appear to have difficulties in understanding the properties of the mind. We were interested in considering whether this might be in some part because of difficulties in picking up on dynamic social meanings conveyed in bodies and faces, and in particular emotions.

There was and still is debate about whether people with ASDs or autism have specific difficulties in perceiving emotions (see Hobson *et al.*, 1988, 1989; Hobson, 1991,1993; and recently Philip *et al.*, 2010). One issue is that any assessment of emotion difficulties is confounded by the use of faces that are used to convey those emotions. As it had also been proposed that children with ASDs may have specific difficulties with face processing, studying the perception of emotional meaning and using PLDs where faces were entirely absent seemed a sensible approach (Moore *et al.*, 1997).

The proposal was that if emotion perception is a general problem for people with ASDs then one might expect children with autism to also be poor at picking up the emotional gestures depicted in human PLDs. However, this issue is further complicated by evidence that people with ASDs may have specific perceptual difficulties, and that aspects of visual perception of motion may be particularly impaired in people with ASDs (e.g., Milne *et al.*, 2005; Mottron *et al.*, 2003; Dakin and Frith, 2005). Consequently, it might be proposed that people with ASDs would have general difficulties in perceiving many levels of meaning of human PLDs because of their problems with detecting motion.

Even now there have been relatively few studies of responses of children with autism to human PLDs. The first (Moore *et al.*, 1997) tested the ability of adolescents with ASD to recognise a moving person's action and emotion-related attitudes when presented in point-light form. Note that in this study we compared the performance of adolescents with autism to both typical children of comparable mental ages and to a group of adolescents with intellectual difficulties who were matched by intelligence quotient (IQ) for mental age (MA) and chronological age (CA). In some recent studies, children with autism have only been compared to typical children.

Surprisingly, in this study, given that people with ASDs have been reported to have deficits in motion perception, we found that adolescents and children with and without autism appeared similarly able to rapidly identify what a PLD represented, whether it was a person or a moving everyday object, suggesting, for this sample of older children at least, that their basic ability to recognise the underlying form of human PLDs was relatively intact. In the first experiment, we used PLDs representing a walking human or moving objects (a rotating chair, rolling ball, moving bicycle and a pair of scissors) to investigate the minimum exposure time required for the naïve participants to recognise the PLDs of people and familiar objects. For each type of display participants were presented with a sequence of brief video clips of increasing durations. After each clip participants were asked to say what was represented by the display. Results showed that the adolescents with autism did not have significantly higher thresholds for identifying PLDs of walking people or moving objects than MA matched controls.

In two further experiments, we evaluated the ability of the same participants to spontaneously describe five displays of a person showing happiness, anger, sadness, fear and surprise in terms of the emotions depicted when just asked to say what was happening (experiment two); and then explicitly asked participants to say what people were doing when presented with PLD that depicted ten actions (e.g. kicking, running, hopping, clapping, walking), and to say how the 'person was feeling' when shown the five emotional displays again along with five displays of other subjective states (i.e. cold, hurt, tired, itchy, bored – experiment three). The displays of emotional states and subjective states were filmed either face on or from the side, and involved the actor dispalying a sequence of actions to convey an emotion. For example for sad, the PLD person moved towards the camera, they then shrugged their arms in a resigned way and then slumped back into a sitting position and put their head in their hands. For happy, the action was simpler with a person jumping around in a happy playful way. For hurt, they walked along and then leaned down to rub their foot as if they had trodden on something sharp. They then rubbed their foot before limping out of shot.

Results revealed that while performance in naming simple actions such as running and walking was the same for the autistic and non-autistic mentally retarded controls, the children with autism were much poorer than the control groups in spontaneously referring to emotional states and also in naming emotional and subjective states even when asked explitly to do so. They did, however, talk about the actions performed in these clips. Taken together, the results suggested that sensitivity to biological motion and abilities to extract global coherence may have developed sufficiently in older autistic individuals to extract basic meaning from these displays, but that there were specific impairments in their abilities to comment on the emotional and subjective states depicted. In these studies we used video technology, but improving digital video technology has made it possible to examine these effects in more detail.

Blake *et al.* (2003) examined this effect in more detail using a discrimination task and explored the abilities of younger children with autism aged 8 to 10 years. Blake *et al.* presented participants with 1-second clips of PLDs which represented a person engaged in actions such as throwing, jumping and kicking, or out-of phase, scrambled, and thereby meaningless, versions of these original actions. Children were not asked to identify the actions but simply asked to decide whether the display represented a person or not. Findings indicated that, compared to typically developing children, children with autism were poorer at discriminating between human and scrambled motion in these brief clips, while being similar in their performance on another visual discrimination task. However, the specific differences in performance between the target and control task in the children with autism may have been a product of general motion perception problems and poorer thresholds of general motion detection in children with autism rather than a product of any specific problem with biological motion. Thus, while there indeed may be problems in motion detection in children with autism that constrain performance in detecting differences in human motion in brief clips it is not yet clear from Blake's findings alone that there are additional specific problems with the detection of human biological motion.

Another source of differences between the findings could rest in the different age range with the autistic participants being younger in the Blake *et al.* (2003) than in the Moore *et al.* (1997) study. It may be that the ability to recognise and discriminate between human and non-human PLDs improves with age. To partly reconcile these issues, Hubert *et al.* (2007) and Parron *et al.* (2008) replicated parts of Moore *et al.*'s (1997) study. To exclude the possible impact of IQ-related effects, Hubert *et al.* explored the responses of high-functioning adults with ASDs who did not have mental retardation. Consistent with Moore *et al.*'s (1997) data, their findings indicated that the children and adults with ASDs performed as well as the comparison group in describing (5-second) point-light movies depicting simple actions and in identifying manipulated objects. In contrast, the high-functioning ASD adults performed significantly less well than comparison participants in the emotion and state labelling condition. The finding that the adults with ASDs had few problems in identifying actions, but had a specific problem with recognising subjective states and actions, suggests that the recognition of higher level subjective meaning may be a core deficit for adults and older children with autism.

Similarly, Parron *et al.* used the same stimuli and found that children with ASDs were impaired in interpreting PLDs depicting emotions, but performed as accurately as typically developing children when point-light movies depicted simple personal actions, subjective states or objects. These results clearly indicate that children with autism understood the task demands and were able to correctly label PLDs. Interestingly, IQ was not found to influence ASD children's overall ability to perceive PLDs. In particular, the low accuracy rates on the emotion condition were unrelated to ASD children's IQ, suggesting that deficits in emotion interpretation in autism are independent of the overall level of functioning, at least with ASD children in the normal IQ range. The second main finding of this paper concerned the absence of a developmental trend in emotional processing in autism. The study demonstrated that while the performance of children and adults with ASDs on object, action and subjective state conditions increased with age, the children with ASDs exhibited difficulties with labelling emotional PLDs, and that these difficulties were similar to those found in adults with ASDs (Hubert *et al.*, 2007). This suggests that difficulties in processing emotional information are a constant throughout the development of individuals with ASDs.

These results appear in line with previous studies showing emotion processing deficits in both ASD adults (e.g. Hefter *et al.*, 2005) and children (e.g. Robel *et al.*, 2004). However, the results are at odds with previous reports demonstrating a developmental trend in several cognitive competences that are supposed to be directly involved in emotion processing, in particular configural processing. For instance, visual configural processing abilities have been shown to increase with age in ASD individuals with meaningless stimuli, such as Gabor patches, (Del Viva *et al.*, 2006) or geometrical stimuli (see Rondan and Deruelle, 2005), and with meaningful facial stimuli (i.e. Rondan and Deruelle, 2004). Our results suggest that while improvements with age may apply to the processing of meaningful objects and human actions, they may not apply to emotional stimuli.

The issue of whether children and adults with autism have difficulties in the perception of biological motion have also recently been taken up by cognitive neuroscientists who wish to examine which aspects of the social brain may be specifically impaired in people with autism.

Interestingly the current data are mixed, with some researchers appearing to confirm Blake *et al.*'s finding of difficulties in discriminating between action stimuli when using brief treadmill clips (see Annaz *et al.*, 2010) and there is some functional magnetic resonance imaging (fMRI) data to support the view that people with ASDs may show different levels of neuronal activation to moving PLDs, although this difference seems to apply both for typical and scrambled displays and does not appear to support a specific deficit in the perception of basic human biological motion (see Freitag *et al.*, 2008). Some have also claimed that the perception of PLDs in children with autism does not develop in the same way for children with autism from age 5 onwards (Annaz *et al.*, 2010).

While this may be true for difficult discrimination tasks with brief video clips it is not yet clear whether this is the case for more naturalistic stimuli where translatory motion is included, and where there is more time to detect some of the higher level of the meanings involved. In addition to the findings reported above (by Moore *et al.*, 1997; Hubert *et al.*, 2007; and Parron *et al.*, 2008) other researchers have also reported no differences between ASDs and matched controls in the perception of the direction of walking of human PLDs that contain translatory motion (see Murphy *et al.*, 2009). Thus, while there may be constraints on the substrates underpinning social perception (Pelphrey *et al.*, 2004) and this may affect the basic level perception of human PLDs, it appears that people with autism are capable of detecting and linking human motion to actions where sufficient time allows.

However, what is intriguing is that while children with autism may be able to develop abilities in the area of action perception, it appears that they are less able or biased towards picking up on those aspects of movement that inform observers about the subjective states of a person. Findings of specific difficulties in perception of emotion in human PLDs reported by my colleagues and me (Moore *et al.*, 1997; Hubert *et al.* 2007; and Parron *et al.*, 2008) have also recently been reported by Atkinson (2009) and there are suggestions that this may be particularly problematic for the expression of fear (see Hadjikhani *et al.*, 2009).

Interestingly Atkinson (2009) also found a relationship between aspects of basic low-level perception of coherence and this higher level emotion recognition difficulty. Thus low-level processing may be a constraint on abilities to process higher levels of meaning for people with ASDs. However, this alone may not be the entire problem as even high functioning adults with ASDs appear to have difficulties with perceiving emotional meanings in PLDs, suggesting that both top-down and bottom-up problems are present in people with ASDs.

Thus, presently it is still not clear what the particular components are that are impaired in people with autism. Indeed the picture is highly incomplete partly because research has yet to take a systematic approach to examining the different levels of meaning and perceptual capacities that underpin the perception of human motion in people with ASDs. Table 7.2 summarises what is known currently, but comparing this to Table 7.1, it is clear that many of the lower level processes that underpin the development of human motion perception in infancy have yet to be systematically explored in this population. We are even further behind when examining the perception of bodily motion in people with other developmental difficulties (although see Moore *et al.*, 1995; Virji-Babul *et al.*, 2006).

Table 7.2 *Evidence for differential sensitivity to levels of motion and form in human PLDs in people with ASDs*

Property of movement to PLDs	Similarities and differences in people with ASDs	Age of participants	Citation
Identification as human	(=) ASD equally rapid as controls in identifying a human PLD as human.	Children and teenagers	Moore *et al.* (1997)
Discrimination of in-phase and out-of-phase human actions	(<) ASD less accurate than typically developing (TD) for displays of 1second duration	Children	Blake *et al.* (2003) Freitag *et al.* (2008) Annaz *et al.* (2010)
Direction of movement of PLDs	(=) No difference between ASD and control group	Adults	Murphy *et al.* (2009)
Naming of actions	(=) No difference to intellectually impaired or TD groups with long clips	Children and adults	Moore *et al.* (1997) Hubert *et al.* (2007) Parron *et al.* (2008)
Naming of emotions and subjective states	(<) ASD poorer than intellectually impaired and TD controls	Children and adults	Moore *et al.* (1997) Hubert *et al.* (2007) Parron *et al.* (2008) Atkinson (2009)

Conclusions

Studies of infant responses to human PLDs reveal changes throughout the first year, with preliminary evidence that an infant's capacity for integrating aspects of form and motion is in place by 6 months. We have proposed (Moore *et al.*, 2007) that from 6 months infants incorporate not only surface information regarding faces and body shape into their developing human prototype, but may also be linking this to unique human-specific patterns of movement. While this speculation is based on only a handful of studies, and requires further investigation, this would seem to be consistent with a developmental story in which infants begin from the middle of the first year to undertake a wholesale representational integration of a number of social perceptual abilities that have been reported to be associated with activity in the superior temporal sulcus (Allison *et al.* 2000).

By the middle of the first year typical infants may be beginning to integrate information relating to body parts (arms, legs, hands) and have begun to form a prototypical whole body representation that is activated by and closely linked to human motion. This would then allow them to begin to utilise these representations to understand that the actions of the human body, while consisting of many parts and many levels of motion, have a single unified intention. This may be an essential bridge towards the understanding of goals and ultimately of psychological phenomena.

Considering the nature of the links between motion and the development of a representation of the human form may also help in understanding developmental difficulties. The different levels of processing involved in understanding of human PLDs may prove to be challenging to populations of people with developmental difficulties. To understand the difficulties that individuals with ASDs have in social perception requires an analysis of their abilities to understand the meaning of stimuli that span a number of different levels. Studies of infancy have helped to reveal the levels of motion perception that contribute to understanding of the human form and basic element of meaning. More work is required to investigate the perception of these levels in populations of people with autism and other intellectual difficulties, and to begin to understand both similarities but also individual differences within these diagnostic groups. To date most studies looking at the neurological substrates of biological motion perception have only explored responses to simple human walking.

What this chapter has emphasised is the need for greater precision in distinguishing between levels of motion that underpin the perception of human motion. We should not confound terms such as biological motion, animacy, biomechanical motion and human motion, and we should be more aware of the critical differences between these levels of meaning. While human motion is biological and contains biomechanical movement that overlaps with that of animals, human motion also has specific properties that convey important social and psychological meanings, and there are therefore levels of subtlety to the patterning of motion of humans that infants need to become attuned to. We need to adopt a more systematic approach to exploring these levels of motion in infants and in children with social difficulties.

In summary, the challenge facing infants is one of trying to understand the relationship between different levels of motion and different aspects of form (see Thirkettle *et al.*, 2009). Therefore, the study of human motion perception should not be restricted simply to the study of the perception of basic biomechanical motion. When trying to understand the development of capacities for understanding social meanings, we must consider what are the critical and salient meanings that human bodily motion conveys, and how these relate to the human form. Importantly, the study of the development of understanding of representations of the human body should not demote the significance of human movement simply to that of an 'attention grabber'. Sensitivity to these different levels of human motion may be integral to an infant's developing representations of the physical, intentional and psychological properties of humans.

References

Allison, T., Puce, A., and McCarthy, G. (2000). Social perception from visual cues: Role of the STS region. *Trends in Cognitive Science*, **4**, 267–278.

Annaz, D., Remington, A., Milne, E., Campbell, R., Coleman, M., and Swettenham, J. (2010). Development of motion processing in children with autism. *Developmental Science*, **13**, 826–838.

Arterberry, M. E. and Bornstein, M. H. (2001). Three-month-old categorisation of animals and vehicles based on static and dynamic attributes. *Journal of Experimental Child Psychology*, **80**, 222–246.

(2002). Infant perceptual and conceptual categorisation: The roles of static and dynamic stimulus attributes. *Cognition*, **86**, 1–24.

Atkinson, A. P. (2009). Impaired recognition of emotions from body movements is associated with elevated motion coherence thresholds in autism spectrum disorders. *Neuropsychologia*, **47**(13), 3,023–3,029.

Atkinson, A. P., Dittrich, W. H., Gemmell, A. J., and Young, A. W. (2004). Emotion perception from dynamic and static body expressions in point-light and full-light displays. *Perception*, **33**, 717–46.

Atkinson, J. (2000). *The Developing Visual Brain*. New York: Oxford University Press.

Bertenthal, B. I. (1993). Infants' perception of biomechanical motions: Intrinsic image and knowledge-based constraints. In C. E. Granrud (ed.). *Visual Perception and Cognition in Infancy* (175–214). Mahwah, NJ: Lawrence Erlbaum Associates.

Bertenthal, B. I. and Pinto, J. (1994). Global processing of biological motions. *Psychological Science*, **5**(4), 221–225.

Bertenthal, B. I., Proffitt, D. R., and Cutting, J. E. (1984). Infant sensitivity to figural coherence in biomechanical motions. *Journal of Experimental Child Psychology*, **37**(2), 213–230.

Bertenthal, B. I., Proffitt, D. R., and Kramer, S. J. (1987). Perception of biomechanical motions by infants – implementation of various processing constraints. *Journal of Experimental Psychology – Human Perception and Performance*, **13**(4), 577–585.

Bertenthal, B. I., Proffitt, D., Kramer, S., and Spetner, N. (1987). Infants' encoding of kinetic displays varying in relative coherence. *Developmental Psychology*, **23**(2), 171–178.

Bertenthal, B. I., Proffitt, D. R., Spetner, N. B., and Thomas, M. A. (1985). The development of infant sensitivity to biomechanical motions. *Child Development*, **56**(3), 531–543.

Blake, R. and Shiffrar, M. (2007). Perception of human motion. *Annual Review of Psychology*, **58**, 47–73.

Blake, R., Turner, L. M., Smoski, M. J., Pozdol, S. L., and Stone, W. L. (2003). Visual recognition of biological motion is impaired in children with autism. *Psychological Science*, **14**, 151–7.

Bonda, E., Petrides, M., Ostry, D., and Evans, A. (1996). Specific involvement of human parietal systems and the amygdala in the perception of biological motion. *Journal of Neuroscience*, **16**, 3,737–3,744.

Booth, A. E., Pinto, J., and Bertenthal, B. I. (2002). Perception of the symmetrical patterning of human gait by infants. *Developmental Psychology*, **38**(4), 554–563.

Christie, T. and Slaughter, V. (2010). Movement facilitates infants' recognition of the whole human form. *Cognition*, **114**, 329–337.

Clarke, T. J., Bradshaw, M. F., Field, D. T., Hampson, S. E., and Rose, D. (2005). The perception of emotion from body movement in point-light displays of interpersonal dialogue. *Perception*, **34**(10), 1,171–1,180.

Cutting, J. E. and Kozlowski, L. T. (1977). Recognising friends by their walk: Gait perception without familiarity cues. *Bulletin of the Psychonomic Society*, **9**, 353–356.

Dakin, S. and Frith, U. (2005). Vagaries of visual perception in autism. *Neuron*, **48**, 497–507.

Del Viva, M. M., Igliozzi, R., Tancredi, R., and Brizzolara, D. (2006). Spatial and motion integration in children with autism. *Vision Research*, **46**, 1,242–1,252.

Dittrich, W. H., Troscianko, T., Lea, S. E. G., and Morgan, D. (1996). Perception of emotion from dynamic point-light displays represented in dance. *Perception*, **25**, 727–738.

Downing, P., Jiang, Y., Shuman, M., and Kanwisher, N. (2001). A cortical area selective for visual processing of the human body. *Science*, **293**, 23–26.

Durand K. and Lecuyer, R. (2002). Object permanence observed in 4-month-old infants with a 2D display. *Infant Behaviour and Development*, **25**, 269–278.

Fox, R. and McDaniel, C. (1982). The perception of biological motion by human infants. *Science*, **218**, 486–487.

Freitag, C. M., Konrad, C., Haeberlen, M., Kleser, C., von Gontard, A., Reith, W., *et al.* (2008). Perception of biological motion in autism spectrum disorders. *Neuropsychologia*, **46**(5), 1,480–1,494.

Frykholm, G. (1983). Perceived identity I: Recognition of others by their kinematic patterns. *Uppsala Psychological Reports*, **351**.

(2005). *How the Body Shapes the Mind*. Oxford, UK: Oxford University Press/ Clarendon Press.

Gergley, G., Bekkering, H., and Kiraly, I. (2002). Rational imitation in preverbal infants. *Nature*, **413**, 755.

Giese, M. A. and Poggio, T. (2003). Neural mechanisms for the recognition of biological movements. *Nature Reviews Neuroscience*, **4**, 179–192.

Grezes, J., Fonlupt, P., Bertenthal, B., Delon-Martin, C., Segebarth, C., and Decety, J. (2001). Does perception of biological motion rely on specific brain regions? *Neuroimage*, **13**(5), 775–785.

Grossman, E. D., Battelli, L., and Pascual-Leone, A. (2005). Repetitive TMS over posterior STS disrupts perception of biological motion. *Vision Research*, **45**, 2,847–2,853.

Hadjikhani, N., Joseph, R. M., Manoach, D. S., Naik, P., Snyder, J., Dominick, K., *et al.* (2009). Body expressions of emotion do not trigger fear contagion in autism spectrum disorder. *Social Cognitive and Affective Neuroscience*, **4**(1), 70–78.

Hefter, R. L., Manoach, D. S., and Barton, J. J. (2005). Perception of facial expression and facial identity in subjects with social developmental disorders. *Neurology*, **65**, 1,620–1,625.

Hirai, M. and Hiraki, K. (2005). An event-related potentials study of biological motion perception in human infants. *Cognitive Brain Research*, **22**(2), 301–304.

Hirai, M., Watanabe, S., Honda, Y., and Kakigi, R. (2009). Developmental changes in point-light walker processing during childhood and adolescence: An event-related potential study. *Neuroscience*, **161**(1), 311–325.

Hobson, R. P. (1991). Methodological issues for experiments on autistic individuals' perception and understanding of emotion. *Journal of Child Psychology and Psychiatry and Allied Disciplines*, **32**, 1,135–1,158.

(1993). *Autism and the Development of Mind*. Hove, UK: LEA.

Hobson, R. P., Ouston, J., and Lee, A. (1988). Emotion recognition in autism: Coordinating faces and voices. *Psychological Medicine*, **18**, 911–923.

(1989). Recognition of emotion by mentally retarded adolescents and young adults. *American Journal of Mental Retardation*, **93**, 434–443.

Hubert, B., Wicker, B., Moore, D. G., Monfardini, E., Duverger, H., Da Fonseca, D., *et al.* (2007). Brief report: Recognition of emotional and non-emotional biological motion in individuals with autistic spectrum disorders. *Journal of Autism and Developmental Disorders*, **37**(7), 1,386–1,392.

Johansson, G. (1973). Visual perception or biological motion and a model for its analysis. *Perception and Psychophysics*, **14**, 201–211.

(1976). Spatio-temporal differentiation and integration in visual motion perception: An experimental and theoretical analysis of calculus-like functions in visual data processing. *Psychological Research*, **38**, 379–393.

Johnson, S. P., Bremner, J. G., Slater, A. M., Mason, U. C., and Foster, K. (2002). Young infants' perception of unity and form in occlusion displays. *Journal of Experimental Child Psychology*, **81**, 358–374.

Johnson, M. H., Mareschal, D., and Csibra, G. (2001). The functional development and integration of the dorsal and ventral visual pathways: A neurocomputational approach. In C. A. Nelson and M. Luciana (eds). *Handbook of Developmental Cognitive Neuroscience*. Cambridge, MA: MIT press.

Kozlowski, L. T. and Cutting, J. E. (1977). Recognizing the sex of a walker from a dynamic point-light display. *Perception and Psychophysics*, **21**, 575–580.

Kuhlmeier, V. A., Bloom, P., and Wynn, K. (2004). Do 5-month-old infants see humans as material objects? *Cognition*, **94**, 95–103.

Kuhlmeier, V. A., Troje, N. F., and Lee, V. (2010). Young infants detect the direction of biological motion in point-light displays. *Infancy*, **15**, 83–93.

Maas, J. B., Johansson, G., and Jansson, G. (1971). *Motion Perception, Parts 1 and 2 (films)*. Boston: Houghton Mifflin.

Marshall, P. J. and Shipley, T. F. (2009). Event-related potentials to point-light displays of human actions in 5-month-old infants. *Developmental Neuropsychology*, **34**(3), 368–377.

Milne, E., Swettenham, J., and Campbell, R. (2005). Motion perception and autistic spectrum disorder: A review. *Cahiers De Psychologie Cognitive (Current Psychology of Cognition)*, **23**(1–2), 3–33.

Moore, D. G., Goodwin, J. E., George, R., Axelsson, E. L., and Braddick, F. M. B. (2007). Infants perceive human point-light displays as solid forms. *Cognition*, **104**(2), 377–396.

Moore, D. G., Hobson, R. P., and Anderson, M. (1995). Person perception: Evidence for IQ-independent perceptual processing? *Intelligence*, **20**, 65–86.

Moore, D. G., Hobson, R. P., and Lee, A. (1997). Components of person perception: An investigation with autistic, non-autistic retarded and typically developing children and adolescents. *British Journal of Developmental Psychology*, **15**, 401–423.

Mottron, K. L., Burack, J. A., Iarocci, G., Belleville, S., and Enns, J. T. (2003). Locally oriented perception with an intact global processing among adolescents with high-functioning autism: evidence from multiple paradigms. *Journal of Child Psychology and Psychiatry*, **44**, 904–913.

Murphy, P., Brady, N., Fitzgerald, M., and Troje, N. F. (2009). No evidence for impaired perception of biological motion in adults with autistic spectrum disorders. *Neuropsychologia*, **47**(14), 3,225–3,235.

Opfer, J. (2002). Identifying living and sentient kinds from dynamic information: The case of goal-directed versus aimless autonomous movement in conceptual change. *Cognition*, **86**, 97–122.

Parron, C., Da Fonseca, D., Santos, A., Moore, D. G., Monfardini, E., and Deruelle, C. (2008). Recognition of biological motion in children with autistic spectrum disorders. *Autism*, **12**(3), 261–274.

Pauen, S. (2000). Early differentiation within the animate domain: Are humans something special? *Journal of Experimental Child Psychology*, **75**, 134–151.

Pavlova, M. and Sokolov, A. (2000). Orientation specificity in biological motion perception. *Perception and Psychophysics*, **62**(5), 889–899.

  (2003). Prior knowledge about display inversion in biological motion perception. *Perception*, **32**(8), 937–946.

Pavlova, M., Krageloh-Mann, I., Sokolov, A., and Birbaumer, N. (2001). Recognition of point-light biological motion displays by young children. *Perception*, **30**(8), 925–933.

Pavlova, M., Sokolov, A., Birbaumer, N., and Krageloh-Mann, I. (2006). Biological motion processing in adolescents with early periventricular brain damage. *Neuropsychologia*, **44**(4), 586–593.

Pelphrey, K., Adolphs, R., and Morris, J. P. (2004). Neuroanatomical substrates of social cognition dysfunction in autism. *Mental Retardation and Developmental Disabilities Research Reviews*, **101**, 259–271.

Perrett, D. I., Harries, M. H., Benson, P. J., Chitty, A. J., and Mistlin, A. J. (1990). Retrieval of structure from rigid biological motion: An analysis of the visual responses of neurones in the Macaque temporal cortex. In A. Blake and T. Troscianko (eds). *AI and the Eye* (181–200). Chichester, UK: New Wiley.

Philip, R. C. M., Whalley, H. C., Stanfield, A. C., Sprengelmeyer, R., Santos, I. M., Young, A. W. *et al.* (2010). Deficits in facial, body movement and vocal emotional processing in autism spectrum disorders. *Psychological Medicine*, **40**, 1,919–1,929.

Pinto, J. and Shiffrar, M. (2009). The visual perception of human and animal motion in point-light displays. *Social Neuroscience*, **4**(4), 332–346.

Rakison, D. H. and Poulin-Dubois, D. (2001). The developmental origin of the animate–inanimate distinction. *Psychological Bulletin*, **127**, 209–228.

Reid, V. M., Hoehl, S., and Striano, T. (2006). The perception of biological motion by infants: An event-related potential study. *Neuroscience Letters*, **395**(3), 211–214.

Reid, V. M., Hoehl, S., Landt, J., and Striano, T. (2008). Human infants dissociate structural and dynamic information in biological motion: Evidence from neural systems. *Social Cognitive and Affective Neuroscience*, **3**(2), 161–167.

Robel, L., Ennouri, K., Piana, H., Vaivre-Douret, L., Perier, A., Flament, M. F. *et al.* (2004). Discrimination of face identities and expressions in children with autism: Same or different? *European Child and Adolescent Psychiatry*, **13**, 227–233.

Rondan, C. and Deruelle, C. (2004). Face processing in high functioning autistic adults: A look into spatial frequencies and the inversion effect. *Journal of Cognitive and Behavioral Psychotherapies*, **4**, 149–164.

(2005). Developmental trends in visuo-spatial abilities in the autistic pathology. *Current Psychology of Cognition*, **23**, 198–204.

Runeson, S. and Frykholm, G. (1983). Kinematic specification of dynamics as an informational basis for person-and-action perception: Expectation, gender recognition, and deceptive intention. *Journal of Experimental Psychology General*, **112**, 585–615.

(1986). Kinematic specification of gender and gender expression. In V. McCabe and G. J. Balzano (eds). *Event Cognition: An Ecological Perspective*. Hillsdale, NJ and London: Lawrence Erlbaum Associates.

Saxe, R., Tzelnic, T., and Carey, S. (2006). Five-month-old infants know humans are solid, like inanimate objects. *Cognition*, **101**, 1–8.

Simion, F., Regolin, L., and Bulf, H. (2008). A predisposition for biological motion in the newborn baby. *Proceedings of the National Academy of Sciences of the United States of America*, **105**(2), 809–813.

Slaughter, V., Heron, M., and Sim, S. (2002). Development of preferences for the human body shape in infancy. *Cognition*, **85**(3), 71–81.

Thirkettle, M., Benton, C. P., and Scott-Samuel, N. E. (2009). Contributions of form, motion and task to biological motion perception. *Journal of Vision*, **9**(3), 1–11.

Troje, N. F. and Westhoff, C. (2006). The inversion effect in biological motion perception: Evidence for a 'life detector'? *Current Biology*, **16** (8), 821–824.

Ungerleider, L. G., and Haxby, J. V. (1994). 'What' and 'where' in the human brain. *Current Opinion in Neurobiology*, **4**(2), 157–165.

Vaina, L. M., Lemay, M., Bienfang, D. C., Choi, A. Y., and Nakayama, K. (1990). Intact biological motion and structure from motion perception in a patient with impaired motion mechanisms – a case-study. *Visual Neuroscience*, **5**, 353–369.

Virji-Babul, N., Kerns, K., Zhou, E., Kapur, A., and Shiffrar, M. (2006). Perceptual-motor deficits in children with Down Syndrome: Implications for intervention. *Down Syndrome Research and Practice*, **10**(2), 74–82.

Yoon, J. M. D. and Johnson, S. C. (2009). Biological motion displays elicit social behavior in 12-month-olds. *Child Development*, **80**(4), 1,069–1,075.

8   How infants detect information in biological motion

Vincent Reid

The ability to detect and then interpret meaning within biological motion is one of the great mysteries of early human development. Human infants are remarkably good at disambiguating aspects of the visual world such that key information is rapidly processed. This is in many ways a marvel of evolution. After all, what information is more complex, continuous, and dynamic than human movement? This ability is particularly surprising when the range of information conveyed spans from "low level" perceptual information, such as organismic structure, through to complicated social knowledge, such as intentions and beliefs embedded within action.

This chapter will outline the current state of our knowledge associated with biological motion (BM) processing by infants, drawing heavily on recent work derived from electrophysiological methodologies (such as electroencephalogram [EEG] and event-related brain potentials [ERPs], see below) rather than behavioral techniques. This emphasis is partly due to the recency of these findings, and partly because they generate important new research questions. As EEGs and ERPs can allow the investigation of infant processing capacities in the absence of overt behavioral responses, these techniques provide an important tool in the arsenal of any given infancy researcher. They do, however, produce different results to work conducted via behavioral paradigms, occasionally making comparisons between the two methodologies problematic when investigating the same research area. In order to present the EEG and ERP area, I briefly outline how these techniques are used. In this review, I focus on the perception of biological motion during infancy. Through the introduction of the concept of the directed attention model of infant social cognition, I present how this capacity cascades via the perception of human movement into a wider corpus of skills present in early social-cognitive processing, including intention detection and interpretation.

Behavioral work

Behavioral research dating from the 1980s using point-light displays (PLDs; where points of light are superimposed on key joints of an otherwise unseen figure), suggests that infants detect biological motion and discriminate it from other forms of motion, such as drifting dots, from 3–4 months of age (Bertenthal, 1993). After a relatively dormant period of research in this area, interest has again been sparked by recent work by Simion *et al.* (2008), who demonstrated via a preferential looking paradigm that 2-day-old infants were capable of distinguishing a BM stimulus from random motion. In this study the BM was a PLD of a chicken translating across the screen. A second experiment indicated that the infants had a sensitivity to upright over inverted versions of the presented BM. Previous work has shown that inversion of BM severely disrupts the perceived biological nature of the stimuli in adults and in infants (see Moore, Chapter 7 of this volume), with the recent suggestion that the basis for this orientation preference may be associated with characteristic motion patterns of the lower visual plane, in those areas surrounding the feet (Troje and Westhoff, 2006). Specifically, the pattern of motion associated with translating movement, with a leg crossing another leg with consequently correlated alignments of PLD movement at any given time, may be critical for this form of detection. The conclusion of Simion *et al.* (2008), that the detection of BM is an intrinsic and innate component of the visual system, stands in stark contrast to earlier work in this area, which had indicated sensitivity for biological motion from around 3–4 months of age (e.g. Fox and McDaniel, 1982; Bertenthal *et al.*, 1987).

The findings of Simion *et al.* (2008) require some consideration, not least because they push down the age of BM detection to soon after birth. Bertenthal (personal communication) maintains that he had always regarded BM processing as something that the human neonate could discriminate from other forms of motion, if provided with the right conditions. It is worth noting that none of his own work has, however, indicated this to be the case. What does this imply for other components of complex visual processing? Should thresholds for the capacity to detect and interpret goals and beliefs also be examined in very early development? This is not a conclusion that many would believe naturally arises from the Simion article, but it is a logical conclusion if one accepts that BM processing is a first step towards processing meaning within these more complex patterns of movement. For further consideration of the history of BM processing via behavioral paradigms, see Chapter 7 by Moore.

Electrophysiological measures: what and why?

Behavioral data, such as that contained in Simion *et al.* (2008), provides a rich source of information on what infants can discriminate, categorize, and learn. There are, however, some issues with behavioral paradigms in terms of what information they convey and how they go about doing it. Typically increased or decreased looking towards one of two stimuli sets has been assumed to indicate discrimination by the infant of those two stimuli sets. Recent work suggests that increased looking time may not necessarily index the assumed cognitive processing of such stimuli. For example, infants' looking time in a violation of expectation task did not correlate with other established indexes of cognitive processing of sustained attention, such as task evoked pupil dilation (Jackson and Sirois, 2009). It is consequently important for the field of infancy for additional work to be conducted on how infants process visual information. One approach to this question is the investigation of infant brain function during the observation of events. One class of electrophysiological measurement of brain activity which is particularly well adapted to work with infants is derived from an electroencephalogram (EEG) and is known as the event-related brain potential (ERP). This technique relies on the non-invasive and painless recording of brain electrical activity measured by electrodes placed on the scalp. An ERP can be defined as the resultant electrophysiological response derived from the onset of a specific stimulus or the execution of a specific action.

ERPs are particularly popular for measuring functional brain activation in infants as it is a technique that is relatively easy to implement and record and it does not have large ethical issues surrounding use. The primary advantage of ERP research over other forms of brain-based methodology is that it provides an excellent temporal resolution for viewing elicited processing, even to the tune of milliseconds (ms). Another advantage is that it is relatively inexpensive when compared to other methods of assessing brain function. However, spatial resolution is highly diminished when compared with haemodynamic measures of brain activity, such as functional magnetic resonance imaging (fMRI). This is due to the fact that (1) electromagnetic fields summate algebraically so that multiple neuronal generators cannot be disentangled from each other; and (2) the positioning of the electrodes means that they do not sample all activity generated by the brain. Many deep structures are not measurable, although exactly how much or little is open to debate as certain frequencies of the EEG (e.g. theta) appear to correlate with the activation of the hippocampus (see Jacobs and Kahana, 2010). Further, there is additional spatial smearing of the resulting EEG activity due to the resistive properties of meninges, cerebrospinal fluid, skull, and scalp.

Despite these drawbacks in terms of poor spatial resolution, there are also distinct advantages for the developmental researcher. One aspect of ERPs that makes them particularly attractive for research in early development is the fact that they do not require an overt behavioral or verbal response in passive paradigms. They consequently permit the study of phenomena that may be difficult or impossible to investigate with behavioral methods alone (see, for example, Striano *et al.*, 2006). This is particularly useful with infants when preferential looking paradigms appear to indicate no discrimination between stimuli sets. A detailed discussion of the functional specifics of key ERP components found across development is far beyond the scope of this chapter (useful reviews are de Haan et al., 2003; Nelson and Monk, 2001).

Importantly, EEG is far more than just ERPs. Recently the investigation of event-related oscillations (EROs) has produced some interesting results that would otherwise have not been detected, were the EEG only analyzed via the ERP technique. The ERP is the component of the EEG that is specifically related to repeated presentations of a stimulus. Effectively the ERP acts as a low pass filter, removing higher frequencies and smoothing the data. Consequently much of the raw EEG is removed when performing ERP research. EROs are bursts of EEG that occur within and across specific frequency bands, including higher frequencies that are lost to ERP analysis. Within the ERO field, two key distinctions appear within EEG oscillation research: evoked and induced oscillations. Evoked gamma is precisely phase locked to the stimulus onset as it is an evoked response to the stimulus. Evoked oscillations are often referred to as transient evoked responses. This is because they appear in the data at the same latency and phase in each trial of the same stimulus, unlike other forms of oscillatory activity. Induced oscillations, unlike evoked oscillations, are produced with a different latency for each stimulus presentation. The induced oscillation therefore has a loose temporal relationship to the stimuli. When standard evoked response averaging techniques are applied to the dataset, the induced oscillation is effectively edited from the final data. This is due to its loose relationship with the stimuli. In order to detect these oscillations, time-frequency analysis of single trials is followed by averaging across trials. For more detail on these techniques, see Csibra *et al.* (2008).

One particular advantage of investigating time-frequency relations is that it is possible to investigate changes over time to the perception of dynamic stimuli, such as film clips. For example, Reid *et al.* (2007) showed 8-month-old infants movies of complete and incomplete goal directed actions. We found that infants at this age could discriminate the two conditions at the behavioral level for one set of stimuli depicting the pouring of liquids from a bottle to a glass, and this was also manifested in their gamma frequency oscillatory activity in left frontal regions of the electrode array.

The ability to present movies to infants allows us to ask new questions that were previously extremely difficult to address due to technical factors. For example, it is difficult to know when to determine which point in time is appropriate as a baseline when viewing dynamic stimuli, such as a movie of someone dancing. For segmentation of an epoch when using the ERP technique, an initial period of brain activity before the stimulus is presented is used as the baseline. The baseline is a period in time where the brain is not processing information related to the stimulus, and is used to ensure that electrical activity seen in the epoch of interest is the result of the stimulus and not due to tonic changes in brain acitivity. The baseline should therefore appear flat in amplitude. In many ERP studies, a central fixation point is presented on the screen before the stimulus is shown, with the baseline period featuring the fixation point. This method cannot work with dynamic stimuli. Should the time lock be placed at the start of the dance passage? If so, the baseline period is psychophysically totally different from the epoch of interest as there would be a static image compared with movement. This would not allow for suitable comparisons. If the time lock is placed during the dance period, then the location of the time lock is essentially random, and no effect would be expected. This issue is partially resolved by investigating oscillatory activity over the period of the display of the dynamic stimuli. With these electrophysiological measures, we are better able to examine subtle differences in how infants process the motion of others.

Electrophysiological understanding of BM in early development

Only a handful of papers on infants' perception of biological motion have been published using electrophysiological techniques. Consequently these studies have started by looking at the most simple elements of biological motion processing – effectively ascertaining concepts already well understood in adult populations. The first EEG paper, by Hirai and Hiraki (2005), examined the simple processing of PLDs of translating human walking biological motion by infants at 8 months of age when contrasted with the same PLD motion cues presented in a scrambled format. They found that right parietal electrodes contained a negative amplitude for biological motion which was not evident for scrambled motion. The same stimuli indicated a similar right parietal response in adult participants. Activation in this area coincides with prior work on biological motion processing in adulthood, suggesting that this location is responsible specifically for biological motion rather than motion detection per se.

One criticism of Hirai and Hiraki (2005) is that the sample size was extremely small – with only seven participants included in the final sample, with a further sixteen rejected as too few trials were collected to create an average ERP for each condition. A further five 6-month-old infants were also tested, but did not display differential processing of the two conditions. This difference from behavioral work, where BM discrimination is clear at 4–5 months of age, may well be due to the extremely small sample size that was reported in this article. The conclusion of the paper was that the neural systems involved in biological motion processing do not become evident until the second half of the first postnatal year, but must emerge prior to 8 months of age as this capacity is present at 8 months of age. It was also speculated that the possible generator of the waveform was located in the superior temporal sulcus (STS) as this would fit with the electrode placement and fMRI work in adult populations. A larger sample of infants may, however, have yielded substantially different results.

Shortly after the Hirai and Hiraki article, Reid *et al.* (2006) investigated the neural correlates of biological motion processing utilizing concepts from a behavioral paradigm that was developed in the 1980s. Bertenthal *et al.* (1987) found that infants displayed a familiarity preference for PLDs depicting adult locomotion when contrasted to the same stimuli presented in an inverted format. Adult participants when shown inverted PLDs failed to recognize the contents of the stimuli despite all psychophysical characteristics being the same between inverted and upright conditions. This led Bertenthal (1993) to suggest that the driving force behind the identification of biological motion was stored knowledge of the human form – thereby implying that experiential rather than innate factors were key in determining how infants detect and interpret biological motion. From a cognitive neuroscience perspective, should the topography of processing of biological motion be similar between adult and infant populations, this could imply that similar processes are occurring in each population when confronted with this form of information. If infants and adults process BM similarly, this would permit us to use the more extensive work with adults to inform our understanding of infants' BM processing. Accordingly, the study investigated event-related potentials associated with observing upright and inverted PLDs of human movement in infants of 8 months of age, predicting that right parietal areas would be involved in processing the upright BM when contrasted with the inverted BM. Our stimuli were of a human adult walking from left to right on the screen (often referred to as translating movement) and of a human adult performing a kicking action in profile. We chose this age as it was the same age that Hirai and Hiraki (2005) had investigated. There was also a degree of pragmatism involved – infants around 7–8 months are very easy to test using ERP techniques (thereby explaining the number of articles using ERP with infants at this age rather than other ages) and any age during infancy would have sufficed to test the hypotheses of the study.

Reid *et al.* (2006) found that 8-month-old infants' processing of upright and inverted PLDs of biological motion elicited a greater right posterior amplitude in the infants' ERPs, for the upright when contrasted with the inverted stimuli, suggesting differential processing of these conditions and providing corroborating evidence for what was already known from behavioral research.

Grossmann *et al.* (2007) suggest that the primary significance of this finding is not specific to biological motion processing. The timepoint where the two conditions diverged was at approximately 290 ms after the onset of the stimuli. This factor and a similar topography of the effect have also been seen in studies involving inverted human faces compared with upright human faces (see Halit *et al.*, 2003). This similarity observed in infants' processing of human face and human motion information suggested to Grossmann *et al.* that the cortical processes underlying the N290 might be more generally tuned to "humanness" independent of the nature of the stimulus. Further, they suggested that as a consequence of the "humanness" processing factor, the N290 effect may be driven by familiarity (Grossmann *et al.*, 2007), although this may now be revised given the previously mentioned results of Simion *et al.* (2008) as these were found with BM depicting a walking chicken.

Almost exclusively the entire field of motion processing within cognitive neuroscience has used PLDs. It has distinct advantages when attempting to investigate the most pure form of motion perception possible. Even within PLDs some information is conveyed regarding the underlying structure of the represented organism. Some joints do rigidly align with each other, such as the two points depicting the shoulders, whereas others, such as the elbow, move in relation to the wrist or hand. Bertenthal *et al.* (1987) presented three light points to infants of five months, with each point of light representing a shoulder, elbow, or wrist. In one condition, all three light points moved in a rigid transformation, appearing biomechanically possible. Another condition moved the PLD out of phase such that the arm display appeared to look disjointed, or biomechanically impossible. The infants discriminated the locally rigid display from the out-of-phase display, suggesting some sensitivity to biomechanical constraints present within the human body.

Only recently have attempts been made to delve deeper into what elements of motion are extracted and interpreted by infants from PLD stimuli. Reid *et al.* (2008) argued that in order for an infant to detect and dissociate biological motion from other forms of motion the infant must first detect some structural parameters of the organism before further processing could proceed. It could not be the amount of movement that allows infants to discriminate biological from nonbiological movement, as otherwise Hirai and Hiraki (2005) would have found no difference in processing between the biological and the scrambled motion conditions. Rather, the movement within the PLD must convey information that suggests coherent underlying schematic representations in the biological motion condition, which in turn must be detected by the infant. The aim of Reid *et al.* (2008) was to investigate the relationship between the capacity for detecting biological motion and the ability to detect alterations in human body schema. We defined "human body schema" to mean the understanding of the biomechanical constraints inherent in the physical makeup of a typical human.

The only problematic issue with investigating this concept was that infant processing of biological motion appears to be well advanced by the end of the first postnatal year, yet current work clearly shows that infants extract a structural representation of the whole human body gradually, beginning in the second half of the first year of life, although this varies as a function of motion included in the stimuli (for a review, see Chapter 5 in this volume by Slaughter *et al.*). The objective of the experiment was therefore to see if the processing of biological motion and schematic information are differentially processed by infants at 8 months of age. We presented three sets of stimuli – the same upright walking and kicking PLD stimuli as in Reid *et al.* (2006); a modified version of the kicking stimuli whereby the kicking leg appeared to detach from the body and spin in a circle before re-attaching to the body; and a modified version of the walking stimuli where the knee point lights were re-arranged so that they circumflexed backwards rather than forwards. The overall effect in this condition was of a person walking but with legs appearing similar to those of a horse. We referred to these three conditions as "normal biological motion," "biomechanically impossible," and "schematically impossible but biologically possible," respectively.

We found that the perception of biological facets of the stimuli was manifested in a parietal location with reduced amplitude effects for normal biological motion when contrasted to the other conditions. This was the expected effect, with dissociation in this area as a function of BM, not of body schema. However, the overall effect was unexpectedly marginally positive rather than negative, conflicting with the earlier work mentioned in this chapter, with the effect located over all parietal electrodes rather than only the right hemisphere. Perhaps the manipulations within Reid *et al.* (2008) were either more visually salient or complex when compared with previous tasks. In the previous work, displays were of simple manipulations to the whole screen, with normal BM versus scrambled BM (Hirai and Hiraki, 2005) or upright BM versus inverted BM (Reid *et al.*, 2006). The relatively subtle manipulations in Reid *et al.* (2008) may in turn result in bilateral parietal activation, where additional visuo-spatial resources are recruited to process the fundamental differences between conditions as a consequence of the enhanced task demands. Irrespective of the differences in amplitude between Reid *et al.* (2008) and previous studies, the fact that parietal activation was related only to the processing of the biological nature of the stimuli suggested that the results were indeed valid.

At a different time and in a frontal location, an early dissociation between the schematically impossible stimuli and the other two conditions was evident. The finding of dissociations between the perception of normal and corrupted body schema were in line with research investigating infants' structural encoding of human bodies. Gliga and Dehaene-Lambertz (2005) found that infants by 3 months are capable of detecting distortions in human body configuration. Reid *et al.* (2008) suggested a similar sensitivity by at least 8 months of age. Using ERPs, Gliga and Dehaene-Lambertz (2005) found a reduction in a P400-like component in bilateral posterior regions for images of distorted bodies and faces. The differences in topography and latency of the effects from Reid *et al.* (2008) and Gliga and Dehaene-Lambertz (2005) are likely to be the effect of static versus moving stimuli coupled with technical factors surrounding the choice of reference electrode during analysis.

Overall, the largest implication of Reid *et al.* (2008) is the suggestion that infants are capable of discriminating differences in human movement in the absence of the ability to perform the specific observed movements themselves. None of the infants tested were capable of walking or of a full body kicking action that involved counterbalancing the weight of the kicking leg with a corresponding shift in weight of the upper torso. This suggests that various associations are made between the observing infant and the actions of an adult. Given the results of Slaughter and Heron (2004), this indicates that these associations are made despite the lack of a mature system for a proprioceptive schema of the infant's own body. It is possible that these associations have been made in the absence of comparisons between the infant's own schematic makeup and the makeup of the observed adult, although further work would be needed to substantiate this claim. Given the current drive to investigate the parameters of mirror neuron systems during development, this capacity within the repertoire of infant abilities is of potential significance. This is particularly the case as it is presumed that the ability to perform an action is related to how action is perceived and vice versa (see, for example, the work on neural correlates of perceiving and producing crawling by van Elk *et al.*, 2008). The result of Reid *et al.* (2008) draws this into question, with the potential for infant's processing abilities for the perception of action more advanced than their ability to produce actions.

Further pushing our knowledge of how infants process biological motion, Marshall and Shipley (2009) investigated how infants at 5 months of age processed human biological motion when contrasted with scrambled motion. The stimuli that they used were more diverse than the walking and kicking stimuli used in prior ERP studies, with the inclusion of running and throwing a ball. Results for the processing of all stimuli were averaged together to create one ERP for biological motion and one for scrambled motion. Given that infants at younger ages tend to produce a more attenuated amplitude response to stimuli, Marshall and Shipley investigated the processing of slow waves over a 2-second period. The resultant ERPs suggest that overall there are effects in parietal locations, which is broadly in line with Reid *et al.* (2006). However, the data from Marshall and Shipley indicate extended amplitude differences between conditions, with changes constant across the 2-second epoch, whereas previous work (Hirai and Hiraki, 2005; Reid *et al.*, 2006) has indicated more transient changes in amplitude, that return to baseline amplitude by the end of the first second. The effect found in Marshall and Shipley is most likely due to the age of the infants as younger infants do produce a greater degree of slow wave activity than older infants. Alternatively, it could be due to the small number of trials contributed to the grand average by each infant, with the inclusion criteria being more than five trials per condition, which is low when contrasted with other infant studies. One substantial contribution of Marshall and Shipley (2009) to BM research is that it indicates the utility of investigating younger ages via these techniques.

The research currently reviewed indicates that there are substantial changes in infant capacities to detect and interpret BM in early infancy. Newborns discriminate upright and inverted walking movements by chickens. Infants at 5 months detect differences in upright and inverted movement for human stimuli, with differences noted in parietal regions (Marshall and Shipley, 2009). By 8 months, infants can discriminate biological from scrambled motion (Hirai and Hiraki, 2005) and upright from inverted human motion (Reid *et al.*, 2006), with activation localized to right parietal regions. This is the same area used by adults to process biological motion. Work investigating relations between the processing of body structure and biological motion is currently at an early stage, although differences in processing these two factors were reported in Reid *et al.* (2008) in 8-month-old infants.

Research into the perception of stable and non-stable body postures in adults suggests that the gamma frequency may be involved in the recognition of postural stability (Slobounov *et al.*, 2000). These authors presented adult participants with an animated human body rocking backwards and forwards on the ankle joint. Results from passive viewing showed that increases in gamma in fronto-central regions and parietal sites correlated with the recognition of postural instability. These results suggest that during visual perception, there are thresholds within human movement that are detectable within the EEG signal. As such, this suggests the existence of neural detectors for biologically possible movements. Consequently we (Reid *et al.*, 2005) presented videos to 8-month-old infants, which depicted actions that were possible or impossible due to constraints of the use of joints in performing actions. The possible condition featured a hand moving towards and grasping the top of a cup. The impossible condition featured a modified film of the possible action, however the arm was manipulated to show a plane of movement that was impossible for the arm to execute, given the biomechanical constraints of the limb. Essentially the elbow could not rotate to the degree needed to complete the action, although we had modified each frame in Photoshop so that the final film showed this impossible action occurring. The infants discriminated the two sets of stimuli, and had a visual preference for the biologically impossible condition relative to the possible condition. Interestingly, when achieving the goal is added as a variable for such stimuli, infants appear to be concerned only about the attainment of the goal, not the biological motion involved in achieving that goal (Southgate *et al.*, 2008).

When the same age group of infants observed the possible and impossible hand-action stimuli while having EEG recorded, it was found via analysis of induced event-related oscillations that the biologically impossible condition produced more gamma activity in right fronto-temporal regions than was observed in the possible condition. We anticipated that this particular region would be activated bilaterally should the superior temporal sulcus (STS) be involved in the processing of this form of information. Further, the assessment of infant motor abilities suggested that it was those infants with relatively high fine motor skills that manifested more gamma power in the impossible condition, whereas this was not the case for infants with relatively low fine motor skills. Reid *et al.* (2005) therefore tentatively suggested that the perception of biological motion may in some way be related to knowledge of the biomechanical constraints of one's own body. Caution in interpreting these results must remain, however, due to the small sample size of eight infants in each motor activity group.

Directed attention?

One substantial challenge to the field of social cognition is explaining how complex social skills emerge from limited experience and despite the relatively poor cognitive capacities of infants throughout the first postnatal year. How, for example, does an infant resolve complex information such as the semantic content of action, or anticipate a goal within a stream of action (e.g. Reid *et al.*, 2007; Reid *et al.*, 2009)? Biological motion and how semantics are extracted from visual information form part of this conundrum. Recently we proposed a simple mechanism that might explain the advanced state of infant social cognitive capacities when contrasted with poor basic cognitive abilities, such as working memory. The directed attention model (DAM; Reid and Striano, 2007, 2008; expanded in Hoehl *et al.*, 2009) suggests that the processing of certain successive elements of social information may facilitate performance on more complex skills.

Broadly speaking, the DAM suggests that key groupings of cognitive tasks must occur in a set sequence in order for the infant to successfully react to a given social situation. Importantly, the infant must process social information in a sequence, conceptualized as five stages, in order to produce socially appropriate complex behaviors. The sequence within each individual stage may vary. The first stage involves the detection of socially relevant organisms. At a purely mechanistic level, in order to produce social responses, the infant must detect those components of the environment that are socially relevant. Following the detection of a conspecific, the infant individuates the socially relevant partner. Once these steps have been taken, the infant can assess the individual's locus of attention and determine the direction of eye gaze in relation to the self (third stage) and in relation to outside objects and other persons (fourth stage). Then provided that these four components of the social situation are successfully appraised, the infant can infer the observed goal, and/or, prepare an appropriate response (e.g. establish contact, offer response).

The first stage of the DAM suggests that other people must first be detected within the environmental scene in order for the infant to engage successfully in social interactions. To detect socially relevant agents, the superior temporal sulcus (STS) is of particular importance as it processes biological motion (Puce et al., 1998; Puce and Perrett, 2003) and is one of the sources of the face sensitive adult N170/infant N290 ERP component (Itier and Taylor, 2004; Johnson et al., 2005).

The second stage of the DAM involves the individuation of social partners. The processing of eye gaze may well play an important role for infants in this activity. For example, Farroni et al. (2007) tested 4-month-olds' recognition of faces depending on eye gaze direction during a habituation phase and a preferential looking test phase. Infants showed a novelty preference for unfamiliar faces only in the direct gaze condition, suggesting that direct gaze enhances the processing and encoding of faces in early infancy. The neural correlates of identification and individuation in early development remain to be examined.

The third stage of the DAM focuses on the detection of another person's locus of attention in relation to the self. Neuroimaging studies with adults have shown that processing the self-relevance of social cues activates the dorsal medial prefrontal cortex (e.g. Schilbach et al., 2005). Recent results suggest that the same structure may be implicated in 4-month-olds' neural processing of direct eye gaze (Grossmann et al., 2007). Though further research is required, these results suggest that an important region of the social brain network may already function in early infancy.

The DAM in the fourth stage involves the detection and processing of another person's attention in relation to external objects or other people. In adults, the perception of averted eye gaze activates regions of the parietal cortex (intraparietal sulcus, IPS) with the STS also playing an important role, not only for the detection of biological motion, but also for the processing of intentions which underlie gaze shifts (Pelphrey *et al.*, 2003). When eye gaze is unexpectedly averted from a visual cue, this area shows increased activation in typically developing children and adults, but not in individuals with autism (Pelphrey *et al.*, 2003, 2005; Mosconi *et al.*, 2005). Given that such relatively low-level aspects of detecting and perceiving others are impaired in autism, this may suggest to some that autism may in part be a simple perceptual skew in early development which may have continuing and exacerbating effects in later life.

The final element of the DAM relates to the ability to predict observed action, and to anticipate a required social response. This stage is not as relevant as the earlier stages of the DAM, given the topic of this chapter. Overall, what the DAM framework strongly suggests is that biological motion processing is key to the most fundamental elements of social cognition. As a model for predicting cognitive abilities during infancy, it has already been beneficial. For example, the DAM predicts that the addition of biological motion (BM) to more complex aspects of the social environment, such as normal and disrupted human body schema, may help facilitate detection of aspects of body schema that would not otherwise be attended. This was shown to be the case in Reid *et al.*, (2008). Similarly, the addition of information from the initial components of the DAM, such as adding more biological cues to later components of the DAM, such as goal anticipation, suggests that this additional information will aid disambiguation of the later elements of the DAM. For example, the addition of head turning to eye gaze should facilitate gaze processing and consequent object processing at younger ages than stimuli that do not involve head turning but contain eye gaze. Of equal interest is whether more complex aspects of information override unexpected cues from lower levels of the DAM. One prediction would be that the low level information is simply less socially relevant and is discarded should complex aspects of social information conform to expectations. Another prediction is that such conflicts will hinder or delay processing of information within the later stages of the DAM, although evidence for the former prediction has already been provided by Southgate *et al.* (2008). In their study, infants did not process differences between biologically possible and impossible movements as goal-directed action was occurring at the same time. It appeared that the presence of a goal skewed the infant to attend to goal-related aspects of the visual scene rather than to the corrupted biological nature of the movement.

Integration and implications: towards a developmental cognitive neuroscience of social cognition?

Little work has been conducted on understanding the processing of biological motion and/or human movement in early development and how this relates to brain development. Investigations using ERP and EEG have revealed that infants as young as 5 months of age process BM as unique from other forms of motion and that this is manifested at the level of neural correlates. Work has also shown that 8-month-old infants use parietal regions for this form of processing, similar to how adults detect and interpret biological motion (Reid *et al.*, 2006). Further, recent work by Reid *et al.* (2008) has shown that, consistent with the DAM, different neural correlates are associated with the processing of BM and body understanding, even when infants do not have the capacity to perform the observed actions themselves. As I have suggested throughout the chapter, these findings have implications for social cognitive research well beyond the topic of biological motion processing.

Currently, the field of early social cognition has been focused on understanding other social factors, such as face and gaze processing. The role of biological motion in these aspects of social information processing will ensure that more work will occur in this field in order to resolve how infants detect and interpret individuals and their behavior. For example, given that there is precious little work conducted on how the human infant individuates individuals – from extracting an individual from a visual scene through to identifying the individual as a specific person – this area is ripe for investigation as it stands to tell us much about the nature and development of early social cognition. Another active issue relates to how the ability to produce actions may relate to the ability to perceive actions. Social cognition as a field has much to gain by understanding the avenues via which complex factors are broken down into elements that can be processed by infants, despite the limited set of skills and capacities for retaining information that are present during infancy. It is clear that BM processing and the ability to detect and process human movement are fundamental to understanding more complex forms of social-cognitive information processing. Such a "bottom up" perspective stands to yield much information on all aspects of social cognition in early development, not merely on how biological motion is processed during infancy.

References

Bertenthal, B. (1993). Infants' perception of biomechanical motions: Intrinsic image and knowledge-based constraints. In C. E. Granrud (ed.). *Visual Perception and Cognition in Infancy* (175–214). Mahwah, NJ: Lawrence Erlbaum Associates.

Bertenthal, B. I., Proffitt, D. R., and Kramer, S. J. (1987). The perception of biomechanical motions by infants: Implementation of various processing constraints. *Journal of Experimental Psychology: Human Perception and Performance*, **13**, 577–585.

Csibra, G., Kushnerenko, E., and Grossmann, T. (2008). Electrophysiological methods in studying infant cognitive development. In C. A. Nelson and M. Luciana (eds). *Handbook of Developmental Cognitive Neuroscience* (2nd edn, 247–262). Cambridge, MA: MIT Press.

de Haan, M., Johnson, M. H., and Halit, H. (2003). Development of face sensitive event-related potentials during infancy: A review. *International Journal of Psychophysiology*, **51**, 45–58.

Farroni, T., Massaccesi, S., Menon, E., and Johnson, M. H. (2007). Direct gaze modulates face recognition in young infants. *Cognition*, **102**, 396–404.

Fox, R. and McDaniel, C. (1982). The perception of biological motion by human infants. *Science*, **218**, 486–487.

Gliga, T. and Dehaene-Lambertz, G. (2005). Structural encoding of body and face in human infants and adults. *Journal of Cognitive Neuroscience*, **17**, 1,328–1,340.

Grossmann, T., Johnson, M. H., Farroni, T., and Csibra, G. (2007). Social perception in the infant brain: Gamma oscillatory activity in response to eye gaze. *Social Cognitive and Affective Neuroscience*, **2**, 284–291.

Halit, H., de Haan, M., and Johnson, M. H. (2003). Cortical specialization for face processing: Face-sensitive event-related potential components in 3- and 12-month-old infants. *NeuroImage*, **19**, 1,180–1,193.

Hirai, M. and Hiraki, K. (2005). An event-related potentials study of biological motion perception in human infants. *Brain Research: Cognitive Brain Research*, **22**(2), 301–304.

Hoehl, S., Reid, V. M., Parise, E., Handl, A., Palumbo, L., and Striano, T. (2009). Looking at eye gaze processing and its neural correlates in infancy – implications for social development and Autism Spectrum Disorder. *Child Development*, **80**, 968–985.

Itier, R. J. and Taylor, M. J. (2004). Source analysis of the N170 to faces and objects. *Neuroreport*, **15**, 1,261–1,265.

Jackson, I. and Sirois, S. (2009). Infant cognition: Going full factorial with pupil dilation. *Developmental Science*, **12**, 670–679.

Jacobs, J. and Kahana, M. J. (2010). Direct brain recordings fuel advances in cognitive electrophysiology. *Trends in Cognitive Sciences*, **14**(4), 162–171.

Johnson, M. H., Griffin, R., Csibra, G., Halit, H., Farroni, T., de Haan, M. *et al.* (2005). The emergence of the social brain network: Evidence from typical and atypical development. *Development and Psychopathology*, **17**, 599–619.

Marshall, P. J. and Shipley, T. F. (2009). Event-related potentials to point-light displays of human actions in 5-month-old infants. *Developmental Neuropsychology*, **34**(3), 368–377.

Mosconi, M. W., Mack, P. B., McCarthy, G., and Pelphrey, K. A. (2005). Taking an "intentional stance" on eye-gaze shifts: A functional neuroimaging study of social perception in children. *NeuroImage*, **27**, 247–252.

Nelson, C. A. and Monk, C. S. (2001). The use of event-related potentials in the study of cognitive development. In C. A. Nelson and M. Luciana (eds). *Handbook of Developmental Cognitive Neuroscience* (125–136). Cambridge, MA: MIT Press.

Pelphrey, K. A., Morris, J. P., and McCarthy, G. (2005). Neural basis of eye gaze processing deficits in autism. *Brain*, **128**, 1,038–1,048.

Pelphrey, K. A., Singermann, J. D., Allison, T., and McCarthy, G. (2003). Brain activation evoked by perception of gaze shifts: The influence of context. *Neuropsychologia*, **41**, 156–170.

Puce, A. and Perret, D. (2003). Electrophysiology and brain imaging of biological motion. *Philosophical Transactions of the Royal Society of London*, **358**, 435–445.

Puce, A., Allison, T., Bentin, S., Gore, J. C., and McCarthy, G. (1998). Temporal cortex activation in humans viewing eye and mouth movements. *Journal of Neuroscience*, **18**, 2,188–2,199.

Reid, V. M. and Striano, T. (2007). The directed attention model of infant social cognition. *European Journal of Developmental Psychology*, **4**, 100–110.

  (2008). The directed attention hypothesis of infant social cognition: Further evidence. In T. Striano and V. M. Reid (eds). *Social Cognition: Development, Neuroscience and Autism* (157–166). Oxford, UK: Wiley-Blackwell.

Reid, V. M., Belsky, J., and Johnson, M. H. (2005). Infant perception of human action: Toward a developmental cognitive neuroscience of individual differences. *Cognition, Brain, Behavior*, **9**(3), 193–210.

Reid, V. M., Csibra, G., Belsky, J., and Johnson, M. H. (2007). Neural correlates of the perception of goal-directed action in infants. *Acta Psychologica*, **124**, 129–138.

Reid, V. M., Hoehl, S., and Striano, T. (2006). The perception of biological motion by infants: An event-related potential study. *Neuroscience Letters*, **395**(3), 211–214.

Reid, V. M., Hoehl, S., Grigutsch, M., Groendahl, A., Parise, E., and Striano, T. (2009). The neural correlates of infant and adult goal prediction: Evidence for semantic processing systems. *Developmental Psychology*, **45**, 620–629.

Reid, V. M., Hoehl, S., Landt, J., and Striano, T. (2008). Human infants dissociate structural from dynamic information in biological motion: Evidence from neural systems. *Social, Cognitive and Affective Neuroscience*, **3**, 161–167.

Schilbach, L., Wohlschlaeger, A. M., Kraemer, N. C., Newen, A., Shah, N. J., Fink, G. R. *et al.* (2005). Being with virtual others: Neural correlates of social interaction. *Neuropsychologia*, **44**, 718–730.

Simion, F., Regolin, L., and Bulf, H. (2008). A predisposition for biological motion in the newborn baby. *Proceedings of the National Academy of Sciences of the United States of America*, **105**, 809–813.

Slaughter, V. and Heron, M. (2004). Origins and early development of human body knowledge. *Monographs of the Society for Research in Child Development*, **69**(2).

Slobounov, S., Tutwiler, R., Slobounova, E., Rearick, M., and Ray, W. (2000). Human oscillatory activity within gamma-band (30–50 Hz) induced by visual recognition of non-stable postures. *Cognitive Brain Research*, **9**, 177–192.

Southgate, V., Johnson, M. H., and Csibra, G. (2008). Infants attribute goals even to biomechanically impossible actions. *Cognition*, **107**, 1,059–1,069.

Striano, T. and Reid, V. M. (2008). *Social Cognition: Development, Neuroscience and Autism*. Oxford, UK: Wiley-Blackwell.

Striano, T., Reid, V. M., and Hoehl, S. (2006). Neural mechanisms of joint attention in infancy. *European Journal of Neuroscience*, **23**, 2,819–2,823.

Troje, N. F. and Westhoff, C. (2006). Inversion effect in biological motion perception: Evidence for a "life detector"? *Current Biology*, **16**, 821–882.

van Elk, M., van Schie, H. T., Hunnius, S., Vesper, C., and Bekkering, H. (2008). You'll never crawl alone: Neurophysiological evidence for experience-dependent motor resonance in infancy. *NeuroImage*, **43**, 808–814.

9   The integration of body representations and other inferential systems in infancy

Kirsten O'Hearn and Susan C. Johnson

Do infants reason about the object kind *human*, as represented by the human body, in a more mature fashion than they do other object kinds? When adults recognize an object as belonging to a certain kind (e.g. dog), this licenses a wide variety of inferences, including kind-specific inferences, like whether the object barks, and more abstract inferences, such as whether the object's behavior is goal-directed. It also allows adults to track or count individuals in ambiguous contexts (Bonatti *et al.*, 2002; Hall, 1998; Hirsch, 1982; MacNamara, 1986; Spelke, 1990; Xu, 1999, 2007; Xu and Carey, 1996; Xu *et al.*, 1999). For example, if a small, furry, white dog goes out the door and sometime later a small, furry, white cat comes back in, adults know they have encountered two individuals because adults understand that dogs do not become cats. Even within a single point in time, kind designations help adults to individuate objects even when they are partially occluded. A tail and a nose poking out from behind opposite sides of a bush suggest one dog, but a tail poking out from behind each side indicates two dogs. Infants, on the other hand, are considerably less able to use kind information in such situations (Xu, 1999, 2007; Xu and Carey, 1996; Xu *et al.*, 1999).

The current studies examine whether infants reason more maturely when the object in question belongs to the kind *human*. This possibility was suggested by Bonatti and colleagues (2002) on the basis of infants' skill with human faces. One suggested explanation for this advantage is the status of humans as the prototypical goal-directed object. The current studies rule out this explanation by showing that (1) when the exemplar object used to represent the kind was a human hand rather than a doll's face, the advantage disappeared, and (2) this was so even when goal attributions to the hand were deliberately primed. Specifically, this series of studies showed that although 9- to 10-month-old infants recognize and represent the human hand "well enough" to encode its behavior in terms of goals, they do not recognize or represent it "well enough" to track a hand through occlusions on the basis of its appearance alone. We use this dissociation to argue for a lack of integration across different types of representational/inferential systems in infancy, specifically with respect to body representations.

Infants can use spatiotemporal information to individuate and track objects

Young infants can do the computations needed to do these tasks – individuate and track objects – if given unambiguous spatiotemporal information, i.e. the location or movement of object surfaces (Baillargeon, 1986; Bower, 1974; Spelke, 1990; Spelke *et al.*, 1992; Wilcox and Baillargeon, 1998; Wynn, 1992). For example, Spelke and Kestenbaum (reported in Spelke, 1990) showed 4-month-old infants a display in which two screens rested side by side on a stage with a visible separation between them. Infants saw an object emerge from behind the outside edge of the screen on the left, turn around, and disappear back behind the screen. Next, an identical object emerged from, and then disappeared behind, the outside edge of the screen on the right. No object ever appeared in the empty space between the two screens. After infants were habituated to these events, the screens were lowered to reveal either one or two objects on the stage. Infants looked significantly longer at the test displays revealing only one object, suggesting that they had expected there to be two objects behind the screens because of the two diverse trajectories. Spelke and others since (Leslie *et al.*, 1998; Xu and Carey, 1996) have argued that this demonstrates the young infant's ability to individuate and track physical objects using spatiotemporal information alone.

In contrast to the ease with which infants use spatiotemporal information, infants struggle to use an object's kind identity to individuate and track physical objects over time and through occlusions. A variety of results from several distinct methodologies support this conclusion (Carey and Xu, 2001; Krojgaard, 2000; Simon *et al.*, 1995; Van de Walle *et al.*, 2000; Xu and Carey, 1996; see Xu, 2007 for a recent review).

In their original finding, Xu and Carey (1996) used a paradigm based on the study by Spelke and Kestenbaum (reported in Spelke, 1990). Infants were habituated to a series of consecutive, non-overlapping emergences of two common objects (e.g. a toy duck and a ball) from behind a single screen. After habituation, the screen was removed, revealing either both or only one of the two toys, and infants' looking time to these displays was measured. Xu and Carey reasoned that, if infants could use kind membership alone to maintain representations of each object during the occlusion, the infants would infer that there were two objects behind the screen and look longer if only one of the objects was revealed. While 12-month-old infants did show this pattern, 10-month-old infants did not. In contrast, replicating previous results, both groups of infants looked longer at the outcome with a single object if provided with unambiguous spatiotemporal information (i.e. simultaneous presentation) of the two objects. Other labs have replicated these basic findings in which younger infants failed to keep track of the number of hidden objects even when the objects used were familiar, well-loved toys (Krojgaard, 2000) or represented familiar individuals (Ernie and Elmo puppets; Simon *et al.*, 1995), or when the test consisted of measuring infants' manual search behavior rather than looking behavior (Van de Walle *et al.*, 2000).

Converging evidence came from an unoccluded object segregation study by Xu *et al.* (1999). In this method, infants were habituated to a display with a toy duck perched on top of a toy car. In test trials, the experimenter reached into the display, grasped the duck and lifted it straight up. If infants segregated the display into two objects, they should have looked longer, relative to any baseline preferences, when the toy car moved upwards with the duck than when it remained behind on the stage floor. While 12-month-old infants did look longer at the unexpected display of the duck and car moving together, 10-month-old infants did not.

One striking exception to these failures has been found in the context of the kind *human*. Bonatti *et al.* (2002) found that 10-month-old infants were quite capable of keeping track of the number of objects in an occluded display when one of the objects was a person, as represented by a doll's head. Bonatti *et al.* (2002: 419) concluded that "infants can use properties common to all and only humans for object individuation [including] seeing a certain body schema." On the basis of this hypothesis, cues that successfully lead to the infant recognizing a human, including parts of the body other than the head and face, should support object individuation and tracking in infants by 10 months of age, before infants do the same with other object kinds.

Privileged representations in infancy: people and the human body

Much research supports the claim that infants' representations of humans are relatively rich and support inductive reasoning. Infants preferentially track and imitate faces at birth (Morton and Johnson, 1991; Meltzoff and Moore, 1983), and can recognize their own mother's face (Walton *et al.*, 1992), voice (DeCasper and Fifer, 1980), and smell (MacFarlane, 1975) by the age of 6 days old. They also discriminate between the biomechanical movements of people and non-people by the middle of the first year (Bertenthal *et al.*, 1985; Fox and McDaniel, 1982). Well before the end of the first year, infants are more likely to smile and vocalize when confronted with people than with similarly moving objects (Ellsworth *et al.*, 1993; Frye *et al.*, 1983; Legerstee *et al.*, 1987; Klein and Jennings, 1979). Expectations about human actions also emerge early. By the middle of the first year infants recognize that hands must make physical contact with objects in order to pick them up (Leslie, 1984), and that people, unlike inanimate objects, do not need an external force in order to initiate movement (Spelke *et al.*, 1995).

By 6 months, infants also recognize that some movements of human hands, but not inanimate objects, are goal-directed (Woodward, 1998). In Woodward

(1998), 5- and 9-month-old infants were habituated to a hand approaching and grasping one of two toys on a stage. The position of the two toys was then reversed, and infants saw test events in which either the path of the hand changed but the target object, or goal, stayed the same, or the hand's target object changed but the path stayed the same. Woodward reasoned that if infants encoded the *relationship* between the hand and the target object, then test trials in which the target object changed would be more novel than those in which the path changed. Indeed, the infants looked longer at the change in the hand's target relative to the change in the hand's path. In contrast, when infants saw the same movements/events performed by an inanimate pincer, they looked relatively longer when the path of the pincer, but not the target object, changed. These disparate patterns of looking behavior imply that infants recognized that the hand and pincer were different kinds of objects, and made different inferences licensed by their distinct category memberships, specifically that hands are capable of goal-directed action and inanimate pincers are not. This conclusion has been confirmed in countless studies over the intervening years (see Caron, 2009, for a recent review of the research on theory of mind in infancy).

Do infants use their knowledge of hands to individuate them?

Recognizing that Bonatti *et al.*'s work was motivated in part by infants' recognition of human agency, including infants' successful attribution of goals to human hands, we were interested in whether infants would also successfully individuate and track human hands. Despite infants' relatively precocious reasoning about humans, even for adults, evidence on brain function suggests that recognition of the human body may be less holistic than subjective impression indicates. The recognition of actions involving faces, hands, and bodies all seem to utilize discrete regions of the ventral stream (Binkofski and Buccino, 2006; Downing *et al.*, 2001, 2006; Haxby *et al.*, 2000; Moscovitch *et al.*, 1997; Pelphrey *et al.*, 2005). Inferences based on one body part (i.e. the face or head), may not be made as readily from another part (i.e. the hands).

We now describe three habituation studies we conducted, each aimed at testing how well infants' representations of hands are integrated with their ability to track and individuate objects and attribute goals. These studies include: (1) a tracking study based on Xu and Carey (1996); (2) a segregation study based on Xu *et al.* (1999); and (3) a tracking study similar to the first but explicitly incorporating goal-directed behavior elicited and measured with Woodward's (1998) paradigm. Like Bonatti *et al.* (2002), we predicted that infants would track the hand on the basis of their kind knowledge of *human*.

In our first study we used a tracking paradigm based on Xu and Carey (1996) to explore whether infants would use objects' kind identities to enumerate and track hidden objects if one of the objects was a human hand. Infants were tested in two conditions: (1) a spatiotemporal condition in which the items were presented simultaneously prior to test; and (2) a kind condition in which infants saw only one object at a time. In the kind condition, infants could potentially represent the two objects using a number of distinctions between the objects including different features (e.g. flesh-toned, skin substance versus red, plastic substance), different basic level kinds (e.g. hand versus cup; human versus non-human), or different superordinate kinds (e.g. agent versus non-agent). We expected that infants would represent two objects using any one, or more, of these distinctions.

Forty 9- to 10-month-old infants were brought into the lab to watch a puppet show involving a human hand, a long set of pincers, and a brightly colored sippy cup. We first measured how long the infants looked at the objects sitting still on the stage before any manipulations were performed. Infants alternatively saw either an inanimate object alone on the stage, or the same inanimate object paired with the hand. All of the objects, including the hand, protruded through a slit cut into the floor of the stage that was wide enough to allow them to travel back and forth but not (seemingly) wide enough to allow them to 'escape' from the stage. This initial measurement allowed us to control for any spontaneous preferences an infant might have. Not surprisingly, and as in other studies (Bonatti *et al.*, 2002; Krojgaard, 2000; Xu and Carey, 1996; Saxe *et al.*, 2006), infants typically looked longer at the whole display if there were two objects on the stage, than if there were only one.

A small blue screen was then introduced on the stage and infants in both conditions were habituated to the two objects, alternately emerging from and then disappearing behind the screen. Once habituated to these emergences, infants' expectations of the number of objects behind the screen were tested. In the spatiotemporal condition, the two objects emerged simultaneously on either side of the screen for a brief instant, then disappeared behind it again. In the kind condition, the two objects emerged one at a time before disappearing. Finally, the screen was lowered, revealing either one or two objects, and infants' attention to the final display was measured. The habituation and test events are shown in Figure 9.1.

The results are shown in Table 9.1. We reasoned that if infants expected two objects when the occluder was removed in the test trials, they would look relatively longer at one object than two object outcomes in the test trials *relative* to the baseline trials, leading to an interaction between experimental phase (baseline vs test trials) and outcome (one vs two objects). Based on the Bonatti *et al.* (2002) results, we predicted that infants would expect two objects in the test trials of both the spatiotemporal and kind conditions. Therefore we predicted just such an interaction in both conditions. However, in contrast to the Bonatti *et al.* results and consistent with the previous results of Xu and colleagues, infants looked relatively longer at the one object test trials only in

Habituation

Test Trials

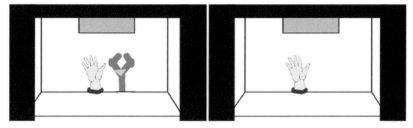

Two objects/expected outcome   One object/unexpected outcome

Figure 9.1 Schematic representation of the tracking task in study (1). Baseline events were just like test events. In the spatiotemporal condition, both objects also emerged simultaneously at the beginning of the habituation phase and before each test trial

the spatiotemporal condition. Infants in the kind condition looked longer at the two object outcomes in both baseline and test.

Non-parametric analyses revealed similar results. More infants looked longer at the one object outcome in test than in baseline in the spatiotemporal condition, but not in the kind condition.

In this first study, we predicted that 9- to 10-month-old infants would use the relevant properties of hands – their shape, color, and texture – to recognize and encode the stimulus hand as a stable individual, distinct from the other object,

Table 9.1 *Looking time data from study (1)*

	Baseline trials		Test trials	
	1 object	2 objects	1 object	2 objects
Spatiotemporal condition				
Looking time in secs (standard deviation)[a]	8.4 (5.6)	11.6 (6.3)	8.7 (6.1)	7.6 (3.2)
Number of subjects looking longer at each outcome[a]	4	16	14	6
Kind condition				
Looking time in secs (standard deviation)	7.2 (4.2)	9.9[b] (4.0)	5.6 (3.4)	6.4[b] (3.6)
Number of subjects looking longer at each outcome	6	14	7	13

[a] $p < .05$ for interactions between experimental phases and outcomes.
[b] $p < .05$ for pairwise comparisons within experimental phases.

even in the absence of disambiguating spatiotemporal information. Infants did use spatiotemporal information with the hand when it was available, expecting two objects in the spatiotemporal condition. However, in the kind condition, when infants received only ambiguous spatiotemporal information, they failed to expect two distinct objects behind the screen, even when one of the objects was the highly recognizable human hand.

The findings from this first study surprised us, since we had hypothesized that infants would use the distinction between humans and non-humans to represent and track the occluded objects in the kind condition. Reasoning that infants' failure might be due to unrelated confounds such as the memory load inherent in occluded paradigms, difficulties with occlusion itself (event monitoring as opposed to event mapping; Wilcox and Baillargeon, 1998; Wilcox and Chapa, 2002), or even the fact that people may behave unpredictably when out of sight (i.e. during an occlusion), we designed a further study. In this second study we tested infants' ability to segregate a fully visible display into its constituent objects, using either spatiotemporal or kind information.

As in the first study, we used the human arm and hand as one stimulus in puppet shows for 9-month-olds. The contrasting, second object was a rounded, pillow-like object the approximate size and shape of a human forearm. Both the arm and pillow were covered in flesh-toned hosiery. Flesh-toned Velcro connected the top of the pillow lengthwise to the hosiery on the underside of one forearm so that the two objects could move together when needed. Though the boundary between the two objects was clearly visible, it did not correlate with information about color or texture; cues that infants can otherwise use to segregate objects at much earlier ages (Needham and Baillargeon, 1997; Needham, 1998). Thus, if infants succeeded in segregating the full display into two objects, as evidenced by looking relatively longer at test outcomes with only one "object" (i.e. the united arm and pillow), it would be more likely that they were using their knowledge and recognition of the human arm to do so.

Before infants were shown the experimental displays, they were briefly familiarized with the hosiery-covered arm and pillow off-stage, including allowing them to touch either one if they chose to. Viewing objects by themselves prior to the study has sometimes helped infants later segregate a display of those objects (Needham and Baillargeon, 1998), though not always (Xu *et al.*, 1999). By doing this, we were at least able to confirm that, as expected, infants appeared to detect the difference between the experimenter's arm and hand and the pillow. More infants touched/grasped and mouthed the pillow than the person's hand (79 percent touched the pillow versus 49 percent touched the hand: $p < .0001$; 10 percent mouthed the pillow versus 0 percent mouthed the hand: $p < .03$). Conversely, more infants socially referenced their caretakers before touching the hand compared to the pillow (69 percent versus 39 percent: $p < .05$) and/or withdrew in the presence of the hand/person compared to the pillow (22 percent versus 2 percent: $p < .001$). Thus, infants distinguished the hand from the pillow and treated them as members of the human and inanimate classes respectively, consistent with other reports in the literature (Legerstee *et al.*, 1987; Palmer, 1989; Ricard and Allard, 1993; Ruff, 1984).

Once introduced to the objects, infants were habituated to displays including either spatiotemporal and kind/property information, or just kind/property information (see Figure 9.2). Infants in the spatiotemporal condition were shown a display in which the experimenter's arm first rested on top of the pillow, then slowly pivoted out once from the elbow in a 90° arc toward the infant and back, before returning to rest on the pillow. In the kind condition, infants saw the same display without the movement. Finally, infants were presented with alternating test trials in which the unseen experimenter lifted her visible hand and arm up from their resting position toward the top of the stage. Either the pillow was lifted with the arm (because it was, in fact, attached) or it remained in place on the floor of the stage. An additional group of infants were tested in a baseline condition to control for any inherent differences in attractiveness of the two outcomes (arm and pillow apart vs together).

The results are shown in Table 9.2. As in the first study, we reasoned that infants would look relatively longer at test outcomes with only one "object" (i.e. the united arm and pillow), if they had used the information in the habituation trials to segregate the display into two distinct objects. As expected, infants in the spatiotemporal condition looked longer at the test event in which the pillow moved with the hand and arm, compared to the infants in the baseline condition.

In contrast, infants in the kind condition did not look longer when the arm and pillow moved together compared to infants in the baseline condition. Infants in

Habituation

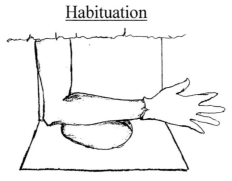

Hand moves forward horizontally in spatiotemporal condition.

Test Trials

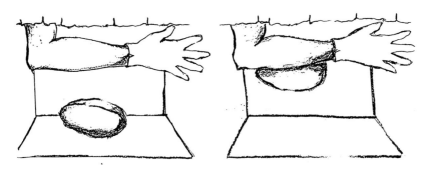

Two objects moving apart
is the expected outcome.

One object moving together
is the unexpected outcome.

Figure 9.2 Schematic representation of the individuation task in study (2). The
habituation trials differed between the conditions. In the spatiotemporal
condition, the hand/arm pivoted forward. In the kind condition, it remained still

both these conditions looked longer overall at the outcomes in which the two
stimuli were positioned apart in the display. Even when infants were first
familiarized to the hand and pillow in person, they did not seem to expect two
discrete objects in the test trials.

Non-parametric analysis revealed similar patterns. More than twice as many
infants in the spatiotemporal condition looked longer when the arm and pillow
moved together (13 out of 21), than did infants in the kind condition (5 out of 20).

Quite unexpectedly, but again like our first study, this visual segregation
experiment failed to find support for a privileged role for the kind *human*.

Table 9.2 *Looking time data from study (2)*

	Test trials	
	1 object (*together*)	2 objects (*apart*)
Baseline condition		
Looking time in secs (standard deviation)[b]	13.2 (5.3)	16.8 (9.8)
Number of subjects looking longer at each outcome	7	13
Spatiotemporal condition		
Looking time in secs (standard deviation)[a]	7.6 (3.7)	6.5 (2.4)
Number of subjects looking longer at each outcome[c]	13	8
Kind condition		
Looking time in secs (standard deviation)[b]	4.9 (2.1)	6.0 (2.5)
Number of subjects looking longer at each outcome	5	15

[a] $p < .05$ for interactions between experimental test and baseline.
[b] $p < .05$ for pairwise comparisons within experimental phases.
[c] $p < .05$ for chi-square comparisons of spatiotemporal and kind test outcomes.

Infants did not interpret the array of a human hand and arm positioned atop a similarly colored pillow as two independent objects unless they had previously seen spatiotemporal evidence to that effect. Infants failed to segregate the objects using their knowledge of the appearance and boundaries of the hand and arm, despite the fact that infants had thoroughly examined both objects prior to the study and shown systematic and appropriate responses to each. The results from this individuation study thus also converge with those from Xu and colleagues' work with inanimate objects.

In our first two studies, we predicted that infants would individuate and track the hand because they recognized it as belonging to the human body, indicating the well-known, inductively rich kind *person*. Surprisingly, they did not do so, despite their ability to make inferences about hands in other sorts of events involving both contact causality (Leslie, 1984; Needham and Baillargeon, 1993) and goals (Woodward, 1998).

If infants' representation of hands supports inferences as sophisticated as goal-directedness, why could they not use that representation to track the hand as a unique individual distinct from an inanimate grabber? One possibility is that we did not give infants enough information to recognize the hand. In previous studies with hands, the hands were shown in action, reaching for an object. Infants might not fully recognize the hand in our experiments because the hand and arm were not moving and behaving in a goal-directed manner. Therefore, in order to give infants more information, we modified the tracking paradigm so that infants saw the hand move toward a target, displaying both biological motion and goal-directed behavior. We hypothesized that infants explicitly shown these behaviors, which in previous studies have led infants to make goal-directed inferences, would be more likely to represent the hand and the inanimate object as two distinct, traceable objects. To provide direct confirmation that infants in this new tracking study in fact recognized the goal-directedness of the hand, the same infants also participated in a replication of Woodward's (1998) goal attribution study.

Twenty 9-month-olds were tested. Every infant participated in both a tracking task and a goal attribution task, in counterbalanced order. The goal attribution procedure was a straightforward replication of the task described in Woodward (1998). Half the infants observed a hand reach out and grasp one of two toy objects during habituation trials. The other half saw an inanimate object perform the same action. At test, the infants saw the "actor" (either the hand or pincer) reach for the other toy. In the original Woodward (1998) study, infants dishabituated and looked longer at test events in which the target object of the actor changed, but not events in which the target's location changed, and only when the actor was a hand, not an inanimate pincer.

For the tracking task we used the same procedure described in the kind condition of the first study above, with one exception. Instead of simply emerging from behind the screen to rest motionlessly in view on the stage, the hand (or inanimate object) reached out from behind the screen to grasp a toy placed on either side of the stage. In this way, the hand was able to demonstrate the complete set of information infants use to recognize a hand and attribute goals to it, whatever those might be. Schematic views of the displays are shown in Figures 9.3 and 9.4.

The results from this study are shown in Table 9.3. As a group, these 9-month-old infants did recognize and distinguish between the hand and the pincer. In the goal attribution task they looked longer at test outcomes in which the hand appeared to change its goal, but not those in which the pincer did so, replicating the now well-established effect first shown in Woodward (1998). In contrast, when the same group of infants observed the same hand and same inanimate object emerge in goal-directed ways from behind a screen, they did not use their kind knowledge to infer that there must be two objects behind the screen. Even when we selected just those infants who showed specific knowledge of the goal-directedness of hands, as evidenced by longer looking to the goal change in the attribution task, we found no evidence that infants expected two objects behind the screen in the tracking task.

In a final control condition, we showed a separate group of infants the same goal-directed behavior in a spatiotemporally unambiguous manner – both the hand and inanimate object emerged from behind the screen and simultaneously moved toward the two goal targets. In this case, infants succeeded in tracking the two objects behind the occluder, showing that the failure in the kind condition of the goal attribution study was not due to the increased complexity of the displays.

Habituation

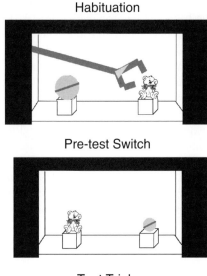

Pre-test Switch

Test Trials

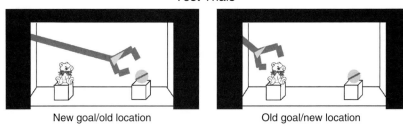

New goal/old location   Old goal/new location

Figure 9.3 Schematic representation of the goal inference task used in study
(3), a replication of Woodward (1998). Infants saw either the hand and arm or
the grabber throughout the experiment

We originally predicted that infants would use the kind membership of
human hands (e.g. *person*) to help them individuate and track hands the
same way they do faces/heads (Bonatti *et al.*, 2002). This would suggest that
they have a relatively complete and holistic representation of the human body,
in that hands and faces activate the same set of inferences. This outcome
seemed particularly likely given that infants know quite a bit about hands.
Hands robustly activate inferences of goal-directedness both in the present
studies and previous ones (e.g. Woodward, 1998). Hands have also been shown
to support a variety of physical inferences, namely solidity in 5-month-old
infants (Saxe *et al.*, 2006) and contact mechanics in 6-month-olds (Leslie,
1984).

Habituation

Test Trials

Two objects/expected outcome   One object/unexpected outcome

Figure 9.4 Schematic representation of the tracking task used in study (3). As in study (1), the two stimuli were also shown simultaneously in the spatiotemporal condition but not in the kind condition

Nonetheless, we repeatedly found that, though 9-month-olds were able to use spatiotemporal information to individuate and track human hands, they were unable to use their recognition of hands per se, in the absence of unambiguous spatiotemporal information, to do the same tasks. That is, infants showed no apparent concern to see a hand and then a grabber disappear behind an occluder, but only a grabber *or* a hand remain when the occluder was removed. Nor did they seem to infer that a visual display involving a hand resting on a pillow involved two distinct objects rather than one conglomerate arm-pillow. These failures remained despite infants' clear

Table 9.3 *Looking time data from study (3)*

Goal task	Test trials	
	New goal	Old goal
Hand condition		
Looking time in secs (standard deviation)[a]	9.2 (4.8)	6.8 (4.2)
Number of subjects looking longer at each outcome[a]	7	2
Grabber condition		
Looking time in secs (standard deviation)	6.5 (4.5)	7.7 (3.3)
Number of subjects looking longer at each outcome	2	8
Tracking task	1 object	2 objects
Baseline		
Looking time in secs (standard deviation)	10.6 (4.7)	12.6 (6.6)
Number of subjects looking longer at each outcome	7	13
Test		
Looking time in secs (standard deviation)[b]	9.3 (5.6)	9.9 (6.1)
Number of subjects looking longer at each outcome[b]	10	10

[a] $p < .05$ for interactions between hand and grabber.
[b] p = ns for interactions between baseline and test outcomes.

recognition of similar moving hands as goal-directed and of inanimate pincers as not goal-directed.

This pattern of results was quite surprising and it has a variety of implications for the relationship between body representations, object recognition, object tracking, and goal-detection in infancy. Object recognition may cue inferences about goal-directedness, but it does not necessarily influence object tracking in infancy, not even when the object belongs to the privileged kind *human*.

While intuitively surprising, this finding is consistent with Xu and colleagues' (Carey and Xu, 2001; Xu and Carey, 1996) original proposal that, prior to the age of 12 months, infants can use spatiotemporal information to individuate objects but do not readily use their knowledge of kinds or kind-specific properties to do the same thing. They point to the distinction between the occipitoparietal and occipitotemporal paths of visual processing (Goodale and Milner, 1992), and their relatively late integration in the developing brain as the explanation for this failure (Kaldy and Leslie, 2003; Leslie *et al.*, 1998; Xu, 1999). Indeed, work by Mareschal and Johnson (2003) has shown that 4-month-olds have considerable difficulty binding the location information processed in the dorsal (occipitoparietal) stream with the more featural information, including faces and color, processed in the ventral (occipitotemporal) stream.

However, this result contrasts with the evidence from Bonatti *et al.* (2002), who showed that, at least by 10 months, infants can individuate and track objects with human faces and argued that the kind *human* may be privileged in infancy, supporting object tracking before other concepts (like "duck" and "truck").

How do we reconcile these two conflicting results? Our conclusion is that they may both be right. Faces are developmentally privileged stimuli in infancy, but probably not because they are embedded in a representation of the kind *human*, at least not in the specific sense intended by Xu and Carey (1996) and not because they belong to goal-directed agents. Indeed, infants may not incorporate faces and hands into a single, complete representation of "person" (or agent) that can support individuation and tracking judgments, as the adult does. Rather, it may be the case that infants successfully traced the identity of the dolls' faces in the Bonatti *et al.* (2002) study because faces help identify individual people, a skill infants display early in life (Pascalis *et al.*, 1995; Walton *et al.*, 1992). If this conjecture is correct, it is not surprising that infants do not do the same with hands, which provide substantial information about goal-directedness but little information about individual people.

Three pieces of evidence suggest that this may be at least a partial explanation. First, when Bonatti *et al.* (2002) tested infants with two distinct dolls' heads (i.e. both belonging to the kind *human*), they predicted that infants would fail to represent them as two distinct individuals, yet infants displayed a trend toward longer looking when only one head was revealed ($p = .08$), suggesting that they may in fact have been tracking individual dolls.

Second, work by Slaughter and colleagues suggests that visuo-spatial representations of the face and body are somewhat independent in infancy, following different developmental trajectories. Unlike the human face, infants do not have strong expectations about the configuration of the human body until 15 to 18 months of age (Slaughter and Heron, 2004; Slaughter *et al.*, 2002, 2004). Similarly, Kuhlmeier and colleagues showed that, when viewing the entire human body moving, 5-month-old infants do not even apply spatiotemporal principles to humans (Kuhlmeier *et al.*, 2004).

Third, the neural substrates supporting the recognition of faces and bodies are distinct, though both are part of the occipito-temporal visual pathways. Indeed, seeing a face or a moving hand may activate not only discrete regions but also different circuits, based at least in part on the inferences generally made about these objects. The circuit of regions active when viewing faces includes the fusiform face area (FFA), prefrontal cortex and amygdala, regions specialized for recognizing individuals and emotions (Haxby *et al.*, 2000; Rothstein *et al.*, 2005; Ryu *et al.*, 2008; but see Pourtois *et al.*, 2005). In contrast, static bodies and body parts, including hands, may be represented in other occipito-temporal areas (the extrastriate body area; Downing *et al.*, 2001), and moving bodies and hands rely particularly on more superior regions in the temporal lobe, namely the superior temporal sulcus (STS; Pelphrey *et al.*, 2005; Jellema *et al.*, 2000).

Furthermore, a parieto-premotor circuit is active when adults see a hand move toward a goal, including premotor regions (inferior frontal gyrus) that are particularly sensitive to the goal-directed movements of the human hand (Blangero *et al.*, 2009; Binkofski and Buccino, 2006; Fabbri-Destro and Rizzolatti, 2008; Filimon *et al.*, 2007; Grol *et al.*, 2007). While it is certainly unclear whether this organization is evident in infancy, the discreteness of these two circuits and their task specificity make it less surprising that infants do not make the same inferences about faces and hands.

Thus, based on the current work, it does not appear likely that it is the potential for goal-directedness that gives faces privileged access to the object individuation and tracking system. The hand used in the current study was clearly seen as goal-directed by infants, yet this did not affect their inability to individuate or track it. It is interesting to note that, unlike object tracking, the pathways for goal-detection do seem to have access to object recognition information very early in infancy. Infants much younger than 12 months attribute goals to hands on the basis of their appearance alone, as demonstrated in the paradigm used by Woodward (Woodward, 1998; Sommerville *et al.*, 2005) and replicated here. This success may be simply because at least some goal-directed actions are represented in terms of particular body actions (Jellema *et al.*, 2000; Gallese and Goldman, 1998).

In summary, while infants can use their representations of faces to individuate and track objects, they have more difficulty using their representations of hands to do so, even when they clearly recognize the hand as goal-directed and the other object as not. While Bonatti's evidence indicates that human-face/not-a-human-face dichotomy supports these abilities in infancy, our evidence indicates that the goal-directed/not-goal-directed dichotomy does not. One possibility for this unexpected set of results is that the need for individual recognition of people – or perhaps the additional attention for faces that comes with it – supports precocious object tracking abilities. By contrast, hands hardly ever require individual recognition. What is important about hands is to figure out what they are reaching for, and infants show early skill in this regard. That the infants' reasoning about different parts of the body reflects their distinct functions helps to explain why the infants' reasoning about the human body may be more piecemeal than that of adults. Indeed, the adults' holistic view of the human body may be a late-emerging component of the concept *human*.

References

Baillargeon, R. (1986). Representing the existence and the location of hidden objects: Object permanence in 6- and 8-month-old infants. *Cognition*, **23**, 21–41.

Bertenthal, B. I., Proffitt, D. R., Spetner, N. B., and Thomas, M. A. (1985). The development of infant sensitivity to biomechanical motions. *Child Development*, **56**,
531–543.

Binkofski, F. and Buccino, G. (2006). The role of ventral premotor cortex in action
execution and action understanding. *Journal of Physiology – Paris*, **99**, 396–405.

Blangero, A., Menz, M. M., McNamara, A., and Binkofski, F. (2009). Parietal modules
for reaching. *Neuropsychologia*, **47**, 1,500–1,507.

Bonatti, L., Frot, E., Zangl, R., and Mehler, J. (2002). The human first hypothesis:
Identification of conspecifics and individuation of objects in the young infant.
Cognitive Psychology, **44**, 388–426.

Bower, T. G. R. (1974). *Development in infancy*. San Francisco, CA: W. H. Freeman and
Company.

Carey, S. and Xu, F. (2001). Infants' knowledge of objects: Beyond object files and
object tracking. *Cognition*, **80**, 179–213.

Caron, A. J. (2009). Comprehension of the representational mind in infancy.
Developmental Review, **29**, 69–95.

DeCasper, A. and Fifer, W. (1980). Of human bonding: Newborns prefer their mother's
voices. *Science*, **208**, 1,174–1,176.

Downing, P. E., Jiang, Y., Shuman, M., and Kanwisher, N. (2001). A cortical area
selective for visual processing of the human body. *Science*, **293**, 2,470–2,473.

Downing, P. E., Peelen, M. V., Wiggett, A. J., and Tew, B. D. (2006). The role of the
extrastriate body area in action perception. *Social Neuroscience*, **1**, 52–62.

Ellsworth, C., Muir, D., and Hains, S. (1993). Social competence and person–object
differentiation: An analysis of the still-face effect. *Developmental Psychology*, **29**,
63–73.

Fabbri-Destro, M. and Rizzolatti, G. (2008). Mirror neurons and mirror systems in
monkeys and humans. *Physiology*, **23**, 171–179.

Filimon, F., Nelson, J. D., Hagler, D. J., and Sereno, M. I. (2007). Human cortical
representations for reaching: Mirror neurons for execution, observation, and
imagery. *Neuroimage*, **37**, 1,315–1,328.

Fox, R. and McDaniel, C. (1982). The perception of biological motion by human infants.
Science, **218**, 486–487.

Frye, D., Rawling, P., Moore, C., and Meyers, I. (1983). Object–person discrimination and communication at 3 and 10 months. *Developmental Psychology*, **19**,
303–309.

Gallese, V. and Goldman, A. (1998). Mirror neurons and the simulation theory of mind-
reading. *Trends in Cognitive Science*, 2(12), 493–501.

Goodale, M. A. and Milner, A. D. (1992). Separate visual pathways for perception and
action. *Trends in Neurosciences*, **15**, 20–25.

Grol, M. J., Majdandzić, J., Stephan, K. E., Verhagen, L., Dijkerman, H. C.,
Bekkering, H. *et al.* (2007). Parieto-frontal connectivity during visually guided
grasping. *Journal of Neuroscience*, **27**, 11,877–11,887.

Hall, D. G. (1998). Continuity and the persistence of objects: When the whole is greater
than the sum of the parts. *Cognitive Psychology*, **37**, 28–59.

Haxby, J. V., Hoffman, E. A., and Gobbini, M. I. (2000). The distributed human neural
system for face perception. *Trends in Cognitive Sciences*, **4**, 223–233.

Hirsch, E. (1982). *The Concept of Identity*. New York: Oxford University Press.

Jellema, T., Baker, C. I., Wicker, B., and Perrett, D. I. (2000). Neural representation for the perception of the intentionality of actions. *Brain and Cognition*, **44**(2), 280–302.

Kaldy, Z. and Leslie, A. (2003). Identification of objects in 9-month-old infants: Integrating "what" and "where" information. *Developmental Science*, **6**, 360–373.

Klein, R. P. and Jennings, K. D. (1979). Responses to social and inanimate stimuli in early infancy. *The Journal of Genetic Psychology*, **135**, 3–9.

Krojgaard, P. (2000). Object individuation in 10-month-old infants: Do significant objects make a difference? *Cognitive Development*, **15**, 169–184.

Kuhlmeier, V. A., Bloom, P., and Wynn, K. (2004). Do 5-month-old infants see humans as material objects? *Cognition*, **94**, 95–103.

Legerstee, M., Pomerleau, A., Malcuit, G., and Feider, H. (1987). The development of infants' responses to people and a doll: Implications for research in communication. *Infant Behavior and Development*, **10**, 81–95.

Leslie, A. M. (1984). Infant perception of a manual pick-up event. *British Journal of Developmental Psychology*, **2**, 19–32.

Leslie, A. M., Xu, F., Tremoulet, P. D., and Scholl, B. J. (1998). Indexing and the object concept: Developing "what" and "where" systems. *Trends in Cognitive Science*, **2**, 10–18.

MacFarlane, A. (1975). Olfaction in the development of social preferences in the human neonate. In Ciba Foundation Symposium (ed.). *Parent–child Interaction*. New York: Elsevier.

MacNamara, J. (1986). *A Border Dispute; the Place of Logic in Psychology*. Cambridge, MA: MIT Press.

Mareschal, D. and Johnson, M. H. (2003). The "what" and "where" of object representations in infancy. *Cognition*, **88**, 259–276.

Meltzoff, A. N. and Moore, M. K. (1983). Newborn infants imitate adult facial gestures. *Child Development*, **54**, 702–709.

Morton, J. and Johnson, M. H. (1991). CONSPEC and CONLERN: A two-process theory of infant face recognition. *Psychological Review*, **98**, 164–181.

Moscovitch, M., Winocur, G., and Behrmann, M. (1997). What is special about face recognition? Nineteen experiments on a person with visual object agnosia and dyslexia but normal face recognition. *Journal of Cognitive Neuroscience*, **9**(5), 555–560.

Needham, A. (1998). Infants' use of featural information in the segregation of stationary objects. *Infant Behavior and Development*, **21**, 47–76.

Needham, A. and Baillargeon, R. (1993). Intuitions about support in 4.5-month-old infants. *Cognition*, **47**, 121–148.

(1997). Object segregation in 8-month-old infants. *Cognition*, **62**, 121–49.

(1998). Effects of experience on 4.5-month-old infants' object segregation. *Infant Behavior and Development*, **21**, 1–24.

Palmer, C. (1989). The discriminating nature of infants' exploratory actions. *Developmental Psychology*, **25**(6), 885–893.

Pascalis, O., de Schonen, S., Morton, J., Deruelle, C., and Fabre-Grenet, M. (1995). Mother's face recognition by neonates: A replication and an extension. *Infant Behavior and Development*, **18**, 79–85.

Pelphrey, K. A., Morris, J. P., Michelich, C. R., Allison, T., and McCarthy, G. (2005). Functional anatomy of biological motion perception in posterior temporal cortex:

An fMRI study of eye, mouth and hand movements. *Cerebral Cortex*, **15**, 1,866–1,876.

Pourtois, G., Schwartz, S., Seghier, M. L., Lazeyras, F., and Vuilleumier, P. (2005). View-independent coding of face identity in frontal and temporal cortices is modulated by familiarity: An event-related fMRI study. *Neuroimage*, **24**, 1,214–1,224.

Ricard, M. and Allard, L. (1993). The reaction of 9- to 10-month-old infants to an unfamiliar animal. *The Journal of Genetic Psychology*, **154**(1), 5–16.

Rothstein, P., Henson, R. N. A., Treves, A., Driver, J., and Dolan, R. J. (2005). Morphing Marilyn into Maggie dissociates physical and identity face representations in the brain. *Nature Neuroscience*, **8**, 107–113.

Ruff, H. (1984). Infants' manipulative exploration of objects: Effects of age and object characteristics. *Developmental Psychology*, **20**(1), 9–20.

Ryu, J., Borrman, K., and Chaudhuri, A. (2008). Imagine Jane and identify John: Face identity after effects induced by imagined faces. *Public Library of Science ONE*, **3**, e2,195.

Saxe, R., Tzelnic, T., and Carey, S. (2006). Five-month-old infants know humans are solid, like inanimate objects. *Cognition*, **101**, B1–B8.

Simon, T. J., Hespos, S. J., and Rochat, P. (1995). Do infants understand simple arithmetic? A replication of Wynn (1992). *Cognitive Development*, **10**, 253–269.

Slaughter, V. and Heron, M. (2004). Origins and early development of human body knowledge. *Monographs of the Society of Research in Child Development*, **69**(2), 1–102.

Slaughter, V., Heron, M., and Sim, S. (2002). Development of preferences for the human body shape in infancy. *Cognition*, **85**, B71–B81.

Slaughter, V., Stone, V. E., and Reed, C. (2004). Perception of faces and bodies: Similar or different? *Current Directions in Psychological Science*, **13**(6), 216–223.

Sommerville, J. A., Woodward, A. L., and Needham, A. (2005). Action experience alters 3-month-old infants' perception of others' actions. *Cognition*, **96**(1), B1–B11.

Spelke, E. (1990). Principles of object perception. *Cognitive Science*, **14**, 29–56.

Spelke, E., Breinlinger, K., Macomber, J., and Jacobson, K. (1992). Origins of knowledge. *Psychological Review*, **99**, 605–632.

Spelke, E., Phillips, A., and Woodward, A. (1995). Infants' knowledge of object motion and human action. In D. Sperman, D. Premack, and A. Premack (eds). *Causal Cognition*. Oxford, UK: Oxford University Press.

Van de Walle, G., Carey, S., and Prevor, M. (2000). Bases for object individuation in infancy: Evidence from manual search. *Journal of Cognition and Development*, **1**, 249–280.

Walton, G. E., Bower, N. J. A., and Bower, T. G. R. (1992). Recognition of familiar faces by newborns. *Infant Behavior and Development*, **15**, 265–269.

Wilcox, T. and Baillargeon, R. (1998). Object individuation in infancy: The use of featural information in reasoning about occlusion events. *Cognitive Psychology*, **37**, 97–155.

Wilcox, T. and Chapa, C. (2002). Infants' reasoning about opaque and transparent occluders in an individuation task. *Cognition*, **85**, B1–B10.

Woodward, A. (1998). Infants selectively encode the goal object of an actor's reach. *Cognition*, **69**, 1–34.

Wynn, K. (1992). Addition and subtraction by human infants. *Nature*, **358**, 749–750.

Xu, F. (1999). Object individuation and object identity in infancy: The role of spatio-temporal information, object property information, and language. *Acta Psychologica*, **102**, 113–136.

(2007). Sortal concepts, object individuation, and language. *Trends in Cognitive Science*, **11**, 400–406.

Xu, F. and Carey, S. (1996). Infants' metaphysics: The case of numerical identity. *Cognitive Psychology*, **30**, 111–153.

Xu, F., Carey, S., and Welch, J. (1999). Infants' ability to use object kind information for object individuation. *Cognition*, **70**, 137–166.

Yet another approach to development of body representations

Kazuo Hiraki

Progress in cognitive science requires a balance between divergence and convergence of approaches. As an interdisciplinary and integrated field for scientific understanding of the human mind, cognitive science has incorporated diverse approaches such as computer modelling and brain imaging. These approaches have brought us not only new findings but also new problems when the findings of different approaches are in conflict with each other. For example, advances in infant looking-time methodologies (e.g. Baillargeon, 1986; Ahmed and Ruffman, 1998) have led to claims that infants know far more about the physical world than previously credited by studies using more traditional methodologies (Piaget, 1954). The current novel emphasis on elec-trophysiological methodologies, such as electroencephalogram (EEG) or evoked response potential (ERP), adds another layer of complexity. As a result, cognitive scientists have had to develop new models of the mind that can integrate empirical evidence across multiple methodologies (e.g. Munakata, 2001) in order to converge on a unified model of cognitive functioning.

The five chapters of Part II are a case in point. These chapters all address questions of when and how infants and young children acquire representations of the bodies of other people. The chapters are remarkably diverse; there are several important distinctions that cut across the chapters and that highlight the fact that representing others' bodies is a complex, multi-layered cognitive process.

In Chapter 5, Slaughter, Heron-Delaney and Christie review their excellent studies on infants' visual discrimination and recognition of the human body shape, and propose an experience-dependent model for the development of visuo-spatial body representations. They systematically used preferential look-ing and visual habituation methods to document infants' responses to typical and scrambled bodies over the first two years of life. Their focus is on an initial, basic aspect of representing others' bodies, which they label 'body detection' and define as the ability to visually discriminate human bodies from other objects. They propose that this fundamental ability develops gradually with experience.

Cox (Chapter 6) discusses human body representations at a much higher level, namely older children's body representations as revealed in their human figure drawings. Although children must certainly access an internal mental representation of the human body when drawing it, Cox suggests that children's drawings may not be direct reflections of their body representations because cultural practices and individual experiences influence how children portray the human figure. Cox concludes that children's drawings may mislead us into underestimating their knowledge about the human body.

Whereas the chapters by Slaughter *et al.* and Cox explore development of structural representations of the body, those by Reid (Chapter 8) and Moore (Chapter 7) focus on the development of human motion perception using point-light displays (PLDs). When moving, the human body reveals not only its underlying structure, but also conveys higher level information such as direction of attention, communicative intent and emotional state. Reid, in Chapter 8, reviews electrophysiological studies showing that infants within the first year of life are sensitive to the structure of human bodies as revealed in unique movement patterns. Moore, in Chapter 7, provides an excellent summary of the development of sensitivity to human bodies in PLDs, moving from apprehension of structural information from human movement to perception of emotions and mental states based on body movement. In his review, Moore nicely demonstrates that there are multiple 'levels of meaning' conveyed in the movement of the human body.

Finally, in Chapter 9, O'Hearn and Johnson address the question of how infants represent others' bodies from a different perspective by considering infants' responses to a highly salient body part: the hand. Based on their studies and contrasting findings from previous researchers, they suggest that infants' representations of different body parts – in particular, hands versus faces – develop independently.

These five chapters exemplify the diversity of approaches to investigating how we represent others' bodies. They use different methods ranging from the explicit production of drawings to more passive looking-time methods to EEG, and they use a range of stimuli from static body images to PLDs to live hands reaching for objects. Furthermore, these chapters address multiple levels of meaning (Moore, Chapter 7) in body representation. In their chapter, Slaughter *et al.* define a continuum of body processing from body detection (recognition that a visual object is a human body and not something else) to body identification (recognition of individual bodies based on shape, posture, movement parameters, etc.) to body meaning (apprehending the social-communicative relevance of body structure, postures and movement). Crossing these two dimensions of explicit-to-implicit methodologies with levels of meaning in body perception, reveals how much research is still required before we can begin to build a comprehensive model of how we represent others' bodies.

In spite of the tremendous diversity, some convergence can be found across the five chapters. For instance, Slaughter *et al.* argue that representations of human faces and bodies develop independently in infancy, and in this they agree with O'Hearn and Johnson who argue that infants' representation of human hands as individual agents lags behind their representations of human faces as individual agents. These two chapters both paint a picture in which the acquisition of body representations occurs bit-by-bit and over a protracted period of development.

Consistent with this developmental picture, all five chapters emphasise the importance of *experience* for the development of body representations. The crucial question then becomes what sort of experience enhances or attenuates infant development. Infants' visual exposure to others' bodies depends on their developmental stage. For example, up to around 6 months of age, infants most often see the faces and hands of care-givers from their position of lying down or being propped up, but in the second half year of life infants can sit alone and thereby observe whole bodies of other people as they move around and interact with objects. From this point infants are also exposed to human body images via books or television; what do they learn from these experiences? Characters in many cartoon animations for young children have strange bodies and as a result also move differently to real human bodies. If representations of others' bodies come about largely via learning, then we must understand how these various sorts of experiences are assimilated.

In our studies of how *experience* affects infants' and children's knowledge of others' bodies, we have been using robots. There are some advantages to using robots in developmental research. First, we can manipulate and control infants' and children's experience of robots, because even in today's technological world, robots are novel stimuli. Second, we can program the motion of a robot so that it is repeated exactly over and over, thereby isolating different specific visual experiences that may be crucial to the developmental process we are studying. As we saw in Chapter 7 (Moore) and Chapter 8 (Reid), most of the motion perception studies use PLDs created by a computer program or a motion tracker system. Thus the stimuli for the studies must be shown in two-dimensional displays whereas robots move in natural (three-dimensional) environments.

In one study (Arita *et al.*, 2005) we investigated whether infants expect people to talk only to other humans, or if they would also accept a robot (whose body is structurally similar to that of a human) as a potential communicative partner. The design was based on Legerstee *et al.* (2000) who showed that infants do not expect people to talk to inanimate objects. In their experiment, infants were shown an actor who talked to something hidden behind a curtain. When the curtain was opened, either a broom appeared or a person appeared. Infants looked longer when the object, compared to the person, appeared from behind the curtain, suggesting that infants were surprised by the anomaly of an actor speaking to an object.

We modified the experimental design of Legerstee *et al.* (2000) in two ways. First, we used a humanoid robot instead of a broom as the inanimate object. Although the humanoid robot would be classified as an inanimate object by knowledgeable adults, it shares many properties with human beings, including equivalent body parts such as a head, a face, hands, arms, a trunk and so on (see Figure C2.1). The second modification was that we added a familiarisation period prior to the test trials, letting infants *experience* how the robot behaved and interacted with people.

We assigned infants to one of four experimental conditions, three of which included a familiarisation period in which the infants observed the robot's actions in 1-minute video clips before the test. In the *interactive robot condition*, infants were shown the robot interacting with a person during the familiarisation period. During this period, the robot and a person talked to each other using a lot of gestures. In the *non-active robot condition*, the robot remained stationary and did not respond to the person talking to it during familiarisation. In the *active robot condition*, the robot displayed humanlike behaviours during familiarisation, as in the interactive robot condition, but this time the person remained stationary and did not respond. The control condition did not include a familiarisation period. In one test trial, infants watched an actor talk to the person and in the other, they watched an actor talk to the robot. If infants expected the robot to be talked to by a person actor, and characterized the robot as a communicative agent, they would not be surprised when the robot was addressed by a person in conversation. But if infants did not expect the robot to be talked to by an actor, and characterized the robot as an inanimate object, they would be surprised when it was addressed by the actor in conversation. We found that infants who had previously observed the interactive robot showed no difference in looking-time between the two types of test events. Thus, they saw the person and the robot as equally likely conversation partners for the actor. Infants in the other conditions, however, looked longer at the test event where the actor talked to the robot, presumably because they did not represent the robot as a potential communicative partner. This study demonstrates that the same body can be seen very differently, depending on how it moves and behaves.

It is worthwhile to note that the results of our experiment suggest that a very short experience (just 1 minute of observation of the interactive robot in a video clip) can alter infants' responses to non-human objects. Although this experiment focused on the body as a communicative entity, a similar process might occur in infants' visual discrimination and recognition of human body shape. Imagine a strange world where infants live for a while with scrambled humans, such as those depicted in Slaughter *et al.*'s chapter. As a result of this experience, infants' responses to a typical human could well be changed. Although it does not seem likely that those infants who spend a lot of time watching cartoon

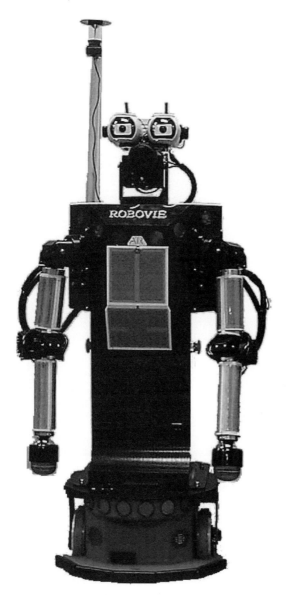

Figure C2.1   The humanoid robot 'Robovie', used in Arita, Hiraki, Kanda, and Ishiguro (2005)

Figure C2.2. Geminoid F, developed by Department of Systems Innovation and ATR Intelligent Robotics and Communication Laboratories. Left: Geminoid F; right: real human (photo by Hiroshi Ishiguro Osaka University and ATR)

animations on television acquire altered representations of human bodies, we should take account of how everyday experiences are assimilated into infants' human body representations.

As technology advances, it is no longer fantasy or fiction that human beings can live with robots. Humanlike robots such as 'ASIMO' (Sakagami, 2002) and 'Geminoid' (Ishiguro, 2005) are being developed for many purposes. Notably, android robots like Geminoid exactly resemble human beings (Figure C2.2). Advances in technology open new questions on the development of *human* body representation. How do infants and/or adults discriminate robots and human beings? How does experience with robots alter infants' knowledge of humans? Currently we are approaching the former question by manipulating the appearance of agents doing the same action (Hirai and Hiraki, 2007; Matsuda *et al.*, 2010; Kamewari *et al.*, 2005). For example, Hirai and Hiraki (2007) compared ERP responses to human action and robotic action among adult subjects. The results demonstrated that appearance information affected neural responses in the occipitotemporal region. That is, even when the motion was identical, the motion sensitive ERP component responded differently to human and robot. Although we need much more research on such issues, such studies illustrate the kinds of novel research on human motion perception and body representation that new technologies make possible.

References

Ahmed, A. and Ruffman, T. (1998). Why do infants make A not B errors in search task, yet show memory for the location of hidden objects in a non-search task? *Developmental Psychology*, **34**(3), 441–453.

Arita, A., Hiraki, K., Kanda, T., and Ishiguro, H. (2005). Can we talk to robots? Ten-month-old infants expected interactive humanoid robots to be talked to by persons. *Cognition*, **95**, B49–B57.

Baillargeon, R. (1986). Representing the existence and the location of hidden objects: Object permanence in 6- and 8-month-old infants. *Cognition*, **23**, 21–41.

Hirai, M. and Hiraki, K. (2007). Differential neural responses to humans vs. robots: An event-related potential study. *Brain Research*, **1,165**, 105–115.

Ishiguro, H. (2005). Android science: Toward a new cross-disciplinary framework. *Toward Social Mechanisms of Android Science: A CogSci 2005 Workshop*. July 25–26, Stresa, Italy, 1–6.

Kamewari, K., Kato, M., Kanda, T., Ishiguro, H., and Hiraki, K. (2005). Six-and-a-half-month-old children positively attribute goals to human action and to humanoid-robot motion. *Cognitive Development*, **20**, 303–320.

Legerstee, M., Barna, J., and DiAdamo, C. (2000). Precursors to the development of intention at 6 months: Understanding people and their actions. *Developmental Psychology*, **36**(5), 627–634.

Matsuda, G., Hiraki, K., and Ishiguro, H. (2010). Evaluation of robot appearance by using a brain science technique. *IEEE/RSJ IROS 2010 Workshop: Human-Robot Symbiosis: Synergistic Creation of Human-Robot Relationships*, Taipei, Taiwan.

Munakata, Y. (2001). Graded representations in behavioral dissociations. *Trends in Cognitive Sciences*, **5**(7), 309–315.

Piaget, J. (1954). *The Construction of Reality in the Child*. New York: Basic Books.

Sakagami, Y. (2002). The intelligent ASIMO: System overview and integration, *Proceedings of 2002 IEEE/RSJ International Conference on Intelligent Robots and Systems*, 2,478–2,483.

Part III

Bodily correspondences: integrating self and other

10 Prepared to learn about human bodies' goals and intentions

Teodora Gliga and Victoria Southgate

Human beings are one of the first and one of the most frequent 'objects' in infants' environment. Infants' interactions with their caregivers are extremely diverse and socially rich. Caregivers provide care, affection and knowledge. It therefore seems trivial to assume that one of the first things human infants will learn is how to identify their conspecifics. The first section of this chapter reviews a series of studies that contradict the above intuition. Experimental research presented in this section has shown that infants, prodigiously good at learning about faces, are slow at learning about the human body appearance. A few explanations have been put forward to integrate these conflicting findings. Faces and bodies are similar in many respects (e.g. they have component parts whose relative position is species-specific; minor variations in the distance between these components occur between individuals) but also different in others (e.g. body parts movement leads to ampler structural changes than face component movements and these movements are often object-oriented). Thus, because movement changes the outline of bodies it may be more difficult to build a prototype of the human body than of the human face. Alternatively it could be that body movement, particularly the goals of human action, grab infants' attention, at the expense of learning about body structure. It has been proposed that infants' learning about the structure of the human face is secondary to their learning about facial communicative cues like eye-contact and eye-gaze (Gliga and Csibra, 2007). In the second section we will review evidence in support of a similar developmental story for acquiring knowledge about body structure. We will show that, before acquiring precise knowledge on humans' appearance, infants are proficient at understanding and anticipating human (body) action. This attentional bias is driven by their need to learn from others, which requires understanding other people's goals and intentions. The final section will attempt to integrate these two lines of research. We will propose that the principles infants use to understand the goals of human actions can also be

This work was supported by the UK Medical Research Council Programme Grant G0701484 ID: 85031.

used to learn about which bodily actions are possible and which are not, and eventually about human body structure. We will bring arguments to support this view from both developmental and adult cognitive neuropsychology.

Protracted learning about human body structure

Despite possessing good visual processing capacities from very early on, which are successfully deployed to learn about objects and faces, human infants are surprisingly slow at learning about the human body structure. A number of studies have shown that it takes between 9 and 18 months to tell apart a scrambled human figure from a typical one, depending on the realism of the figure (Slaughter and Heron, 2004; Slaughter *et al.*, 2002, Chapter 5 in this volume). These results are surprising, considering that, at only a few months old, infants are able to acquire visual categories based on a variety of visual dimensions. For example, presented with a succession of differently shaped triangles, 4-month-olds will notice the shape similarity and look longer if a different shape is presented in a habituation design (Quinn, 1987). As they grow older infants become able to learn categories based not only on one common feature but also on combinations of shapes or parts (Younger and Cohen, 1986), one of their most well-known abilities in this sense being their face processing skills. In a task equivalent to the body discrimination study discussed above, infants as young as 2 months look longer towards a normal face than towards a scrambled one (Maurer and Barrera, 1981). By 5 months of age, infants would even notice a change in the orientation of only one face element, within an otherwise typical face (Bhatt *et al.* 2005). These studies show that even young infants possess detailed knowledge about the human face structure. Brain imaging studies measuring event related potentials (ERPs) have shown that neural specialization for face processing parallels the behavioural findings. Two posterior components, the N290 and the P400, are recorded in infants in response to visual stimulation (Gliga and Dehaene-Lambertz, 2005), and are considered to be the precursors of the adult N170, a face sensitive component (Carmel and Bentin, 2002). The N400 is stronger for typical than for scrambled faces in 3-month-olds (Gliga and Dehaene-Lambertz, 2005) and at 12 months of age the N290 differentiates between inverted and upright human faces but not monkey faces (Halit *et al.*, 2003).

In contrast to their knowledge of human faces, infants' knowledge about the human body structure seems very limited. Like faces, human bodies are processed within specialised brain areas in the adult brain (Taylor *et al.*, 2007), and evoke similar electrophysiological responses to the N170 (Gliga and Dehaene-Lambertz, 2005). Bodies and faces seem to be processed in a similar way, e.g. both show an inversion effect (Reed *et al.*, 2003; Stekelenburg and de Gelder, 2004). This parallel between face and body perception has motivated research into the development of body representations, which were expected to closely follow that of face representations. In one of these studies, a preferential looking paradigm was used to investigate whether infants aged 12, 15 and 18 months could discriminate between a typical and a scrambled body shape (Slaughter *et al.*, 2002). Only at 18 months did infants show a preference for the scrambled body, suggesting that only these older infants found the scrambled body to be unexpected. When more realistic body representations are used, i.e. real people in movement, infants as young as 9 months or 4–6 months show discrimination of scrambled and intact bodies (see Slaughter *et al.*, Chapter 5 in this volume). These results contrast with infants' performance with a class of artificial objects. These objects were similar to bodies in the sense that they also had a number of component parts whose relative position could vary. Even 12-month-old infants succeeded at discriminating the prototypical from 'scrambled' versions of these objects (Slaughter and Heron, 2004). What is it about bodies that makes it so difficult to grasp their typical configuration?

To account for the relatively poor knowledge about the structure of human bodies, Slaughter and Heron (2004) make an interesting observation: when bodies are in movement, the relative position of the limbs on the body or the body symmetry are frequently violated. The many possible positions in which the human body may be viewed (e.g. upright, seated, kneeling) may thus be the reason behind young infants' failure to build a human body category. This may also explain the fact that 4-month-olds (unlike 7-month-olds) who are habitu-ated to various exemplars of human figures, in different positions, do not subsequently dishabituate when they see a picture of an animal (Quinn, 2004). Infants' experience with people might be too variable to lead to a narrowly defined human body category. While animals can be equally versatile, it is possible infants have seen more two-dimensional depictions of animals (in probably prototypical postures) than real life exemplars.

While body movement might prevent infants from learning the normal configuration of the human body, movement in itself can be a source of valuable information. Adults use body motion to gain information about a person's emotional state, identity, gender or the action accomplished (Blake and Shiffrar, 2007; Hill and Johnston, 2001). A great proportion of the studies investigating the perception of body motion employed point-light displays (PLDs), in which the movement of the body is conveyed in the absence of any surface feature information. Despite the poverty of these displays, adults immediately perceive them as representations of humans in motion. Infants as well seem to be 'recognizing' biological movement in these displays. For example, 2-day-old infants prefer human PLDs to scrambled PLDs, in which the dots' positions and movements are randomised (Simion *et al.*, 2008). Infants also discriminate and prefer upright human PLDs to inverted PLDs (Bertenthal, 1996; Reid, Chapter 8 in this volume). Inversion effects are taken as evidence for specialised processing of certain object configurations which, in this case, imply that infants also posses some knowledge about the typical body config-uration. While these studies suggest that there are some similarities between how infants and adults perceive PLDs, we are still far from knowing whether infants can gather the same amount of information from these displays as adults do, i.e. gender, identity and actions. It is still unknown whether infants even perceive PLDs as representations of their conspecifics, and as equivalent to a picture of a human body.

Telling apart biological and non-biological movement is useful but it is equally useful to know the range of possible body movements. As adults we are highly sensitive to movements that go beyond what is humanly acceptable (e.g. a contortionist's movements). When brain activity is measured in adults in response to human actions, possible actions evoke stronger parietal activity (Costantini *et al.*, 2008; Stevens *et al.*, 1999). Attempts to show similar knowl-edge about constraints in body movements in infancy have been inconclusive (Beier and Spelke, personal communication). In these studies infants showed no preference when presented with video sequences depicting possible or impos-sible arm or body rotations (e.g. someone's arm doing a 360° rotation or someone making a sharp bend backwards).

What the studies briefly reviewed here clearly show is that infants possess knowledge about biological motion and, as we will see further, human actions, from very early on, before they acquire knowledge about the structure of human bodies. We will see in the next section that young infants ignore body structure knowledge when involved in understanding the meaning of human body actions.

Early understanding of actions

Unlike knowledge about human bodies, infants appear to have a much earlier understanding of human action, and researchers agree that infants interpret actions as goal-directed from at least 6 months of age. This is not a trivial feat. Most actions occur within a continuous and unsegmented stream, and in order to find intentional, goal-directed actions, individuals must be capable of segmenting this continuous stream into meaningful units (Zacks *et al.*, 2001). Evidence that infants are able to do this comes from studies by Wynn (1996) and Baldwin *et al.* (2001). For example, 6-month-old infants habituated to a puppet jumping twice look longer when shown an event in which a puppet jumps three times than infants who were habituated to a three-jump event (Wynn, 1996). This is the case even when these jumping events are embedded in a continuous stream of motion, suggesting that they were able to parse this dynamic event into discrete units. In a different study, Baldwin and colleagues presented 10- to 11-month-old infants with dynamic events (someone cleaning the kitchen) in which the events were paused either at time points coinciding with the actor's goal or at points which interrupted the actor's pursuit of a goal. Infants in this study looked longer at the interruption events than at the completion events. Furthermore, even when these dynamic events were unfamiliar, infants were still able to detect the endpoints of intentional actions (Saylor and Ganea, 2007). Recent evidence measuring brain activity suggests that 8-month-olds also detect these interruptions in dynamic events, exhibiting an increase in gamma-band activity when they are presented with an incomplete pouring event but not a completed pouring event (Reid *et al.*, 2007).

Infants are also able to predict human action outcomes. Employing eye-tracking technology, Falck-Ytter and colleagues showed infants small balls either being placed by a hand into a container, or moving by themselves into the container. 12-month-old infants made predictive saccades, anticipating the action outcome, only when the balls were moved by the human hand (Falck-Ytter *et al.*, 2006). In another study, 10- to 12-month-olds were repeatedly shown the end of a throwing event in which a previously shown inert beanbag landed on a stage floor in front of them. Crucially, they did not see what caused the beanbag to land on the stage. In test trials, they were shown a human hand appearing, either from the side from which the beanbag had emerged, or the opposite side. Infants looked significantly longer at the event in which the hand appeared from the opposite side, suggesting that they expected that a hand would have been the cause of the event and were surprised when it appeared from a side incongruent with this expectation (Saxe *et al.*, 2005). In a follow-up study, 7-month-old infants were shown a similar beanbag event, but this time on test trials they were first briefly shown the location of a hand. Then, the beanbag either appeared from this location or from another location. Infants looked longer at the event in which the beanbag appeared from the location without the hand (Saxe *et al.*, 2007). Together, these studies suggest that infants have an early understanding of the causal role that human hands play in the movements of inert objects.

This early ability to detect intentional action units, even within novel streams of action, alludes to a brain prepared to detect goals in the actions of others. This is unsurprising given the immense advantage such ability would offer. Detecting goals enables individuals to predict outcomes as well as intervening actions, and prepare one's own actions for coordinated interaction with others (Csibra and Gergely, 2007). Furthermore, for young learners, goal detection may provide a valuable basis for imitative behaviour in the absence of ostensive cues to disambiguate which elements of a demonstration are worthy of imitation (Bekkering *et al.*, 2000; Call *et al.*, 2005).

Goal attribution in infancy is also evidenced by their behaviour in another paradigm, developed by Amanda Woodward. In this paradigm, infants are habituated to a person repeatedly reaching for one of two toys. In test trials, the two toys switch locations and the person either continues to reach for the 'old' toy in its new location, or reaches for the 'new' toy in the old location. Infants from 6 months of age look longer when the person reaches for the new toy (despite the pathway the arm takes being the perceptually more familiar one) than when the person reaches for the old one, suggesting that they had encoded the person's goal as the toy that they were repeatedly reaching for, and were surprised when the person reached for the other toy.

This section has revealed a puzzling contrast between the late acquisition of knowledge on human body appearance, and the impressive early capacities to understand and predict the goals of human action. Infants' 'obsession with goals' (Csibra and Gergely, 2007) derives from their high dependence on people for both survival and knowledge acquisition. To predict other people's actions (e.g. Is mummy preparing my bottle?) or to learn from others (e.g. That's the way you open the toy box!), infants have to first identify the goals of their actions. We propose here that it is their 'obsession' with goals early in life that directs infants' attention away from learning about the detailed structural properties of the human body to first learning about body actions. Some evidence exists to show that infants pay more attention to object-directed actions than to object appearance (Perone *et al.*, 2008). In this study, 6- to 7-month-olds were habituated to events in which a hand acted on an object to produce a sound. In the test phase infants robustly responded to changes in action type e.g. squeeze or roll, but did not respond to changes in object appearance, e.g. colour and shape. By 10 months of age, infants' attentional abilities improve and they manage to encode both the actions and the sounds of objects as well as the relationship between specific object appearances and actions (Perone and Oakes, 2006). One could test in a similar way the hypothesis that younger infants are biased towards the goal of the action and not the agent's body properties. One could familiarise infants with goal-directed actions and non-goal-directed actions and subsequently measure their ability to detect a change in structural properties of the agent or in the action. Based on the evidence that infants are particularly interested in goal-directed actions, we also make the prediction that infants will encode body properties better when the action cannot be interpreted as goal-directed.

We proposed here that infants' poor knowledge about the human body configuration stems from their preferential interest in what one does and not who does it. A similar bias was previously proposed to explain the excellent gaze-processing abilities infants have early in life, at a time when their face recognition is still poor (Gliga and Csibra, 2007). In the case of the face it is the need to interact with others rather than recognising them that induces the early attentional biases to the eyes and away from other face parts and their relationships. Recognising conspecifics is an equally important ability but it may be that the richness of the multi-modal cues available for discriminating individuals, e.g. the odours, the voices, can compensate for the lack of visual expertise and is initially sufficient to tell apart the small number of relevant individuals in a toddler's environment.

The principles used to understand the goals of human actions could drive learning about the human body

A debate has arisen over how the ability to attribute goals emerges. On one side there are researchers who advocate the view that this ability develops slowly through experience, both observing other people's actions and carrying out actions themselves (Woodward *et al.*, 2001). This view is supported by a growing number of studies. For example, 3-month-olds, who do not make purposeful reaches and grasps themselves, do not look longer when a person reaches for a new toy in test events on the Woodward paradigm. However, Sommerville and colleagues have shown that if 3-month-old infants are given some experience with grasping objects – they give them experience wearing Velcro mittens that enables their swipes at objects to result in obtaining the object – they do subsequently look longer at someone else's reach for a new object with the Velcro mittens (Sommerville *et al.*, 2005). In another demonstration of the important role that experience plays, Sommerville and Woodward showed infants an event in which an actor pulled one of two cloths to obtain an out-of-reach toy. Only those infants who themselves were adept at cloth-pulling looked longer when the actor now pulled a cloth to obtain a different toy (Sommerville and Woodward, 2005).

An alternative view is that infants do not need experience with actions and agents in order to attribute goals to them – this feat is achieved through the deployment of abstract principles that are insensitive to the type of agent, and goals are attributed whenever an action is efficient with respect to a goal (Gergely and Csibra, 2003). These researchers propose that infants apply a non-mentalistic inferential principle in order to interpret actions as goal direc- ted. Specifically, infants (like adults) assume that actions bring about goals through the most efficient means possible, given the particular situational constraints. Indeed, infants do appear to be willing to attribute goals to a wide range of actions and agents, for example to small geometric animations, agents that are presumably completely new to the infant, if the efficacy principle is satisfied. In the original demonstration of this principle at work, 12-month-old infants were habituated to animations in which a small red ball jumped over a wall and came to rest next to a blue ball. Then, infants saw two test events in which the wall was no longer there and the red ball either moved in a straight path towards the blue ball or continued the jumping path even though it was now unnecessary. Despite the jumping action being the perceptually more familiar action, infants in fact looked longer at this action than the straight pathway. However, if infants were habituated to an agent that was not behaving in an efficient way (jumping when the location of the wall did not necessitate it), they did not look longer at either of the two test events, suggesting that in this condition infants have not inferred the goal of the small red ball to be that of approaching the blue ball (Gergely *et al.*, 1995). In a number of variations on the

Woodward paradigm, researchers have shown how infants will attribute goals to an unfamiliar mechanical claw (Biro and Leslie, 2007).

In the same way as infants use situational constraints (i.e. the presence of a barrier) to infer action goals, they can infer the presence of a constraint to explain the inefficient path taken to achieve a goal. If no obstacle blocks the path from the hand to an object one wants to grasp, infants expect the hand to follow the shortest path to the object (Kiraly *et al.*, 2003; Southgate *et al.*, 2008). Nonetheless, if a non-efficient means is repeatedly used to attain a goal, infants infer the existence of a constraint. This is what happens in a follow-up study to Gergely *et al.* (1995). This time all infants see is the small ball jumping to approach the other ball (i.e. an inefficient way of achieving that goal) but they do not see the barrier, which is hidden from view by an occluder (Csibra *et al.*, 2003). When the occluder is removed, in the test trials, 12-month-old (but not 9-month-old) infants look longer in the wall absent versus the wall present condition, suggesting that they inferred the existence of a barrier the agent has to jump over. 9-month-old infants, who succeeded at inferring which path the small ball will take, in the absence of the barrier, fail at making the reverse inference.

These latter studies strongly suggest that it is not necessary for infants to identify the perpetrator of an action as human, and hence paying attention to human-specific body structure is not necessary in order to successfully interpret their actions as goal-directed. Indeed, one particular study demonstrates the redundancy of body structure knowledge for successful goal attribution. In this study, having been habituated to an event in which a human arm behaves efficiently to obtain a small ball, 6-month-old infants then saw two test events in which a box now obstructed a direct reach for the ball (Southgate *et al.*, 2008). In the first test event, infants watched the arm move the box out of the way and then reach for the ball. In the second test event, the human arm was seen 'snaking' around the box in a biologically impossible manner. However, if it were possible, the second event would be a more efficient route to the goal as it would not require the effort of moving the box out of the way first. 6-month-olds apparently agreed, as they looked significantly longer at the possible (but less efficient) than the impossible (but more efficient) test event. This is a striking finding because it suggests that knowledge about body structure is unnecessary for goal attribution, and that goal attribution in this case is driven by the recognition of an efficient action relative to the goal state.

In their daily lives infants only experience a limited (though rich) variety of body movements. The movements we can make are constrained by the rigidity of bones and by limited rotation permitted by the anatomy of joints. Young infants seemed to be unaware of these constraints (Southgate *et al.*, 2008). We propose that the same principles used to infer situational constraints (i.e. the presence of a barrier that forced the ball to take a curvilinear trajectory [Csibra *et al.*, 2003]), will allow infants to infer the existence of human body constraints and, therefore, to learn about human body structure. The principle of efficacy states that infants expect goals to be reached through the most efficient means (Gergely and Csibra, 2003). If, when reaching for an object, arms repeatedly take a longer route than the expected efficient route, and if no external barrier is present, this would make infants infer constraints internal to the human body (Figure 10.1). When would infants start making these inferences? Both the amount of exposure to human actions and their ability to make inferences about hidden properties are limiting factors. Remember that only 12-month-olds, but not 9-month-olds, inferred the presence of a hidden barrier in Csibra et al. (2003). It is thus possible that we would not find evidence of knowledge about possible and impossible body movements before 1 year of age.

There are other routes to learning about possible body movements. Infants could make use of their powerful statistical learning skills to extract a prototype of 'possible actions' based on the most frequent movements encountered. Statistical learning is slow, however, as it would require frequent exposures to a variety of possible actions. Making use of their ability to infer body constraints when seeing inefficient goal-directed actions can give infants an additional, powerful learning strategy. Based on only a few instances in which the observed bodily movement does not correspond to what was expected in that context, i.e. not efficient, infants can make predictions about the whole range of impossible movements (e.g. the whole rotation range that is beyond the point at which the arm stopped, is inferred to be 'impossible').

Observing other people's actions is, of course, not the sole source of information about body movements. Infants' proprioceptive and visual experience with their own body may provide equally rich information about which movements can or cannot be achieved. This is illustrated in a study of action perception in which participants were people born with or without arms. When presented with images of two successive arm positions, all participants experienced an illusory arm movement. However, while control participants saw a biologically possible but longer path movement, participants born without arms, who had never experienced this movement themselves, reported seeing the most efficient albeit biologically impossible illusory arm movement (Funk et al., 2005).

Research on body perception in infancy placed the emphasis on infants' ability to learn the structural properties of bodies, probably inspired by previous work on face perception. However, body movement makes this task difficult, as it continuously modifies the outline of the body and the position of limbs with respect to each other (which does not happen in the case of faces). On the other hand, although problematic for learning configural properties, body movement and more particularly the goal-directedness of human actions (of others or one's own), may be part of the key information infants use to eventually learn about their conspecifics' appearance, in their first years of life. Although infants

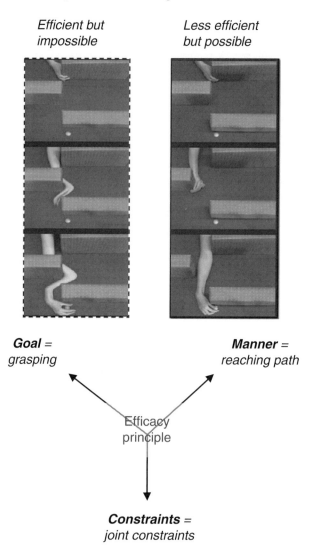

Figure 10.1 Inferential learning of bodily mechanical properties based on the 'efficacy' principles. 6-month-olds do not find the biologically impossible but efficient arm movement unexpected (Southgate *et al.*, 2008), but older infants, having experienced the non-efficient possible movement more often, might reverse their expectancies

seem to be able to grasp the meaning of goal-directed action from very early on, a full-blown understanding of the principles involved, e.g. inferring action constraints when efficacy is not attained, may take longer, making body perception in infancy less prodigious, but not less fascinating a topic.

Conclusions

Infants' knowledge about the structure of the human body improves slowly during the second year of life. In contrast, they already make use of the ability to understand and predict the goals of human actions before their first birthday (Southgate *et al.*, 2010). We attempted to explain this discrepancy by raising the hypothesis that infants have a bias to attend to action goals (i.e. what people do) and not to structural body properties (i.e. who does the action). Young infants possess limited attentional resources and the existence of processing biases is crucial for acquiring essential initial knowledge. Anticipating other people's actions may be of greater urgency in the first year of life, than discriminating people from other animate agents or identifying people based on their body silhouettes. The body structure will contribute eventually to individual recognition, but faces are sufficient, initially, to allow recognition of the few caregivers infants rely upon. From very early on, nonetheless, infants have to anticipate and respond to other people's actions. By paying attention to body actions and their constraints, infants will learn about body structure. Although highly speculative, this chapter provides a coherent explanation for what seemed like a paradox in infants' cognitive development. We hope to have inspired a new approach to studying body perception in infancy and perceptual development in general.

References

Baldwin, D. A., Baird, J. A., Saylor, M. M., and Clark, M. A. (2001). Infants parse dynamic action. *Child Development*, **72**(3), 708–717.

Bekkering, H., Wohlschlager, A., and Gattis, M. (2000). Imitation of gestures in children is goal-directed. *Quarterly Journal of Experimental Psychology*, **53**(1), 153–164.

Bertenthal, B. I. (1996). Origins and early development of perception, action, and representation. *Annual Review of Psychology*, **47**, 431–459.

Bhatt, R. S., Bertin, E., Hayden, A., and Reed, A. (2005). Face processing in infancy: Developmental changes in the use of different kinds of relational information. *Child Development*, **76**, 169–181.

Biro, S. and Leslie, A. M. (2007). Infants' perception of goal-directed actions: Development through cue-based bootstrapping. *Developmental Science*, **10**(3), 379–398.

Blake, R. and Shiffrar, M. (2007). Perception of human motion. *Annual Review of Psychology*, **58**, 47–73.

Call, J., Carpenter, M., and Tomasello, M. (2005). Copying results and copying actions in the process of social learning: Chimpanzees (pan troglodytes) and human children (homo sapiens). *Animal Cognition*, **8**(3), 151–163.

Carmel, D. and Bentin, S. (2002). Domain specificity versus expertise: Factors influencing distinct processing of faces. *Cognition*, **83**(1), 1–29.

Costantini, M., Committeri, G., and Galati, G. (2008). Effector- and target-independent representation of observed actions: Evidence from incidental repetition priming. *Experimental Brain Research*, **188**(3), 341–351.

Csibra, G. and Gergely, G. (2007). 'Obsessed with goals': Functions and mechanisms of teleological interpretation of actions in humans. *Acta Psychologica (Amsterdam)*, **124**(1), 60–78.

Csibra, G., Biro, S., Koos, O., and Gergely, G. (2003). One-year-old infants use teleological representations of actions productively. *Cognitive Science*, **27**, 111–133.

Falck-Ytter, T., Gredeback, G., and von Hofsten, C. (2006). Infants predict other people's action goals. *Nature Neuroscience*, **9**(7), 878–879.

Funk, M., Shiffrar, M., and Brugger, P. (2005). Hand movement observation by individuals born without hands: Phantom limb experience constrains visual limb perception. *Experimental Brain Research*, **164**(3), 341–346.

Gergely, G.and Csibra, G. (2003). Teleological reasoning in infancy: The naive theory of rational action. *Trends in Cognitive Sciences*, **7**(7), 287–292.

Gergely, G., Nadasdy, Z., Csibra, G., and Biro, S. (1995). Taking the intentional stance at 12 months of age. *Cognition*, **56**(2), 165–193.

Gliga, T. and Csibra, G. (2007). Seeing the face through the eyes: A developmental perspective on face expertise. *Progress in Brain Research*, **164**, 323–339.

Gliga, T. and Dehaene-Lambertz, G. (2005). Structural encoding of body and face in human infants and adults. *Journal of Cognitive Neuroscience*, **17**(8), 1,328–1,340.

Halit, H., de Haan, M., and Johnson, M. H. (2003). Cortical specialisation for face processing: Face-sensitive event-related potential components in 3- and 12-month-old infants. *Neuroimage*, **19**(3), 1,180–1,193.

Hill, H. and Johnston, A. (2001). Categorizing sex and identity from biological motion of faces. *Current Biology*, **11**, 880–885.

Kiraly, I., Jovanovic, B., Prinz, W., Aschersleben, G., and Gergely, G. (2003). The early origins of goal attribution in infancy. *Consciousness and Cognition*, **12**(4), 752–769.

Maurer, D. and Barrera, M. (1981). Infants' perception and distorted arrangements of a schematic face. *Child Development*, **52**, 196–202.

Perone, S., Madole, K. L., Ross-Sheehy, S., Carey, M., and Oakes, L. M. (2008). The relation between infants' activity with objects and attention to object appearance. *Developmental Psychology*, **44**(5), 1,242–1,248.

Perone, S. and Oakes, L. M. (2006). It clicks when it is rolled and it squeaks when it is squeezed: What 10-month-old infants learn about object function. *Child Development*, **77**(6), 1,608–1,622.

Quinn, P. C. (1987). The categorical representation of visual pattern information by young infants. *Cognition*, **27**(2), 145–179.

(2004). Is the asymmetry in young infants' categorization of humans versus nonhuman animals based on head, body or global gestalt information? *Psychonomic Bulletin and Review*, **11**, 92–97.

Reed, C. L., Stone, V. E., Bozova, S., and Tanaka, J. (2003). The body-inversion effect. *Psychological Science*, **14**(4), 302–308.

Reid, V. M., Csibra, G., Belsky, J., and Johnson, M. H. (2007). Neural correlates of the perception of goal-directed action in infants. *Acta Psychologica*, **124**, 129–138.

Saxe, R., Tenenbaum, J. B., and Carey, S. (2005). Secret agents: Inferences about hidden causes by 10- and 12-month-old infants. *Psychological Science*, **16**(12), 995–1,001.

Saxe, R., Tzelnic, T., and Carey, S. (2007). Knowing who dunnit: Infants identify the causal agent in an unseen causal interaction. *Developmental Psychology*, **43**(1), 149–158.

Saylor, M. M. and Ganea, P. (2007). Infants interpret ambiguous requests for absent objects. *Developmental Psychology*, **43**(3), 696–704.

Simion, F., Regolin, L., and Bulf, H. (2008). A predisposition for biological motion in the newborn baby. *Proceedings of the National Academy of Sciences of the USA*, **105**(2), 809–813.

Slaughter, V. and Heron, M. (2004). Origins and early development of human body knowledge. *Monographs of the Society for Research in Child Development*, **69**(2).

Slaughter, V., Heron, M., and Sim, S. (2002). Development of preferences for the human body shape in infancy. *Cognition*, **85**(3), B71–B81.

Sommerville, J. A. and Woodward, A. L. (2005). Pulling out the intentional structure of action: The relation between action processing and action production in infancy. *Cognition*, **95**(1), 1–30.

Sommerville, J. A., Woodward, A. L., and Needham, A. (2005). Action experience alters 3-month-old infants' perception of others' actions. *Cognition*, **96**(1), B1–11.

Southgate, V., Johnson, M. H., and Csibra, G. (2008). Infants attribute goals even to biomechanically impossible actions. *Cognition*, **107**(3), 1,059–1,069.

Southgate, V., Johnson, M. H., El Karoui, I., and Csibra, G. (2010). Motor system activation reveals infants' on-line prediction of others' goals. *Psychological Science*, **21**, 355–359.

Stekelenburg, J. J. and de Gelder, B. (2004). The neural correlates of perceiving human bodies: An ERP study on the body-inversion effect. *Neuroreport*, **15**(5), 777–780.

Stevens, J. A., Fonlupt, P., Shiffrar, M., and Decety, J. (1999). New aspects of motion perception: Selective neural encoding of apparent human movements. *Neuroreport*, **11**(1), 109–115.

Taylor, J. C., Wiggett, A. J., and Downing, P. E. (2007). Functional MRI analysis of body and body part representations in the extrastriate and fusiform body areas. *Journal of Neurophysiology*, **98**, 1,626–1,633.

Woodward, A. L., Sommerville, J. A., and Guajardo, J. J. (2001). How infants make sense of intentional action. In B. Malle, L. J. Moses, and D. A. Baldwin (eds). *Intentions and Intentionality: Foundations of Social Cognition* (149–169). Cambridge, MA: MIT Press.

Wynn, K., (1996). Infants' individuation and enumeration of actions. *Psychological Science*, **7**, 164–169.

Younger, B. A. and Cohen, L. B. (1986). Developmental changes in infants'perception of correlations among attributes. *Child Development*, **57**, 803–815.

Zacks, J., Tversky, B., and Iyer, G. (2001). Perceiving, remembering, and communicating structure in events. *Journal of Experimental Psychology: General*, **130**(1), 29–58.

11 Imitation in infancy and the acquisition of body knowledge

Susan Jones and Hanako Yoshida

This chapter is about how the study of imitation in infancy can contribute to our understanding of the origins of body knowledge. If we define imitation as the voluntary reproduction of the movements of another, then imitation clearly requires a good deal of such knowledge. The accomplished imitator must know their own body parts – their locations, their interrelations, the possible movements of each, and how to create those movements (singly and in combination) so as to achieve different actions. They must also be able to recognize and represent all of these same aspects of the body and actions of the person to be imitated, and to reliably map their knowledge of their own body onto those representations.

The study of the origins of imitation, then, could also be one way to study the origins of body knowledge. We say "could" because at this time the literature on imitation in infancy has surprisingly little to say about when and how infants develop the requisite knowledge, motor abilities, and motivation to voluntarily reproduce the behaviors of others. However, we believe that new research focused on the mechanisms that account for the emergence and development of imitation will lead to new discoveries and new theoretical directions. In this chapter, we will present data from one study that we believe illustrates this potential – a case study of the development of behavioral matching in one infant across a 12-month period. Data from this study are especially interesting for what they suggest about how infants acquire the body knowledge and body mappings on which the ability to imitate depends.

The fact that so much remains to be discovered about imitation's origins and underpinnings reflects the historical focus of the field. Until the late1970s, mainstream North American researchers attempted to explain imitation as a product of associative learning (e.g. Abravanel *et al.*, 1976; Parton, 1976; Uzgiris and Hunt, 1975). Piaget's (1945) constructivist description of the infant's slow development of imitation was at that time unknown to most American psychologists. The North American discovery of Piaget (e.g. Elkind and Flavell, 1969) was followed by a brief period of developmental research confirming his major observations in American children. However, this enterprise was soon displaced by research seeking counter-examples to Piaget's stage theory of cognitive development, and in particular to his characterization of the cognitive abilities of infants.

Research on the origins of imitation has provided a particularly startling counter-example, in reports that infants from birth can imitate some simple behaviors from memory, including behaviors that they cannot even see themselves perform (see Anisfeld, 1996; Butterworth, 1999; Meltzoff, 2005 for summaries of this research). These reports have necessarily led theorists to propose that infants are able to represent and compare their own and other people's body parts and body part configurations from birth (e.g. Meltzoff, 2005; 2007a; 2007b; Meltzoff and Moore, 1997). Thus, newborn imitation implies that at least some body knowledge is innate.

Research on infant imitation has produced a range of claims of precocious cognitive feats in both newborns and older infants, including the proposals that newborn infants use imitation to probe the identities of their social partners (Meltzoff and Moore, 1992, 1994), and that older infants choose whether to imitate a model on the basis of their reasoning about contextual and motivational constraints on the model's actions (Gergely *et al.*, 2002; Schwier *et al.*, 2006; Zmyj *et al.*, 2009). However, researchers have paid less attention to questions concerning the development of imitation itself – for example, to the questions of what kinds of behaviors are matched by infants at different ages, or of how and why the quality of infants' behavioral matches may change over time.

The widespread belief that the ability to imitate is innate is likely a major reason for the small amount of work on the development of imitation. The assertion that a feature is innate often acts as a barrier to further psychological research. But many behaviors that appear to be innately hardwired have turned out on further study to have surprising developmental histories (e.g. Gottlieb, 1976, 2007; Kuo, 1932; Lehrman, 1953). For example, the ability of rat pups to find, attach to, and nurse from the mother immediately after birth turns out to depend crucially on prenatal, perinatal, and postnatal learning enhanced by specific sensory experiences provided by the behavior and body contours of the dam and by the compressions of birth itself (Alberts, 2008). Thus, the fact that a behavior appears to be innate should not discourage its study.

Furthermore, there is reason to doubt that the ability to imitate is in fact innate. Below, we will briefly review and weigh both the evidence that newborn infants can imitate and the evidence for an alternative explanation of those findings. We will conclude that the empirical basis for the widespread belief in an innate ability to imitate is not strong: thus, that belief should not discourage research aimed at producing a detailed, empirically based account of the postnatal emergence of imitation.

With such an account in mind, we will next present an overview of the comparatively sparse evidence on infants' imitative abilities beyond the newborn period. In general, the data indicate that infants are not able to imitate specific motor movements before their second year, although they may reproduce *effects* that they have observed – that is, they may *emulate* (Tomasello, 1998) – at earlier ages. The evidence also suggests that the ability to imitate is not a modular competency of the sort that could be inherited as a unit. Instead, it appears more likely to be a dynamic system – that is, a gradually emerging product of a complex of different cognitive, social, and motor competencies, each developed from a mixture of inherited and acquired features (e.g. Thelen and Smith, 1994).

In the remainder of the chapter we will focus on the particular component of imitation that is relevant to the topic of this book. That component is a competency in matching one's own body parts and actions to the body parts and actions of others. We will describe the development of behavioral matching in one infant from 3 to 15 months of age. The nature of this infant's progress in matching the behaviors modeled by her mother suggests that a potential mechanism for acquiring early body representations and body mappings is embedded in everyday imitative interactions between infants and their social partners. The mechanism we have in mind does not involve infants' imitations of others, for which body representations and interpersonal body mapping may well be prerequisites. Instead, it depends on the high number of interactions in which others imitate the infant.

Can newborn infants imitate?

The central questions in the study of cognitive development concern the origins of knowledge and of the processes by which knowledge is acquired, stored, retrieved, processed, and applied. The claim that newborn infants can imitate is a very important claim for the field because imitation requires quite a bit of knowledge, and imitation in newborns would be evidence that at least some of the required knowledge is innate. Meltzoff (2007a, 2007b; Meltzoff and Moore, 1997) has proposed that newborn infants possess a mechanism that automatically matches visual input from the behavior of others to mental representations of the infant's own behaviors to produce imitation. Similarly, neuroscientists have cited newborn imitation as support for the idea that a system of "mirror neurons" automatically matches observed behaviors with motor programs for performance of those same behaviors from birth (e.g. Iacoboni *et al.*, 1999; Rizzolatti and Craighero, 2004). Because the claim that newborns imitate is so important (and, on the face of it, so improbable), we should not accept it unless compelled by the evidence to do so. In our view, the best evidence for imitative abilities at birth is open to a second, more plausible explanation. Jones (2009a, 2009b) has recently laid out this view in some detail, and we will not repeat the entire discussion here, but will summarize the evidence and arguments.

The evidence for newborn imitation consists of multiple reports that newborn infants have selectively increased their rates of production of certain behaviors when in the presence of a model producing the same behaviors. What is actually observed in such studies, however, is not imitation. What is observed is behavioral matching: and imitation is only one of several reasons why the behaviors of two people might match (e.g. Want and Harris, 2002). While we follow the convention of referring to "newborn imitation" studies, we should bear in mind that behavioral matching is the observed phenomenon, whereas imitation is an interpretation of the observed phenomenon.

Infants in newborn imitation studies have reportedly matched adult models of a range of behaviors, including mouth opening, tongue protruding, sequential finger movements, pouting (e.g. Meltzoff and Moore, 1977), tongue protruding to the side (Meltzoff and Moore, 1994), head-circling (Meltzoff and Moore, 1989), and index finger movements (Nagy *et al.*, 2007). The list is made up entirely of behaviors that newborn infants commonly do. On the one hand, this is necessarily true: an experimenter cannot ask a neonate to imitate a behavior that is not yet in the infant's repertoire. On the other hand, we could be much more confident that an infant was imitating if they matched a behavior that they were very unlikely to produce spontaneously. For example, if an older infant watched a model put a puppet on his head, then put the puppet on their own head, we would infer that the infant's behavior was imitative because the probability that the infant would spontaneously put the puppet on their head was small.

Unfortunately, we cannot think of a single novel action by which imitation of low probability behavior in newborns could be tested. Still, the fact that all of the behaviors matched by infants in imitation experiments are also frequently produced by infants in everyday contexts raises questions about the usual conditions for production of those behaviors, and about whether those same conditions play a role in the increased rate of performance observed in imitation experiments. One obvious candidate cause for an increase in frequency of a common newborn behavior in both contexts is an increase in arousal.

Meltzoff and Moore (e.g. 1977, 1983) argued that newborn infants' matching of adult behavior could not be due to an increase in arousal. Increased arousal would be expected either to indiscriminately increase the frequencies of many behaviors, or to increase the frequency of the same "arousal response" across different situations. But newborn infants reportedly match only the specific behaviors they see modeled; and they reportedly match a range of different behaviors. Infants' selective matching of a variety of different behaviors can only be explained as imitation.

However, Meltzoff and Moore's (1977, 1983) characterization of newborn infants' behavior in imitation experiments was challenged by Anisfeld (1996, 2005), who carried out a meta-analysis of the entire body of data on newborn imitation and found that only one behavior – tongue protruding – was consistently matched. Anisfeld (1996) suggested that tongue protruding might in fact be an arousal response. This proposal is consistent with reports that newborn infants have increased their tongue protruding in response to a range of potentially arousing sensory experiences, including tactile stimulation of their palms (Humphrey, 1970); auditory stimulation from snippets of the *Barber of Seville Overture* (Jones, 2006); and visual stimulation from advancing and retreating objects (a pen and a small ball: Jacobson, 1979; Jacobson and Kagan, 1979), glimpses of the colorful interior of an opening and closing box (Legerstee, 1991), colored lights, and dangling toys (Jones, 1996). Given increased newborn tongue protruding in response to stimulation in three sensory modalities, it seems fair to conclude that tongue protruding is in fact a general arousal response in very young infants. Furthermore, it is likely that the sight of a tongue protruding model is just another interesting visual stimulus evoking that arousal response (Jones, 1996, 2009a).

In short, the evidence that newborn infants imitate is not compelling. And if there is no compelling evidence that newborn infants imitate, then there is no evidence that either the ability to imitate, or any of the body knowledge that imitation demands, is innate.

Infant imitation beyond the newborn period

If we do not have strong evidence that newborn infants can imitate, do we have other evidence to indicate when the ability to imitate does emerge? Jones (2009a) has recently addressed this question, so we will again summarize the evidence and conclusions from that review.

A small number of studies have tracked infants' matching of tongue protruding and mouth opening into the months just after the newborn period. The data show that matching of tongue protrusions rapidly declines and then disappears by 2 or 3 months of age (Fontaine, 1984; Heimann *et al.*, 1989; Jones, 1996). By the arousal account, this decline would reflect a change in the arousal value of the stimulus – the sight of the tongue protruding model – to the infant.

Other studies have attempted to document early infant imitation during natural social interactions (e.g. Kokkinaki, 2003; Kokkinaki and Kugiumutzakis, 2000; Masur and Rodemaker, 1999; Papousek and Papousek, 1989; Pawlby, 1977). These studies have found that *parents* imitate *infants* at prodigious rates in the first semester; but that infants match their parents' behaviors so infrequently that those matches must be attributed to chance.

Delayed or elicited imitation by infants between 6 and 12 months of age has been reported many times (e.g. Bauer, 1998; Barr *et al.*, 1996). However, in most cases, what is measured is the infants' reproduction of the *outcome* of the model's actions – that is, emulation (Tomasello, 1998; Want and Harris,

2002) – rather than the reproduction of those actions themselves. Emulation may reflect the infant's learning about the features and affordances of objects from watching another person interact with the object; but emulation does not require the infant to even notice, much less copy, the specific actions of the other person, or to have any cognitive access to representations of their own behavioral choices. For example, Barr and her colleagues (e.g. Barr *et al.*, 1996) have reported that infants as young as 6 months of age have imitated a model's 3-action sequence: removing a mitten from a puppet's hand, shaking the mitten to ring a bell inside, and replacing the mitten on the puppet's hand. However, a large majority (75 percent) of infants actually did only one of the actions – pulling off the puppet's mitten. It seems likely that infants might pull off the puppet's mitten, once they saw that this could be done, without any intention of imitating the model. In short, without more attention to how infants actually move in such studies, we cannot say that infants' matching of a model's actions on objects reflects any imitative intention or ability.

Meltzoff (1985, 1988a, 1988b) reported that infants 9, 14, and 20 months of age were able to remember modeled actions for later imitation. However, all of these were actions on objects, and the possibility that infants were emulating rather than imitating was not ruled out. For example, one action was shaking a plastic egg that contained small rattling objects when shaken by the experimenter. If an infant remembered that the egg had made a rattling sound, and if they had produced similar sounds by shaking objects in the past, then they might shake the egg during test and be credited with imitation despite having no memory at all of the experimenter's action on this object.

One behavior in Meltzoff's set is not subject to this criticism, as it involves a novel pairing of action and outcome. Matching of this behavior by infants, then, would be evidence that they did observe and reproduce the specific movements of the model. The behavior was tapping the forehead on the translucent surface of a box, to turn on a light inside the box. Unfortunately, Meltzoff (e.g. 1988b) credited infants with imitation not just when they tapped the box with their foreheads but also when they bent their heads to within 10 cm of the box. Because frequencies of these two behaviors were not separately reported and because infants could have other reasons for bending over the box – for example, to look into it – we cannot know how many of the infants in these studies actually imitated the model's movement. The same criticism applies to more recent reports of "rational" imitation by infants using the same light-box task scored in the same way (e.g. Gergely *et al.*, 2002; Zmyj *et al.*, 2009).

In an attempt to pin down the age range during which infants typically begin to imitate modeled movements (not when they begin to reproduce modeled outcomes), Jones (2007) tested infants from 6 to 20 months of age for their ability (or willingness) to imitate eight simple behaviors likely to be found in most infants' repertoires. Each infant's parent modeled four of the eight behaviors, giving the infant plenty of time (up to 3 minutes) and encouragement to match each behavior. Two of the behaviors – sequential finger movements and tongue protruding – were chosen from among those that newborn infants reportedly imitate.

The major measures in this study were the proportions of infants at each age level who produced each modeled behavior (1) during the period in which that behavior was modeled; and (2) during the modeling of each of the other three behaviors. Jones argued that infants should not be accorded the ability to imitate any of the behaviors until the age at which the proportion of infants matching the behavior while it was being modeled significantly exceeded the proportion spontaneously producing that same behavior while an entirely different behavior was being modeled. Only one behavior – making "Aah" sounds – met this criterion before the age of 12 months. The other behaviors met the criterion for imitation at different ages ranging from 12 to 18 months. The two behaviors reportedly imitated by newborn infants – sequential finger movements and tongue protrusions – did not meet the criterion for imitation until 16 and 18 months of age, respectively. By the age of 20 months – the maximum in this study – substantial proportions of the infants still failed to reproduce each of the tested behaviors.

Other studies have similarly reported limited imitative abilities in infants well into their second year. Masur (1998; Masur and Rodemaker, 1999) reported that infants aged 10 and 13 months old produced less than one instance of behavioral matching during experimental sessions. At 17 and 21 months, however, infants produced four or five instances on average. Abravanel *et al.* (1976) found that 15-month-olds reproduced only about one-third of twenty-two simple actions modeled for them. Nielsen and Dissanayake (2004) did not observe imitation until 18 to 21 months of age.

Together these studies indicate that there is no single answer to the question of when infants begin to imitate. Imitation of specific actions is sparse but detectable in the first half of the second year. However, imitation does not appear to be typical until later in the second year. Even at 18 or 20 months of age, the imitative abilities of infants are patchy, and depend on the specific actions modeled for them.

The wide spread in the ages at which infants in these descriptive studies begin to imitate different behaviors argues against the general idea that imitation is a unitary ability – a dedicated module, say, of the sort that might be inherited. The similarly wide spread in the ages at which different infants in Jones (2007) began to imitate the same behavior argues against the idea that the origins and developmental course of imitation are the same in different infants. Thus, if there is some biological preparation for human imitation, it clearly requires considerable elaboration by mechanisms that are sensitive to the idiosyncratic experiences of individuals.

Behavioral matching in one infant from 3 to 15 months of age

The descriptive data consistently depict imitation as a competency with an extended period of emergence later in infancy. However, those data do not have much to say about the mechanism(s) by which the ability to imitate emerges. In this section, one infant's behavioral matching through most of her first year and into her second will be described. Observations of this one infant suggest that the ability to match the behaviors of others is rooted in the thousands of social interactions in which the parent imitates the child (Jones, 2005). We do not mean to suggest that infants directly learn to imitate from being imitated – that they imitate imitation, so to speak. Rather, we propose that parental imitation provides infants with the body knowledge that is essential to the ability to imitate. In particular, the interactions we observed between this one infant and her parent presented the infant with the right kinds of information at the right times to teach her about the equivalencies between her body parts and actions, and the body parts and actions of her social partner.

Observing Yo

The subject of the study is Yo Anne, the daughter of the second author. Yoshida began the study as a subject rather than an investigator. She was invited to participate with her daughter in a longitudinal study of "mother–infant inter-action" that would focus on playful behaviors. One stated purpose among others was "to look at the baby's early imitative behavior." No mention was made of the fact that the mother's imitation of the infant would also be studied; and nothing was said about what the first author expected to observe.

Yo was videotaped between the ages of 3 and 15 months, as far as possible on a weekly schedule. Because Yo suffered the usual minor illnesses of infancy and also traveled a lot with her parents, the final record consists of thirty-one sessions distributed unevenly over the 12-month period.

In each session, Yo's mother played and talked with Yo for a minimum of 9–10 minutes. During this time, Yo was seated in either a reclining infant seat (to age 10 months, 16 days) or a high chair. Mother and infant were each videotaped by separate cameras feeding to a split screen with time and date superimposed on the combined image. Yoshida was made aware of the true purpose of the study and became a co-investigator when Yo was 7 months of age. Thereafter, the investigation became more experimental, as we attempted to elicit imitation from Yo in a variety of ways. Mother and infant interacted without any other objects until the fifteenth session, when Yo was 10 months 16 days of age. From that point on, toys and actions on toys became the focus of the interactions.

The videotapes were all transcribed as running narratives of time-marked behaviors produced by mother and infant. The two primary coders were unaware of the purpose of the study and knew little about research on imitation. The transcripts were examined for instances of behavioral matching – either the mother's matching of the infant's behavior or the infant's matching of the mother's behavior – within a 3-second timeframe. A 3-second maximum delay between observation and performance of the same action was chosen to minimize Type 1 errors and also to reflect the pace of turn-taking in this mother-daughter pair. Coding focused on each infant behavior and asked whether the mother had produced the same behavior as the infant within a 3-second period before the infant's behavior (infant imitation of mother) or within a 3-second period after the infant's behavior (mother imitation of infant).

Like parents and infants in previous studies (e.g. Kokkinaki and Kugiumutzakis, 2000; Parton, 1976), this mother consistently imitated her infant at high frequencies and this infant matched her mother's behaviors at what appeared to be chance levels. It soon became clear, however, that the most theoretically interesting aspects of the events which we were witnessing were not the frequencies with which each partner imitated the other. The new information on the development of behavioral matching was found instead in the descriptive narratives of the sequences of behavior produced by mother and infant at each session. Thus, it is from the narratives that the following observations are largely drawn.

The observations

At 2 months 29 days of age (2:29), in the first recorded session, Yo lay in an infant seat while her mother spoke to her, sang to her, tickled her, and played "peek-a-boo." Yo's mother did not model tongue protrusions, but Yo produced tongue protrusions in abundance: Yo's mean rate of tongue protruding across that session was 6.3 tongue protrusions per minute. The rate typically reported in neonatal imitation experiments is about 2.5. Thus, Yo's rate of tongue protruding in response to her mother's voice and touch was quite high and supports the proposal that tongue protruding is an arousal response in young infants.

In each of the next several sessions, Yo's mother *did* model tongue protrusions. In response to the sight of her mother's moving tongue, Yo simply stared. Like other infants beyond the newborn period (Fontaine, 1984; Heimann *et al.*, 1989; Jones, 1996), Yo did not produce any tongue protrusions while watching her mother model tongue protrusions. It is possible that Yo was captured by a strong orienting response to her mother's tongue movements, and that she might have produced tongue protrusions if her mother had become still, as adult models do in imitation experiments. However, the fact is that Yo at 3 months gave no indication that she could voluntarily find her tongue: and, despite having done countless tongue protrusions in her brief life, she gave no indication that she possessed a mechanism that would automatically map the tongue protrusions she saw onto a motor plan for tongue protrusions (Iacoboni *et al.*, 1999; Meltzoff, 2005, 2007a, 2007b). On the contrary: at 3 months and for many months thereafter, Yo did not match tongue protrusions – or anything else that her mother did.

Yo's mother, on the other hand, imitated Yo *a lot* throughout the study. This observation is consistent with the findings mentioned above (Kokkinaki and Kugiumutzakis, 2000; Masur and Rodemaker, 1999; Papousek and Papousek, 1989; Pawlby, 1977) that parents very frequently imitate their young infants during social interactions. In the early sessions, Yo's mother was not aware that her own behavior would be analyzed. Thus, the mother's spontaneous imitation of the infant could be measured. As the study progressed, Yo's mother began to actively participate in attempts to elicit imitation from Yo, so that the mother's imitation of the infant was no longer naïve and spontaneous. Nevertheless, as will become clear below, we had abundant evidence that both of Yo's parents frequently imitated certain actions across the entire period of the study.

In early sessions, Yo's mother frequently imitated Yo's vocalizations, facial expressions, and head movements. In the first session, Yo's mother imitated Yo thirty times in 9 minutes ($M = 3.33$ instances per minute). Nineteen of these were imitations of sounds the baby made: eleven were instances of actions – tilting the head, raising eyebrows, facial expressions, and touching the face with a hand. At that rate, assuming something like 1–2 cumulative hours of interaction with parents and other social partners each day, Yo could have experienced from 200 to 400 instances of imitation of her own sounds and actions in a single day. In 1 month, she could have experienced 6,000 to 12,000 instances; in 6 months, 36,000 to 72,000 instances.

Imitation appears to be the parent's attempt to make a social connection with the very young infant, and it is doubtful that the initially high rates of parental imitation persist as the infant becomes increasingly responsive. However, even by more conservative estimates, Yo must have been imitated tens of thousands of times in her first year. It is these thousands of instances of parents imitating their infants that we think may be a key source of body knowledge for infants, and thus a key source of one indispensable component of the ability to imitate. Every time Yo's mother imitated Yo's behavior, Yo's sensorimotor experiences – including visual, auditory, and proprioceptive sensations produced by her own action – were immediately followed by her sensory experiences – visual, auditory, and/or somatosensory – of her mother's matching action. This experience was certainly repeated many times for some specific actions that became familial play routines. Given the likely number of repetitions of these contiguous events, it would be remarkable if Yo did *not* form strong associations among all of these sensory and motor experiences both within and across modalities. Thus, it is very likely that Yo learned to associate her own movements with the same movements produced by her mother; and to associate the parts of her body that produced those actions with the parts of her mother's body that produced the contiguous actions.

Such an associative learning mechanism could be very important in developing the infant's ability to match her own actions and body parts to those of others, given that the perceptual matches between these objects and events from the first-person and second-person perspectives are often not very good. It seems very *un*likely that Yo would initially be aware of matches between her own actions and the same actions produced by her imitating mother. Nevertheless, Yo would be acquiring a mapping of her body parts and actions to the body parts and actions of her mother in the form of associative links – and this mapping would prepare her to eventually recognize the match between her mother's actions and her own. In short, Yo could acquire a lot of the grounding for the body knowledge and body mapping ability she needed to imitate others as a product of her multiple experiences of *being imitated by* others.

Although body knowledge is necessary for imitation, it is obviously not sufficient. Other components, including some social understanding, and the motivation and intention to imitate are also needed, and we do not know when these develop. So we would not expect Yo to begin imitating as soon as she had learned to associate her body parts and actions with those of her social partners. However, we *would* expect to see Yo *match* her mother's behaviors before all of these components were in place, because some of her mother's behaviors had become learned cues for infant behaviors that just happened to match. That is, once an association was formed between an action produced by Yo and an immediately imitative action by Yo's mother, we would expect to see the mother's action gain the power to elicit a very similar action from Yo.

And that is what we believe we saw. Yo's first matches of her parents' actions appeared to be responses to learned sensory/perceptual cues. What is remarkable to us is that *all* of this infant's behavioral matches, up to 15 months of age, appeared to be responses to acquired cues. We did not see a single clear instance of imitation in any of our taped sessions.

Yo produced her first behavioral match in the lab at age 10:16. The first matched action was "air kissing" – making loud kissing sounds with pursed lips. Yo had often done this spontaneously at home, and both parents had often imitated her. During our session at 10:16, Yo's mother was first to make the air-kissing sound; and after many repetitions, Yo eventually made a similar sound. Again, this was the first instance of Yo's behavioral matching recorded in the lab after more than 7 months of observations! It seemed likely that Yo's air kissing was not imitation but rather a response to the sound cue provided by her mother's air kissing.

Along with "air kissing" with sounds, Yo's mother imitated Yo's "la-la-la" babbles, using exaggerated open-mouthed tongue movements. Yo's mother also frequently reproduced Yo's hand actions, for example imitating Yo's hand smacks on the high chair tray. Often, Yo's mother imitated an action performed by Yo, and added to it an interpretation and a unique sound: so, for example, when Yo extended one arm or both arms forward in a horizontal plane, her mother would say "Gimme five!" and lightly slap one of Yo's palms with her own.

Eventually, Yo's mother could produce an action with an accompanying sound, and Yo would respond on cue with the same action. But this was not imitation. Instead, in every case, Yo appeared to be responding to an acquired sound cue. Yo gave no evidence that she could imitate any behaviors outside of well-practiced routines, or that she was in any way aware that her behavior matched that of her mother.

Crucially, *all* behavioral matches produced by Yo were actions (1) originally initiated by Yo herself, (2) that either produced or were accompanied by sounds, and (3) that Yo's parents imitated (either imitating Yo's sounds or supplying a standard accompanying sound) repeatedly over many weeks, until (4) the day came when Yo's mother produced the behavior and sound first, and Yo responded with the same behavior.

The importance of the sound cues is evident in an example at age 11:7. Yo's mother held a toy raccoon, tapped the high chair tray with its plastic nose, then gave the raccoon to Yo. Yo pushed the raccoon aside in order to smack the tray with her open palm. It seemed clear that Yo's intention was to reproduce the sound of the tapping, not her mother's action on the object. When Yo was aged 11:21, her mother modeled tonguing twice – first with "la-la" sounds and several minutes later without intentionally making sounds, although one could hear slight sloppy noises as her tongue moved. Yo responded to her mother's tonguing with "la-la" sounds by moving her own tongue in and out of her mouth. However, she responded to her mother's tonguing without "la-la" sounds with air kissing – apparently responding, not to the sight of her mother's moving tongue, but to the slight sounds that her mother's moving tongue produced.

So it appeared that Yo, at almost 1 year of age, still could not find her tongue based on visual input from her mother's behavior. What does this say, then, about newborn tongue protruding? It does not seem likely that a newborn could imitate tongue protruding, when an 11-month-old could not. And what does this say about the likelihood that Yo was born with a mechanism that automatically matched visual input from others' behaviors to motor programs for behaviors in her own repertoire (Iacoboni *et al.*, 1999; Meltzoff, 2007a, 2007b)? If Yo possessed such a mechanism, the sight of the mother's tongue movements should have been automatically matched with Yo's well-practiced motor program for the production of tongue protrusions, resulting at least sometimes in Yo's production of tongue protrusions. But there was no evidence that any of this took place.

Yo had already matched her mother's tonguing *with* sounds at age 10:16 – but then, the tonguing sounds (the "la-la-las") were something Yo frequently

produced by herself in repetitive sequences. It is likely, as Piaget (1945) proposed, that her mother's tonguing sounds functioned in the same way as Yo's
own sounds, to cue repetitions of the tongue movements in a circular reaction. Yo
did not match the very same tongue movements *without* sound until age 13:25.

Here is another example: Yo, like many infants, sometimes raised both arms
and vocalized, as though asking to be picked up. For months, whenever Yo did
this, her mother responded with her own bilateral arm raises and an enthusiastic
"Bonsai!". At the 11:7 session, Yo's mother repeatedly showed Yo bilateral arm
raises while silent, and then several minutes later showed the same arm movements while saying the word "Bonsai!". Yo did not respond with any upward
arm movements, either to the sound cue or to silent arm raises. Instead, when
her mother raised her arms and said "Bonsai!", Yo first looked up, then pointed
at the ceiling. Because Yo's mother was imitating Yo's own arm raises, there
is no doubt that the "motor program" for arm raises should have been in the
baby's repertoire. But Yo did not imitate arm raises when she saw them. Yo first
did arm raises after the sound cue "Bonsai!" at 12:14. She did not raise her arms
at the sight of her mother's *silent* arm raises until aged 14:2.

As with these arm raises, all of Yo's matching of movements with no sounds
in the late stages of the study was confined to actions that had previously been
associated with sounds in one or another of the well-practiced routines – only
now, Yo could do them without the sound cues. So Yo's actions were still
learned associates, not imitations, of her mother's actions. And there were still
doubts about whether any of the behaviors were cued by visual input alone. For
example: when Yo was 12:7, Yo's mother had for several weeks been modeling
putting an object on her own head, with no effect on Yo's behavior. During this
session, Yo's mother tapped the top of her own head with a cone-shaped object
(about 16 cm tall), then handed the object to Yo. Yo brought the object close to
the side of her head and we thought that she was finally going to imitate her
mother's action. However, what Yo had noticed and we had not was that Yo's
mother, while tapping her own head with the cone, had been repeating in the
same rhythm a single nonsense sound. Instead of tapping her head with the cone
as we expected, Yo held the object against her ear as though it was a telephone,
and vocalized. Yo's mother interpreted Yo's action just this way, laughing and
saying "hello" in Japanese – a word that sounds very like the syllables she
had previously repeated. Yo's mother reported that she often said "hello!" when
Yo touched her ear with an object. Thus, once again, Yo appeared to be acting
in response to learned sound cues, not to the visual input from her mother's
modeled action.

One week later (age 12:15), Yo's mother modeled tapping her own head with
a plastic stacking ring, again with accompanying sound cues. She repeatedly
offered the ring to Yo, who repeatedly handed it back. However, during one of
these exchanges, while Yo still held the ring, Yo's mother touched the top of

Yo's head with her hand, then lifted the plastic ring, still in Yo's two hands, to lie flat on the top of Yo's head. When Yo's mother let go, Yo lowered the ring, still in her two hands, then raised her hands again and replaced the ring on her head.

An observer seeing this single exchange in isolation might easily have taken it for an instance of imitation. However, the whole sequence suggested instead that Yo was reproducing, not the action she saw, but the sensations (the touch to the top of her head) that she had just felt. This interpretation is supported by one more observation. A few minutes later, Yo's mother again modeled putting the object on her own head, but did not touch Yo's head. She then handed the ring to Yo. But Yo did not attempt to put it on her own head – we think because this time, there was no immediately preceding sensory experience (of a touch to her head) to reproduce.

That Yo knew how to reproduce the sensation of the ring touching the top of her head was in its own way impressive – but once again, it was not imitation. It was not imitation because the infant did not reproduce her mother's specific movements: rather, she reproduced the outcome of her mother's action. Thus, at best, this was an instance of emulation.

When Yo was 13:4, her mother put a stacking ring on her own head, then bent her head to let the ring slide off. Yo immediately put a ring on her own head. Thus, the sight of her mother's action by itself was now enough to elicit a similar action from Yo. Note, however, that the infant's matching of the mother's behavior was still at least partially elicited by a learned cue. Yo's mother had been doing the same action in every session (and at home) for several weeks by this time, and had many times raised Yo's hand with a plastic ring grasped in it to make Yo's ring touch the top of her head. Thus, Yo had had ample opportunity to learn to associate the sight of her mother's action with her own arm movements that brought the ring to the top of her head, and/or to associate the sight of her mother's action with a sensation of touch on her head that she was independently able to produce. She might thus have been cued by the sight of her mother's action to produce an action – contacting her own head with the ring she held – that was associated with that sight, without necessarily knowing that the two actions matched. Thus, we have no evidence that the infant acted *in order to* reproduce her mother's behavior, and so no evidence that Yo's action was imitation.

To really convince us that she was imitating her mother, Yo would have had to reproduce one of her mother's actions the first time she saw it. But reproduction of actions on the first day they were introduced was not observed *at all* during the entire study. Instead, every attempt to get Yo to match an action of her mother's that was not already part of a play routine was a failure. Again, we are talking about actions that Yo had often spontaneously produced and that therefore should have been "motor plans" in her repertoire. For example: when Yo was 12:0, her mother gave her one of two identical stuffed bears, then modeled kissing and hugging of the second bear. Kissing and hugging were certainly actions that Yo had in her repertoire. Yo, at 1 year of age, just watched her mother with interest while dangling the bear from one hand.

We were forced by circumstances to stop filming at 15 months. By that time, Yo readily and accurately matched a variety of her mother's behaviors with no hesitation, and generalized matched behaviors – for example, kissing – to new objects. However, right to the end of the study, we did not observe even one instance of Yo's immediate reproduction of a modeled behavior, either transitive or intransitive, that was not part of a familiar play routine that had evolved out of parental imitation of the infant's behavior.

Insights from observing Yo

The findings from this case study are consistent with and bolster those from the normative study of 6- to 20-month-old infants. Yo's developmental course suggests that the ability to imitate is not innate, and that there is no functional "mirror system" or "supramodal act space" available to infants – at least until sometime beyond 15 months of age.

Importantly, the study strongly suggests that *the experience of being imitated* provides associative learning opportunities that may be vital to the development of the ability to imitate. Specifically, parental imitation of an infant's actions puts the visual, auditory, and/or somatosensory input from the parent's movements side-by-side with the infant's sensory-perceptual feedback from her own movements. This is so common in parent–infant interaction that we can assume that the infant forms associations among all of the sensory-perceptual features of the two experiences.

Yo's data suggest that the first associations to affect the infant's behaviors are associations between the sounds made by the infant and the imitating parent. Piaget (1945) believed that this was true, though he did not write in terms of learned associations. Next we see evidence of associations between those sounds and specific movements. Finally, we see evidence of associations between visual input from the actions of others and the infant's experiences of her own actions, as the silent movements of another come to elicit similar movements from the infant.

We propose one further step – one that Yo may have taken but that our method did not reveal – in which the matching behaviors that are first produced by the parent alone, and that are subsequently produced as cued responses by the infant, are eventually recognized by the cognitively more sophisticated infant as behaviors belonging to the same category. This recognition may be facilitated when the behaviors become functionally linked – that is, when the infant observes that the associated behaviors achieve the same outcomes on objects – or when those outcomes are labeled with the same words.

Thus, the strong tendency of infants' social partners to imitate the infants' behaviors is likely to contribute substantially to the development of cognitive representations of the appearance and locations of infants' own body parts; of the relations among them; and of the movement capabilities of those parts, by association with infants' observations of the body parts and movements of others. This learning process is a long one: the data from Yo and from several cross-sectional studies (Abravanel *et al.*, 1976; Horne and Erjavec, 2007; Huang and Charman, 2005; Jones, 2007; Masur, 1998; Vallotton and Harper, 2006) indicate that it extends well into the second year. Our everyday experience suggests that behavioral matching acquired from being imitated extends even further into childhood. As a last example: one visitor to our lab described to us how her adult daughter, having read about newborn imitation of tongue protrusions in her baby book, stuck out her tongue whenever her newborn son protruded his tongue even slightly. Now, at age 2½, our visitor's grandson responds to tongue protrusions performed by his mother and grandmother by poking just the tip of his tongue through his lips. His mother has repeatedly tried to correct him, saying "No, like this!" and sticking out her tongue to its full extent – but her son continues to respond with tiny tongue protrusions. This boy's behavior makes sense if his tiny tongue movements are not attempts to imitate his mother, but are instead the movements that he associates with the sight of his mother's tongue protrusions. If he is responding to her behavior but not imitating her behavior, then he may not only be unconcerned that his behavior doesn't match very well – he may not know that it matches at all.

Conclusions

True imitation – the ability to freely reproduce the movements of others – requires extensive and detailed representations of the bodies of both the imitator and the entity being imitated, and mappings of each to the other. For this reason, research on the development of imitation can be a good source of information about when and how such representations and mappings develop.

Our case study of behavioral matching by Yo suggests that parents' imitation of their infants is central to the development of two crucial components of a dynamic imitation system – the infant's knowledge of her own body parts and actions, and the infant's ability to map that knowledge onto her knowledge of the body parts and actions of others. As other contributions to this volume will illustrate, there are many potential sources of infants' body representations. However, we believe that acquired associations between closely contiguous sensory experiences produced by one's own action and the same action produced by an imitating social partner may provide an important route to infants' awareness of their own actions; to their ability to isolate and identify sensations produced by their own actions; and thus to their eventual ability to reproduce those actions at will. Parental imitation of infant actions may be even more important as a route to infants' body mapping abilities – that is, to infants' abilities to recognize the body parts and actions of others as like their own, and to analyze those actions into sequences of specific movements of specific body parts by association with their own action experiences.

At present, we can only offer this sketchy description; but we believe that a view of imitation as a multi-component dynamic system with an extended, piecemeal, and complex developmental course provides the best fit to existing empirical evidence and the most promising approach to future research on how the components of the imitation system develop and combine to enable the free, voluntary reproduction of the actions of others.

References

Abravanel, E., Levan-Goldschmidt, E., and Stevenson, M. B. (1976). Action imitation: The early phase of infancy. *Child Development*, **47**(4), 1,032–1,044.

Alberts, J. R. (2008). The nature of nurturant niches in ontogeny. *Philosophical Psychology*, **21**(3), 295–303.

Anisfeld, M. (1996). Only tongue protruding modeling is matched by neonates. *Developmental Review*, **16**(2), 149–161.

(2005). No compelling evidence to dispute Piaget's timetable of the development of representational imitation in infancy. In S. Hurley and N. Chater (eds). *Perspectives on Imitation: From Cognitive Neuroscience to Social Science*, Vol. II (107–131). Cambridge, MA: MIT Press.

Barr, R., Dowden, A., and Hayne, H. (1996). Developmental changes in deferred imitation by 6- to 24-month-old infants. *Infant Behavior and Development*, **19**(2), 159–170.

Bauer, P. (1998). Development of memory in early childhood. In N. Cowan and C. Hulme (eds). *The Development of Memory in Childhood* (83–112). New York: Psychology Press.

Butterworth, G. (1999). Neonatal imitation: Existence, mechanisms and motives. In J. Nadel and G. Butterworth (eds). *Imitation in Infancy* (63–88). New York: Cambridge University Press.

Elkind, D. and Flavell, J. H. (eds) (1969). *Studies in Cognitive Development: Essays in Honor of Jean Piaget*. New York: Oxford University Press.

Fontaine, R. (1984). Changes in imitative behavior during early infancy. *Infant Behavior and Development*, **9**, 415–421.

Gergely, G., Bekkering, H., and Kiraly, I. (2002). Rational imitation in preverbal infants. *Nature*, **415**(6,873), 755.

Gottlieb, G. (1976). The roles of experience in the development of behavior and the nervous system. In G. Gottlieb (ed.). *Neural and Behavioral Specificity* (25–54). San Diego, CA: Academic Press.

(2007). Probabilistic epigenesis. *Developmental Science*, **10**(1), 1–11.

Heimann, M., Nelson, K. E., and Schaller, J. (1989). Neonatal imitation of tongue protrusion and mouth opening: Methodological aspects and evidence of early individual differences. *Scandinavian Journal of Psychology*, **30**, 90–101.

Horne, P. J. and Erjavec, M. (2007). Do infants show generalized imitation of gestures? *Journal of the Experimental Analysis of Behaviour*, **87**, 63–87.

Huang, C.-T. and Charman, T. (2005). Gradations of emulation learning in infants' imitation of actions on objects. *Journal of Experimental Child Psychology*, **92**(3), 276–302.

Humphrey, T. (1970). The development of human fetal activity and its relation to postnatal behavior. In H. W. Reese and L. P. Lipsitt (eds). *Advances in Child Development and Behavior*, Vol. V (2–57). New York: Academic Press.

Iacoboni, M., Woods, R. P., Brass, M., Bekkering, H., and Mazziotta, J. C. (1999). Cortical mechanisms of human imitation. *Science*, **286**, 2,526–2,528.

Jacobson, S. W. (1979). Matching behavior in the young infant. *Child Development*, **50**, 425–430.

Jacobson, S. W. and Kagan, J. (1979). Intepreting "imitative" responses in early infancy. *Science, New Series*, **205**(4,402), 215–217.

Jones, S. S. (1996). Imitation or exploration? Young infants' matching of adults' oral gestures. *Child Development*, **67**(5), 1,952–1,969.

(2005). Why don't apes ape more? In S. Hurley and N. Chater (eds). *Perspectives on Imitation: From Cognitive Neuroscience to Social Science*, Vol. I (297–301). Cambridge, MA: MIT Press.

(2006). Exploration or imitation? The effect of music on 4-week-old infants' tongue protrusions. *Infant Behavior and Development*, **29**(1), 126–130.

(2007). Imitation in infancy: The development of mimicry. *Psychological Science*, **18**(7), 593–599.

(2009a). The development of imitation in infancy. *Philosophical Transactions of the Royal Society B*, **346**, 2,325–2,335.

(2009b). Imitation and empathy in infancy. *Cognition, Brain, Behavior*, **13**, 391–413.

Kokkinaki, T. (2003). A longitudinal, naturalistic and cross-cultural study on emotions in early infant–parent imitative interactions. *British Journal of Developmental Psychology*, **21**, 243–258.

Kokkinaki, T. and Kugiumutzakis, G. (2000). Basic aspects of vocal imitation in infant–parent interaction during the first 6 months. *Journal of Reproductive and Infant Psychology*, **18**, 173–187.

Kuo, Z. Y. (1932). Ontogeny of embryonic behavior in Aves, Vol. IV. The influence of embryonic movements upon the behavior after hatching. *Journal of Comparative Psychology*, **14**, 109–122.

Legerstee, M. (1991). The role of person and object in eliciting early imitation. *Journal of Experimental Child Psychology*, **51**, 423–433.

Lehrman, D. S. (1953). A critique of Konrad Lorenz's theory of instinctive behavior. *The Quarterly Review of Biology*, **28**(4), 337–363.

Masur, E. F. (1998). Mothers' and infants' solicitations of imitation during play. *Infant Behavior and Development*, **21**, 559.

Masur, E. F. and Rodemaker, J. E. (1999). Mothers' and infants' spontaneous vocal, verbal, and action imitation during the second year. *Merrill-Palmer Quarterly*, **45**, 392–412.

Meltzoff, A. N. (1985). Immediate and deferred imitation in 14- and 20-month-old infants. *Child Development*, **56**, 62–72.

(1988a). Infant imitation and memory: 9-month-olds in immediate and deferred tests. *Child Development*, **59**, 217–225.

(1988b). Infant imitation after a 1-week delay: Long-term memory for novel acts and multiple stimuli. *Developmental Psychology*, **24**(4), 470–476.

(2005). Imitation and other minds: The "like me" hypothesis. In S. Hurley and N. Chater (eds). *Perspectives on Imitation: From Neuroscience to Social Science*, Vol II (55–78). Cambridge, MA: MIT Press.

(2007a). "Like me": A foundation for social cognition. *Developmental Science*, **10**(1), 126–134.

(2007b). The "like me" framework for recognizing and becoming an intentional agent. *Acta Psychologica*, **124**, 26–43.

Meltzoff, A. N. and Moore, M. K. (1977). Imitation of facial and manual gestures by human neonates. *Science*, **198**(4,312), 75–78.

(1983). Newborn infants imitate adult facial gestures. *Child Development*, **54**(3), 702–709.

(1989). Imitation in newborn infants: Exploring the range of gestures imitated and the underlying mechanism. *Developmental Psychology*, **25**, 954–962.

(1992). Early imitation within a functional framework: The importance of person identity, movement, and development. *Infant Behavior and Development*, **15**, 479–505.

(1994). Imitation, memory, and the representation of persons. *Infant Behavior and Development*, **17**(1), 83–99.

(1997). Explaining facial imitation: A theoretical model. *Early Development and Parenting*, **6**, 189–192.

Nagy, E., Kompagne, H., Orvos, H., and Pal, A. (2007). Gender-related differences in neonatal imitation. *Infant Child Development*, **16**, 267–276.

Nielsen, M. and Dissnayake, C. (2004). Pretend play, mirror self-recognition and imitation: A longitudinal investigation through the second year. *Infant Behavior and Development*, **27**, 342–365.

Papousek, M. and Papousek, H. (1989). Forms and functions of vocal matching in interactions between mothers and their precanonical infants. *First Language*, **9**, 137–158.

Parton, D. A. (1976). Learning to imitate in infancy. *Child Development*, **47**, 14–31.

Pawlby, S. (1977). Imitative interaction. In H. R. Schaffer (ed.). *Studies in Mother–Infant Interaction* (203–223). London: Academic Press.

Piaget, J. (1945). *Play, Dreams, and Imitation in Childhood*. New York: W. W. Norton.

Rizzolatti, G. and Craighero, L. (2004). The mirror-neuron system. *Annual Review of Neuroscience*, **27**, 169–192.

Schwier, C., van Maanen, C., Carpenter, M., and Tomasello, M. (2006). Rational imitation in 12-month-old infants. *Infancy*, **10**(3), 303–311.

Thelen, E. and Smith, L. B. (1994). *A Dynamic Systems Approach to the Development of Cognition and Action*. Cambridge, MA: Bradford Books/MIT Press.

Tomasello, M. (1998). Emulation learning and cultural learning. *Behavioral and Brain Sciences*, **21**, 703–704.

Uzgiris, I. C. and Hunt, J. McV. (1975). *Assessment in Infancy*. Urbana, IL: University of Illinois Press.

Vallotton, C. D. and Harper, L. V. (2006). Why don't they just let it go? *Infant Behaviour and Development*, **29**(3), 373–385.

Want, S. C. and Harris, P. L. (2002). How do children ape? Applying concepts from the study of non-human primates to the developmental study of "imitation" in children. *Developmental Science*, **2**, 1–41.

Zmyj, N., Daum, M. M., and Aschersleben, G. (2009). The development of rational imitation in 9- and 12-month-old infants. *Infancy*, **14**(1), 131–141.

12   Infants' perception and production of crawling and walking movements

Petra Hauf and Michelle Power

Learning to move from one place to another is a major milestone in infants' development. First crawling and later walking, infants start to discover and explore the world around them from a new and independent perspective. Now they are able to crawl or walk to reach a desired toy without relying on help. Crawling and walking infants spend about half of their time during the day moving around, but most of the time that infants could move around, they do not (Adolph, 2002). Instead, they also spend time exploring and manipulating objects and watching others do the same. From early on, infants show a distinct preference for objects in motion. They enjoy watching the mobile moving above the crib, and enjoy even more moving the mobile by kicking it. The cat sneaking around or the dog running across the backyard catches their attention and often makes them squeal with glee. Long before infants are actually able to move on their own, they are attentive observers of motion in general and movements performed by others in particular.

Previous research in the area of motor development has focused on the question of when and how infants learn to crawl and walk (Adolph, 2008), while another branch of research has focused on how infants perceive motion (Bertenthal *et al.*, 1984). It has been demonstrated that before six months of age infants discriminate between walking point-light displays (PLDs) and randomly moving dots (Bertenthal *et al.*, 1984, 1987), indicating an early understanding of movements performed by others. Beyond that, it has been suggested that infants are born with a preference for biological motion (Simion *et al.*, 2008). But, the question of whether perception and production of crawling and walking movements are interlinked has been neglected in infant research so far. This is surprising given the fact that a link between the onset of self-locomotion and developmental changes in perception and cognition has been suggested for decades (Gibson, 1988; Piaget, 1953; for a review, see Campos *et al.*, 2000).

We would like to thank Virginia Slaughter and Celia Brownell for the motivation they provided on this project. This research was supported by the Canada Research Chair (CRC) Program in conjunction with the Canada Foundation for Innovation (CFI) and a grant from the Natural Sciences and Engineering Research Council of Canada (NSERC) to Petra Hauf.

This notion is further supported by recent research demonstrating that the ability to crawl enhances 9-month-old infants' flexibility in memory retrieval (Herbert *et al.*, 2007). The onset of crawling and walking also seems to correspond with major advances in social development as indicated by changes in social looking behaviour in relation to motor skills (Clearfield, 2011). In addition, infants need stimulating physical surroundings and warm care-giving to promote active exploration of the environment and proper attainment of developmental motor milestones (Bendersky and Lewis, 1994). But, the questions of how the perception and production of crawling and walking movements are linked to each other and how they influence each other remain open.

The current chapter will approach the issue of how the perception and production of major motor movements might be interrelated by incorporating a similar framework from the area of action understanding, which highlights bidirectional linkage of perceived and produced actions, into the field of motor development. Based on a short introduction of this notion of bidirectional influences, the current chapter will then present an overview of how infants learn to crawl and walk and of how infants perceive crawling and walking movements performed by others. What kind of challenges do they have to master before they are experienced crawlers and walkers and how do they perceive body movements like crawling and walking? Are they able to discriminate between bodily possible and impossible movements? Following this, the main section will relate infants' motor capacities to how they perceive motor movements. For example, do infants identify moving dots as crawling or walking? And do they have to be able to crawl and/or walk themselves to understand these movements? Finally, the idea of a bidirectional linkage between movement perception and production will be discussed with respect to possible implications for motor development and cognitive development.

Bidirectionality of perception and production in action understanding

Actions are defined as movements towards a goal associated with a desired effect. Interestingly, we perform and perceive actions in our everyday lives on a regular basis, often without paying much attention to them. For example, we reach for and grasp a cup to get a sip of coffee, almost automatically adjusting our motor movements to the environmental constraints of the action. We enlarge the opening of the hand if we grasp for the whole mug or we prepare our thumb and index finger if we plan to grasp the handle. In doing so, our actions are prepared and executed by an impressive interplay of sensory system, e.g. what we see, and motor system, e.g. how we move. But how is this interplay actually functioning?

Research on action control has focused on this question for many years. Whereas more traditional theories postulated a 'transformation system' to explain how sensory information stored in the sensory system can be co-ordinated with motor information stored in the motor system, newer approaches deny such a system exists. Any transformation between different systems would take too much time to enable us to act and react effectively. Therefore, the *common coding* approach introduced by Wolfgang Prinz (1990, 1997) argues that sensory information and motor information are stored in a shared representational system. These shared representations include visuospatial representations based on perception experience as well as sensorimotor representations based on motor experience and are used by both the sensory system during action perception to understand perceived actions and the motor system during action production to exhibit actions. This notion is supported by empirical evidence in different domains of adult cognitive psychology as demonstrated by studies investigating such areas as the timing of movements, compatibility effects, sequence learning and action perception (for an overview, see Hommel *et al.*, 2001; Prinz, 2002). Furthermore, research in neuroscience has demonstrated that the same brain regions are activated both when an action is observed and when it is produced (e.g. Decety, 1996; Decety *et al.*, 2002; Gallese, 2003; Hamilton *et al.*, 2004; Iacoboni, 2005). For example, the motor system is automatically activated during movement perception and when the observed behaviour is subsequently reproduced (see Brass and Heyes, 2005 for a recent review).

Importantly, the notion of common shared representations not only provides a framework to understand how perception possibly guides action production, it also suggests that motor experience influences how we perceive and understand actions performed by others. Despite the fact that the notion of shared representations of perceived and produced actions has been widely established in adult action understanding, the idea of such a bidirectional linkage has only recently been extended to infant action understanding (Hauf, 2007; Hauf and Prinz, 2005; Meltzoff, 2002, 2007). Current research suggests that a bidirectional linkage between perceived and performed actions is already established during the first year of life (Hauf, 2007; Longo and Bertenthal, 2006; Sommerville and Woodward, 2005), which raises the question of whether such an interdependence of sensory and motor systems is restricted to actions or might also be involved in motor movements per se. We will come back to this idea in more detail in the last section of this chapter. However, in order to consider the possibility of bidirectionality in motor development, we first need to establish how infants learn to move, how they come to understand movements performed by others and how the development of both might be interrelated.

How do infants learn to crawl and walk?

The onset of self-locomotion is a very important developmental accomplishment during the first year of life, closely related to the development of other – less obvious – psychological functions. Motor skills, such as crawling and walking among others, are developing in conjunction with perception and cognition (Adolph and Berger, 2005; Gibson and Pick, 2000). Infants' perception helps them to evaluate the current situation and informs them how to move and where to go. This perceptual information guides their movements and provides feedback about the consequences of moving (Adolph and Joh, 2007). In addition, cognitive processes are involved in crawling and walking. While infants move around they learn about their environment, they think about their goals and how to obtain them. They also need to remember where to move and why. Problem-solving is required to find a way to overcome obstacles and to discover new solutions for challenging motor problems. Supporting adequate development, motor actions, in turn, provide new information for the perceptual system as well as for cognition (Gibson, 1988; Piaget, 1953).

At around 4 to 5 months of age, infants rapidly gain eye–head control and are able to explore the world around them simply by looking from a distance. Later on, with the development of manual skills, they learn about objects and materials by reaching, grasping and manipulating them. A major milestone in motor development is accomplished when infants develop independent locomotion. Now, they can explore objects and surfaces in various locations on their own without relying on others' help. But how do they actually manage this developmental challenge? Are motor skills developing in a series of stages or do infants exhibit individual trajectories? And how much impact does the environment have on this development?

The onset of self-locomotion is typically happening in the first six months of life. Infants move their bodies by rolling from their bellies to their backs, not only changing positions but also moving from one location to another (Bly, 1994). Infants show individual preferences in moving: shuffling in a sitting position, crabbing on their backs, or pivoting. The same variety in moving is evident in crawling styles (Adolph *et al.*, 1998). Some infants begin crawling on their stomachs; others use only their arms and drag their legs behind. They might alternately use all four limbs at once before they actually fully crawl on their hands and knees. Not all infants crawl on their stomachs; some of them skip it and proceed straight to the hands-and-knees crawling, which occurs at approximately 8 months of age. Still others never crawl at all; instead their first successful self-locomotion is walking.

Recent research demonstrated that improvements in locomotor skills are experience-dependent (Adolph *et al.*, 1998). Not only does infants' crawling become faster with each week of crawling experience, but this experience is also a reliable predictor of developing advanced crawling skills. For example, infants with experience in prone movements were more skilful crawling on hands and knees than infants who did not crawl on their stomachs before (Adolph *et al.*, 1998), suggesting that infants use crawling patterns acquired earlier to enhance crawling skills later on.

With the mastery of crawling, infants are able to move effectively from one location to another. But, their hands are still occupied while moving, which compromises their possibilities to explore the world. Therefore, the next major achievement is to free up their hands by pulling themselves to standing and moving in an upright position (Bly, 1994). Typically this is done first by moving sideways, holding onto furniture or a helping hand for support (Adolph, 1997; Adolph *et al.*, 1998). At around their first birthday, infants begin taking independent walking steps (Bly, 1994). Again, improvements in walking are driven by experience. The first steps are tiny with their legs being splayed wide and toes pointing outward. This provides them with extra stability for keeping balance. The first walking movement is uneven because they try to keep both legs on the ground for as long as possible and lift each leg only for a very short time (Bril and Breniere, 1989, 1993). During the first months of walking, infants make rapid improvements: step length increases, step width and external rotation decreases and more time is spent with one foot in the air and less time with both feet on the ground (Adolph *et al.*, 2003).

As with crawling, walking experience predicts improvements in infants' walking skills better than their body dimensions or age (Adolph *et al.*, 2003), but there seems to be no transfer from one locomotion skill to another. For example, experienced crawlers avoid a steep, and therefore unsafe, slope when tested while crawling, indicating their ability to properly evaluate the environmental constraints. However, the same infants attempted to walk down the same slope when tested in their novice, and thus unfamiliar, walking posture (Adolph, 1997). So far, there is no evidence indicating any transfer from earlier developed postures to those developing later (Adolph, 2000, 2005, 2008). But how do infants actually manage the transition from crawling to walking? Recent research focuses on the challenges infants have to master before they are experienced crawlers and walkers and what this transition in self-locomotion looks like.

Typically, infants display a transition from crawling to sideways and forward cruising before they actually walk independently. Interestingly, the first steps cruising sideways require the infants to hold onto some kind of support, thus, still occupying their hands. Nevertheless, this change from 'crawling on four limbs' to 'moving upright with four limbs' (Vereijken and Adolph, 1999: 141) is an important precursor for independent walking. A longitudinal study by Adolph and colleagues (2003) demonstrated that most infants cruised sideways using separate and successive limb movements, in contrast to the consistent diagonal gait pattern in crawling. During the cruising period, limb movements increasingly overlap and the pauses between the movements decrease. Also, limb movements become more variable, changing quickly into forward cruising and then independent walking (Adolph *et al.*, 2003). Without any support, infants modify their walking to maintain upright balance resulting in shorter steps, higher cadence, less variability in interlimb phasing and more consistent step lengths, but with increasing experience in independent walking infants regain their balance and stability. Over weeks of walking, infants take longer steps, display smaller lateral distances between their feet, point their feet more straight ahead and maintain a straighter path of progression. In addition, step-to-step variability decreases (Adolph *et al.*, 2003). These findings suggest that deficiencies in infants' first weeks of walking may actually result from poor balance control during periods of standing on one foot (Adolph, 1997; Bril and Breniere, 1993) indicating a transition from walking with support to walking without support.

Ongoing practice with balance and locomotion is closely related to behavioural flexibility and problem-solving skills because motor experience facilitates infants' ability to manage novel and challenging tasks (Adolph and Joh, 2007). As demonstrated in recent research, everyday locomotor experience enhances speed and size of infants' crawling (Adolph *et al.*, 1998) and walking steps (Adolph *et al.*, 2003). Nevertheless, learning from practice typically requires more than one exposure. For example, in contrast to experienced walkers and adults who showed one-trial learning, novice walkers required several trials before they learned that a particular patch of ground would not support their weight even though the foam pit was distinctly marked by salient visual cues (Joh and Adolph, 2006). Also, experienced walkers take into account the environmental constraints while crossing bridges (Berger and Adolph, 2003). When bridges were wide, infants crossed the bridge without even noticing a handrail. But, when the bridges were narrower, infants crossed only when the handrail was available and solid (Berger *et al.*, 2005).

The onset of self-locomotion is the most dramatic motor achievement in the first year of life. First crawling and later walking reflect radical changes in infants' body structure, coordination and control. As infants' motor skills improve, new features of the environment are available for exploration. But the developing skills of crawling and walking, especially balance control, are challenged by the properties of the environment (Adolph *et al.*, 1993), which infants seem to master with practice (Adolph *et al.*, 2003). Experience, therefore, is a strong predictor and an important developmental factor for infants' accomplishment of crawling and walking movements (Adolph *et al.*, 1998, 2003). Furthermore, research suggests that motor skills develop in close interrelation with perception and cognition (Adolph and Berger, 2005; Adolph *et al.*, 2003; Gibson and Pick, 2000). Obviously perceptual information from the environment guides movements and is thus involved in crawling and walking, but how do infants perceive movements performed by others?

How do infants perceive crawling and walking?

From the first hours following birth, infants begin to take in the world around them. Some theorists believe that humans have an innate mechanism to perceive biological motion (Simion *et al.*, 2008). From a developmental perspective, this sensitivity to detect biological movement combined with infants' early abilities to recognise human body forms (Bertenthal *et al.* 1987; Moore *et al.*, 2007), has led to much research on how such perceptions evolve as infants gain exposure and visual experience by watching other walkers, and eventually as they themselves begin to crawl and walk. While infants' first experience with self-locomotion almost always begins with crawling behaviours, very little research has looked at infants' perception of crawling. Rather, most of the research focuses on infants' ability to detect biological motion, specifically normal human walking.

Visual experience observing others walking provides valuable information to young infants, and is the starting point of their knowledge base of human forms, recognition of their own and others' body shapes and schemas and their perception of different types of biological movement. Bertenthal (1993) suggests that such early exposure and increasing familiarity with human walking movements allows infants to store and later retrieve knowledge of a human form. This emerging body schema provides a framework for infants to organise sensory and motor information from their own bodies to create a picture of what their body looks like, such as where specific limbs are located and how they move, but it also helps organise infants' perceptions of other people's bodies, allowing them to understand and make predictions about a human body in motion.

Infants' early ability to distinguish biological motion from other types of motion is evident from research using PLDs. Biological motion, as reflected in adult human walkers, is reproduced by attaching lights to the head and major joints involved in locomotion (shoulders, elbows, hips, knees, ankles) and displaying the point lights against a black background with all human form removed (Bertenthal *et al.*, 1987; Johansson, 1973). Infants as young as 3 months preferentially look at the biological motion depicted in the normal human walking PLD compared to other types of motion such as randomly moving dots (Bertenthal *et al.*, 1987).

Beyond the preference they show for biological motion, infants' perception of differences in biologically possible and impossible human walking behaviour is particularly acute. 3-month-old infants discriminate between normal walking PLDs and ones that have spatially and temporally shifted the pattern of lights (Bertenthal *et al.*, 1987; Proffitt and Bertenthal, 1990). Additionally by 4 months of age, infants are aware of differences in the orientation of PLDs as evidenced by their ability to distinguish between upright and inverted human walkers (Bertenthal *et al.*, 1984).

While research has clearly shown that the ability to perceive motion and detect subtle perturbances in typical human locomotion is present very early in infants, less is known about what additional information infants may be extracting from the biological motion of the human walker PLDs they observe. Studies using PLDs have shown that 3-month-old infants are able to detect information about the action being performed, such as distinguishing walking from running (Booth *et al.*, 2002). Kuhlmeier *et al.* (2010) further examined whether 6-month-old infants could detect directionality in displays of point light walkers. The PLDs depicted walkers moving on either a leftward or rightward trajectory, but without translating movement across a horizontal plane. The PLD conveyed dynamic motion as if the figure were walking on a treadmill. Once habituated to PLDs moving in one direction, infants were able to detect changes in the direction of motion of upright human walkers. The effect was not observed when the PLD walkers were inverted, possibly due to the difficulty detecting a global human form in this orientation. Kuhlmeier *et al.* (in press) suggest that irrespective of the possible processing mechanisms underlying the ability to detect direction, infants do appear to be extracting information about the action being depicted in the display of biological motion.

If infants are able to extract action-related information from biological motion, is it possible that they also perceive features of the actor? That is, are infants able to gather information from human walking PLDs that helps to inform their developing body schema? Reid *et al.* (2008) filmed bodily possible human walking movements and then digitally manipulated them to create bodily impossible human movements (PLDs with knee joints circumflexing backwards in the manner of the rear legs of a horse). Using electroencephalogram (EEG) recordings to measure brain activity and calculate event-related potentials (ERPs), Reid and colleagues found that 8-month-old infants distinguished between bodily possible and impossible human movements. Further, these infants were able to perceptually discriminate normal human body schema from an altered one, suggesting that they detected violations to their developing representations of human body forms. In fact, the PLDs may be activating a whole-body schema in infants of this age, which makes bodily distortions more salient.

As infants begin to incorporate a body schema and apply it to their perception of biological motion in walking PLDs, they also begin to attribute physical properties to their representations of human forms. One such physical dimension of human bodies is solidity. Moore *et al.* (2007) speculate that when infants see biological motion in the form of walking human PLDs, their body schema is invoked and they attribute physical characteristics to the point-light figures. As a result, Moore and colleagues predicted infants would be more sensitive to motion that violates their human prototype, in particular the violation of solidity.

To test this notion, Moore *et al.* (2007) designed a series of experiments for 6- and 9-month-old infants. Initially, infants were habituated to a walking human PLD on a computer screen and then shown repeated trials of the PLD moving behind a table. In the final phase of the experiment, the PLD appeared to walk through the table – an impossible event for a solid human form and violation of the principle of solidity. Both age groups looked longer at the last display indicating the PLD triggered a body schema to which they had attributed a solid form. Interestingly, additional trials with inverted PLD figures and scrambled, non-human PLDs did not show the effect, suggesting that infants attribute the principle of solidity only to upright human forms.

While PLDs provide an effective method of studying infants' perception of biological motion, they are limited in what they can tell us about how infants overlay human body schemas on a display of moving dots. Biological motion in the human walker PLD appears to trigger a human body schema, but what physical or psychological properties of a human prototype are being translated is more difficult to determine. Previous findings suggest that in the first six months of life, infants perceive human locomotion and use it as an implicit foundation for their emerging prototype of human form, which includes basic features such as orientation, direction and action. Such a prototype of the human form helps provide young infants with a framework to begin to understand the movements, goals and intentions of others. As infants mature, however, so too does their body schema. Therefore, it is important to examine infants' understanding of the whole human body.

Slaughter *et al.* (2002) showed 12-, 15- and 18-month-old infants typical and scrambled pictures of human bodies. The stimuli included both line drawings and photographs of typical body shapes and bodies that had been scrambled to violate typical form (e.g. legs attached to shoulders and arms attached at hips). Slaughter *et al.* found that only 18-month-old infants looked longer at the scrambled bodies, suggesting that infants' understanding of the whole body form does not fully develop until after their first year of life. However, a more recent follow-up study by Heron and Slaughter (2010) claims that improving the realism of body form stimuli presented to infants (i.e. showing real people as opposed to drawings and photographs) greatly improved infants' ability to detect distortions in the body form. In the latter study, infants as young as 9 months distinguished typical from atypical body shapes, which implies that infants of this age do have elaborate representations of the human body. The more similar the stimuli are to actual human bodies, the more likely infants' body schema will be triggered.

Research on motion perception indicates that by around 9 months of age infants are able to discriminate between normal human walking PLDs and randomly moving dots; extract information about direction, actions and solidity from moving PLDs; and access an increasingly elaborate body representation. But how is this understanding related to their motor skills?

Relation of infants' motor production and perception

Recently, research in infancy started to focus on questions emphasising the relation of motor skills and movement perception. Infants start to move on their own at around 6 months of age. At first, they do so by rolling, but soon they are crawling and walking (Adolf, 2008; Bly, 1994). At this age infants are also able to discriminate between randomly moving dots and walking PLDs (Bertenthal *et al.*, 1987). But, how do they come to understand movements performed by others and how might this understanding be related to their own motor skills?

Reid *et al.* (2005) investigated 8-month-old infants' ability to perceive possible and impossible human grasping actions. Interestingly, infants with high fine motor skills in pressing buttons, holding objects and twisting toys, looked longer at impossible versus possible body movements. Furthermore, Gamma frequency analysis of EEG recordings indicated that infants with high fine motor skills processed the stimuli differently than those same-aged infants with low fine motor skills (Reid *et al.*, 2005).

A similar relation of motor experience and perception of movements performed by others has been demonstrated in experienced crawlers (van Elk *et al.*, 2008). 14- to 16-month-old infants watched a video display of a crawling and walking toddler while their EEG was recorded. A stronger mu- and beta-desynchronisation was only found for watching the crawling movement, not for watching the walking movement. Interestingly, the effect was strongly associated with the infants' own crawling experience, indicating a close relation of motor experience and motor perception (van Elk *et al.*, 2008). Sanefuji *et al.* (2008) used PLDs of crawling and walking adults to examine whether crawling and walking infants display a preference for watching one movement or the other. The findings revealed a clear looking preference related to the level of motor skills: crawling infants preferred to look at the crawling PLD, whereas walking infants preferred to watch the walking PLD. Infants seem to change their looking preference for the type of locomotion that corresponds to their current motor skills.

In line with this assumption, Christie and Slaughter (2009), using a body perception task, specifically investigated the relation of sensorimotor representation based on motor experience and visuospatial body knowledge. Infants' body representation was tested via a human body visual discrimination task (see Slaughter and Heron, 2004 for a detailed description). In this task, infants aged 6 to 15 months were habituated to a typical body image and then tested with a series of scrambled body images (e.g. legs attached to the head, arms coming out of the hips). Fine and gross motor skills were assessed as well as the gross motor activity during the body discrimination task. Clear age-dependent trends in recognition of the human body shape and sensorimotor development were found, but the data did not reveal a consistent correlation between infants' motor skills and their perception of body images (Christie and Slaughter, 2009). These findings suggest that by 15 months of age, visuospatial and sensorimotor body representations are not yet linked to each other. However, this does not contradict the notion that motor experience and movement perception are closely linked to each other early in life. It could easily be argued that experience producing and perceiving movements is involved in the development of both sensorimotor and visuospatial body knowledge.

In order to look at this possibility in more detail, a study by Hauf, Giese, and MacDonald (in preparation) investigated the relation of motor experience and movement perception in infants and toddlers. The study focused on the question of whether infants and toddlers identify moving dots as crawling and walking humans and whether different levels of motor skills influence the perception of these movements performed by others. Eye-tracking technology was introduced to record infants' looking behaviour in detail. 6.5-month-old non-crawling and non-walking infants, 9.5-month-old crawling but non-walking infants and 13.5-month-old crawling and walking infants watched six videos presenting adult crawling and walking PLDs. Each of the movements was presented in a normal version, a phase-shifted version and as randomly moving dots. All stimuli presented biological motion, but only the normal crawling and walking movements were bodily possible movements, whereas the phase-shifted version violated body constraints by altering the temporal ratio of the movement. A 45/100 ratio was used to shift the point lights in the bodily impossible version. Infants' eye movements were recorded with respect to the overall display and special areas of interest (AOI). The lower body AOI covered the body parts performing the actual movement (arms, hands, knees and feet for the crawling movement, and feet, knees and legs for the walking movement), whereas the upper body AOI covered the rest of the body parts, those not directly involved in the movement production. In addition, infants' motor skills were assessed using the Fine and Gross Motor Scales of the Bayley Scales of Infant and Toddler Development III (Bayley, 2006).

The motor assessment confirmed profound differences in the fine and gross motor skills between the age groups, whereas infants within each age group demonstrated comparable fine and gross motor skills. Eye tracking data revealed no differences in overall looking time. The infants of all age groups watched the different crawling and walking movements equally long. Also, no differences were found for the upper body AOI, which covered the body parts

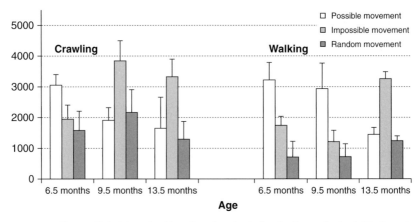

Figure 12.1 Mean looking duration (ms) for the lower body AOI. Data is depicted for 6.5-, 9.5- and 13.5-month-old infants while watching possible and impossible movements as well as randomly moving dots

not directly involved in the movement production. In contrast, differences in looking time were found for the lower body AOI (see Figure 12.1). Non-crawling infants (6.5 months old) looked longer at the lower AOI while watching the normal crawling compared to the phase-shifted, thus bodily impossible, crawling and the randomly moving dots. On the contrary, crawling infants (9.5 and 13.5 months old) looked longer at the lower AOI while watching the bodily impossible crawling movement compared to the normal crawling and the randomly moving dots. All groups of infants discriminated between the stimuli, but displayed different looking behaviour for the lower AOI of the crawling movement depending on their crawling experience (Hauf, Giese, and MacDonald, in preparation). A similar result pattern was found for the looking behaviour while watching the walking movement. Non-walking infants (6.5 and 9.5 months old) looked longer at the lower AOI while watching the normal walking compared to the bodily impossible walking and the randomly moving dots, whereas walking infants (13.5 months old) looked longer at the lower AOI while watching the bodily impossible walking compared to the normal walking and randomly moving dots. Again, all groups of infants discriminated between the stimuli, but displayed different looking behaviour for the lower AOI of the walking movement depending on their walking experience (Hauf, Giese, and MacDonald, in preparation). These findings indicate that the level of motor experience – here crawling versus walking – influences how infants look at these movements. Infants not yet able to perform a certain movement look longer at the normal display, whereas infants experienced in producing the movement look longer at the display violating body constraints (Hauf, Giese, and MacDonald, in preparation).

Research on motor development has shown that improvements in motor skills depend on experience. Crawling becomes faster with each week of crawling experience, and novice walkers show different movement patterns than experienced walkers (Adolph *et al.*, 1998, 2003). Therefore, it could be assumed that novice walkers perceive walking movements differently than experienced walkers. But what about movements that children are capable of, but do not regularly perform anymore? A comparison of novice and experienced walkers revealed interesting differences in the perception of crawling and walking PLDs (Hauf, Geangu, and Williams, in preparation). The same crawling and walking movements as in the previous study were now presented to experienced walkers (3-years-old). No differences in the overall looking time and the upper body AOI were found. However, the toddlers spent more time looking at the lower body AOI while watching the bodily impossible walking movement compared to the normal walking and the randomly moving dots. These findings duplicate the looking behaviour of the novice walkers, indicating that increased motor experience did not influence motor perception. However, differences in looking behaviour were found with respect to the crawling movement. Whereas the novice walkers, who were also experienced crawlers, demonstrated the same looking pattern for the crawling and the walking movement, this was not the case for the toddlers. The 3-year-old experienced walkers looked equally long at the lower body AOI while watching the normal and bodily impossible crawling movement and the randomly moving dots (Hauf, Geangu, and Williams, in preparation). These findings suggest that several aspects of motor experience influence movement perception. The capability to perform the crawling or walking movement is only one factor. Whether the respective movement is actually used for self-locomotion on a regular basis seems to have an equally important impact on the perception of movements.

Taken together, recent research suggests that the level of motor skills influences the way infants perceive crawling and walking movements performed by others. But, how closely are motor perception and production linked to each other and does the perception of movements impact their production as well?

Bidirectionality of perception and production in motor development

The onset of self-locomotion is an important achievement in infancy. Being able to crawl and walk provides infants with a dramatically increased number of opportunities to explore the world around them on their own. Therefore, it is not surprising that motor skills like crawling and walking exert a far-reaching influence during infancy. As previously outlined, infants' ability to crawl and walk influences how they perceive and process crawling and walking PLDs

(Sanefuji *et al.*, 2008). Furthermore, it seems that the onset of self-locomotion coincides with major developmental changes in other psychological domains. For instance, a study by Herbert *et al.* (2007) revealed that independent locomotion is associated with more flexible memory retrieval. Although both crawling and non-crawling 9-month-old infants performed well in a retention task, there was a profound difference in the flexibility of their memory retrieval. Only infants with crawling experience performed the target action when tested with a different stimulus in a different context. Most likely, crawling experience provides infants with new opportunities to retrieve their memories in a range of different situations facilitating memory retrieval more generally. Moreover, major changes in locomotor development may also be connected to major changes in social development. Clearfield (2011) explored the relation of developmental changes in motor skills and social cognition by testing walking and non-walking age-matched 9- to 12-month-old infants in a 10-minute free play session with a stranger and ambiguous toys. Interestingly, infants' social looking behaviour changed as they made the transition from crawling to walking. Walkers were far more actively engaged than crawlers, as indicated by an increased number of approaches and offers for social interaction. Walkers spent more time playing with toys and interacting with their mothers and they also displayed more undirected and directed vocalizations. Clearfield (2011) also investigated crawlers who were placed in a baby walker providing these infants with a hands-free upright posture. Even though these infants were able to move like walkers their social engagement was similar to the crawling infants, indicating that independent walking marks an important transition in social and exploratory behaviour.

These few examples demonstrate that self-locomotion enhances at least some aspects of cognitive development (for a review, see Campos *et al.*, 2000). The onset of self-locomotion seems to provide infants with a range of new experiences that might boost their existing cognitive skills to new levels. But what about the experience provided by watching others? Could it be possible that watching others' movements provides infants with information, which in turn can be used to explore new ways of moving on their own?

Support for a possible bidirectional linkage of movement perception and production could be derived from studies on infant action understanding. For example, Sommerville and Woodward (2005) tested 10-month-old infants' ability to successfully perform a means–end task (pulling a cloth to reach a toy) and investigated how this action production was related to the understanding of a similar task presented visually. Only those infants who completed the task on their own understood the means–end sequence performed by another person, thus indicating a link between action production and action perception. Longo and Bertenthal (2006) addressed the same issue using a task eliciting the Piagetian A-not-B error. The 9-month-old infants watched an overt reaching action and were then given the chance to look for the hidden toy themselves. Interestingly, infants displayed only perseverated behaviour following observation of an ipsilateral reaching action, which they were able to produce, but not contralateral reaching, which infants at this age usually do not do. A close link between action perception and action production is also evident in studies on imitation. Infants' ability to imitate perceived actions and also to recognise being imitated by another person indicates shared common representations (Agnetta and Rochat, 2004; Meltzoff, 2007; Meltzoff and Moore, 1999).

Although these findings indicate a close relation between action perception and action production, only a few studies have investigated the assumed bidirectionality explicitly. For example, Sommerville *et al.* (2005) tested 3-month-old infants in a production and perception task. In the production task, infants were wearing special mittens allowing them to pick up a toy. In the perception task, infants' looking behaviour was assessed while watching an adult actor reaching for and grasping one of two toys. All infants participated in both tasks, but the sequence of perception and production tasks was manipulated. Interestingly, only infants with previous reaching experience understood the perception task as indicated by accordant looking time. On the contrary, no evidence was found that previous action perception experience influenced subsequent grasping actions.

A study by Hauf *et al.* (2007) demonstrated a profound influence of action production on action perception in 9- and 11-month-old infants. First, infants gained action experience by playing with a selected toy for 90 seconds. Following this, infants were seated and centred in front of two monitor screens. Both screens simultaneously displayed two female adults acting with either the same toy the infant had played with before or a novel toy. Acting time during the action production session and looking time during the action perception session were analyzed. 9- and 11-month-old infants preferred to watch the same-toy action. These and control results indicate that infants' action experience influenced their interest in actions performed by others (Hauf *et al.*, 2007). To investigate the reciprocity of action perception and production, infants participated in another study providing them with action perception experience prior to assessing their action performance (Hauf, in preparation). In this study, infants first watched a video presenting two adults facing each other across a table with two toys available. For 90 seconds the two adults took turns in playing with one toy while consistently ignoring the other available toy. During the subsequent action production session, infants were seated at a table with both toys available. 9- and 11-month-old infants selected the same toy as the adults did in the video and played significantly longer with it. These and control results suggest an influence of action perception on production.

Taken together, the reported findings support the notion that the relation between action perception and action production is indeed bidirectional.

Infants improve their perception of actions performed by others through self-experience *and* they learn about their possibilities through watching others' actions. The idea of a functional equivalence of perceived and produced actions emphasises that representations of one's own actions are similar to representations of others' actions (Hauf, 2007). The perceptual system and the motor system both use these representations to understand and guide action. In line with the idea that common representations support both perceived and performed actions, one could suggest that infants' perception and production of body movements are linked to each other in a comparable bidirectional way.

As previously outlined, infants' motor skills clearly influence how they perceive and process crawling and walking movements performed by others. In addition, Bertenthal (1993) suggests that the perception of movements provides infants with important information to develop their body representation, which in turn will facilitate movement production. A bidirectional model of motor development would suggest that body representations are actually based on both visuospatial and sensorimotor information gained through movement perception and production, and that this information in turn is shared and used while perceiving movements performed by others and while producing movements.

Recent findings in adults support this close linkage as outlined previously. For example, action perception activates the same motor representations that guide to-be-produced actions (Decety *et al.*, 2002). Additionally, a functional linkage between visuospatial and sensorimotor systems appears to be at play in observers' sensitivity to human movement (Jacobs *et al.*, 2004). In their study, Jacobs and colleagues found that adult observers were more sensitive to differences in the speed of PLD walkers when they were presented with possible gaits compared to impossible gaits. Interestingly, no difference was found when observers witnessed familiar (e.g. normal walking) or unusual (e.g. short, fast-paced stepping) gaits, suggesting that it is the ability to produce the gait pattern, rather than visual experience alone, that guides our perception of human movement.

From a developmental perspective it is of particular importance that, by as early as 15 months of age, infants demonstrate equally developed access to visuospatial and sensorimotor body representations (Christie and Slaughter, 2009) indicating an early development of functional equivalence of body representations. But, how might a possible linkage of body representations actually develop and how might this be related to motor development in more general ways? For example, will an infant with delays in motor development establish their body representations in the same way infants normally do, possibly only a bit later? Or will they develop comparable body representations in the same time line by compensating the missing motor experience with more visuospatial information based on watching others' movements more intensively? Recent findings demonstrate that motor experience has a major impact on how infants watch bodily possible and impossible crawling and walking movements (Hauf, Giese, and MacDonald, in preparation). These findings might reflect differences in motor and/or body representations, which allow infants to focus on information about movements they cannot yet perform as well as to detect inconsistencies in movements they are already capable of producing. Furthermore, the notion that body representations are closely linked to experience in perceiving and producing motor movements implies that infants' body representations change with increasing gross motor skills and possibly fine motor skills as well.

Based on the findings in the field of action understanding, it seems to be reasonable that the perception and the production of movements share common representations and that input from perception and production is essential to implement and develop these representations. Additional research is needed to evaluate this idea and to further establish what is known about the impact of self-locomotion on movement perception and to address how movement perception might influence movement production.

References

Adolph, K. E. (1997). Learning in the development of infant locomotion. *Monographs of the Society for Research in Child Development*, **62**(3), Serial No. 251.

(2000). Specificity of learning: Why infants fall over a veritable cliff. *Psychological Science*, **11**, 290–295.

(2002). Learning to keep balance. In R. Kail (ed.). *Advances in Child Development and Behavior*, Vol. 30 (1–30). Amsterdam: Elsevier Science.

(2005). Learning to learn in the development of action. In J. Lockman, J. Reiser, and C. A. Nelson (eds). *Action as an Organizer of Perception and Cognition during Learning and Development: Minnesota Symposium on Child Development*, Vol. 33 (91–122). Mahwah, NJ: Lawrence Erlbaum Associates.

(2008). Learning to move. *Current Directions in Psychological Science*, **17**, 213–218.

Adolph, K. E. and Berger, S. (2005). Physical and motor development. In M. H. Bornstein and M. E. Lamb (eds). *Developmental Science: An Advanced Textbook* (5th edn, 223–281). Hillsdale, NJ: Lawrence Erlbaum Associates.

Adolph, K. E. and Joh, A. S. (2007). Motor development: How infants get into the act. In A. Slater and M. Lewis (eds). *Introduction to Infant Development* (2nd edn). New York: Oxford University Press.

Adolph, K. E., Eppler, M. A., and Gibson, E. J. (1993). Crawling versus walking infants' perception of affordances for locomotion over sloping surfaces. *Child Development: Special Issue on Biodynamics*, **64**, 1,158–1,174.

Adolph, K. E., Vereijken, B., and Denny, M. (1998). Learning to crawl. *Child Development*, **69**, 1,299–1,312.

Adolph, K. E., Vereijken, B., and Shrout, P. E. (2003). What changes in infant walking and why. *Child Development*, **74**, 475–497.

Agnetta, B. and Rochat, P. (2004). Imitative games by 9-, 14-, and 18-month-old infants. *Infancy*, **6**(1), 1–36.

Bayley, N. (2006). *Bayley Scales of Infant and Toddler Development* (3rd edn). San Antonio, TX: Harcourt Assessment.

Bendersky, M. and Lewis, M. (1994). Environmental risk, biological risk, and developmental outcome. *Developmental Psychology*, **30**, 484–494.

Berger, S. E. and Adolph, K. E. (2003). Infants use handrails as tools in a locomotor task. *Developmental Psychology*, **39**, 594–605.

Berger, S. E., Adolph, K. E., and Lobo, S. A. (2005). Out of the toolbox: Toddlers differentiate wobbly and wooden handrails. *Child Development*, **76**(6), 1,294–1,307.

Bertenthal, B. I. (1993). Perception of biomechanical motions by infants: Intrinsic and knowledge-based constraints. In C. Granrud (ed.). *Carnegie Symposium on Cognition: Visual Perception and Cognition in Infancy* (175–214). Hillsdale, NJ: Lawrence Erlbaum Associates.

Bertenthal, B. I., Proffitt, D. R., and Cutting, J. (1984). Infant sensitivity to figural coherence in biomechanical motions. *Journal of Experimental Child Psychology*, **3**, 213–230.

Bertenthal, B. I., Proffitt, D. R., and Kramer, S. J. (1987). The perception of biomechanical motions by infants: Implementation of various processing constraints. *Journal of Experimental Psychology: Human Perception and Performance*, **13**, 577–585.

Bly, L. (1994). *Motor Skills Acquisition in the First Year*. San Antonio, TX: Therapy Skill Builders.

Booth, A. E., Pinto, J., and Bertenthal, B. I. (2002). Perception of the symmetrical patterning of human gait by infants. *Developmental Psychology*, **38**(4), 554–563.

Brass, M. and Heyes, C. (2005). Imitation: Is cognitive neuroscience solving the corresponding problem? *Trends in Cognitive Science*, **9**, 489–495.

Bril, B. and Breniere, Y. (1989). Steady-state velocity and temporal structure of gait during the first six months of autonomous walking. *Human Movement Sciences*, **8**, 99–122.

(1993). Posture and independent locomotion in early childhood: Learning to walk or learning dynamic postural control? In G. J. P. Savelsbergh (ed.). *The Development of Coordination in Infancy* (337–358). Amsterdam: Elsevier/North Holland.

Campos, J. J., Anderson, D. I., Barbu-Roth, M. A., Hubbard, E. M., Hertenstein, M. J., and Witherington, D. (2000). Travel broadens the mind. *Infancy*, **1**, 149–219.

Christie, T. and Slaughter, V. (2009). Exploring links between sensorimotor and visuo-spatial body representations in infancy. *Developmental Neuropsychology*, **34**(4), 448–460.

Clearfield, M. W. (2011). Learning to walk changes infants' social interaction. *Infant Behavior and Development*, **34**, 15–25.

Decety, J. (1996). Do imagined and executed actions share the same neural substrates? *Cognitive Brain Research*, **3**, 87–93.

Decety, J., Chaminade, T., Grèzes, J., and Meltzoff, A. N. (2002). A PET exploration of the neural mechanisms involved in reciprocal imitation. *Neuroimage*, **15**, 265–272.

Gallese, V. (2003). The manifold nature of interpersonal relations: The quest for a common mechanism, *Philosophical Transactions of the Royal Society of London*, **358**, 517–528.

Gibson, E. J. (1988). Exploratory behavior in the development of perceiving, acting and the acquiring of knowledge. *Annual Review of Psychology*, **39**, 1–41.

Gibson, E. J. and Pick, A. D. (2000). *An Ecological Approach to Perceptual Learning and Development*. New York: Oxford University Press.

Hamilton, A., Wolpert, D., and Frith, U. (2004). Your own action influences how you perceive another person's action. *Current Biology*, **14**, 493–498.

Hauf, P. (2007). Infants' perception and production of intentional actions. In C. von Hofsten and K. Rosander (eds). *Progress in Brain Research: From Action to Cognition*, Vol. 164 (285–301). Amsterdam: Elsevier Science.

(in preparation). *Baby See – Baby Do! How Infants Learn from Other Persons' Actions*. St. Francis Xavier University.

Hauf, P. and Prinz, W. (2005). The understanding of own and others' actions during infancy: 'You-like-me' or 'me-like-you'? *Interaction Studies*, **6**(3), 429–445.

Hauf, P., Aschersleben, G., and Prinz, W. (2007). Baby do – baby see! How action production influences action perception in infants. *Cognitive Development*, **22**, 16–32.

Hauf, P., Geangu, E., and Williams, A. (in preparation). *The Perception of Crawling and Walking Point-light Displays in Toddlers and Adults*. St. Francis Xavier University.

Hauf, P., Giese, M., and MacDonald, K. M. (in preparation). *Are You Moving? How Motor Experience Influences Infants' Perception of Crawling and Walking Point-light Displays*. St. Francis Xavier University.

Herbert, J., Gross, J., and Hayne, H. (2007). Crawling is associated with more flexible memory retrieval by 9-month-old infants. *Developmental Science*, **10**(2), 183–189.

Heron, M. and Slaughter, V. (2010). Infants' responses to real humans and representations of humans. *International Journal of Behavioral Development*, **34**(1), 34–45.

Hommel, B., Müsseler, J., Aschersleben, G., and Prinz, W. (2001). The theory of event coding: A framework for perception and action planning. *Behavioral Brain Sciences*, **24**, 849–937.

Iacoboni, M. (2005). Neural mechanisms of imitation. *Current Opinion in Neurobiology*, **15**, 632–637.

Jacobs, A., Pinto, J., and Shiffrar, M. (2004). Experience, context, and the visual perception of human movement. *Journal of Experimental Psychology*, **30**(5), 822–835.

Joh, A. S. and Adolph, K. E. (2006). Learning from falling. *Child Development*, **77**, 89–102.

Johansson, G. (1973). Visual perception of biological motion and a model for its analysis. *Perception and Psychophysics*, **14**, 201–211.

Kuhlmeier, V. A., Troje, N. F., and Lee, V. (2010). Young infants detect the direction of biological motion in point-light displays. *Infancy*, **15**, 83–93.

Longo, M. R. and Bertenthal, B. I. (2006). Common coding of observation and execution of action in 9-month-old infants. *Infancy*, **10**(1), 43–59.

Meltzoff, A. N. (2002). Elements of a developmental theory of imitation. In A. N. Meltzoff and W. Prinz (eds). *The Imitative Mind: Development, Evolution, and Brain Bases* (19–41). Cambridge: Cambridge University Press.

(2007). The 'like me' framework for recognizing and becoming an intentional agent. *Acta Psychologia*, **124**(1), 26–43.

Meltzoff, A. N. and Moore, M. K. (1999). Persons and representation: Why infant imitation is important for theories of human development. In J. Nadel (ed.). *Imitation in Infancy: Cambridge Studies in Cognitive Perceptual Development* (9–35). New York: Cambridge University Press.

Moore, D. G, Goodwin, J. E., George, R., Axelsson, E. L., and Braddick, F. M. B. (2007). Infants perceive human point-light displays as solid forms. *Cognition*, **104**, 377–396.

Piaget, J. (1953). *The Origins of Intelligence in the Child*. London: Routledge and Kegan Paul.

Prinz, W. (1990). A common coding approach to perception and action. In O. Neumann and W. Prinz (eds). *Relationships Between Perception and Action: Current Approaches* (167–201). Berlin: Springer.

   (1997). Perception and action planning. *European Journal of Cognitive Psychology*, **9**(2), 129–154.

   (2002). Experimental approaches to imitation: In A. N. Meltzoff and W. Prinz (eds). *The Imitative Mind: Development, Evolution, and Brain Bases* (143–162). Cambridge: Cambridge University Press.

Proffitt, D. R. and Bertenthal, B. I. (1990). Converging operations revisited: Assessing what infants perceive using discrimination measures. *Perception and Psychophysics*, **47**, 1–11.

Reid, V. M., Belsky, J., and Johnson, M. H. (2005). Infant perception of human action: Toward a developmental cognitive neuroscience of individual differences. *Cognition, Brain, and Behavior*, **9**(2), 35–52.

Reid, V. M., Hoehl, S., Landt, J., and Striano, T. (2008). Human infants dissociate structural and dynamic information in biological motion: Evidence from neural systems. *Social Cognitive and Affective Neuroscience*, **3**, 161–167.

Sanefuji, W., Ohgami, H., and Hashiya, K. (2008). Detection of the relevant type of locomotion in infancy: Crawlers versus walkers. *Infant Behavior and Development*, **31**, 624–628.

Simion, F., Regolin, L., and Bulf, H. (2008). A predisposition for biological motion in the newborn baby. *Proceedings of the National Academy of Sciences*, **102**(2), 809–813.

Slaughter, V. and Heron, M. (2004). Origins and early development of human body knowledge. *Monographs of the Society for Research in Child Development*, **69**(2), 1–102.

Slaughter, V., Heron, M., and Sim, S. (2002). Development of preferences for the human body shape in infancy. *Cognition*, **85**(3), B71–B81.

Sommerville, J. A. and Woodward, A. L. (2005). Pulling out the intentional structure of action: The relation between action processing and action production in infancy. *Cognition*, **95**, 1–30.

Sommerville, J. A., Woodward, A. L., and Needham, A. (2005). Action experience alters 3-month-old infants' perception of others' actions. *Cognition*, **96**, B1–B11.

van Elk, M., van Scheie, H. T., Hunnius, S., Vesper, C., and Bekkering, H. (2008). You'll never crawl alone: Neurophysiological evidence for experience-dependent motor resonance in infancy. *Neuroimage*, **43**(4), 808–814.

Vereijken, B. and Adolph, K. E. (1999). Transitions in the development of locomotion. In G. J. P. Savelsbergh, H. L. J. van der Maas, and P. C. L. van Geert (eds). *Non-linear Analyses of Developmental Processes* (137–149). Amsterdam: Elsevier.

13   The body in action: the impact of self-produced action on infants' action perception and understanding

Jessica A. Sommerville, Emily J. Blumenthal,
Kaitlin Venema and Kara D. Sage

Perceiving, representing, and reasoning about the human body is an incredibly difficult task; the fact that we traffic in this ability with such ease is no mean feat. After all, bodies are more than complex objects. They are more than a collection of parts that co-articulate, more than things that can be acted on, more than entities that are in the world and of the world. Rather, bodies act *on* the world. Bodies, by definition, are bodies in action: limbs move, joints articulate, digits bend and curl. Critically, many of these actions convey meaning: they are *about* the world. And it is precisely this meaningfulness of the human body in relation to the world that makes the task of perceiving, representing and reasoning about the human body both so complex and so critical.

Among other things, understanding the human body is central to our everyday social reasoning and social interactions: we perceive the body to read the mind. Goals and intentions, in particular, while generated by the mind, are instantiated in bodily acts. An event in which an arm moves at a 45-degree trajectory, and a rate of 15 centimeters a second, culminating in contact with a wine glass, is more than the collection of its surface features. It signifies an actor's goal (obtaining the wine glass), reveals the actor's underlying intention (getting a drink of wine), and can be a window into the actor's proclivities and dispositions (liking wine).

Recent evidence suggests that adults are not the only rich readers of bodily actions. Infants, too, attribute meaning to both simple acts and action sequences. 6-month-old infants, after seeing an actor repeatedly reach for and grasp one of two toys sitting side by side on a stage, show enhanced attention to a change in the actor's goal object, but not changes to the spatiotemporal features of the event (Woodward, 1998). Several months later, infants identify the goal of referential acts (points, eye gaze; Woodward, 2003; Woodward and Guajardo, 2002) and simple action sequences (e.g. opening a box in order to get a toy within

This work was supported by a University of Washington Royalty Research Fund grant and NICHD grant (1R03HD053616–01A1), both to the first author.

the box; Sommerville and Woodward, 2005; Woodward and Sommerville, 2000). Infants, like adults, think goals and intentions are important, and recover them from bodily acts. How do infants develop this ability?

The importance of self-produced action for understanding others' actions

The ability to recognize the goal structure of action likely derives from many contributors and experiences. Infants' experience producing goal-directed actions has long been hypothesized to act as one strong contributor to their understanding of others' actions. Scholars have suggested that infants' understanding of others as intentional agents depends in large part upon their own newly emerging forms of intentionality in sensori-motor actions (e.g. Frye, 1991; Tomasello, 1999) or that imitation of others' actions allows infants to determine their intentions (Meltzoff and Moore, 1995). These theoretical speculations have recently been given support by findings demonstrating that neural representations that subserve action are also automatically invoked during action observation, leading to the suggestion that such representations provide the basis for action understanding (e.g. Gallese, 2009; Rizzolatti and Sinigaglia, 2010; Sommerville and Decety, 2006).

To test the hypothesis that infants' own experience-producing action may serve as a catalyst for developments in their understanding of goals and intentions, we systematically tested two predictions that derive from this hypothesis. First, we predicted that there should be an intimate link between infants' developing ability to perform goal-directed actions and their understanding of these actions. In one series of experiments, we investigated infants' understanding of a cloth-pulling sequence, in which an actor pulled a cloth to obtain an out-of-reach toy that it supported, as well as infants' ability to perform the sequence in their own actions (Sommerville and Woodward, 2005). Past work suggested that there are significant developments between 8 and 12 months of age in infants' ability to successfully perform a range of means–end sequences (Piaget, 1953). Thus, we tested infants at both 10 and 12 months of age in a visual habituation paradigm; 10-month-old infants also received an accompanying action task designed to assess their own ability to use the cloth as a means to obtain the toy.

During the habituation paradigm, infants saw an actor grasp one of two cloths, each supporting different out-of-reach toys, pull the cloth toward her and grasp the toy it supported. The question was whether infants recognized that the actor's actions on the cloth signified an intention to retrieve the toy (rather than obtain the cloth itself). To address this question, following habituation trials, the locations of the toys were reversed and infants saw the actor act on a new cloth toward the same toy she had initially pursued, or act on the same cloth she had initially toward a different toy. We found that infants at 12 months of age looked longer to events that changed the actor's ultimate goal (versus the cloth she acted on). At 10 months of age infants were variable in their habituation performance, and this variability was related to their skill at performing the cloth-pulling sequence in their own actions: infants who were skilled at solving the problem looked longer to the change in the actor's ultimate goal, whereas infants who were unskilled showed the opposite pattern of findings, looking longer to the change in cloth the actor acted on. Thus, our results showed that by 12 months of age infants were able to identify the goal of a simple action sequence, and that prior to this age infants' ability to do so was tightly interwoven with their own ability to perform such a sequence.

Given our findings indicating a close inter-connection between infants' action production and understanding, we tested our next prediction: that intervening to facilitate infants' ability to produce goal-directed actions would enhance their ability to identify the goal structure of actions produced by others. To do so, we focused on younger infants' ability to interpret a reach and grasp event as goal-directed.

Past research provides evidence for developmental change in infants' ability to produce proficient goal-directed reaches between 3 and 6 months of age (Clifton et al., 1991; Robin et al., 1996; von Hofsten and Ronnqvist, 1988; Yonas and Hartman, 1993). Over this same time frame, there are changes in infants' perception of the goal of a simple reach and grasp action: whereas 6-month-old infants selectively encode the goal object of the reach and grasp event (Woodward, 1998), 3-month-old infants do not (Sommerville et al., 2005).

We investigated whether providing pre-reaching 3-month-old infants with an intervention designed to bolster their ability to produce goal-directed reaches would impact their ability to encode the goal object of another person's reach and grasp. Either directly prior to (reach-first infants) or directly after (watch-first infants) a visual habituation paradigm designed to investigate infants' understanding of a reach and grasp event as goal-directed (cf. Woodward, 1998), infants received an action task designed to facilitate their ability to reach for and grasp objects. This was accomplished by fitting infants with Velcro mittens, and providing them with toys with the opposing side of Velcro attached to them, such that when they swiped or batted at the toys they were able to apprehend and move them. This intervention significantly impacted infants' ability to contact and apprehend the objects. It also enhanced infants' ability to understand the goal structure of the reach and grasp event. Infants in the reach first group showed enhanced attention to test trials that changed the actor's goal object versus test events that manipulated the spatio-temporal features of the event; infants in the watch-first group looked equally to both types of events.

Taken together, the aforementioned findings suggest that action production and perception are intertwined: naturally occurring variability in infants' ability to produce action sequences predicts infants' ability to understand the goal-directed nature of these sequences, and intervening to facilitate infants' ability to produce goal-directed action also facilitates their ability to view simple actions as goal-directed. In subsequent work in the lab, we have investigated whether the ability to produce goal-directed action exerts a unique impact on infants' action perception and understanding.

Is self-produced action special? Comparing active and observational experience

The findings just discussed suggest that action experience may play a pivotal role in shaping action perception. In everyday life, however, active experience and observational experience are correlated: by acting infants are provided with more behavioral exemplars of a given act. Thus, it is possible that changes in visual experience, that is the number of exemplars of a given action that infants are exposed to, account for subsequent changes in action perception. Indeed, others have suggested that observational experience provides infants with important information about human action, such as knowledge of action effects (Hauf *et al.*, 2004), sensitivity to behavioral regularities signaling goal attainment (Baldwin *et al.*, 2001), and an understanding of object affordances (Gibson and Pick, 2000).

We subsequently sought to test an alternate hypothesis: that active experience may play a unique or privileged role in infants' action perception. We did so by providing 10-month-old infants with experience using a novel tool (a plastic cane) to obtain an out-of-reach toy, and assessing the impact that this tool use training had on their perception of others' tool use acts (Sommerville *et al.*, 2008). Initial work in our lab established that at 10 months of age, infants rarely spontaneously use the cane as a tool. However, their ability to do so improves rapidly as a function of training and experience (Sommerville *et al.*, in preparation). We reasoned that if active experience plays a privileged role in infants' action understanding, then infants should demonstrate greater understanding of the goal-directed nature of the tool use sequence following active training than following matched observational experience.

Infants were randomly assigned to one of three conditions: a no experience condition, a training condition and an observation condition. All infants took part in a habituation paradigm to assess their ability to identify the goal of a sequence in which an adult actor used a plastic cane to retrieve an out-of-reach toy. This task was structurally analogous to Sommerville and Woodward (2005). During habituation trials infants saw an actor sitting in front of a stage that supported two perceptually distinct canes, each of which surrounded a different toy. The actor repeatedly used one of two canes to bring within reach the out-of-reach toy and grasp it. On test trials, the locations of the toys were reversed, and infants saw two test events in alternation. On new toy trials, infants saw the actor reach for and grasp the same cane as she had during habituation trials, which now surrounded a new toy. On new tool trials, the actor grasped a new cane, which surrounded the same toy the actor acted toward on habituation trials. We anticipated longer looking to the new toy event if infants recognized that the actor's intention during habituation trials was to act on the cane in pursuit of the toy (rather than in pursuit of the cane itself).

Prior to the habituation paradigm, infants received either active training and practice using the cane to retrieve out-of-reach toys (training condition), matched observational experience (observation condition), or no experience at all (baseline condition). Infants in the training condition first received two pre-test trials to assess their ability to spontaneously use the cane tools to retrieve out-of-reach-toys. During these trials, the adult experimenter who acted as the trainer (henceforth, trainer) placed a toy out of the infants' reach in the crook of the cane and infants were encouraged to get the toy. No assistance was given to the infants on these trials, and infants were not rewarded for obtaining the toy. Pre-test trials were followed by training trials, in which the trainer used a variety of methods designed to enhance infants' ability to use the cane to retrieve various bath toys. These methods were individually tailored to the challenges that infants faced with the task. They included methods such as tapping on the toy, tapping on the cane, helping infants pull the cane, demonstrating cane-pulling, using canes that moved in a set of tracks to enable infants to more readily pull the canes, and praising infants after they obtained the toy. Following training trials, infants received two post-test trials (identical to pre-test trials) to assess improvements in their ability to use the cane tools to retrieve toys. Infants received up to nine training trials, and proceeded to test trials after they had received a minimum of four opportunities to act on the cane to get the toy and after they used the cane to get the out-of-reach toy on at least three consecutive trials.

The observation condition was designed to mimic the training condition, except that during the pre-habituation session the infant acted as an observer rather than a participant. Thus, infants in the observational experience condition witnessed two adult experimenters interacting in the context of the cane task. One experimenter acted as the modeler: she used the cane to retrieve out-of-reach toys in a manner that was designed to parallel infants' actions in the training condition. A second experimenter acted as the trainer, providing guidance to the modeler as she solved the task. Infants sat directly facing the modeler but several feet away. Neither the modeler nor the trainer interacted with infants during the observation session, in order to provide infants with a third-party observational experience. During observation trials, the modeler solved the task accurately and efficiently, because it would have been difficult for the modeler to accurately reproduce the exact actions of infants in the training condition. This ensured that, if anything, the quality of problem-solving attempts that infants saw exceeded those of the attempts that infants in the training condition performed. Infants watched the same number of cane-pulling trials that training infants completed. An on-line observer verified that infants watched all training trials.

During observation trials, the trainer used the same training cues that were used most frequently by the experimenter in the training condition: infants saw the trainer demonstrate pulling the cane once (following the pre-test trials) and the trainer tapped on the toy twice during each trial. After solving each trial the modeler maintained a neutral facial expression similar to that produced by infants in the training condition and played with the toy for the same average duration as infants in the training condition (approximately 5 seconds). The trainer praised the modeler after each training trial, to a level that matched the training condition. The length of the observation session was matched to the training session. Infants in the baseline condition proceeded directly to the habituation paradigm.

We found that infants' looking preferences to the test events in the habituation paradigm varied as a function of condition. Whereas infants in the baseline and observation conditions looked equally to the new toy and new cane events, infants in the training condition showed a significant preference for the new toy events. Moreover, recovery to the test events differed across conditions. Infants in the baseline condition recovered attention to the new cane event uniquely, infants in the observation condition recovered attention to both the new cane and new toy events, and infants in the training condition recovered attention selectively to the new toy event. Taken together, these findings suggest that active training and experience using the tool led infants to selectively encode the goal of the tool use sequence.

We next investigated whether infants' responses in the training condition varied as a function of the ultimate expertise they had attained with the tool. We divided infants into two groups on the basis of their post-test performance. Eleven infants achieved a high level of expertise during training, performing perfectly on post-test trials. Seven infants showed improvement during training, but did not receive perfect scores on post-test trials. Subsequent analyses revealed that high expertise infants alone accounted for the group-level effect of longer looking to the new toy versus new cane events. These findings suggest that in order for active training and experience to impart an impact on infants' perception of tool use sequences, infants must become highly skilled with the tool.

Taken together, the results support the hypothesis that active training impacts infants' understanding of another person's tool use actions over and above observational experience.

Recent empirical work: addressing two critical questions

Existing research on the role of self-produced action in action understanding leaves two critical questions unaddressed. We sought to address these questions through a series of three experiments.

The first question concerns the process or mechanism underlying the impact of self-produced action on infants' action perception and understanding. Several authors have recently claimed that the activation of a motor resonance system during action observation has important consequences for action perception and understanding. In particular, such a system is hypothesized to play an important role in the ability to anticipate upcoming actions and action outcomes (e.g. Sommerville and Decety, 2006; Wilson and Knoblich, 2005). Our findings (Sommerville et al., 2005, 2008) are consistent with recent claims that a motor resonance mechanism is present and operative in infancy (Longo and Bertenthal, 2007; Falck-Ytter et al., 2006; Nystrom, 2008); however, whether such a system contributes to action anticipation in infants is an open question. We sought to directly test whether self-produced action experience leads infants to anticipate particular action outcomes using a novel paradigm in experiment (1).

The second question raised by prior work concerns whether the difference between self-produced experience and observational experience is absolute or relative. Although Sommerville et al. (2008) found that only infants in the training condition selectively encoded the tool use goal, observational experience did exert some effects on infants' attention to the test events. Whereas infants in the baseline condition recovered attention selectively to the new cane event, infants in the observation condition recovered attention to both the new cane and the new toy events. Moreover, the impact of observational experience was mediated by the quality of infants' attention to the observational experience session (coded as the frequency of look aways during the observational session that lasted 1 second or less): infants who were high-quality observers showed a trend toward longer looking to the new toy event, whereas low-quality observers showed a trend toward longer looking to the new cane event. Thus, it is possible that observational experience enhanced infants' attention to the goal of the tool use event, but perhaps not to the same extent as did active training or experience. Perhaps given more behavioral exemplars, or richer exemplars, the effects of observational experience would parallel that of active training and experience.

In addition, the tool use exemplars that infants in the observational experience condition witnessed differed from that of infants in the active training condition in terms of their degree of success. In the observational experience condition infants only viewed successful tool use acts. In contrast, infants in the active training condition showed improvement from fledgling tool use attempts, to proficient use. Thus, one possibility is that infants given observational experience that more closely mimics that of active training experience will reap greater benefits to their action processing. Indeed, recent work demonstrates that 3-year-old children learn from observing another person's tool use success and failure (above only witnessing tool use success; Want and Harris, 2001). It is possible that infants will glean more from observational experience if they witness the modeler produce both tool use success and tool use failure. We investigated this possibility in experiment (2).

In experiment (3), we pushed the boundary between active training and observational experience. In the Sommerville *et al.* (2008) experiment, infants acted as third-party observers during the observational session. Infants sat across from the modeler, and the modeler did not attempt to engage the infant prior to performing their demonstration. Recent work, however, suggests that the way in which infants engage with observational exchanges can have marked effects on their attention to, and learning from, such exchanges. First, infants appear to be sensitive to a range of ostensive cues, and use these cues to determine whether an adult seeks to communicate culturally relevant information about a referent object or an individual disposition toward that object (Csibra and Gergely, 2009). Second, infants only detect what others know and perceive when they are directly involved in joint engagement with their social partner, and not when they watch acts of joint engagement from a third-person perspective (Moll *et al.*, 2007). Third, children's learning and memory from others' actions relies on whether they are a collaborator in the exchange, or a mere observer (Sommerville and Hammond, 2007). These findings led us to investigate whether infants' ability to learn from observational experience was impacted by whether they were involved in joint engagement during the observational session, or whether they acted as a third-party observer.

Experiment (1): the role of training and observational experience in infants' anticipation of tool use outcomes

In experiment (1) we investigated whether active training and practice using a cane as a tool led 10-month-old infants to anticipate that actions on the tool were directed toward retrieving the out-of-reach toy. To investigate the influence of active training and experience on action anticipation, we created a novel violation-of-expectation paradigm that we named the cane-as-tool (CAT) procedure (see Figure 13.1). On each trial, the screen was lowered and infants saw an actor sitting in front of a cane that surrounded an out-of-reach toy. Infants saw the actor look at the toy, and reach toward and grasp the stalk of a cane that surrounded the out-of-reach toy. As soon as the actor grasped the stalk of the cane a screen that separated the display from the infant was raised to just above the actor's head, obscuring the event from infants' view, and giving the impression that an in-progress event had been interrupted. When the screen was lowered, infants were presented with one of two outcomes in alternation: the actor holding the cane, or the actor holding the toy. Infants saw two trials of each type, for a total of four trials.

Our question of interest was whether, upon seeing the actor grasp the stalk of the cane, infants would anticipate the outcome of the tool use sequence as

Screen Up

Toy Outcome   Cane Outcome

Figure 13.1 Cane-as-tool (CAT) procedure

attainment of the toy. If so, we reasoned that infants should show longer looking to the cane outcome, because they expected the actor to act on the cane in service of the toy, rather than the cane itself. In contrast, if infants anticipated that the actor grasped the cane to obtain the cane then longer looking to the toy outcome was expected. Finally, if infants failed to anticipate a particular outcome, equivalent looking to the outcomes was predicted.

Infants in the training condition (*n* = 20; *mean age* = 9 months, 27 days) received active training and experience using the cane to retrieve the toy. Infants sat in a high chair in front of a table that supported a yellow cane made from PVC piping and an out-of-reach toy. Infants received two pre-test trials and two post-test trials, in which they were given the opportunity to spontaneously solve the cane problem. On these trials, the same yellow PVC cane and toy used in the subsequent CAT procedure were used.

The pre- and post-test trials were separated by a training session. During training, infants also acted on a yellow PVC cane. However, this cane was equipped with furniture sliders on the underside, which made the cane easier for infants to wield. The training session began with the trainer demonstrating the correct solution to the problem. Infants were then given the opportunity to use the cane to retrieve an out-of-reach toy on multiple trials. On these trials, the trainer used a number of different training techniques to improve infants' ability to use the cane to obtain the toy. First, on some trials the infants acted toward a large ball that was set into motion when the cane was pulled, such that it rolled toward the infant. Second, the trainer used various interventions to assist infants' performance, including drawing infants' attention to the toy, helping to correct awkward motor strategies (e.g. preventing the cane from flipping over and dislodging the toy from the crown), helping infants to pull the cane, and rewarding infants for obtaining the toy. These techniques were tailored to the difficulties expressed by individual infants. Infants received training trials until they had solved three out of four trials in a clearly intentional manner (e.g. looked at the toy, maintained attention to the toy while pulled the cane, and quickly obtained the toy when it came within reach). Infants received an average of seven training trials (*range* = 3 to 15).

Infants in the observation condition (*n* = 20; *mean age* = 9 months, 23 days) watched two adult experimenters interact in the context of solving the cane problem: a modeler and a trainer. The modeler solved pre-test and post-test trials, and also participated in an intervening training session. An on-line observer verified that infants watched each of the pre- and post-test trials, as well as the training trials. To investigate whether the effect of observational experience varied according to the number of behavioral exemplars, infants in the observation condition were yoked to infants in the training condition. Thus, infants observed an average of seven training trials, with the number of training trials ranging from three to fifteen, depending on the training infant to whom the observation infant was yoked. On all trials the modeler solved the problem successfully and proficiently, and was rewarded by the trainer for doing so. As in Sommerville *et al.* (2008), the infant was a third-party observer to the observational exchange: she sat across the table several feet from the display and neither the trainer nor the modeler directly interacted with her. This enabled us to manipulate this feature of the observational session in experiment (3).

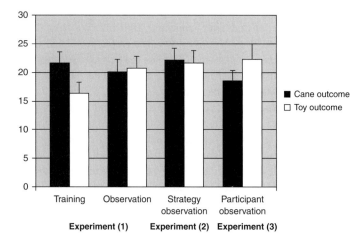

Figure 13.2 Looking times to the test outcomes as a function of condition and experiment

Infants' looking times to the test events are depicted in Figure 13.2. To compare infants' responses to the test events, infants' looking times to the outcomes of each type were entered with outcome (cane versus toy) as the within-subjects variable, and condition (training versus observation) as the between-subjects variable. This analysis revealed a condition by trial type interaction and no other significant effects ($F(1,38) = 4.2$, $p < .05$). Planned comparisons revealed that whereas infants in the training condition looked longer to the cane outcome ($M = 21.6$, $SE = 2.9$) than the toy outcome ($M = 16.3$, $SE = 2.0$; $t(19) = 2.4$, $p < .03$), infants in the observation condition looked equally to both outcomes (cane: $M = 20.1$, $SE = 2.2$; toy: $M = 20.7$, $SE = 2.1$; ns). These findings suggest that infants in the training condition antici- pated that the actor acted on the cane in order to obtain the out-of-reach toy, and thus showed enhanced attention when the actor was depicted holding the cane. Infants in the observation condition showed no preference for either outcome, suggesting that they anticipated neither the toy nor the cane as the actor's goal.

We subsequently investigated whether the number of training trials that infants in the observation condition watched was related to their performance on the CAT procedure. In Sommerville *et al.* (2008), all observation infants received the same number of training trials. One possibility is that active training and experience exert similar impacts on infants' action perception when infants are given an increased number of behavioral exemplars. To investigate this possibility we undertook a correlational analysis, relating infants' preference for the cane out- come (total looking to the cane outcome minus total looking to the toy outcome) to the number of training trials witnessed. This analysis revealed no relation between the two variables (*ns*). We subsequently split the sample into two groups based on the number of trials they witnessed, and entered infants' looking times into an ANOVA with trials witnessed (high exemplars = seven trials or more versus low exemplars = six trials or fewer) as the between-subjects variable and outcome (cane versus toy) as the within-subjects variable. This analysis revealed no significant main effects or interactions (*ns*).

The results of experiment (1) replicate and expand on those of prior work (Sommerville *et al.*, 2008). They suggest that active training and experience using the cane as a tool influences infants' tool use perception, whereas equated observational experience does not. Critically, these findings build on prior work by demonstrating that active training and experience not only influence infants' representations and interpretations of completed tool use sequences, but also provide infants with a basis upon which to identify upcoming action outcomes. Thus, these results are consistent with the claim that active training and experience may lead infants to establish motor representations that are activated during action observation, and provide a basis for action *anticipation*. Moreover, our findings suggest that, at least within the range tested, infants who watched more cane-pulling exemplars reaped no greater benefits than those that watched fewer behavioral exemplars. These findings suggest that either active training and experience exerts a qualitatively different effect on infants' action anticipation, than does observational experience, or that in order for infants to reap the same benefits from observational experience infants require many more exemplars than they would from active training and experience.

Experiment (2): the impact of observing tool use success and failure on action anticipation

In experiment (2), we sought to present infants with observational experience that more closely paralleled the type of experience that infants in the training condition received. Whereas infants in the observational experience condition witnessed the modeler use the tool proficiently to obtain the toy on each and every trial, using a canonical solution, infants in the training condition showed improvement from early in training until late in training, and often used a variety of different motor strategies to solve the task. In experiment (2), we investigated whether providing infants with observational experience in which the modeler (a) showed continued improvement across the training session, and (b) used a number of different strategies to solve the problem, might lead infants to correctly anticipate toy attainment as the tool use outcome.

Infants in experiment (2) took part in the strategy observation condition. Infants (*n* = 20; *mean age* = 9 months, 21 days) participated in the CAT procedure, which was identical to experiment (1), preceded by an observational experience session. This observational experience session was identical to that of experiment (1), except that the strategies that the modeler produced were designed to more closely parallel the actual strategies that infants used during the training condition of experiment (1).

In order to closely match the strategies that infants were exposed to during the observational experience session to those of the active training condition, we first coded and categorized the strategies that infants in the training condition from experiment (1) produced during the training session. Coding of each trial included a description of the actions infants took, as well the accompanying actions used by the experimenter to support infants' attainment of the toy. We next calculated the frequency of each of these strategies, and tabulated their relative distribution over the course of the training session. We then selected the four most frequently occurring strategies, and used their distributional tally, and the total of number of trials that infants would view ($n = 7$, matched to the average number in the training condition, since experiment (1) revealed that infants' performance did not differ as a function of the number of exemplars they saw) to determine the number of models that the infant would see of a particular strategy (e.g. if a given strategy occurred on 40 percent of trials in the training condition, then the modeler would produce this strategy on 40 percent of trials in the observation session). Finally, we arranged trials in order of success and efficiency, such that infants saw strategies that were less efficient and less successful early in the observational session followed by strategies that were more efficient and more successful later in the observational session.

Infants' looking times to the test events did not differ. Planned comparisons revealed that infants in the strategy observation condition did not distinguish between cane ($M = 22.2$, $SE = 2.0$) and toy ($M = 21.6$, $SE = 2.0$) outcomes (*ns*). These results suggest that infants in the strategy observation condition, as a group, did not anticipate the toy as the actor's goal. However, an ANOVA comparing infants' looking times to those of infants in the training condition of experiment (1) with condition (training versus strategy observation) as the between-subjects variable and outcome (cane versus toy) as the within-subjects variable failed to reveal any significant effects, suggesting that infants in the strategy observation condition did not differ in their responses to the test event in comparison to training infants. Thus, we next sought to determine whether individual differences in infants' ability to solve the cane-pulling problem in their own actions mediated their learning from the observational session.

A subset of infants ($n = 14$) received four post-test trials in which they were given the opportunity to spontaneously solve the cane problem in their own actions following the CAT procedure. We related infants' success at using the cane to infants' preference for the cane outcome (looking to cane outcome minus looking to toy outcome). This analysis revealed a marginal relation between infants' expertise at using the cane to retrieve the toy, and their preference for the cane outcome ($r(13) = .40, p < .09$; note that although this relation is marginal, it is a medium effect and would likely reach significance with a larger sample size). These findings are consistent with one of two possibilities. First, some infants may be naturally more skilled tool users than others, and it is these infants that showed a greater preference for the cane outcome. Second, some infants may have benefited more readily from the observational experience session, which subsequently impacted their perception of the tool use event, and their ability to use the tool. Of course, these two alternatives need not be mutually exclusive: it may be the case that infants with greater tool use skill reaped more benefit from the tool use observation session, which enhanced any pre-existing differences that might have existed in their ability to anticipate the tool use outcome.

To summarize, our results suggested that varying the degree of success and the motor strategies used by the modeler did not lead infants' ability to antici-pate the tool use outcome following observational experience at a group level, although our findings did provide some indication that infants' ability to benefit from this type of observational experience may be mediated by their own tool use skills. One interpretation of these findings is that there are age-related changes in children's ability to learn from tool use failures: Want and Harris (2001) found that 3-year-olds, but not 2-year-olds, benefited from observing another person's tool use success and failure (above only witnessing their success). Alternately, or in addition, it is possible that infants' ability to benefit from tool use failure and success relies, in part, on their own skill at using the tool to obtain the toy. Future work can test these possibilities by testing infants and children at different ages, and by assessing infants' own tool use abilities prior to their participation in an observational experience session.

Experiment (3): the impact of joint engagement on infants' action anticipation

In experiment (3) we took a different approach to manipulating the observational experience session. We sought to change infants' role in the session. In prior work (Sommerville *et al.*, 2008), infants watched the observational experience session as third-party observers. They sat across a table, several feet away from the modeler, and the modeler did not directly address or interact with the infant. Given recent evidence that the role that infants and children play in everyday exchanges can dramatically impact their attention and learning from such exchanges (Moll *et al.*, 2007, Sommerville and Hammond, 2007), we investigated whether enhancing communicative and pedagogical cues during the observational session would lead infants to anticipate tool use outcomes during the CAT procedure. Our goal was to give infants the impression that they were active participants in the exchange.

In experiment (3), infants ($n = 18$; *mean age* = 9 months, 24 days) received the CAT procedure with a preceding observational experience session (participant observation condition). As in experiment (1), the modeler produced successful solutions to the cane problem. We chose this approach over the approach in experiment (2) (tool use failure and success) because when adults engage infants in teaching situations they typically produce well-formed actions that infants have the opportunity to benefit from (Brand *et al.*, 2007). The observational experience session differed from experiment (1), however, in several important ways. First, the infants had a first-person perspective on the event; they sat adjacent to the modeler, directly in front of the table that supported the toy and cane, with the trainer on their right side. At the start of the session the modeler greeted the infants and engaged with them using infant-directed speech. On each trial, after the problem was set up, the modeler drew infants' attention to the toy: by calling the infants' names, directing their attention to the toy (by saying "Look!" and pointing at the toy). She then instructed the infants to watch ("Watch this!"). The modeler then pulled the cane and retrieved the toy, saying, "I got it!", and then showed the toy to the infants, saying "See?". Our intention was to provide infants with the message that the event was produced for their benefit in order to teach them how to solve the problem. Infants watched a total of seven training trials (as well as two pre-test and two post-test trials), matched to the average number of training trials completed by infants in the training condition.

Infants' looking times to the cane outcome ($M = 18.6$, $SE = 1.8$) and toy outcomes ($M = 22.3$, $SE = 2.7$) did not differ (*ns*). An ANOVA on infants' looking times to the test events with condition (training versus first-party observation) and outcome (cane versus toy), revealed a condition by outcome interaction ($F(1, 36) = 6.5$, $p < .02$). Thus, infants failed to anticipate the goal of the actor's actions on the tool as the toy.

Taken together, the findings suggest that our changes to the observational session did not lead infants to correctly anticipate the tool use outcome. As prior work has primarily demonstrated an impact of communicative and pedagogical cues on learning from exchanges in older infants and children, it may be the case that infants in our study were transitional in their ability to benefit from such cues. It is possible that infants of this age require more explicit or concrete cues that the witnessed behavior has communicative relevance, such as guided hands-on involvement in tool use activities. Finally, it is possible that there are individual differences in infants' ability to capitalize on communicative cues that influence their ability to learn from observing others. Future work can directly test this possibility.

To summarize, the results of experiments (1) to (3), along with preceding work (Sommerville *et al.*, 2005, 2008), suggest that before the end of the first year of life, active, hands-on experience appears to have a more powerful effect than does observational experience on infants' subsequent action perception and understanding. Our findings also suggest, however, that the extent to which an individual infant benefits from observational experience may hinge on individual difference variables, such as pre-existing action expertise that infants bring to the experimental context. Critically, our results do not suggest that active, hands-on experience produces greater benefits to infants' learning under all circumstances, or for all domains of learning. Indeed there are other domains in which observational experience may be a richer source of information than active experience, or for which only observational experience is possible, and past research has documented the power of observational learning in infancy (Meltzoff, 2005). Rather, our findings demonstrate that doing it oneself may be particularly important early in infancy for interpreting or anticipating the actions of others.

Outstanding questions and future directions

Our recent findings have begun to unpack the relative contributions of active and observational experience to infants' action understanding within the first year of life. The aforementioned results suggest that infants' own developing ability to produce goal-directed actions provides a window into the actions of others. However, if all of infants' action understanding was built through their actions on the world, then infants, and indeed adults, would be at a loss to understand a wide range of actions. A critical charge for developmentalists, then, is to determine the range of mechanisms that contribute to early action understanding, their respective contributions to different aspects of action understanding, and the extent to which such mechanisms are integrated in the service of development.

One way in which we are addressing this question is by examining whether particular observational experiences that facilitate or necessitate anticipation of action outcomes impact infants' action understanding in ways that are commensurate with active experience. Our guiding hypothesis is that self-produced action trumps observational experience because effective action on the world requires anticipation but mere observation does not. Whereas failing to anticipate the trajectory of a tennis ball as an observer may lead one to miss a sizzling counter-play, failing to anticipate the trajectory of a tennis ball as a player could result in a blow to the head. Thus, acting on the world leads to the creation of prospective motor plans that are invoked during and inform infants' action observation. However, the underlying process by which this happens (e.g. through anticipation) need not uniquely be accessed through acting on the world. According to our hypothesis, should other types of experience or pieces of evidence either facilitate or necessitate anticipation of action outcomes, these types of experience or evidence will have consequences for infants' action understanding. We are testing this hypothesis through three lines of studies.

In one study, we (Sommerville and Crane, 2009) provided infants with prior observational information that an actor tended to habitually select one toy over another: infants saw an actor repeatedly reach for, grasp, and pick up one of two toys directly in front of her. We then placed the toys out-of-reach on supporting cloths, and tested infants in a cloth-pulling habituation paradigm that paralleled Sommerville and Woodward (2005). Our underlying idea was that prior knowledge of an actor's habitual action tendencies may lead infants to anticipate the outcome of the cloth-pulling sequence (that the actor would use the cloth to obtain a particular toy) and hence enhance their ability to identify the goal of the sequence. Our results provided support for this hypothesis: when given prior evidence of which of two toys an actor tended to act toward, 9.5-month-old infants identified the goal of the cloth-pulling sequence; in the absence of this evidence, they did not.

In a second study, we provided infants with a different piece of evidence that the actor had an enduring disposition to one of two objects (Sommerville et al., in press). 10-month-old infants saw an actor choose between two toys on habituation trials. In one condition, the actor accompanied her toy selection with a general remark about the object ("Look. Wow!"), in another she accompanied her toy selection with a remark indicating her disposition toward the object ("I like frogs"). Test trials occurred in another room. Infants who heard the dispositional statement looked longer when the actor reached for a new object (versus to a new side), whereas infants that heard the general remark looked equally to both events. Moreover, infants' performance in the dispositional statement condition was correlated with parental reports of receptive vocabulary. These findings support the possibility that when provided with appropriate linguistic evidence for an enduring disposition toward the object, infants anticipated that the actor would continue to pursue her prior goal object in a new room.

Finally, in an ongoing experiment in our lab, we are investigating the influence of collaborative exchanges on infants' action understanding. Collaboration involves anticipating your partners' actions in order to coordinate your actions effectively. Consider helping a friend move a couch up a flight of stairs: successfully coordinating your actions with hers involves anticipating how and when she will lift her end of the couch as she heads up a bend in the stairs. This need to anticipate our social partners' actions during collaborative activities appears to have consequences for memory and learning of others' actions: pre-school age children show better internalization of others' actions after working in collaboration with their social partner, than after working independently of their social partner (Sommerville and Hammond, 2007). In our current study, the infant and an adult experimenter work together to jointly solve a tool use problem. The experimenter uses a plastic cane to pull a toy within the infant's reach, so that the infant is able to grab the toy. Infants are then tested in the CAT procedure. Despite the fact that infants in this condition have no motor experience using the cane (just like in prior observational conditions), we predict that they will correctly anticipate the tool use outcome in the CAT procedure (e.g. recognize the actions on the cane as directed toward the toy). These findings would suggest that any type of experience that has anticipatory consequences may have facilitated infants' subsequent action understanding. Taken together, the aforementioned studies will help to identify the *process* by which action understanding is achieved, and lead to a systematic prediction regarding the types of experience that should facilitate action understanding.

Conclusions

The findings reviewed in this chapter suggest that infants are keen observers of the human body, and that they, like adults, see bodily actions as rife with meaning. Moreover, these findings suggest that changes in infants' own bodies and, in particular, changes in their bodily capabilities, lead to changes in their understanding of the bodies and bodily actions of others. Despite the complexity involved in perceiving, representing, and understanding the human body, infants have made significant strides in their bodily understanding within the first year of life.

References

Baldwin, D. A., Baird, J. A., Saylor, M. M., and Clark, M. A. (2001). Infants parse dynamic action. *Child Development*, **72**, 708–717.

Brand, R. J., Shallcross, W. L., Sabatos, M. G., and Massie, K. P. (2007). Fine-grained analysis of motionese: Eye gaze, object exchanges, and action units in infant-versus adult-directed action. *Infancy*, **11**, 203–214.

Clifton, R. K., Rochat, P., Litovsky, R. Y., and Perris, E. E. (1991). Object representation guides infants' reaching in the dark. *Journal of Experimental Psychology: Human Perception and Performance*, **17**, 323–329.

Csibra, G. and Gergely, G. (2009). Natural pedagogy. *Trends in Cognitive Sciences*, **13**, 148–153.

Flack-Ytter, T., Gredebäck, G., and von Hofsten, C. (2006). Infants predict other people's action goals. *Nature Neuroscience*, **9**, 878–879.

Frye, D. (1991). The origins of intention in infancy. In D. Frye and C. Moore (eds). *Children's Theories of Mind: Mental States and Social Understanding* (15–38). Hillsdale, NJ: Lawrence Erlbaum Associates.

Gallese, V. (2009). Motor abstraction: A neuroscientific account of how action goals and intentions are mapped and understood. *Psychological Research*, **73**, 486–498.

Gibson, E. J. and Pick, A. D. (2000). *An Ecological Approach to Perceptual Learning and Development*. Oxford: Oxford University Press.

Hauf, P., Elsner, B., and Aschersleben, G. (2004). The role of action effects in infants' action control. *Psychological Research*, **68**, 115–125.

Longo, M. R. and Bertenthal, B. I. (2007). Common coding of observation and execution of action in 9-month-old infants. *Infancy*, **10**, 43–59.

Meltzoff, A. N. (2005). Imitation and other minds: The "like me" hypothesis. In S. Hurley and N. Chater (eds). *Perspectives on Imitation: From Neuroscience to Social Science, Vol. II: Imitation, Human Development, and Culture* (55–77). Cambridge, MA: MIT Press.

Meltzoff, A. N. and Moore, M. K. (1995). Infants' understanding of people and things: From body imitation to folk psychology. In J. Bermúdez and N. Eilan (eds). *The Body and the Self* (43–69). Cambridge, MA: MIT Press.

Moll, H., Carpenter, M., and Tomasello, M. (2007). Fourteen-month-olds know what others experience only in joint engagement. *Developmental Science*, **10**, 826–835.

Nystrom, P. (2008). The infant mirror neuron system studied with high density EEG. *Social Neuroscience*, **3**, 334–347.

Piaget, J. (1953). *The Origins of Intelligence in the Child*. London: Routledge and Kegan Paul.

Rizzolatti, G. and Sinigaglia, C. (2010). The functional role of the parieto-frontal mirror circuit: Interpretations and misinterpretations. *Nature Reviews Neuroscience*, **11**, 264–274.

Robin, D. J., Berthier, N. E., and Clifton, R. K. (1996). Infants' predictive reaching for moving objects in the dark. *Developmental Psychology*, **32**, 824–835.

Sommerville, J. A. and Crane, C. C. (2009). Ten-month-old infants use prior information to identify an actor's goal. *Developmental Science*, **12**, 314–325.

Sommerville, J. A. and Decety, J. (2006). Weaving the fabric of social interaction: Articulating developmental psychology and cognitive neuroscience in the domain of motor cognition. *Psychonomic Bulletin and Review*, **13**, 179–200.

Sommerville, J. A. and Hammond, A. J. (2007). Treating another's actions as one's own: Children's memory of and learning from joint activity. *Developmental Psychology*, **43**, 1,003–1,018.

Sommerville, J. A. and Woodward, A. L. (2005). Pulling out the intentional structure of action: The relation between action processing and action production in infancy. *Cognition*, **95**, 1–30.

Sommerville, J. A., Crane, C. C., and Yun, J. E. (in press). Once a frog lover always a frog lover? Infants construe object choices as reflecting enduring preferences based on appropriate evidence. *Frontiers in Developmental Psychology*.

Sommerville, J. A., Hildebrand, E. A., and Crane, C. C. (2008). Experience matters: The impact of doing versus watching on infants' subsequent perception of tool use events. *Developmental Psychology*, **44**, 1,249–1,256.

Sommerville, J. A., Feldman, E., and Dillon, A. (in preparation). Factors influencing infants' early problem-solving performance.

Sommerville, J. A., Woodward, A. L., and Needham, A. N. (2005). Action experience alters 3-month-old infants' perception of other's actions. *Cognition*, **96**, B1–11.

Tomasello, M. (1999). Having intentions, understanding intentions and understanding communicative intentions. In P. D. Zelazo, J. W. Astington, and D. R. Olson (eds). *Developing Theories of Intention: Social Understanding and Self-control* (63–75). Mahwah, NJ: Lawrence Erlbaum Associates.

von Hofsten, C. and Ronnqvist, L. (1988). Preparation for grasping an object: A developmental study. *Journal of Experimental Psychology: Human Perception and Performance*, **14**, 610–621.

Want, S. C. and Harris, P. L. (2001). Learning from other people's mistakes: Causal understanding in learning to use a tool. *Child Development*, **72**, 431–443.

Wilson, M. and Knoblich, G. (2005). The case for motor involvement in perceiving conspecifics. *Psychological Bulletin*, **131**, 460–473.

Woodward, A. L. (1998). Infants selectively encode the goal object of an actor's reach. *Cognition*, **69**, 1–34.

(2003). Infants' developing understanding of the link between looker and object. *Developmental Science*, **6**, 297–311.

Woodward, A. L. and Guajardo, J. J. (2002). Infants' understanding of the point gesture as an object-directed action. *Cognitive Development*, **17**, 1,061–1,084.

Woodward, A. L. and Sommerville, J. A. (2000). Twelve-month-old infants interpret action in context. *Psychological Science*, **11**, 73–77.

Yonas, A. and Hartman, B. (1993). Perceiving the affordance of contact in four- and five-month-old infants. *Child Development*, **64**, 298–308.

Commentary on Part III

Body and action representations for integrating self and other

Moritz M. Daum and Wolfgang Prinz

The topic of Part III of the present book is the integration of the two previous sections that either focus on the representation of one's own body or on the representation of another individual's body. The four contributions of Part III document how these two aspects are integrated during development. In the present commentary, we will first briefly recapitulate the four chapters included in Part III. We will then integrate these finding into a broader picture and suggest a developmental course of body representations. Finally, we will provide an outlook on how future research should approach the topic of the integration of self and other, what the shortcomings of previous research are, and share ideas on how they can be overcome.

Recapitulation

The authors of the four chapters approach the topic of integrating self and other from four different perspectives. Gliga and Southgate (Chapter 10) emphasize the role of actions in infants' development of body representations. They discuss findings that show that infants first come to build representations about the function of the human body, including goal-directed and intentional actions, before they develop representations about the structure of the human body.

The main focus of Jones and Yoshida (Chapter 11) lies in the presentation of a single case study that reports longitudinal data about the development of imitation, and the relation of imitation in the development of representations about one's own and others' bodies. In their view, infants build a representation of both their own body and the bodies of others through interaction with their caregivers and especially through the caregiver imitating the infant.

Hauf and Power (Chapter 12) report a series of studies they conducted investigating the interrelation of infants' own locomotor abilities (crawling and walking) and the perception of others' locomotion depicted as point-light displays (PLDs). Their findings suggest a close relationship of the infants' locomotion production and their perception of others' locomotion. Following the idea of a shared representation of action perception and production as assumed by the principle of common coding (Prinz, 1990, 1997), Hauf and Power suggest that a bidirectional link between perception and production of bodily movements is already established early in life.

Finally, Sommerville, Blumenthal, Venema, and Sage (Chapter 13) present a series of three training studies investigating the link between action perception and production. Infants were trained with novel tasks either by giving them active, hands-on experience or only observational experience. Subsequently, the infants were tested in a perception task where their comprehension of the trained action was measured. The reported findings convincingly show that active experience outperforms observational experience in helping infants to discriminate between expected and unexpected action outcomes.

Integration

The four chapters take different approaches to the topic of integrating self and other. However, at the same time, all four chapters do – to a greater or lesser degree – emphasize two aspects of the representation of one's own body: structure and function. It is not the shape of the body that is in the focus of interest, it is primarily the body in action. This raises the question of whether representations about one's own and another's body can be built at all without the involvement of bodily movements and actions. A second question is whether a developmental course exists from representing function towards representing structure, as suggested by Gliga and Southgate (Chapter 10) when they summarize that "Anticipating other people's actions may be of greater urgency in the first year of life than discriminating people from other animate agents or identifying people based on their body silhouettes."

Emphasizing the functional aspects of the human body or parts of the human body lies at the heart of the definition of body representation. According to Slaughter and Heron (2004), body representations include visuo-structural as well as functional aspects. Reed and colleagues (2006: 231) have defined body representation as "where form and motion meet." These definitions gain support from various studies, for example, Kourtzi and Kanwisher (2000). These authors showed that cortical areas involved in the analysis of human motion, in particular areas that process observed human motion like medial temporal (MT) cortex and medial superior temporal (MST) cortex, are also engaged during the observation of static pictures of a human body in motion, which do not include real but only implied motion information. Their conclusion was that the processing of a particular object category (e.g. a human body) entails the processing of particular attributes that are associated with that object (e.g. movement).

Maravita (2006) suggests that a body representation should not be considered as a static picture or a map of a body surface but rather as a dynamic representation of a body in space. In other words, when we see the picture of a human body, we do not solely perceive the configuration of the body: we additionally infer how the body has moved to end up in the respective posture and what further movements arising from this respective posture are possible. This might imply that a body representation is built not only on the structure of an observed human body but is likewise inferred from the movement that is needed in order to achieve the respective posture.

Representing structure and function

In the following section, we will elaborate on the suggestion put forward by Gliga and Southgate (Chapter 10) that infants first come to build a representation of the function of the human body before they develop a representation of the structure of the human body. First, we speculate whether body structure and body function can be separated that strictly at all. Based on the literature reviewed above, body representations entail both representations of structure *and* function. The relationship between these two facets is an asymmetrical one. Knowledge about the structure of a body part can be acquired without any involvement of the function of the respective body part. Infants learn around the age of 9 months, for example, that a human body has four limbs, which are connected to the body at clearly defined locations (Heron and Slaughter, 2010). In contrast, it is more difficult, if possible at all, to acquire knowledge about function without information about the structure involved. This would mean that one acquires knowledge about an action as such, without the presence of a body or the body part performing the action. Investigating the acquisition of knowledge about structure is thus possible, but investigating the acquisition of knowledge about the function of a body part is not possible without the involvement of the structure of a body part.

In the following, we will put forward the idea that representations of structure and function – or of body and action – do not develop independently from each other but in close relation follow an integrative developmental course. This developmental course is based on the *relevance* a body part or the full body has concerning both an infant's own body and the bodies of others in the infant's world. With relevance, we mean how important a respective body part is for the infant at different points during development.

First, at birth, infants need to distinguish between relevant agents, preferably biological agents such as their caregivers, and less relevant agents like non-human agents and non-biological objects. To distinguish relevant from irrelevant agents, newborns might primarily rely on two aspects; whether the perceived agent has a face and whether the agent moves biologically or non-biologically. Likewise, infants' own skills in communicating with their environment are based on the same two skills; their facial expression and the style of their movements. We know that at birth, infants are tuned to preferably perceive both biological motion over non-biological motion (Simion *et al.*, 2008) and facelike patterns over non-facelike patterns (Cassia *et al.*, 2001; Valenza *et al.*, 1996). Second, later, at around the age of 3 to 4 months, infants start to use their limbs to manipulate their environment. At this age, intentional reaching and successful grasping towards static or slowly moving objects emerges (von Hofsten and Lindhagen, 1979). At the same time, infants detect congruencies between their own leg movements and observed leg movements (e.g. Bahrick and Watson, 1985) and realize that their own leg movements can cause an effect in the environment (e.g. Rovee-Collier, 1989). At approximately the same time, they start to interpret manual actions as goal-directed (Daum and Gredebäck, 2011; Woodward, 1998). Finally, again some months later, infants start to use their full body to locomote through their environment first by crawling, later by cruising along objects (e.g. furniture), and then by walking.

In the following, we will go into the details of each level of relevance and present evidence from our own and others' research showing that from very early on, infants are sensitive to the structural information of body parts. The conclusion of this section will be that as soon as a body part becomes relevant for the infant, the infant acquires knowledge of both structure and function.

Faces   Faces in general, and eye gaze in particular, are important sources of information, especially with regard to others' direction of attention, emotional states, and communicative intentions (Baron-Cohen, 1995). The fact that faces are objects of high relevance in the young infant's world is reflected by the fact that, at birth, infants already have a preference for facelike compared to non-facelike patterns. Newborns also prefer to look at faces that have their eyes open (Batki *et al.*, 2000). From birth, they prefer to look at faces that return their gaze compared to those that avert their gaze (Farroni *et al.*, 2002). A further aspect of the processing of faces is that the direction of gaze is an effective cue to direct an observer's covert attention. Recent research has shown that newborns already make faster saccades to a peripheral target that was cued by the gaze direction of a schematic face, suggesting that newborns already have the rudimentary ability to follow another's gaze (Farroni *et al.*, 2004). Shortly thereafter, beginning at the age of 3 months, infants attend in the same direction as the eyes of an adult face, indicated by the latency of orienting towards a probe appearing at a location that is congruent or incongruent with the gaze direction (Hood *et al.*, 1998).

At the same time that infants start to build representations of others' faces, they start to produce intentional facial expressions. Newborns are already able to form different facial expressions, which were reported to not be random at all.

Rather, they already seem to be organized and follow predefined temporal patterns (Oster, 1978; Oster and Ekman, 1978). Infants' own facial expressions are thought to not reflect precursors of adults' facial expressions but should be regarded as age-related adaptations that are crucial for the infant's survival and normal development (Oster, 1997; Oster et al., 1992). Studies on newborn imitation have shown that infants can produce tongue protrusions and mouth opening, and imitate mouth opening, pouting, and head turning. Whether or not newborns really do imitate is a matter of debate; for further discussion see Jones and Yoshida (Chapter 11, this volume) or Anisfeld (1996). What is clear is that newborns do form various facial expressions. Further evidence comes from newborn infants' facial expressions elicited by different tastes (Rosenstein and Oster, 1988). Two-hour-old infants produced differential facial responses to sweet versus non-sweet tastes as well as to bitter, sour, and salty tastes. The ability to produce a crying facial expression, even without vocalizing a cry, is likewise present from birth if not earlier (Humphrey, 1970).

Biological motion   Similar to the recognition of faces, infants differentiate biological from non-biological motion immediately after birth. Two-day-old infants were shown to selectively prefer to look at the display of a walking point-light chicken compared to a scrambled point-light chicken or an inverted walking chicken (Simion et al., 2008). This sensitivity develops further over the following months. For a detailed review of the development of the perception and interpretation of biological motion displays, see Chapters 7 and 8 by Moore and Reid (this volume). In short, at the age of 3 months, infants discriminate between biologically possible and impossible displays of human point-light walkers (presented upright and inverted). When they are two months older, they discriminate between the upright displays and no longer between the inverted PLDs (Bertenthal et al., 1987). Furthermore, at the age of 3 months, infants distinguish between biologically possible and impossible moving point-light spiders and cats, but at 5 months they no longer do so (Pinto, 1994). Thus, from early on, infants are able to discriminate biological from non-biological movements.

Pinto (2006) argues that early in life, infants categorize perceived motion on a lower level of organization – they perceive an object as moving biologically or not. They have not (yet) acquired knowledge about the form of a human body and accordingly have not yet built a representation of the vertical and hierarchical structure of the human body. This hypothesis is supported by the fact that in contrast to 3-month-olds, 5- and 7-month-old infants can discriminate between a canonical point-light walker and a distorted point-light walker created by offsetting the upper and lower halves of the body (Pinto, 1996). 3-month-olds do not yet seem to pay attention to the correct organization of the body and ignore the principal (vertical) axis of the human body. They rather attend to the organization and movement within limbs and differentiate between what is biologically moving and what is not.

The relation between self and other with respect to biologically moving bodies is that infants' discrimination skills reflect their own motor skills. As long as "being and moving upright" is not a relevant issue in the infants' life, they differentiate biological from non-biological motion no matter whether it is perceived as upright or not and no matter whether it is a human or animal body moving biologically. With the increased experience and relevance of being themselves in an upright position and perceiving other human beings as vertically coherent entities, the vertical axis of the human body becomes more salient.

Limbs: feet   Feet are not necessarily used for intentional action at an early age. Nevertheless, at around the age of 3 to 5 months, infants coordinate their own leg movements with a crib mobile that is attached to their legs (Rovee and Rovee, 1969) and with perceived images of their own legs. At this age, they discriminate between a perfectly contingent live display of their own leg motion and a non-contingent display of their own or a peer's legs (Bahrick and Watson, 1985; Rochat and Morgan, 1995; Schmuckler, 1996). Importantly, infants only differentiate between contingent and non-contingent displays of two pairs of legs when the contours of the legs are available. When the overall featural configuration of the legs was occluded (i.e. the infant's legs were hidden in bulky socks), the infants no longer discriminated between the two displays (Morgan and Rochat, 1997).

Following this line of research, we tested whether infants are able to detect a match or mismatch of visual information and bodily sensations that arise independent of movements of their own body (Zmyj *et al.*, 2011). Infants were presented with two video displays of lifelike baby doll legs. In both video displays, the doll's left leg was stroked, and the timing of the stroking differed between the two video displays. In addition, the infant's left leg was stroked contingently to one of the video displays but not the other. The results showed that starting between 7 and 10 months of age, infants looked significantly longer at the contingent compared to non-contingent display. In a second experiment, we tested the role of morphological characteristics in contingency detection. The doll's legs from the first experiment were replaced by two oblong wooden blocks of approximately the same size as the doll's legs. Here, no preference was found for either the contingent or the non-contingent display. This suggests that the sensitivity to detect a match or mismatch between visual and afferent body-related information develops at around the same age in ontogeny as the ability to detect a match or mismatch of visual and efferent motor-related information. This further suggests that motor experience of actions and afferent experiences of one's own body are intricately related, and both contribute to the developing perception of the self. Together with the findings of

Morgan and Rochat (1997), our findings suggest that infants do indeed possess a representation of the structure of their legs and feet. It is only if the morphology of a perceived pair of feet matches this representation that infants match afferent and efferent information available to them with what they observe.

Limbs: hands The same link between infants' representation of structure and function is valid for hands. Hands are highly important tools. Manual grasping is used for the exploration and the reshaping of our environment (Flanagan and Johansson, 2002). Newborns already aim their arm movements towards interesting objects (von Hofsten, 1982). Intentional reaching and successful grasping towards static or slowly moving objects emerges a few months later, at the age of 3 to 4 months (von Hofsten and Lindhagen, 1979). Shortly afterwards, at 5 to 6 months, grasping has become proficient enough for infants to extrapolate object motions on linear paths well ahead in time (Hespos *et al.*, 2009; von Hofsten *et al.*, 1998). 9-month-olds adjust their hand aperture relative to the size of the target object (von Hofsten and Rönnqvist, 1988) and 1-year-olds develop pincer grasps (e.g. Johnson and Blasco, 1997). As in adults, infants' grasping movements are predictive and future-oriented (von Hofsten, 2004).

Within the first year of life, infants also develop a remarkable sensitivity to the goal of observed grasping actions. At the age of 6 months, infants attribute goals to observed manual grasping actions (e.g. Woodward, 1998). Their perception of actions is already future-oriented. At 6 months, infants encode the goal of an uncompleted grasping action (Daum *et al.*, 2008; Hamlin *et al.*, 2008) and infer the size of an invisible target from the aperture size of the actor's hand during the grasp (Daum *et al.*, 2009). At this age, infants even perceive the directionality of a grasping hand; they shift their covert attention in the direction of the grasp and are faster in detecting a target that appears at a location that is congruent with the grasping direction compared to incongruent targets (Daum and Gredebäck, 2011). In contrast, when the grasping action is performed by a mechanical device instead of a human hand, the infants neither attribute goals to a non-human agent (Hofer *et al.*, 2005; Woodward, 1998) nor shift their covert attention in the direction of the grasping (Daum and Gredebäck, 2011). These findings again suggest that infants have already acquired knowledge about the structure of a human hand early in life, at a time when both their own and others' grasping actions become relevant to them.

Full body Finally, after acquiring knowledge about faces, biological movements, and limbs, infants start to integrate the different pieces of the puzzle. During the development of their first year of life, infants start to increasingly use their full body to act on their environment (for detailed overviews, see Adolph and Berger, 2006; Bertenthal and Clifton, 1998). Infants start to sit with support at around 3 to 4 months (Bertenthal and von Hofsten, 1998). They then move into an upright position using "tripod" sitting and soon thereafter sit hands-free. Infants start to locomote by crawling on their stomach, then on their hands and knees. They pull themselves into a standing position and shortly afterwards start to cruise along furniture. Supported standing is replaced by free standing, cruising is replaced by free walking. In short, during their first year of life, infants develop from being completely immobile to being completely mobile and being able to autonomously explore the world. These developments, which include upright positioning and free locomotion, entail the use and the coordination of the whole body. During this development, at around the age of 5 months, infants start to become aware of the vertical body axis and the fact that the human body has a top and a bottom.

Until recently, infants were thought to represent the shape of the full human body only at the age of 18 months (Slaughter *et al.*, 2002). More recent research has shown that the discrimination of typical and scrambled bodies starts earlier. Infants already discriminate typical and scrambled dolls at the age of 12 months. Similarly, infants as young as 9 months are sensitive to the human body configuration when three-dimensional and life-sized bodies are used as stimuli (Heron and Slaughter, 2010; see also Slaughter *et al.*, Chapter 5). Thus, by the time infants reach the age at which they start to use their whole body to locomote, they are sensitive to the structure of the full human body. However, a first study comparing the sensitivity to human body configuration and motor development has not yet found a correlation between the two (Christie and Slaughter, 2009). Nevertheless, focusing more on the development of full body motor skills including locomotion might yield different results.

To conclude, infants are sensitive to the structure of human body parts before the age of 9 months. Their knowledge about the structure of the body seems to be dependent on the relevance of the respective body part for the infant, both with regard to the self and in others. The relationship of how knowledge about the structure and function of body parts is acquired is depicted in Figure C3.1. *Target selection* indicates the body part that becomes relevant for the infant. This selection is based on the saliency of the body part – that is how prominent a body part is in the infant's perception, a mouth that often moves is, for example, more salient compared to a cheek that moves much less. The selection is furthermore based on the relevance the body part has both in the self and in others – that is, how often and how sophisticatedly they can use it, and how important the use of the respective body part is in observed others. *Knowledge acquisition* refers to the knowledge the infants acquire about a respective body part. With regards to knowledge acquisition, no differentiation can be made between structure and function. Knowledge about *what* a body part is *for* is always related to the knowledge about *how* the body part looks.

Target selection   **Knowledge acquisition**

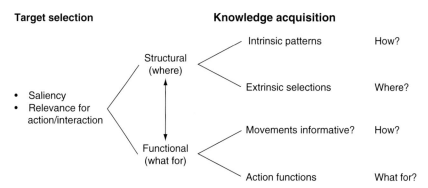

Figure C3.1 The relationship between how knowledge about the structure and function of body parts is acquired in infancy

The acquisition of structural knowledge can furthermore be divided into the knowledge about *intrinsic patterns*, that is, information about the structure of a respective body part (e.g. the fact that a hand has five digits and where each of these is attached to the hand) and knowledge about *extrinsic relations*, that is, where in relation to other body parts the respective part is located (e.g. an arm is attached to the shoulder and not to the hips). The acquisition of knowledge about the function of a respective body part can likewise be subdivided into information about *movements* (i.e. how a body part can move) and information about function in action (i.e. what a body part can be used for).

Further empirical evidence is needed to support the suggestions outlined above. The distinction made between structure and function is mainly based on different empirical criteria used. Knowledge about structure is usually tested by presenting differently arranged body parts and measuring infants' surprise reactions to incorrect arrangements. Research using this approach has mainly been performed with faces, indicating sensitivity from birth (Valenza *et al.*, 1996), and full bodies, indicating sensitivity from around 9 months of age (e.g. Slaughter and Heron, 2004). Knowledge about function is investigated by presenting actions and measuring surprise reactions to the incorrect use of a body part or the unexpected outcome of an action. Parallelizing the two approaches, for example, by testing the sensitivity of 6-month-olds to the structure of a hand, would enhance our knowledge about the relations between the acquisition of structure and function in development.

Continuation

The four contributions in Part III of the present book add important information to the existing literature on the integration of self and other in development.

However, it still remains an open issue how exactly self and other are integrated early in development. We do not yet know whether infants develop a representation of their bodily self based on their representation of the bodies and actions of others, or whether it is exactly the opposite, and infants develop a representation of the bodies and actions of others based on the representation of their own bodily self. Or might it even be that both representations develop in parallel? The four contributions yield no consistent conclusion on this topic. Sommerville and colleagues (Chapter 13) emphasize the importance of an infant's own action experience on the understanding of others (i.e. the self leading the other). Hauf and Power (Chapter 12) suggest a bidirectional influence of action and perception (i.e. the self and other developing in parallel). In this section, we will not provide a conclusive answer to this question but would like to use the opportunity to focus on one important aspect that should be considered in future research in order to solve this debate.

From comparing different mechanisms to comparing similar mechanisms

An important aspect that should be taken into consideration to a much greater degree in future research is the comparability of the tasks used to measure action perception and production in infants. Action production per se includes the anticipation of a goal (von Hofsten, 2004). Performing a goal-directed action automatically entails the anticipation of a future state of the action. The processing timeline of a performed action is unidirectional from the past to the future. It is only the part of the action that has not yet been performed that can be controlled by the actor (von Hofsten, 2003).

Infants' perception skills, in contrast, are predominantly measured via their responses to an action that is finished. Most of the established paradigms use what we call the *post-hoc approach* and measure whether a completed action or the final state of an action either fulfils or violates the infant's expectations about the observed action. The dependent variable that is most often used in this approach in infant studies is looking time (e.g. Gergely *et al.*, 1995; Woodward, 1998), either in forced-choice preferential looking paradigms (Cicchino and Rakison, 2008) or habituation paradigms (Sommerville *et al.*, 2008; Sommerville and Woodward, 2005). Other dependent variables that are used in this approach are electroencephalography (EEG; e.g. Reid *et al.*, 2007), or pupil size (Gredebäck and Melinder, 2010; Jackson and Sirois, 2009).

In contrast to a self-performed action, these post-hoc measures are not sensitive to processing during the observation of an ongoing action. Post-hoc measures allow comparisons between final states of an action that vary in how expected or unexpected they are, but they do not entail prediction. Recent advances in eye tracking methodologies provide the possibility to create paradigms for action perception tasks that are more comparable to action production tasks. Using eye tracking, it is possible to measure infants' processing of an observed action *online* either through shifts of overt attention measured via predictive gaze shifts (Falck-Ytter *et al.*, 2006; Gredebäck *et al.*, 2009) or through shifts of covert attention measured via reactive saccade latencies (Daum and Gredebäck, 2011). With this measure, expectations about forthcoming action can be measured while they are built in anticipation of the final state or goal of the action.

Both post-hoc and online measures have revealed similarities in onset and development of action expectations. However, the amount of information available and the time constraints of the processing at the different points in time of measurement strongly differ. In the case of a post-hoc measurement, the infant's expectation is compared to the outcome of an action *after* it has been completed. The information about the action is *complete* and the processing time extended. In contrast, in the case of online measurement, the measurement takes place *prior to* the completion of an observed action. The information about the action available is thus *incomplete* and the processing time strongly reduced.

Very little research comparing the different measures used in infant action comprehension tasks exists. This research has shown that the two measures are not necessarily correlated (e.g. Gredebäck and Melinder, 2010). Measures that assess infants' action processing post hoc were found to indicate a much earlier comprehension of action goals in infants than measures that assess the *anticipation* of an action outcome. Gredebäck and Melinder, for example, presented 6- and 12-month-old infants with a person feeding another person and recorded the infants' eye movements. The 12-month-olds were able to anticipate rational (food was brought to the mouth) and irrational (food was brought to the other person's hand) feeding actions, but the 6-month-olds were not. In contrast, the pupils of both 6- and 12-month-olds dilated while observing the non-rational feeding actions, indicating certain sensitivity to the irrationality is already present at 6 months, which was not (yet) reflected in their gaze shifts.

This might suggest that the computational processes that are involved in processing observed actions can be dissociated early in life and only later become associated: early in life, action processing and goal attribution needs time and a substantial amount of information. With increasing age, the information and time needed become less, and children become increasingly able to infer action goals from fragmentary information. A question that remains unsolved at the moment is whether the nature of this dissociation is temporal or procedural.

The *temporal interpretation* implies that the dissociation between the two measures reflects two successive states on the processing timeline of one common underlying mechanism. Action expectations measured post-hoc and online would thus rely merely on the different amount of information available, and this information becomes richer the more parts of the action are available during observation. Early in life, infants can only derive goals through post-hoc comparisons of their expectations with an observation when sufficient information and processing time are available. Only later in life can they already derive goals more quickly online during the observation of an ongoing action.

In contrast, according to the *procedural interpretation*, the dissociation between the two measures reflects a dissociation between two different mechanisms involved. These two mechanisms could be separate early in life and only later become integrated.

Conclusion

To sum up, the four chapters of Part III present insight to the interesting question of how self and other are integrated early in life. The common ground of the four contributions lies in the fact that the relevance of the body and its parts is a driving factor to represent both structure and function, which are both important for infants in order to build representations of the full body or parts of it. It further seems that the importance of the functional aspect decreases with increasing age. Towards the end of the first year of life, infants differentiate between correct and scrambled configurations of static human bodies. The question of whether action perception drives action production, or whether it is the reverse, and action production drives action perception, is still a matter of debate. This is shown nicely by the different findings of the four contributions. In order to solve this debate, future research in the field should focus more on causal relations than on correlations, and much more should be done to ensure that the tasks that are used to compare self and other do indeed focus on the same underlying mechanisms and do not differ in the demands and the requirement of cognitive load.

References

Adolph, K. E. and Berger, S. A. (2006). Motor development. In D. Kuhn and R. S. Siegler (eds). *Handbook of Child Psychology: Vol II: Cognition, Perception, and Language* (6th edn, 161–213). New York: John Wiley & Sons.

Anisfeld, M. (1996). Only tongue protrusion modelling is matched by neonates. *Developmental Review*, **16**, 149–161.

Bahrick, L. E. and Watson, J. S. (1985). Detection of intermodal proprioceptive visual contingency as a potential basis of self-perception in infancy. *Developmental Psychology*, **21**, 963–973.

Baron-Cohen, S. (1995). *Mindblindness: An Essay on Autism and Theory of Mind*. Cambridge, MA: MIT Press.

Batki, A., Baron-Cohen, S., Wheelwright, S., Connellan, J., and Ahluwalia, J. (2000). Is there an innate gaze module? Evidence from human neonates. *Infant Behavior and Development*, **23**, 223–229.

Bertenthal, B. I. and Clifton, R. K. (1998). Perception and action. In D. Kuhn and R. S. Siegler (eds). *Handbook of Child Psychology: Vol. II. Cognition, Perception, and Language* (5th edn, 51–102). New York: John Wiley & Sons.

Bertenthal, B. I. and von Hofsten, C. (1998). Eye, head and trunk control: The foundation for manual development. *Neuroscience and Biobehavioral Reviews*, **22**, 515–520.

Bertenthal, B. I., Proffitt, D. R., and Kramer, S. J. (1987). Perception of biomechanical motions by infants – implementation of various processing constraints. *Journal of Experimental Psychology – Human Perception and Performance*, **13**, 577–585.

Cassia, V. M., Simion, F., and Umilta, C. (2001). Face preference at birth: The role of an orienting mechanism. *Developmental Science*, **4**, 101–108.

Christie, T. and Slaughter, V. (2009). Exploring links between sensorimotor and visuospatial body representations in infancy. *Developmental Neuropsychology*, **34**, 448–460.

Cicchino, J. B. and Rakison, D. H. (2008). Producing and processing self-propelled motion in infancy. *Developmental Psychology*, **44**, 1,232–1,241.

Daum, M. M. and Gredebäck, G. (2011). The development of grasping comprehension in infancy: Covert shifts of attention caused by referential actions. *Experimental Brain Research*, **208**, 298–307.

Daum, M. M., Prinz, W., and Aschersleben, G. (2008). Encoding the goal of an object-directed but uncompleted reaching action in 6- and 9-month-old infants. *Developmental Science*, **11**, 607–619.

Daum, M. M., Vuori, M. T., Prinz, W., and Aschersleben, G. (2009). Inferring the size of a goal object from an actor's grasping movement in 6- and 9-month-old infants. *Developmental Science*, **12**, 854–862.

Falck-Ytter, T., Gredebäck, G., and von Hofsten, C. (2006). Infants predict other people's action goals. *Nature Neuroscience*, **9**, 878–879.

Farroni, T., Csibra, G., Simion, F., and Johnson, M. H. (2002). Eye contact detection in humans from birth. *Proceedings of the National Academy of Sciences*, **99**, 9,602–9,605.

Farroni, T., Massaccesi, S., Pividori, D., and Johnson, M. H. (2004). Gaze following in newborns. *Infancy*, **5**, 39–60.

Flanagan, J. R. and Johansson, R. S. (2002). Hand movements. In V. S. Ramachandran (ed.). *Encyclopedia of the Human Brain*, Vol. II (399–414). San Diego, CA: Academic Press.

Gergely, G., Nadasdy, Z., Csibra, G., and Biro, S. (1995). Taking the intentional stance at 12 months of age. *Cognition*, **56**, 165–193.

Gredebäck, G. and Melinder, A. M. D. (2010). Infants' understanding of everyday social interactions: A dual process account. *Cognition*, **114**, 197–206.

Gredebäck, G., Stasiewicz, D., Falck-Ytter, T., Rosander, K., and von Hofsten, C. (2009). Action type and goal type modulate goal-directed gaze shifts in 14-month-old infants. *Developmental Psychology*, **45**, 1,190–1,194.

Hamlin, J. K., Hallinan, E. V., and Woodward, A. L. (2008). Do as I do: 7-month-old infants selectively reproduce others' goals. *Developmental Science*, **11**, 487–494.

Heron, M. and Slaughter, V. (2010). Infants' responses to real humans and representations of humans. *International Journal of Behavioral Development*, **34**, 34–45.

Hespos, S. J., Gredebäck, G., von Hofsten, C., and Spelke, E. S. (2009). Occlusion is hard: Comparing predictive reaching for visible and hidden objects in infants and adults. *Cognitive Science*, **33**, 1,483–1,502.

Hofer, T., Hauf, P., and Aschersleben, G. (2005). Infants' perception of goal-directed actions performed by a mechanical device. *Infant Behavior and Development*, **28**, 466–480.

Hood, B. M., Douglas, W. J., and Driver, J. (1998). Adult's eyes trigger shifts of visual attention in human infants. *Psychological Science*, **9**, 131–134.

Humphrey, T. (1970). Function of the nervous system during prenatal life. In U. Stave (ed.). *Physiology of the Prenatal Period: Functional and Biochemical Development in Mammals*, Vol. II (751–796). New York: Appleton-Century-Crofts.

Jackson, I. and Sirois, S. (2009). Infant cognition: Going full factorial with pupil dilation. *Developmental Science*, **12**, 670–679.

Johnson, C. P. and Blasco, P. A. (1997). Infant growth and development. *Pediatrics in Review*, **18**, 219–251.

Kourtzi, Z. and Kanwisher, N. (2000). Activation in human MT/MST by static images with implied motion. *Journal of Cognitive Neuroscience*, **12**, 48–55.

Maravita, A. (2006). From "body in the brain" to "body in the space". In G. Knoblich, I. M. Thornton, M. Grosjean, and M. Shiffrar (eds). *Human Body Perception from the Inside Out*. New York: Oxford University Press.

Morgan, R. and Rochat, P. (1997). Intermodal calibration of the body in early infancy. *Ecological Psychology*, **9**, 1–23.

Oster, H. (1978). Facial expression and affect development. In M. Lewis and L. Rosenblum (eds). *The Development of Affect*. New York: Plenum.

   (1997). Facial expression as a window on sensory experience and affect in newborn infants. In P. Ekman and E. Rosenberg (eds). *What The Face Reveals: Basic and Applied Studies of Spontaneous Expression using the Facial Action Coding System (FACS)* (320–327). New York: Oxford University Press.

Oster, H. and Ekman, P. (1978). Facial behavior in child development. *Minnesota Symposium on Child Psychology*, **11**, 231–276.

Oster, H., Hegley, D., and Nagel, L. (1992). Adult judgments and fine-grained analysis of infant facial expressions – testing the validity of a priori coding formulas. *Developmental Psychology*, **28**, 1,115–1,131.

Pinto, J. (1994). Human infants' sensitivity to biological motion in pointlight cats. *Infant Behavior and Development*, **17**, 871.

   (1996). Developmental changes in infants' perceptions of point-light displays of human gait. Unpublished doctoral dissertation, University of Virginia, Charlottesville.

   (2006). Developing body representations – a review of infants' responses to biological-motion displays. In G. Knoblich, I. M. Thornton, M. Grosjean, and M. Shiffrar (eds). *Human Body Perception from the Inside Out*. New York: Oxford University Press.

Prinz, W. (1990). A common coding approach to perception and action. In O. Neumann and W. Prinz (eds). *Relationships Between Perception and Action* (167–201). Berlin: Springer-Verlag.

   (1997). Perception and action planning. *European Journal of Cognitive Psychology*, **9**, 129–154.

Reed, C. L., Stone, V. E., and McColdrick, J. E. (2006). Not just posturing: Configural processing of the human body. In G. Knoblich, I. M. Thornton, M. Grosjean, and M. Shiffrar (eds). *Human Body Perception from the Inside Out* (229–258). New York: Oxford University Press.

Reid, V. M., Csibra, G., Belsky, J., and Johnson, M. H. (2007). Neural correlates of the perception of goal-directed action in infants. *Acta Psychologica*, **124**, 129–138.

Rochat, P. and Morgan, R. (1995). Spatial determinants in the perception of self-produced leg movements by 3- to 5-month-old infants. *Developmental Psychology*, **31**, 626–636.

Rosenstein, D. and Oster, H. (1988). Differential facial responses to four basic tastes in newborns. *Child Development*, **59**, 1,555–1,568.

Rovee, C. K. and Rovee, D. T. (1969). Conjugate reinforcement of infant exploratory behavior. *Journal of Experimental Child Psychology*, **8**, 33–39.

Rovee-Collier, C. (1989). The joy of kicking: Memories, motives and mobiles. In P. R. Solomon, G. R. Goethals, C. M. Kelley, and B. R. Stephens (eds). *Memory: Interdisciplinary Approaches*. New York: Springer.

Schmuckler, M. A. (1996). Visual-proprioceptive intermodal perception in infancy. *Infant Behavior and Development*, **19**, 221–232.

Simion, F., Regolin, L., and Bulf, H. (2008). A predisposition for biological motion in the newborn baby. *Proceedings of the National Academy of Sciences of the United States of America*, **105**, 809–813.

Slaughter, V. and Heron, M. (2004). Origins and early development of human body knowledge. *Monographs of the Society for Research in Child Development*, **69**(2).

Slaughter, V., Heron, M., and Sim, S. (2002). Development of preferences for the human body shape in infancy. *Cognition*, **85**, B71–B81.

Sommerville, J. A. and Woodward, A. L. (2005). Pulling out the intentional structure of action: The relation between action processing and action production in infancy. *Cognition*, **95**, 1–30.

Sommerville, J. A., Hildebrand, E. A., and Crane, C. C. (2008). Experience matters: The impact of doing versus watching on infants' subsequent perception of tool-use events. *Developmental Psychology*, **44**, 1,249–1,256.

Valenza, E., Simion, F., Cassia, V. M., and Umilta, C. (1996). Face preference at birth. *Journal of Experimental Psychology – Human Perception and Performance*, **22**, 892–903.

von Hofsten, C. (1982). Eye–hand coordination in the newborn. *Developmental Psychology*, **18**, 450–461.

(2003). On the development of perception and action. In K. J. Connolly and J. Valsiner (eds). *Handbook of Developmental Psychology* (114–140). London: Sage.

(2004). An action perspective on motor development. *Trends in Cognitive Sciences*, **8**, 266–272.

von Hofsten, C. and Lindhagen, K. (1979). Observations on the development of reaching for moving objects. *Journal of Experimental Child Psychology*, **28**, 158–173.

von Hofsten, C. and Rönnqvist, L. (1988). Preparation for grasping an object: A developmental study. *Journal of Experimental Psychology: Human Perception and Performance*, **14**, 610–621.

von Hofsten, C., Vishton, P., Spelke, E. S., Feng, Q., and Rosander, K. (1998). Predictive action in infancy: Tracking and reaching for moving objects. *Cognition*, **67**, 255–285.

Woodward, A. L. (1998). Infants selectively encode the goal object of an actor's reach. *Cognition*, **69**, 1–34.

Zmyj, N., Jank, J., Schütz-Bosbach, S., and Daum, M. M. (2011). Detection of visual-tactile contingency in the first year after birth. *Cognition*, **120**, 82–89.

Index